African Participation at the World Trade Organization

Graduate Institute of International and Development Studies

VOLUME 13

The titles published in this series are listed at brill.com/giis

African Participation at the World Trade Organization

Legal and Institutional Aspects, 1995–2010

By

Joan Apecu Laker

MARTINUS NIJHOFF PUBLISHERS

LEIDEN • BOSTON
2014

Cover illustrations: Enhanced Integrated Framework Secretariat.

Library of Congress Cataloging-in-Publication Data

Apecu Laker, Joan.
African participation at the World Trade Organization : legal and institutional aspects : 1995–2010 / by Joan Apecu Laker.
p. cm. — (Graduate institute of international and development studies ; Volume 13)
Includes bibliographical references.
ISBN 978-90-04-25670-5 (hardback : alk. paper) — ISBN 978-90-04-25671-2 (e-book) 1. World Trade Organization—Africa. 2. Foreign trade regulation—Africa. I. Title.

K4610.A96 2014
382'.92096—dc23

2013025852

This publication has been typeset in the multilingual "Brill" typeface. With over 5,100 characters covering Latin, IPA, Greek, and Cyrillic, this typeface is especially suitable for use in the humanities. For more information, please see www.brill.com/brill-typeface.

ISSN 1572-5618
ISBN 978-90-04-25670-5 (hardback)
ISBN 978-90-04-25671-2 (e-book)

This book is printed on acid-free paper.

DEDICATION

For my parents, Augustine Apecu and Rhoda Aryemo Apecu and my grand parents, Mzee Yokoyadi Jwee and Perina Akello (all of blessed memory). The values and teaching you instilled in me about sustained hard work, commitment and professionalism have been always been my driving force.

Also, for my daughters Amelia Aryemo-Chika and Adela Lagen-Apecu. Let nothing deter you in your quest for knowledge and excellence.

This book is my contribution to African Members of the World Trade Organization. My hope is that the results of this research assists African WTO Members to critically review their participation in the first 15 years of the WTO's existence, address their participatory weaknesses, and, identify specific areas to which they could allocate more resources, and invest greater efforts in order to significantly scale-up their systemic participation.

CONTENTS

LIST OF ANNEXES AND CHARTS

Annexes

Charts

FOREWORD

African countries represent over one quarter of the World Trade Organisation (WTO) membership. Their trade profiles and economic weight are very diverse but their participation in the global trading system has received limited attention by researchers. Joan Apecu's research is a commendable effort to fill this gap. Her book investigates the legal and institutional aspects of Africa's participation at the WTO. The roots of African trade policy behaviour from its origins in the GATT, through the founding of the WTO in 1995 to 2010 are researched. Her work focuses on the quality and effectiveness of African participation in the rules-based, multilateral trading system.

The solidity and value of her research are three-fold. First, on the basis of a systematic accumulation of evidence over a 15-year period, the book describes African trade policy behaviour. There has been no similar study of such range based on original data. She concludes that Africa's participation has been rather limited and she argues that there is wide scope for improvement. Some may disagree. However, data for the conclusions are original and the arguments and logic are compelling.

Second, based on the current transitions in the global economy, the author encourages African Members of the WTO to break from the "inertia of a special and differential exemption orientation", align the trade policy behaviour of African Capitals with the Geneva "Frontline" and, ensure adequacy of deployed resources to three core areas of WTO work: dispute settlement; administration of existing Agreements and, multilateral negotiations.

Third, in the last chapter she reviews each policy area of the WTO work suggesting ways for African policy makers to maximize the benefits of their global trade integration and WTO Membership. She argues that significant improvements in Africa's participation at the WTO will depend on whether African countries consciously operate on global best practices; and, explicitly links domestic reforms, including the rule of law and good governance to substantive participation in their trade policy behaviour. I strongly support her recommendation that African countries use Aid for Trade, the initiative which I launched at the start of my tenure as WTO Director-General, to build trade capacity at home. Mainstreaming trade into domestic development strategies has proven a key instrument to help African countries reap the benefits of the global trading system.

A compelling case is made for mainstreaming trade capacity-building, Aid for Trade, into national development plans.

By carefully examining the past, Joan's work can help African countries build a bridge to an effective trade policy for the future. A must read for policy makers and scholars interested in Africa's trade policy.

Pascal Lamy
Director-General
World Trade Organization

ACKNOWLEDGEMENTS

I wish to acknowledge the guidance, support and assistance provided by several people in the writing of this book. First, I am heavily indebted to Professor Joost Pauwelyn, who gave so much of his time in systematically guiding me in writing this book and ensuring clarity of thought and direction. This book would not have been completed without his relentless and sharp criticism as well as timely encouragement. I am equally indebted to Professor Jean-Louis Arcand, who made me believe that non-statisticians could crunch numbers. Thank you for putting before me this great challenge and for making this research richer, more meaningful and cross-cutting. My appreciation also to Dr Bernard Hoekman, for very useful and insightful comments that helped in enriching this research. Finally, special thanks to WTO Director-General Pascal Lamy for valuable suggestions and comments.

My thanks and appreciation to the African WTO delegates in Geneva that responded to the questionnaire on different aspects of African Participation in the WTO. Your insights and contributions gave this research more meaning.

I am indebted to several colleagues in the WTO Secretariat who provided valuable comments and support. First, Chiedu Osakwe. Without your constant and punishing critique at all stages of my work, drawing on your vast wealth of expertise and experience in WTO African Trade Policy, this book would have probably taken a different turn. I am deeply indebted. Second, Dayong Yu, Roy Santana and Bekele Tamenu for statistical and econometric guidance for the regression for this research. I benefitted from your experience and expertise and I appreciate your contributions. Nadia Ferdi, Celine Schmitt, Deidre Lynch, Edith Rambla, Samantha Morgan and Helen Favez thank you for valuable work in data collection and formatting the document.

Finally, gratitude is due to my family, the Apecu family, who have supported me through the years and in the period spent in writing of this book. Linda, Stella, Florence, Tom, Samuel and David, you have always remained true to your support in my challenges. I value your support.

The views expressed in this research are those of the author and do not represent the views of the WTO, its Members individually or collectively nor it's Secretariat.

ABBREVIATIONS

ACP	African, Caribbean, and Pacific
ACWL	Advisory Centre on WTO Law
AD	Anti-dumping
AGOA	African Growth and Opportunity Act
ANDEAN	Comunidad Andina (Customs Union of Bolivia, Colombia, Ecuador and Peru)
AoA	Agreement on Agriculture
APEC	Asia-Pacific Economic Cooperation
ASEAN	Association of Southeast Asian Nations
ATC	Agreement on Textiles and Clothing (expired)
AU	African Union
C4	Cotton-Four countries (Benin, Burkina Faso, Chad, Mali)
CARIBCAN	Caribbean-Canada Trade Agreement
CARICOM	Caribbean Community and Common Market
CBD	Convention on Biological Diversity
CBERA	Caribbean Basin Economic Recovery Act
CEFTA	Central European Free Trade Agreement
CITES	Convention on International Trade in Endangered Species
CoA	Committee on Agriculture
CRO	Committee on Rules of Origin
CTD	Committee on Trade and Development
CTG	Council for Trade in Goods
CTS	Council for Trade in Services
CVA	Customs Valuation Agreement
DDA	Doha Development Agenda
DSB	Dispute Settlement Body
DSU	Understanding on Rules and Procedures Governing the Settlement of Disputes
EC	European Communities
ECOWAS	Economic Community of West African States
EFTA	European Free Trade Association

EPA	Economic Partnership Agreement
EU	European Union
FTA	Free Trade Agreement
G10	Group of Ten Countries (WTO Agriculture negotiations)
G20	Group of Twenty Countries (WTO Agriculture negotiations)
GATS	General Agreement on Trade in Services
GATT	General Agreement on Tariffs and Trade
GCC	Gulf Co-operation Council
GDP	Gross Domestic Product
GPA	Government Procurement Agreement
GRULAC	Group of Latin American and Caribbean Countries
HWP	Harmonization Work Programme
IGDC	Informal Group of Developing Countries
ILC	Import Licensing Committee
IMF	International Monetary Fund
ITA	Information Technology Agreement
ITBC	International Textiles and Clothing Bureau
ISO	International Organization for Standardization
LDC	Least Developed Country
MEA	Multilateral Environmental Agreement
MERCOSUR	Southern Common Market
MFN	Most-Favoured Nation
NAMA	Non-Agricultural Market Access
NFIDCs	Net Food Importing Developing Countries
OAPI	Organisation Africaine de la Propriete Intellectuelle
OAU	Organization of African Unity
RAMs	Recently Acceded Members
RTA	Regional Trade Agreement
SAARC	South Asian Association for Regional Cooperation
SCM	Subsidies and Countervailing Measures
SGA	Safeguards Agreement
SDT	Special and Differential Treatment
SPS	Sanitary and Phytosanitary
SSG	Special Safeguard
SSM	Special Safeguard Mechanism
STC	Specific Trade Concern
SPS Agreement	Agreement on the Application of Sanitary and Phytosanitary Measures
Sutherland Report	Report by the Consultative Board to the Director-General Supachai Panitchpakdi, *the Future of the WTO: Addressing Institutional Challenges in the New Millennium* (*WTO, 2004*)
SVEs	Small and Vulnerable Economies
TBT Agreement	Agreement on Technical Barriers to Trade
TNC	Trade Negotiations Committee
TPR	Trade Policy Review

TRIMs	Trade-Related Investment Measures
TRIPS	Trade-Related Aspects of Intellectual Property Rights
TRIPS Agreement	Agreement on Trade-Related Aspects of Intellectual Property Rights
TRM	Transitional Review Mechanism (for China – now expired)
UNCTAD	United Nations Conference on Trade and Development
UNECA	United Nations Economic Commission for Africa
UNEP	United Nations Environment Programme
UNFCC	United Nations Framework Convention on Climate Change
WTO	World Trade Organization
WTO Agreement	Marrakesh Agreement Establishing the World Trade Organization.

CHAPTER ONE

INTRODUCTION: PROBLEMATIQUE AND THESIS

1. Introduction

In spite of a significant membership share in relation to other WTO regional groups,[1] the participation of the 42 African WTO Members in regular committee work, the Doha negotiations, and, dispute settlement has been nominal, minimal and largely ineffective. In these areas, African countries have exercised minimal institutional engagement and influence. In the course of the on-going Doha Round negotiations, the positions adopted by African countries, most of which are least-developed, have been mainly oriented towards seeking exemptions or differentiated treatment from concessions to be made and draft rules being developed. In the WTO's Dispute Settlement system, African countries have participated minimally in relation to other Members as grouped in this study. African WTO Members have had limited recourse to legal mechanisms in the DSU, either to address any nullification and impairment of benefits, obtain remedies or monitor issues of systemic interest by undertaking third party rights. What explains this discrepancy between a large membership share, relative to other regional groups, and minimal, nominal and largely ineffective participation?

There has been a considerable volume of research regarding developing country participation in the trading system. These studies have reflected a wide range of dependent variables. They have tended to singular focus on the areas of either dispute settlement, or regular work or negotiations. Furthermore, there has been a pattern to extrapolate from broader developing country participation, conclusions and findings and generalize to African participation. Current research has made useful contributions in suggesting explanations for developing country participatory strengths and weaknesses. These have revolved around a range of factors such as a baseline of passivity, low technical capacity, cost limitations, disinterest with the original GATT agenda perceived as developed-country oriented and initial developing country attraction to UNCTAD in preference to

[1] See Annex I showing WTO Members, grouped into six regional groupings specifically for this study.

the GATT/WTO. This study builds on earlier research and goes further. It contributes by analysing more recent evidence and over a longer period – 1995 to 2010 – in changed circumstances, and extends analysis simultaneously across the three core areas of regular committee work, dispute settlement and negotiations. The primary focus of this study is on African WTO membership.

Although this research has taken an empirical approach, it is legally grounded as its main focus is on participation in the World Trade Organization – a rules-based system grounded on legal Agreements binding on every Member. The value and systemic importance of participation rests on the fact that multilateral trade rules serve an important domestic political-economic function. Increasingly they form part of national strategies of external liberalization. Binding reciprocal commitments engender the necessary locking in of policy, forestalling domestic policy reversals and uncertainty and unpredictability of national trade policy. It is therefore important to participate in the shaping of trade rules that will ultimately require domestic implementation. For instance, in regular committee work, Members' engagement is focused on administering the rules that bind all Members in a system of balanced rights and obligations. In trade negotiations, such as the on-going Doha negotiations, legal texts emerge from technical drafting processes underscoring the value of actively participating and contributing to shaping final outcomes that would be legally binding on each Member party to the negotiations. Each member would have to implement the results. In dispute settlement, although the ability for effective engagement and participation in panel and Appellate Body work inter-alia depend on expert and competent legal capacity in delegations, it is equally important to participate from a systemic view point and contribute to the shaping of "precedents" of panels and the Appellate Body.

Building on previous research, it has been argued in this study that, since the establishment of the WTO, across the three core areas of regular committee work, negotiations and, dispute settlement, the minimal participation of African countries, in contrast to its large membership share is explained by the continuing inertia of a "special and differential exemption orientation";[2] misalignment in coordinating capital-driven domestic trade policy and economic reforms with the African WTO "Geneva frontline"; misallocation of negotiators across the core areas of work; a small trade share (exports and imports); and, to a lesser extent, specialized capacity handicaps. It has also been observed that the degree of engagement and impact of participation of African WTO Members has been explained by the personal commitment and professional engagement of individual negotiators despite existing constraints and weaknesses. Furthermore, the analysis of African participation has suggested that participation of delegates from municipal systems with fragile democracies and weak governance structures has been tentative, largely inactive, inconsistent and largely ineffective.

This study has investigated the inter-relationships between the institutional engagement of African countries in the regular work of the Organization, the Doha negotiations, and the extent of legal participation in the dispute settlement system. It has been

[2] For clarity, special and differential treatment encompasses and is larger than the narrower concept of preferences, the latter specifically applying to market access.

argued that the combined investigation of this three-way inter-relationship enhances understanding on African participation in these key areas of the multilateral rules-based trading system.

2. Questions Investigated

This research sought to address seven broad questions. It was acknowledged that investigation of these questions does not provide the last word. Further research is required.

1. Why has individual and collective African participation in the WTO been nominal, minimal and largely ineffective?
2. Has the existence of the WTO African Group made any difference in African participation?
3. In what ways have African WTO Members used issue-specific, regional and non-regional coalitions to compensate for their individual and collective participatory weaknesses?
4. Why has the posture of African countries in WTO negotiations been essentially oriented towards seeking exemptions or differentiated treatment from concessions to be made and draft rules being developed?
5. How does the level of personal commitment and professional engagement of an African negotiator impact on capacity for effective and result-oriented engagement in regular committee work, negotiations and dispute settlement?
6. What best practices within African membership and beyond exist to improve the level of engagement/participation of African WTO Members?
7. Beyond the activity levels of African engagement/participation at the WTO, what are the linkages between trade policies of African Members at the WTO, on the one hand, with domestic reform, growth, the rule of law and governance, on the other hand?

3. Overview of Developing Country Trade Performance

There are 159 Members of the World Trade Organisation.[3] The vast majority are developing countries. (Figure 1) of which 42 are African countries.[4] Africa accounts for approximately 27 per cent of total WTO membership and 35 per cent of developing country membership. (Figures 2 and 3)

[3] In the period 2012–2013, six new Members acceded to the WTO: Montenegro, Samoa, the Russian Federation, Vanuatu, Lao People Democratic Republic and Tajikistan. This however, does not affect this study which was conducted on the basis of a membership of 153.

[4] The definition of developing countries in this book is the operative definition used in WTO Secretariat reports including for statistical purposes. In this definition, developing countries are all countries or separate customs territories with the exception of Australia, Canada, European Union (27), Iceland, Japan, New Zealand, Norway, Switzerland and the United States. Least Developed Countries are recognized as a legal sub-category of the developing country group. Furthermore, WTO Member status is by self-designation.

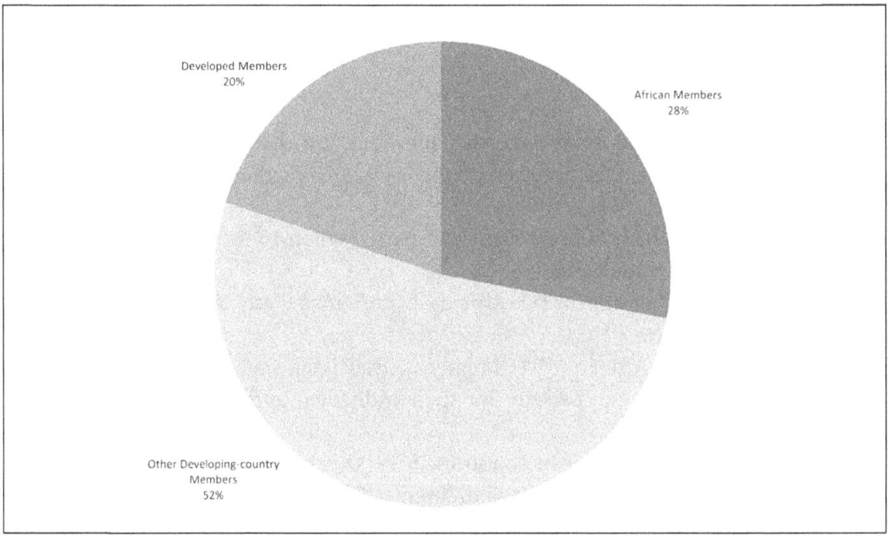

Figure 1. Share of WTO membership.

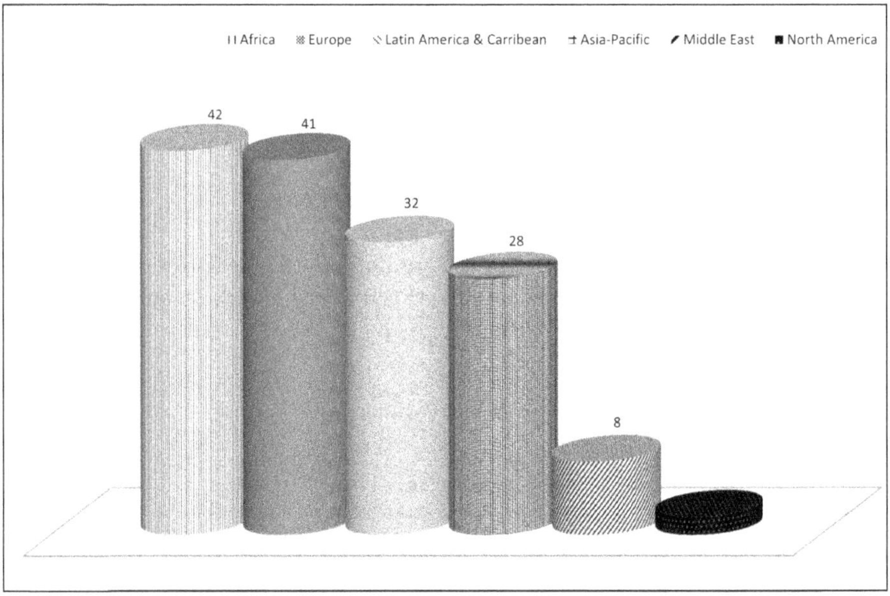

Figure 2. WTO members by region as grouped for this study.

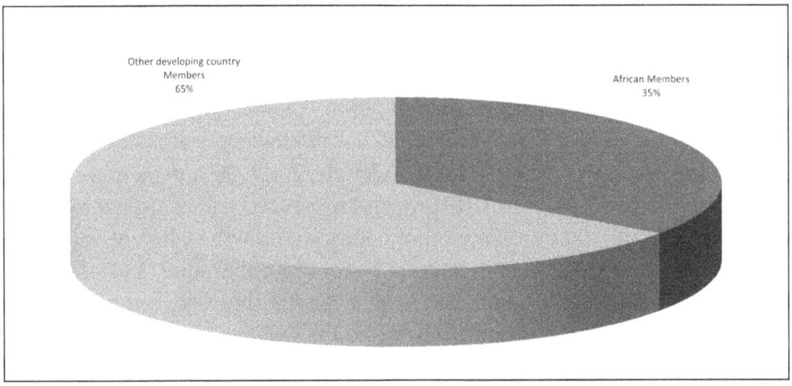

Figure 3. Developing-country members.

In the period of research covered, the role of developing countries as a whole significantly increased. The importance of their role was due in part to their numbers, but also to their trade policy behaviour since the end of the Uruguay Round and the emergence of the WTO (Finger, Michael (2010), Osakwe, Chiedu, (2010)). Several developing countries (now referred to as "emerging economies") have become important players in the global economy and look to trade as a vital tool for development. In general, the share of developing countries as a group in world trade has steadily been increasing. In 2007 for example, developing countries recorded, on average, a growth rate of 7 per cent. This was against a backdrop of a decline in global economic growth from 3.7 per cent to 3.4 per cent. Growth in the developing regions was nearly three times the rate recorded in the developed regions and the contribution of the developing countries to global output growth in 2007 exceeded 40 per cent.[5] The economic performance of developing countries particularly emerging economies has been the subject of intensive analysis in the aftermath of the 2008/2009 global financial and economic crisis. The results of ongoing analysis strongly indicates that developing countries cope better and now appear to be "new engine for global growth" and with the capacity to "partially rescue advanced economies" (Canuto, Otaviano, 2010: 33–47). It has been argued that the reforms they undertook in the past decade are now paying off.

Although there have been improvements in African trade and economic performance, since the domestic reforms of the late 1980s and 1990s, overall, the majority have seen the share of their world trade decline partly due to unfavourable commodity prices.[6] In the period analysed, Africa's share of global trade was the lowest of all regions at less

5 World Trade Report 2008, at pg. 1.

6 However, the World Trade Report 2008 highlights that for the least-developed countries (many of whom are in Africa), trade performance was stronger than that of developing countries over the past seven years largely to higher commodity prices, and the expansion of merchandise exports. Least developed country exports are estimated to have increased by about 16 per cent, to US$120 billion in 2007. At 0.9 per cent, their share in world merchandise exports remained at its highest level since 1980. See pg. 8.

than four per cent of world merchandise exports. Only two African countries featured on the list of leading traders.[7] Mainly oil exporting ones performed well, but this has cycled with the global price of oil.[8] However, it has been observed that after three decades of stagnation and decline, and the crisis of 2008/2009 notwithstanding, Sub-Saharan countries were now growing at the same rate as all developing countries (save for China and India) (Aryeetey, Devarajan, Kanbur and Kasekende, 2012). Seventeen non-oil-exporters sustained better that four per cent GDP growth for over a decade before the crisis. It has been observed however that in many other countries, growth stalled because of political instability or other internal and external factors.[9] Furthermore, and of more direct relevance to this study, is the apparent tenuous relationship between greater activism in domestic level trade and economic reforms on the one hand, and the minimal, nominal and largely ineffective participation in the WTO, on the other hand. Why is it that African WTO trade negotiators, including those from countries pursuing far reaching domestic reforms (on the basis of World Bank and IMF country programmes and trade rules agreed in the Uruguay Round) participate minimally, nominally and ineffectively?

4. Developing Country Participation in the Multilateral Trading System: Research "*L'État d'Avancement*"

There has been considerable initial useful work on the participation of developing countries in the trading system from the GATT to the WTO. This work reflected minimal specificity to African participation, but provided vital analytic perspectives that could be broadly applied to African participation in the trading system. Part of the reason for the research gap in the analysis of African participation was because, to a large extent, African "interest and participation" in the multilateral trading system only emerged and became apparent with the 1995 establishment of the WTO. There was also considerable research interest on the question of the implementation difficulties that confronted African countries with regard to the legal results from the Uruguay Round.

At the first and second African Trade Ministers meetings in Harare, Zimbabwe and Algiers, Algeria in 1998 and 1999 respectively, African Trade Ministers stated that they were unaware of the details of the Uruguay Round results unto which they had signed. At the Fourth Ordinary Session of the OAU/AEC in Abuja, Nigeria (September 2001), OAU/AEC Trade Ministers stated that, African countries continued to be constrained by limited technical and institutional capacities to fully adapt their national laws and fulfil their obligations as required and take full advantage of the provisions of multilateral trade agreements.[10]

---

[7] Nigeria and South Africa. *See International Trade Statistics 2008*, WTO Secretariat, pg. 12.

[8] According to the World Trade Report 2008, somewhat, unexpected is the finding that imports of the non-oil exporting African countries increased as rapidly as those of the oil-exporting countries. See pg. 8.

[9] Aryeetey, Devarajan, Kanbur and Kasekende, the *Oxford Companion to the Economics of Africa*, Oxford University Press, 2012

[10] OAU/AEC/TD/MIN/Decl.2 (IV) Rev.3, 19–23 September 2001.

The range of research on developing country participation in the multilateral trading system encompassed a wide range of dependent variables that required explanation. It cleared the underbrush and pointed the way forward to how the participation of different developing country groups in the rules-based system could be further researched and analysed. This study has built on earlier research on developing country participation with specific application to Africa. Several of the explanations with evident applications to African participation could be grouped as follows:

(i) *Passivity and Defensiveness*: initial research exploring for the low level of developing country institutional engagement in the early years of the GATT, started from the thesis baseline that developing countries as a whole adopted a largely passive and defensive attitude, did not engage in significant ways in the mutual exchange of concessions, and sought exceptions from GATT obligations and code of behaviour (Hudec, 1987, edited in 2009 and 2011).[11] Scholars built on this classic analysis by Robert Hudec. Variants of this thesis, applied to different periods, were reinforced by various scholars. Research noted the shift from the original passivity, defensiveness and special and differential treatment approach in developing country trade policy behaviour to reform and trade liberalizing behaviour by the mid-1980s. (Whalley, 1982; Srinivasan, 1998; Michalopoulos, 1999; Tussie and Lengyel, 2000; Page, 2001; Narlikar, 2004; Bhagwati, 2005; Kessie and Apea, 2006, Trachtman, 2009).

(ii) *Developing Countries as Satellite-Type Regimes*: based on the fact that many developing countries, in the immediate post-independence period were satellites of former colonial authorities, their participation levels were low and they were quiescent in trade policy exchanges. These satellite-type regimes were heavily influenced by former colonial authorities through whom GATT was de facto applied (Kessie and Apea, 2006; Wilkinson and Scott, 2007).

(iii) *Developing Countries – Quiet By-Standers*: literature also suggests that developing countries were quiet bystanders, lacking expertise or political representation to participate fully and attempt to redress the biases in the institution's design. (Croome, 1995; Srinivasan, 2000; Hoekman and Kostecki, 2001; Tussie and Lengyel, 2002; Narlikar, 2004; Bhagwati, 2005).

(iv) *Rule-Making Front – Developing Countries Insulated from Engagement*: On the rule-making front, most developing countries especially the smaller and poorer ones were largely insulated from pressure to engage in rules-related commitments other than those acquired at the time of accession to GATT (Low, 2007). This study explored this point further and argued that wholesale exemption of African countries, particularly least developed countries from WTO rules and procedures, based on current evidence, compromises the effective participation and integration of such countries into the WTO system. Building on the classic analysis of Robert Hudec.

11 Hudec Robert (1987). Developing Countries in the GATT Legal System. London: Trade Policy Research Centre. Edited in 2009 with an afterword by Joel P. Tractchman; re-issued in 2010 by Cambridge University Press with an introduction by Michel Finger.

(v) *Developing Countries' "Activism" in the GATT – Revisionism*: Some researchers have taken an opposite view to argue that developing countries were not excluded from participating in the activities of the GATT. They argue that developing countries were active and sought to participate in the day-to-day running of the GATT from its outset and to influence major events in its institutional development. (Wilkinson and Scott, 2007; Ismail, 2008). They also argue that despite documented constraints of developing country participation, these countries were heavily involved in the ITO negotiations, in tariff cutting negotiations and subsequent negotiations to adjust GATT to better reflect their interests. Developing countries provided chairs and vice chairs of committees from the outset and were represented in all negotiating committees. (Wilkinson and Scott, 2007).[12] The evidence adduced and analysed by these researchers requires further discussion. For instance some of the countries at the founding of the GATT that are now designated as developing countries such as South Africa were actually grouped as developed countries in the period.

(vi) *Special and Differential Treatment Approach in the GATT*: there are suggestions in the literature that the special and differential treatment approach by developing countries in the early years of the GATT provided these countries with no incentive for effective engagement and participation in the system. In other words, the exemption-orientation approach essentially weakened these countries and reduced their ability for effective engagement (Hudec 1987, edited in 2009, 2010).

(vii) *Principal Supplier Rule and Developing Countries*: it has been suggested that developing countries participation was limited by the principal supplier rule on which tariff negotiations took place on a commodity-by-commodity basis, because most of them were not such suppliers. (Page, 2001; Narlikar, 2004; Wilkinson, 2006).

(viii) *The GATT Classic Agenda*: literature suggests that developing country issues including agriculture and textiles and clothing were not high on the agenda of GATT till after 1986, accounting for their low levels of participation (Page, 2001; Narlikar, 2004); Other commentators argue that developing country interests were excluded because of their choice not to engage in reciprocal tariff bargaining which allowed industrialised states to maintain high levels of protection on developing country exports (Hoekman and Kostecki, 2001; Bhagwati, 2005).

(ix) *UNCTAD Rather Than GATT – "Developing Country Institution"*: literature also reveals that in the 1960s and 70s developing countries viewed UNCTAD rather than the GATT as the main institution through which they could promote their interests in international trade. (Hudec, 1987 and 2010; Michalopoulos, 1999; Page, 2001). Therefore, developing country participation was high at UNCTAD and low at the GATT.

(x) *WTO Decision-Making and Participation*: Some have established a relationship between decision-making, on the one hand, and participation, on the other. They have analysed this relationship as having affected more Least-Developed Countries (LDCs),

[12] Some of the documented constraints mentioned include – technical expertise, human resources and financial constraints. Wilkinson and Scott emphasize that the focus of their study is on participation and not aimed at determining whether participation was effective or influential.

most of which are African countries. (Michalopoulos, 1999; Tussie and Lengyel, 2002; Low, 2007).

(xi) *Rational Choice by Countries to Be Inactive*: The rational choice thesis has applied to the analysis of participation. It is argued, that the inactive participation of developing countries including African countries is the result of rational behaviour. Countries with limited trade policy capacity or limited capacity to engage in sustained analysis of trade issues might do well to focus internally rather than externally including on issues like infrastructure, human resource development and stable macro-economic development. (Dunoff, 2007). To be plausible, however, it is argued that this conclusion would have to assume rationality. It is not always obvious that the behaviour of appointed negotiators in all cases is rational. There is a diversity of idiosyncratic propensities. Attributing rationality to all positions and behaviour of trade negotiators exaggerates the rationality assumption and absolutely excludes the interplay of irrationality either in the psychology and/or misreads behaviour linked to domestic circumstances of the negotiators. In addition, while policy objectives or priorities are never clear or straight forward in the face of multiply challenges that confront policy makers, greater engagement in the rules-based multilateral trading system and the global economy carry greater welfare and competitiveness gains. However one may analyse the question of rational ignorance, it is argued in this study that it is a mistake and irrational for African policy makers not to focus on multilateral institutions such as the WTO to assist them with their domestic reforms. WTO Agreements through their binding nature engender the necessary locking in of policy and forestall policy reversals and uncertainty and unpredictability of national trade policy.

4.1 *Changes in Developing Countries' Trade Policy Behaviour and Participation-Levels from the mid-1980s*

A series of events from the mid-1980s modified the attitude of developing countries as a whole to the GATT-based multilateral trading system. In 1986, the Uruguay Round was launched. On the agenda of the Round were issues of real commercial interest to developing countries. These included: agriculture, textiles and clothing and a unique development orientation to trade in services. In the mid-1980s, developing countries embarked on massive domestic reforms in response to the shocks between 1979 and 1981 and the consequent global economic recession.

(i) *Waning of Scepticism to Trade Liberalization*: research by scholars argued with evidence that scepticism to trade liberalization began to wane amongst developing countries as these countries undertook wide-ranging domestic reforms. Reduction in resistance and ambivalence to the trading system was reinforced by the 1991 collapse of the Soviet Union and the lessons drawn over a 10-year period from the former centrally planned command economies to market economies (Rajapatirana, (2000); Sharer, (2000); Hoekman B and Kostecki (2009), Hoekman (2010)). Disillusionment took hold with the negative returns to policies of import substitution. In an afterword on the work of Hudec on developing countries, it is observed that Hudec's model could not anticipate the significant amount of unilateral liberalization effected by developing countries since 1987. It is observed further that much of this liberalization did not take place in a formal reciprocal context, although it is possible that it constituted asynchronous reciprocity or was motivated by the desire to have a reciprocal threat to use to hold open foreign markets (Trachtman, 2009).

(ii) *Effectiveness of Special and Differential Treatment Questioned*: questions emerged about the effectiveness of special and differential treatment (Croome, 1995; Kessie and Apea, 2006; Kessie, 2007). It was observed however in this study that in the context of the Doha Round, initiatives were on-going to strengthen and make more precise and operational special and differential treatment for developing countries. Is this an indication of the change in outlook about the potential utility of special and differential treatment? As it has been observed, in light of Hudec's 1987 work and subsequent developments, the questions that need to be asked are which obligations should not be imposed on/accepted by developing countries, which obligations should be imposed on/accepted by developing countries, and how and when should these latter obligations be contingently relaxed. (Trachtman, 2009). These are indeed some of the fundamental questions currently facing negotiators in the Doha Development Round.

(iii) *Developing Countries Become Major Exporters*: Developing countries had become major exporters of manufactured goods and the opening up of their markets became high on the agenda.

(iv) *Developed Countries Unwilling to Accept Continued Free-Riding*: Literature suggests that developed countries were no longer willing to accept free-riding on a number of areas including on services and intellectual property. Two occurrences during the Uruguay Round have been mentioned as changing the face of rule-making for developing countries – (i) enactment of new agreements including on services and intellectual property and changes to the Tokyo Round Agreements; (ii) the single undertaking, which removed the option that developing countries had of choosing whether or not to participate in agreements going beyond what they had signed on, on assuming membership. (Page, 2001; Kessie and Apea, 2006; Low, 2007).[13]

4.2 *"Africa-Specific" Literature on Participation*

In contrast to the overarching research explaining changes in developing country participation in the trading system, there are some studies specifically related to Africa's institutional and substantive engagement. These researches focused on institutionally precise questions of participation (poor performance and low level of representation) and related questions of "achievements", "capacity to offer concessions" and the effect of negotiating procedures, such as the "single undertaking" on the participation of African countries.

With specific regard to Africa, it has been argued that African countries achieved little because they failed to liberalize their own trade policies. (Yeo, 2005). Others observed that African countries received fewer concessions in comparison to other developing

[13] It has been observed that while African and developing countries initially balked at the idea of adopting a single undertaking approach, they eventually accepted it on the condition that there would be disciplines in areas of interest to them particularly textiles and clothing. (Kessie and Apea, 2006)

countries in the Uruguay Round because they offered few concessions. (Wang and Winters, 1997). African countries paid little attention to external developments that affected their trade and trade prospects. They have traditionally not been active or assertive participants in multilateral trade negotiations. (Lyakurwa, 2005). In addition, there were inadequate domestic policy response and supply side constraints in African countries hindering the ability of African countries to gain much from the Uruguay Round. (Croome, 1995). These areas need to be explored further in light of changes to trade policy behaviour and participation of African countries in the WTO in more recent years.

Cost and capacity constraints: cost and capacity constraints have been limitations that scholars have considered as applying more severely to Africa than other developing country regions. Most scholars draw a relationship to cost and capacity constraints, particularly human resources devoted to WTO activities in Geneva and in capitals (Croome, 1995; Blackhurst, Lyakurwa and Oyejide, 2000; Ohiorhenuans, 2005; Low et al., 2006; Nordstrom, 2007; Wilkinson and Scott, 2007). Blackhurst and Lyakurwa (1999) identify the problem of non-resident delegations, which was acute until the late 1990s. Capacity has also been articulated to relate to analytical capacity for developing of proposals, articulating positions and understanding the implications of agreements and weak institutional capacities in public and private sectors.

5. Critique of Existing Literature on African-Country Participation in the WTO and Justification for Research

The results of initial research so far, have cleared the underbrush and made important contributions. The bulk of these studies have focused on overarching developing country participation in the trading system with some studies more specific to African participation.

Analysis of the behaviour of African countries has been extrapolated from thesis and conclusions from the undifferentiated developing country category. This is too-broad a category that requires differentiation and where analysis has to be more precisely targeted to explain African country behaviour in the trading system in the light of recent evidence. Existing analysis requires update to take into account changed circumstances.

A range of plausible explanations have resulted from current research. These have relevance to the research questions for this study. However, more work is required. For instance, research still needs to explain why African engagement and participation remains largely minimal, tentative and defensive, even with the correction and/or mitigation over time of some of the factors considered to handicap participation particularly cost, and human resource capacity (including the question of knowledge-deficit). Initial human capacity constraints including representation in Geneva have been largely addressed. Logistic issues have to a large extent been resolved for small delegations for the coverage of meetings. Cost considerations for dispute settlement are being addressed through an increasing number of law firms with growing opportunities for *pro bono* assistance and training. The WTO Secretariat has focused most of its technical assistance activities on developing countries particularly on African countries. Development agencies and multilateral institutions are also providing considerable assistance with a focus on African countries. This study draws on existing research of developing country participation with specific and focused application to African WTO membership. On the basis of more recent evidence, African participation in the three core areas of WTO regular committee work, the Doha negotiations and, dispute settlement, from 1995–2010 was investigated.

6. Propositions/Hypothesis Tested

1. Trade shares, income and development levels correlate with the degree of participatory effectiveness in the GATT/WTO system. Participation of Members with higher trade shares and GDP levels tends to be higher than those with lower levels, although this could be mediated by "competitiveness rankings".
2. Inextricable interrelationships exist in the three core areas of WTO work although more intensive systemic engagement in dispute settlement has tended to yield greater systemic payback.
3. Wholesale exemption from WTO rules and procedures has undermined the effective participation of African Members in the GATT/WTO System.
4. Preoccupation with a special and differential treatment approach, resistance to reciprocity and a predisposition to waivers are strongly associated with participation levels.
5. Members accustomed to the rule of law and transparency in governance at the municipal level are more likely to effectively engage in WTO regular work, negotiations and dispute settlement.
6. Despite existing constraints, professional commitment and sustained hard work by individual delegates, positively impacts participation levels.
7. Low levels of technical expertise, capacity constraints and high costs have limited the participation of African countries.

CHAPTER TWO

PARTICIPATION – THE CAPACITY FACTOR

1. Introduction

At the coming into force of the WTO and up until the launch of the Doha Round in 2001, African Members of the WTO maintained the position that they had not participated in the Uruguay Round with full knowledge. They took the position that trade policy technical skill levels had been and were low. As a consequence, the Organization had to focus on implementation, training and developing the trade policy capacity levels of African WTO Members. They conditioned agreement on any new round of trade negotiations to significant investments in training and capacity building.[1] In summary, the rudimentary capacity question raised by African countries in 1995 was that they had neither fully understood the Uruguay Round Agreements they had signed, nor the complex functioning of the rules-based system in its initial years.

The capacity question researched in this study related to the existence of expert and specialized skills of African delegations to operate skilfully and competently in the rules-based multilateral trading system. Specifically, it related to the development and presentation of proposals in regular work or negotiations; request for consultations in the dispute settlement system, establishment of dispute settlement panels, drafting submissions and sustaining arguments, and serving as panellists or Appellate Body Members. In regular committee work and negotiations, skilled capacity was linked to sustaining negotiations for building consensus on proposals; systematically analysing proposals of counter-parties; and, sustained engagement throughout the informal and formal process.

This chapter examines the "capacity-factor question" in relation to African Members' WTO participation. Specifically, it reviewed the capacity factor question of African Missions to the WTO, from 1995 to 2010. The following questions were examined:

- In relation to other regions, what was the average size of African Missions to the WTO in the period examined? Where these based in Geneva?

[1] Organization of African Unity/African Economic Community, Joint Statement Circulated by Ministers of Trade at the Second WTO Ministerial Conference, 18 May 1998, WT/MIN (98)/ST/72. Cairo Declaration, 27 April 2000, WT/L/348.

- Did legal capacity for WTO work exist? In what ways did the level of legal capacity affect use of the DSU?
- What measures were taken to offset or compensate for insufficient levels of WTO capacity?
- In what ways has the African Group, or its individual Members endeavoured to address the question of analytical capacity?
- In what ways has the level of capacity affected systemic WTO participation?

The broad question of the level and quality of participation of developing countries, including African countries, in the GATT/WTO system, has been linked to capacity constraints, unaffordable costs and human resource limitations in capitals and Geneva missions of these Members (Croome, 1995; Blackhurst, Lyakurwa and Oyejide, 2000; Ohiorhenuans, 2005; Low et al., 2006; Nordstrom, 2007; Wilkinson and Scott, 2007). On the basis of evidence, it is argued in this study that weak institutional capacities, in the public sectors of developing countries, explain only in part, and only in the "start-up" years of the WTO, the nominal, minimal and largely ineffective participation of African countries as a sub-set of the developing country group in WTO negotiations, regular committee work and dispute settlement. It is to be noted however that the existence of non-resident delegations in Geneva which was acute in the early years of the WTO compounded the factor of capacity constraint. It has been argued in this study that physical establishment of trade policy negotiators, on site, at the WTO in Geneva carry effects for the effectiveness and quality of legal and institutional participation/engagement in the rules-based multilateral trading system.

2. Location of African Missions to the WTO: 1995, 2001, 2005 and 2010[2]

It is suggested that the specific years of 1995, 2001, 2005 and 2010 are important milestones for reviewing the evolution of the "capacity factor constraint" and its robustness as an explanation of the effectiveness and quality of African WTO Members' engagement/participation in the rules-based multilateral trading system. Evidently, the capacity factor exercised a significant influence in 1995. The question remains the degree of influence this factor continued to exercise 15 years later in 2010.

(a) *The State of Play in 1995*

With the establishment of the WTO in 1995, half of the 33 African WTO Members had representation in Geneva.[3] However, the 50 per cent Geneva-based representation was the lowest in comparison with Members in other regions. For example, representation for North America and the Middle East were 100 per cent of their WTO Members; 96.5

[2] 1995 marked the establishment of the WTO; the DDA negotiations were launched in 2001; 2005 was original mandate to conclude the DDA; 2010 reflected the 15 year end period of this study.

[3] About 30 per cent of African WTO Members had representation in Brussels; 13 per cent were represented directly through their capitals and 7 per cent in other locations, mostly in other European cities – Bonn, London, and Paris.

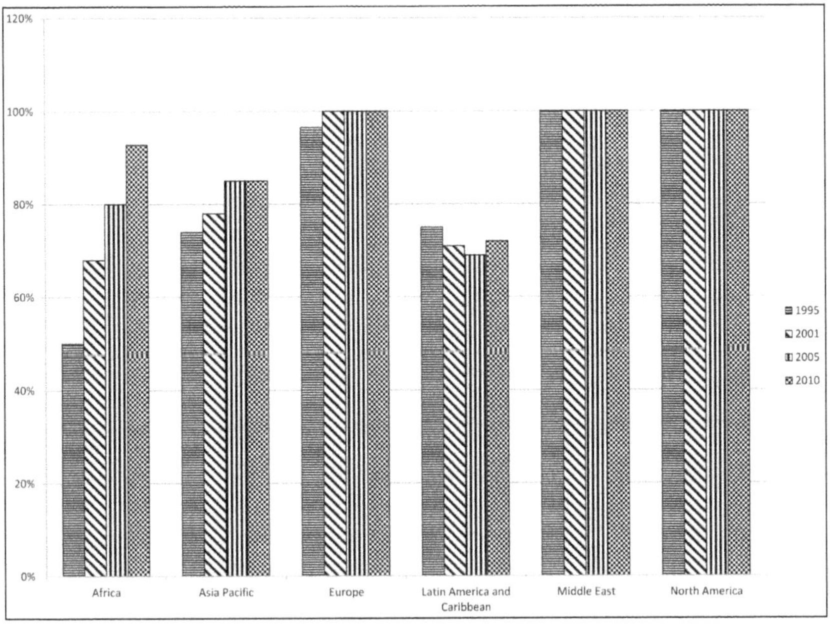

Figure 4. Members with WTO missions in Geneva.

per cent for Europe; 74 per cent for Asia-Pacific; and, 75 per cent for Latin American and Caribbean. (Figure 4).

(b) *State of Play in 2001*

Figure 4 shows that in 2001, coinciding with the launch of the Doha Development Agenda (DDA) negotiations, there was relative improvement across all regions in Geneva-based representation to the WTO, compared to 1995. African WTO Member representation improved to 68 per cent – an increase of 36 per cent – the highest in comparison to regions that did not have 100 per cent representation in 1995. With the launch of the DDA negotiations, African Members, like others, committed more resources to the negotiations to improve capacity to participate in the negotiations. Their individual statements indicated that they wanted to influence the shaping of future rules that would govern the multilateral trading system. In their judgement, they saw this as an opportunity to rebalance the system and improve on the Uruguay Round results.

With the expiry of a number of transition periods for the implementation of WTO Agreements, there was pressure on African delegations to improve institutional participation, with legal effects, through compliance with their obligations such as notifications and elimination of WTO-inconsistent obligations. Physical establishment in Geneva was therefore necessary for improved legal and institutional participation. African delegations understood that there was a relationship between effective participation, on the one hand, and the size and capacity of their delegations on the other hand. The question was whether their knowledge and assessment of the capacity factor question could be resolved by their national "sending" authorities.

(c) *State of Play in 2005*

In 2005, there was further increase in African representation, in comparison to 1995 and 2001. The year 2005 was the original mandated timeline for concluding the Doha negotiations. In 2005, 80 per cent of African-WTO Members had missions in Geneva. All Members in North America, Europe and Middle-East had Geneva missions. In the Asia-Pacific, 85 per cent of WTO Members, had representation in Geneva. The Latin American and Caribbean region had the lowest presence with 69 per cent of Members in that region having a mission in Geneva. The overall improvement in representation to the WTO during this period was an indicator of the importance and priority that WTO Members, including African countries, attached to the DDA negotiations.

(d) *State of Play in 2010*

In 2010, the percentage of African representation in Geneva further increased to 92.8 per cent compared to 80% in 2005, 68% in 2001 and 50% in 1995. This was further indication of the understanding by African Members of the relationship between capacity and effective participation. The question however still to be answered was whether improvement in nominal capacity was matched by qualitative improvement in capacity, technical expertise and engagement of individuals to enhance effectiveness. In other words, increase in nominal capacity does not necessarily increase effective capacity.

More broadly, as of December 2010, of the 42 African WTO Members, 39 had a mission in Geneva. Three African Members were non-resident in Geneva.[4] All three non-resident African WTO Members were represented through their respective embassies in Brussels. Three African Members, Egypt, Nigeria and South Africa had specific commercial offices dedicated to WTO work.

By 2010, Africa had registered an 85.6 percentage increase of its members represented in Geneva from 1995 when the WTO was established and a 36.4 per cent increase since the launch of the Doha Development Agenda negotiations in 2001. Only 7.2 per cent of African Members were non-resident, compared to 32 per cent in 2001 and 50 per cent in 1995. However, as is illustrated in the following sections, although there were relative nominal increases, the human resources actually allocated by African missions to WTO work remained low.

The state of play, 15 years after the establishment of the WTO, therefore revealed that the situation of very low representation in Geneva, as significantly hampering African participation in the WTO had significantly improved. The question that remained was why was it that with the "correction"/mitigation of one of the key participation constraining factors African engagement and participation still remained nominal, minimal and ineffective? Other factors such as mission size, legal capacity and capital support were also examined.

[4] These were Gambia, Malawi and Sierra Leone. As of 2011, Sierra Leone was in the process of establishing its Geneva Mission.

3. Size of WTO Missions: 1995 and 2010

(a) *State of Play in 1995*

Figure 5 shows that in 1995, sizes of missions of the 33 African WTO Members were very small in relation to the mission sizes of Members in other regions. The total number of African delegates, that is, in all missions was 97. This was low in comparison to the number of delegates in other regions with fewer members. This research explored through regression whether there was a correlation between trade and GDP levels and the size of missions. The results suggested that although mission size could be related to trade shares and GDP and consequently commercial interests, the regression results in charts 9, 10, 25, and 26 in Annex III suggested that trade shares and GDP did not matter for mission size. Whether a Members' GDP/trade share level was low or high did not seem to affect mission size. One possible explanation could be that the WTO is about *rules* and not simply about "*commercial interests*". In other words, WTO Members have interests in both commercial matters and rules pertaining to trade law and regulation, including and in particular in "behind-the-border" measures regardless of trade shares and GDP levels and commit resources depending on the priority they attach.

The total number of delegates of European Members was 125 (29 Members); Latin America and Caribbean 95 (27 Members); Asia-Pacific, 104 (18 Members); Middle East, 7 (3 Members) and North America 20 (2 Members). The average number of delegates in the mission of Members in North America was 10; 5.7 for the Asia-Pacific; 4.3 for Europe; 3.5 for Latin America & Caribbean countries; 3 for African countries; and, 2.3 for the Middle East.

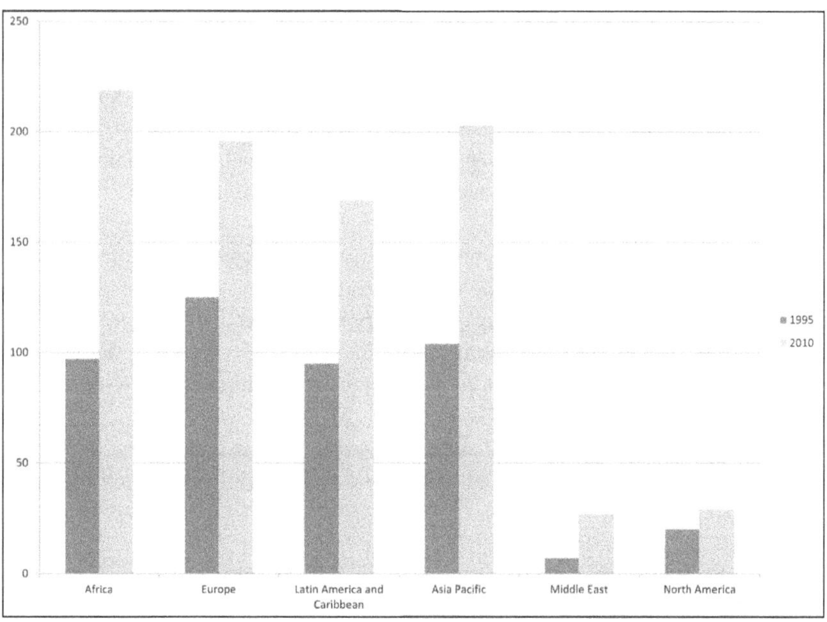

Figure 5. Size of country missions by region 1995 and 2010.

(b) *State of Play in 2010*

2010 shows a significantly improved situation across all regions. (Figure 5). The Middle East had the highest percentage increase – 286 per cent – with a total of 27 delegates, representing 3.4 delegates per mission. Africa had a percentage increase in number of delegates of 125, from 1995, with a total of 218 delegates. This translated to an average of 4 delegates per mission. The Asia-Pacific region with 203 delegates, had a 95 per cent increase, an average of 7 delegates per mission. The Latin America & Caribbean with a total of 169 delegates had a 78 per cent increase, with 5.3 delegates per mission. Europe with a total of 196 delegates had a percentage increase of 57 per cent, translating into an overall average of 5 delegates per mission and, North America with a total of 29 delegates had a 45 per cent increase in delegates, which represented an average of 15 delegates per mission.

By 2010, the evidence indicated that the average size of African WTO missions had relatively improved, although it remained low relative to other regions. But, this relative increase was also reflected in their level of engagement/participation in regular committee work, in such areas as SPS, TBT, TRIPS, and trade policy reviews. This relative improvement in engagement and participation was most reflected in the Doha negotiations. Cotton, special and differential, intellectual property, trade facilitation and other development-related areas were the most evident and illustrative. However, engagement and participation in the dispute settlement system remained self-evidently low despite increases in mission size and capacity building, even with 15 years of the existence and functioning of the WTO and its dispute settlement system. This issue is elaborated more in chapter six.

Although the Middle East and Africa registered relatively significant percentage increases in the number of delegates per missions in comparison to other regions, it should be recalled that their "base" figures were very low, at an average of 2.5 delegates per mission. The increases although important, do not compare to number of delegates in Members in relatively advanced or emerging economies such as in the North America, Europe, Asia Pacific and Latin American regions, with generally higher shares of global trade and traditions of trade policy negotiations. The capacity factor remains relevant in explaining, in part, participation/engagement. The original argument by Professor Hudec should be recalled, namely that,

"The relative novelty of the developing-country problem should be borne in mind when viewing its evolution during the next 40 years. Not only was there no golden age to point towards as a goal but, perhaps more important, there had been no past failures that could serve as a lesson about what not to do – nothing resembling the lesson that developed countries had been taught by the beggar-thy-neighbour policies of the 1930s." (Hudec, 1987): 7 and Hudec, 2011: 27).

While it could be concluded that overall, the size of missions to the WTO significantly increased across all regions,[5] which seemed to be mainly as a result of decisions

[5] Research showed a trend towards an overall downturn in delegate numbers in a number of missions in 2009. It could partly be explained by the state of progress in the DDA negotiations, which had been the focus of work for most delegations in the past 8 years. In addition, several missions have national-policy diplomatic rotation on a four-yearly basis.

by national governments to allocate more resources to WTO work including the DDA negotiations, some regions more rationally allocated human resources than others. Although the proposition has been consistently argued that the more the number of officials allocated to WTO work, the better the level of participation and engagement, this explanation is partial. Other factors were at play because although the size of African delegation was low, it nominally increased, but not always with effective improvements/ engagement, in an even distribution across the three core areas of regular committee work, negotiations and dispute settlement.

North America and certain Asia-Pacific and European countries had the highest numbers of delegates per mission across the 15 year period (1995–2010) studied. Japan had the highest average number of delegates in its mission – 25 delegates. Korea followed with an average of 20 delegates. Other Asia-Pacific countries that had a relatively high average number of delegates included China (16), Thailand (16), Chinese Taipei (15) and Australia (8). Several of these countries are high or middle-income countries and have domestically taken decisions to specifically devote resources to WTO work. Several of them are leading traders[6] with significant commercial interests. They attach institutional priority to the WTO as a rules-based system. These Members actively participate in WTO regular work, dispute settlement and trade negotiations.

In the period reviewed, there were countries in the Asia-Pacific region, whose average number of delegates in missions was comparable or even less than those in Africa – Sri Lanka and Solomon Islands (2 on average) and Maldives (1). Like the majority of African WTO Members, most of these are low-income countries.[7]

In Europe, European Union member-states had relatively higher average of delegates including Spain (12); Belgium (11) and Germany (10). Turkey also had a relatively high average of delegates – 12. However, there were a number of mostly small low-income developing countries with average numbers of delegates that were relatively low – Moldova; FYR Macedonia, Kyrgyz Republic – an average of two delegates. Other European countries with low delegate averages included Lithuania; Latvia; Croatia and Bulgaria. However, any capacity constraint of individual EU Members was compensated for by the fact that the European Commission is mandated to negotiate and speak on their behalf. This therefore assisted in mitigating any capacity constraint pressures.

Some countries in the Latin-American and Caribbean region had on average, a relatively high number of delegates in their missions: Argentina (10), Brazil (16), Mexico (10) and Uruguay (9). The Caribbean countries in general had relatively low average numbers of delegates, examples included Dominica (1.45) Belize (1.7); Grenada (1.6) and Saint Kitts & Nevis and St Vincent and Grenadines – one (1).

In Africa, Egypt (12), Nigeria (8), South Africa (8) and Mauritius (7) had a relatively higher average number of delegates than other African Members. Djibouti and Guinea Bissau had an overall very low average of delegates at one delegate. Notable was the case

6 WTO Secretariat, International Trade Statistics, 2010.

7 The data was mainly collected from the WTO's directory – "the blue book", which indicates a Members' delegation each month. In terms of data accuracy, it observed that in supplying information to be used in the directory, some Members do not distinguish between delegates whose sole responsibility is WTO work from other UN or other international bodies duties; nor is there in some cases a clear distinction between professional and administrative officers.

of Benin, which up to 2005 had an average delegate count of three (3). This increased to an average count of 7.5. A plausible explanation was the emergence of its offensive interest in the negotiations on agriculture; the sectoral initiative on cotton, launched in May 2003, with a mandate for negotiations established in the 1 August 2004 General Council Decision – "The July Package". Three East African countries also had relatively high number of delegates in their missions. These were: Kenya (5), Uganda (5) and Tanzania (7.6).

The data reviewed found an average of four (4) delegates per African mission. In 2009, there were 147 meetings per week. The scope, volume, complexity and technical expertise required for participation in these meetings exceeded the capacity of a mission with four delegates on the average.[8] This situation was compounded by the fact that most African delegations are accredited to and have to cover the activities of other international organisations headquartered in Geneva. However African delegations that responded to the questionnaire administered to them said that on average they allocated 74 per cent of their time to WTO work. This seemed to suggest that African delegates prioritise WTO work. However, respondents consistently pointed to the challenge of limited human resource capacity in their missions.

The point must be made that mission size to the WTO in Geneva is not a standalone factor. The mission-size factor is related to Geneva/capital coordination and how particular Members organize and use their capacity for WTO engagement/participation. Therefore, while the mission size of a Member may be "small", it may not matter, if there is tight coordination with capitals. For instance, Geneva/capital coordination was tight, steady and institutionalized for WTO Members such as the US, EU, Japan, Brazil, India, China, Argentina and some others, while for many African Members, Geneva-based mission size is extraordinarily significant because of the continuing weaknesses in Geneva-capital coordination.

With specific regard to African WTO membership, although the situation with regard to size of missions relatively improved over the past 15 years, there continued to be a capacity deficit that limited effective participation and was compounded by weaknesses in Geneva-capital coordination. Increase in nominal capacity does not necessarily increase effectiveness in participation levels. This is an area that would require greater analysis. There is yet scope for qualitative improvements in participation.

At this time, the key question is for domestic national policy decision-making: the value and priority a government assigns to trade and the WTO as a national policy objective. It has been argued in this study that overall capacity for trade policy is necessary. Even with the pressures and dilemmas for the allocation of resources to competing priority demands, specialized capacity for trade is critical. Trade is an engine for growth. The Doha Round negotiations have made it clear that specialized capacity for trade is not only about securing gains from trade, it is also about regulating Africa's relationship with other WTO Members and defining the place of the Continent in the global

[8] In 1995 it was estimated that the WTO held 454 meetings, averaging 11 meetings per week. This work load has significantly increased. As of 2009; there were 322 formal meetings; 237 informal multilateral and plurilateral meetings; and, 6536 private meetings (appellate body, panels, Chair consultations, bilateral meetings). This came to a total of 7,095 (half-day meetings).

economy. African engagement in trade at the WTO also provides the vital nexus to the achievement of development priorities. The WTO is more than trade negotiations. It has emerged as one of the principal pillars for global governance in the trilateral relationship between trade, finance and development. In close to now 20 years of its functioning, it has rapidly and firmly established, not only as a forum for trade negotiations, but also as a forum for international cooperation. As a consequence, allocation of resources and prioritization of trade are not optional extras or choices. They stand and should stand at the top of the scale of priorities in resource allocation for trade capacity development.

4. Capital Support

In assessing the participation of a Member, the "support" and "communication" received from capital authorities are crucial in, at least, three respects. First, clarity of instructions. Second, supply of required background, including legislative and regulatory information. Third, increased capacity back-up when the delegation is overstretched, or the subject matter requires specialized and technical capital-based expertise.

This section analysed the responses to the questionnaire administered to African WTO Members, on the "*level and quality of technical support and the content clarity of communication*" provided from capitals. (See Annex IV for questionnaire sample and the tabulated results)

Thirty-nine (39) questionnaires were provided to the coordinator of the African Group to cover the universe of the 39 African WTO Members, resident in Geneva, and that participate at the weekly meetings of the WTO African Group. After one year of constant reminders, there was a poor return of nine (or 23% of Geneva-resident African WTO Members). The poor returns corroborate the thesis of minimal, nominal and largely ineffective levels of participation. In the nine responses to the question on "*level and quality of technical support and the content clarity of communication*", from capitals, one respondent gave a rating of "satisfactory"; another, "moderate"; and, seven, "minimal". These responses suggested that for several African WTO Members, the *level and quality of technical support and the content clarity of communication from their capitals was minimal and inadequate.* One of the respondents that expressed "satisfaction" with support referred not to substantive technical support, but to funding and "flexibility" that its mission received to manage its own policy. Coordination between Geneva and capitals was described as challenging and in some cases this suggested that the absence of effective and clear communication from capitals acted as a disincentive to effective engagement in the WTO. In other words, the low level of communication between capitals and African delegates was a demoralizing factor.

In addition to the analysed results from the questionnaire, interviews were conducted. These interviews underscored the low level of systematic support from capitals. Furthermore, the problem of coordination across government ministries and departments was identified. Support provided was diverse and frequently without a connecting rationality. This situation highlights the often complex domestic problem of inter-agency coordination and the challenges of collaboration in formulating coherent and consistent trade policy which ultimately reflect on participation in international organizations, including the WTO. However, the results of the analysis showed that when "support" and "instructions" were provided from capital authorities to negotiators in Geneva missions, and support and instructions were clear, consistent and based on domestic regulations and laws, there was a positive effect through increased levels of participation.

5. Legal Capacity in African WTO Missions

WTO Agreements are binding on its Members. In regular committee work, Members' engagement is focused on administering the rules, in a system of balanced rights and obligations. In trade negotiations, such as the on-going Doha negotiations, legal texts emerge from technical drafting processes. The results would be binding on all Members party to the negotiations. In dispute settlement, the ability for effective engagement in panel and Appellate Body work depends on expert and competent legal capacity in delegations.

This section undertook an inventory of existing legal capacity in African WTO Geneva missions, required to analyse, negotiate and draft legal texts and results of multilateral negotiations, with the caveat that in some Members the core work is undertaken in tight and sustained coordination between capitals and Geneva and sometimes drawing on the legal resources of private law firms. This inventory of legal capacity was used as an indication of the competent capacity of African delegations to effectively engage in the three areas of regular work, negotiations and dispute settlement.

In WTO dispute settlement this included providing in-house counsel, if the need arose.[9] In this research, legal capacity was determined on whether or not a mission had a lawyer or specialised trade lawyer dedicated to WTO work, and any experience of counsel, in terms of number of years spent specializing in WTO law. This study did not address "quality" of legal capacity, that is, type of training or where training was acquired.

For this study, a questionnaire was administered to African delegations in Geneva requesting their responses on the question of legal capacity to participate in dispute settlement, trade negotiations and regular committee work. Of the nine delegations that responded, four said that they had a lawyer in the delegation; five, that they did not have a lawyer. Of the four that said they had a lawyer, only three had ever been involved in some form in WTO dispute settlement. One was a least developed country. Of the five that said they did not have a lawyer, three had been involved in WTO dispute settlement, two had not. What conclusions could be drawn from these returns? First, the overall policy context is relevant namely that, African countries have not effectively engaged/

[9] Busch, Reinhardt and Shaffer (2008) – *Does Legal Capacity Matter? Explaining Dispute Initiation and Antidumping actions in the WTO*, ICTSD, defines legal capacity as the institutional resources required to prepare, prosecute and monitor a case, including legal, economic and diplomatic staff. They look beyond the number of staff to include broader bureaucratic apparatus that supports a government's interpretation of its obligations and enforcement of its rights under trade law. Their study focused on WTO dispute settlement and anti-dumping and not on legal capacity in relation to other areas of WTO work – regular work, negotiations, monitoring and surveillance. However, the results of their study hold true for these areas as well.

participated in the WTO dispute settlement system.[10] Second, taken together, very little could be drawn based on the poor returns and the results from the questionnaire. Broadly, however, the results showed the following:

- in total, nine African delegations (or 23%), of the Africa's WTO membership resident in Geneva, responded;
- 4 (or 10% of Africa's membership resident in Geneva, or 44% of those that responded) had legal capacity and 5 (or 12.8% of Africa's WTO membership resident in Geneva, or 55% of those who responded) had no legal capacity;
- 3 lawyers each from the two sub-sets, with and without legal capacity had participated/engaged in the WTO dispute settlement system.

This level of engagement was ineffective and, at best, minimal in relation to the number of African delegations. However, it needs to be added that African delegations have co-sponsored proposals for reform of the WTO Dispute Settlement Understanding. In regular committee work, participation/engagement has also been limited and legal capacity has not appeared to play an effective role for example in the area of notification defaults.

Participation in trade negotiations appear to be at a level of relative improvement over dispute settlement and regular committee work. This could be explained by the fact that the skill-set required in trade negotiations, although involved, entail *more* policy knowledge and *lower* levels of specialized legal technical competence and capacity and jurisprudential knowledge.

Respondents were asked from which government departments their trade delegates were drawn. Of the nine responses, seven (7) indicated that their delegates were drawn from the departments of commerce or the economy. Two (2) indicated that their delegates were drawn from the Foreign Affairs department. None of the respondents mentioned the department of Justice and/or Legal Affairs, which had been presented as an option. Although caution must be exercised because of the extremely poor rate of returns, this nonetheless strongly suggested that legal expertise appeared not to be a priority for several African countries in composing their delegations to a rules-based system operating on the strict parameters of the rule of law in trade.

Overall and consistent with the earlier finding of inadequate technical human resources in WTO missions, the results of this survey revealed that many countries in Africa did not deploy specialised legal staff dedicated to WTO work. Some factors could explain this situation. First, several of these countries do not seem to perceive the need and role of legal experts compared to for instance trade/commercial experts in WTO work – the prime business of the WTO being commerce or trade facilitation not necessarily dispute resolution; second, financial constraints to commit to specialised legal expertise; third, generally low levels of technical knowledge of WTO law and, fourth, no reason to have an "in-house" lawyer as several of these countries minimally or do not engage in WTO dispute settlement either as complainants; respondents or even third parties or where they do, can acquire "outside" legal assistance including pro bono services.

---

10 See Annex II (methodology) for the indices for dispute settlement participation/engagement namely, number of chairmanships, initiation of disputes(complainant roles), respondent (defendant) roles, third party roles, panellist roles, Appellate Body Member roles.

6. WTO African Cooperation – Case Study of the WTO African Group

To improve participation levels and mitigate insufficient levels of WTO capacity, African WTO Members have taken measures. An informal WTO African Group was established in 1995 to coordinate the positions of African delegations in the WTO, provide a forum for exchange of views on how best to improve Africa's participation in the multilateral trading system, including on Africa's participation in the precedent Uruguay Round of Multilateral Trade Negotiations. The structure, functioning and focus of the African group provide insights into the strengths and capacity shortfalls of the Group.

Interviews conducted with several coordinators of the Group, including its founding coordinator(s) revealed that the African Group has always acknowledged its strength in its numbers, but its limited engagement and equally limited results achieved. Establishment of the Group was motivated by the objective to mobilize the potential coalitional strength of the largest informal WTO regional grouping and also compensate for capacity, expert and other weaknesses. Participation in the Group is open to all African WTO Members and observer countries. The African Union office in Geneva and the Geneva liaison office of the UN Economic Commission for Africa undertake analysis and make policy suggestions with options for the Group.

(a) *Mandate of the WTO African Group*

The mandate of the African Group is established by African Ministers responsible for WTO matters in their annual meetings and at extraordinary sessions held inter-alia in preparation for WTO ministerial conferences.[11] Since the launch of the DDA negotiations in 2001, the mandate from Ministers has focused mostly on the negotiating aspect of WTO work.

(b) *Functioning of the WTO African Group*

The WTO African Group meets at two levels: ambassadors and officials. Ambassador-level meetings are aimed at providing direct political direction and guidance to the work of officials. Official meetings focus on technical aspects. The Group is co-ordinated on a rotational basis, in alphabetical order, by one of its members for a period of six-months. This term could be extended to one year. The coordinating African country derives its mandate from the Group as a whole. Proposals or statements made on behalf of the Group require the Group's prior approval.

The African Group meets at least once a week at the officials' level to discuss WTO issues, prepare proposals and exchange views on how to increase Africa's participation in the multilateral trading system. Overtime it has become an important forum for discussion, formulation of general positions and development of proposals of a more specific nature in those areas of WTO work and negotiations where common agreement can be found.

[11] A list of Communiqués/Declarations by African Ministers responsible for Trade which highlight African priorities in the WTO is in Annex V.

The African Group has developed a subject-focal point system, to pool resources together as a way of compensating for capacity deficits in individual African delegations. A focal point is responsible for representing the Group at respective meetings and reporting back to the Group. Focal points also initiate proposals to be tabled by the Group; arrange for meetings with other WTO delegations and organise briefing sessions for members of the Group.

Although there seem to be no formal rules on the conduct of affairs of the Group – being an informal grouping, focal points would be expected to operate on a rotational basis. However, certain countries have "traditionally" been the focal points for particular subjects. This could be attributable to the personality and professionalism of those particular delegates[12] designated focal point; the national interest of a delegation in a subject area hence time to follow it through; and the fact that other delegations are usually reluctant to take on these roles because of inadequate human resources in their missions bearing in mind that most of them are also responsible for the work in other international organisations in Geneva.

As of 2010, there were nine focal points in subject areas of the DDA negotiations.[13] The structure of focal points established in the African Group, the assignment of responsibilities and the pattern of work in the Group demonstrate near exclusive focus on the Doha negotiations. Regular work in WTO bodies and committees and dispute settlement are mainly handled by individual delegations, depending on commercial/systemic interest and the extent/timing of the application of obligations in WTO Agreements.

In response to the need to assist in addressing the capacity and resources problem in African WTO missions, the WTO African Group is one of the few informal grouping serviced directly by the WTO Secretariat. In addition to servicing meetings of the African Group, the WTO funds an intern to assist the coordinating African WTO Member.

(c) *Effectiveness of the WTO African Group*

All respondents to the questionnaire administered to African delegations in Geneva expressed dissatisfaction with the level of effectiveness and cooperation in the WTO African Group.[14] Of the nine respondents, four said that the level of effectiveness and cooperation was "work in progress" and five indicated "unsatisfactory". One respondent stated that it was difficult to reconcile positions of members at variant levels

12 For instance, a Kenyan delegate was the focal point for Special and Differential Treatment and NAMA. This delegate vigorously followed these issues. Even after the delegate left Geneva, Kenya was requested to take over responsibilities for these issues. The same can be said about the focal points on Cotton, which have seemed to rotate amongst the Cotton Four countries (Benin, Chad, Burkina Faso, and Mali).

13 The focal points are on Agriculture (Egypt); Cotton (Benin, Burkina Faso); NAMA (Kenya); Services (Morocco); Trade Facilitation (Rwanda); Special and Differential Treatment (Kenya, Egypt); TRIPS (Nigeria); Rules (Ghana). Generally, these focal points seem to suggest commercial or systemic interests by the holders in the subject areas.

14 This level of dissatisfaction has not always been so. In an interview with the founding coordinator, there was a high level of satisfaction and enthusiasm at the starting point of the African Group in 1995. However, this may have been more euphoria at the creation of the Group.

of development, adding that interests in the WTO were commercial in nature which rendered "solidarity" challenging.

Another respondent stated that the major difficulty lay in the ability of the African Group to take informed decisions. Positions were reached based on influence from countries/groups outside the African Group. A participant observer assessed the African Group as follows: "although they have considerable weight for political decisions and to be represented in small groups, they do not generally agree on any particular position…"[15]

Overall, the assessment was that the Group was minimally effective.

(d) *Challenges Facing the WTO African Group*

In interviews with WTO Secretariat officials that covered the African Group, the greatest challenge cited was reconciling frequently diverse commercial interests so as to distil a unified African Group position for its 42 members. In the Group there are least-developed countries that typically band together in the LDC Consultative Group and are differently treated by the System. In the LDC Group, there are non-African LDCs who make a claim for LDC benefits because of LDC status. In the on-going Doha negotiations, African WTO Members belong to a number of formal or informal groupings depending on national interest (NAMA 11; G33; G20, see Annex VII). For instance, South Africa is ambitious in agricultural liberalization, while Mauritius is defensive and co-sponsors defensive agricultural positions with Switzerland, Norway, Korea, Chinese Taipei, Iceland, Liechtenstein, Israel and Japan, its G10 partners. Furthermore, there are tensions and differences between the North African members and African delegations south of the Sahara, with North African WTO Members belonging both to the WTO Arab Group and the WTO African Group.

There are language challenges. The francophone respondents cited "language differences" as a challenge for effective co-operation in the African Group and for overall participation in WTO work. One respondent stated that documents were usually first distributed in English, making it not only difficult to engage in discussions for non-English speakers, but also delaying transmission of information to capitals for action and instructions.

One respondent stated that positions in the Group were reached based on influences from countries/groups outside the African Group. This situation has generated opposition by several in the Group who oppose issues they judge as "extraneous" in the position of "other" delegations, whom they consider as acting as a proxy for "others".

All respondents highlighted serious capacity constraints. One respondent stated that delegations were very thin and were therefore not readily available to undertake work for the Group. Another respondent stated that inadequacy of personnel was an impediment to participation.

---

[15] Manzoor Ahmed, Director, FAO Liaison Office, Geneva (Former Pakistan Ambassador to the WTO 2002–2008) "*Negotiating mechanisms, the various interest groups and their functioning*", Presentation to senior Vietnamese Trade Negotiators, IDEAS Centre, 23 September 2009.

(e) *Improving and Strengthening Cooperation on WTO Matters amongst African Delegates*

Respondents to the questionnaire administered were asked to recommend areas of action for improving or strengthening cooperation on WTO matters amongst themselves. All respondents said that it was important to improve "substance" by improving knowledge and expert analytical capacity in subject areas of the WTO, including through cooperation with other delegations. Related to this, most stated that contributions from other multilateral institutions and civil society would be important in enhancing cooperation within the African Group and with other WTO delegations.

The francophone respondents mentioned addressing language-related problems, particularly, timing of distribution of documents in all three official working languages of the WTO. This was important for their improved participation and cooperation within the African Group and also with other WTO delegations. Other areas for improvement within the African Group mentioned by respondents were coordination of the Group; the role of focal points and enhancing the technical and analytical support of the AU and UNECA Geneva liaison offices to the African Group.

The combined results of interviews and responses to questionnaires strongly indicated that the level of engagement/participation of the African Group had been relatively effective in trade negotiations and limited in regular work and dispute settlement. Although there had been gains, the original objectives of the Group had not been fully realized. Although the Group had given support to decisions in favour of LDCs, most of which are African countries, LDCs had themselves preferred to pursue their interests within their dedicated forum – the Least Developed Countries' Consultative Group.

But despite its challenges and weaknesses, the Group had had utility in pooling scarce resources together, creating synergies, providing a necessary forum for countries to exchange views and engage in coordination with other groupings and providing "the weight for numbers", in a non-voting institution for political decisions and for African representation in small group consultations. The latter is part of a "constituency" system, which has become the *modus operandi* in WTO work to facilitate consensus decision-making amongst WTO Members. The African Group thus has an important role on cross-cutting and issues of general interest to its members. The African Group could consider equally focusing its attention on WTO regular committee work and systemically, on dispute settlement.

7. WTO Technical Assistance and Capacity Building for African Countries

Analytical and technical capacity has frequently been mentioned as a participation constraint for African delegations. This section analysed to what extent this constraint had been mitigated through WTO Secretariat technical assistance activities to African countries. The proposition examined at the onset, subject to caveats such as rate of turnover of trade officials in Geneva and in government departments responsible for WTO matters, was that the higher the number of technical assistance/training activities received, the higher the rate of the mitigation of the technical/analytical capacity constraints and as a result, the higher the likelihood of increased participation. The WTO technical assistance/training programme places particular emphasis on providing assistance to African Members and to least developed countries (LDCs), whose integration into the multilateral trading system remains a WTO priority.[16]

Overall, the amount of technical assistance to WTO Members increased since the establishment of the WTO. Data analysed[17] indicated that WTO-specific technical assistance and capacity building to African WTO Members increased from a total of 324 activities in 2000 (the selected baseline) by 281 per cent to a total of 1235 activities in 2005 and by 366 per cent to 1513 activities in 2010. These were massive increases in technical assistance and capacity building by the WTO Secretariat alone, excluding very many other TA/CB suppliers. In the period researched, WTO technical assistance and capacity building steadily improved as confirmed by independent evaluators and auditors of the WTO. The question that remained was why, after 15-years of supposedly accumulated experience and capacity-building, the level of African engagement/participation had not significantly scaled-up? Questions remained about the appropriateness of candidates nominated by African delegations for training and, subsequent, national efficiency in the allocation of individual African negotiators so trained and whose capacity had been developed.

African countries also benefit from a range of other trade-related technical assistance programmes. These include the Netherlands Trainee programme (for junior public officials who spend up to 10 months within the WTO Secretariat or at Geneva-based missions) and the reference centre programmes (a network of centres where relevant information on the WTO can be assessed). African LDCs benefit from the Enhanced Integrated Framework programmes and three weeks introduction courses for LDCs.

In addition, there are "newer" programmes on building trade capacity for developing countries including those in Africa in the form of the Aid for Trade Initiative, the Standards and Trade Development Facility[18] and the 2011 China LDCs' Accession and Internship Programme.

Current evidence therefore confirmed that overall, trade-related technical assistance to WTO Members particularly developing countries in Africa had been on the increase. It was noted, however, that the rule in the revised administrative measures for Members in

---

[16] WTO Annual Report, 2010, p. 117. The same treatment for African countries with regard to receipt of technical assistance holds for the early days of the WTO. In the annual report of 1998, it was stated that "*since the creation and entry into force of the World Trade Organization, over 600 technical cooperation activities have been organized through mid-1998. Major efforts have been directed towards assisting African countries, while activities for countries in other regions have been maintained. Africa continues to be covered in large measure under specific programmes*". WTO Annual report 1998, pg. 128.

[17] See Annex VI for the grand total and individual African WTO Member disaggregation. (WTO Technical Assistance Database).

[18] The Aid for Trade Initiative was launched in 2005 at the sixth WTO Ministerial Conference in Hong Kong. It aims to assist developing countries, particularly least-developed countries, develop the trade-related skills and infrastructure that are needed to implement and benefit from WTO agreements and to expand trade. The Standards and Trade Development Facility is a joint initiative in capacity building and technical cooperation aimed at assisting developing countries to implement international sanitary and phytosanitary standards and thereby gain and/or maintain market access.

arrears, classified in category IV as inactive, that such Members would be denied access to training or technical assistance other than that necessary to meet their WTO Article XIV:2 obligations (implementation of its obligations in multilateral trade agreements), had of the writing of this study not been fully implemented in the area of technical assistance.[19] A number of African Members had been in arrears of contributions to the WTO budget and been classified as inactive. However, several of African Members have proposed payment plans to liquidate their arrears and administrative measures been accordingly suspended.

The question needing answers was whether the increase in technical assistance had facilitated the participation of African countries in regular work, negotiations and dispute settlement. Evidence suggested that African participation overtime had been relatively improved with WTO technical assistance. However, factors that went beyond technical assistance and capacity building were at play. For instance, explanations were still necessary as to why the level of African participation/engagement in regular work and dispute settlement was still minimal, nominal and largely ineffective in relation to other groupings and individual Members, despite massive increases in technical assistance and capacity building to African WTO Members.

There are limitations to the technical assistance and capacity building provided by all technical assistance providers. In the technical assistance provided by the WTO Secretariat, the Secretariat still has to ensure its neutrality, including in the review of cases either sub-judice, or in reference to issues that could potentially be raised in disputes. However, the universe of technical assistance providers ensures that all angles are covered. There is for instance technical assistance supplied by the ACWL, private law firms that offer technical assistance pro bono, and other international organizations like UNCTAD with lesser policy advice constraints. What emerged therefore was that the responsibility still lay with African delegations and individual negotiators to coherently approach the consumption and use of WTO and other technical assistance. Such improvements should be undertaken through improved domestic coordination, better municipal domestic institutions, and strengthening capital-Geneva frontline coordination.

[19] The General Council's approval of the Revised Administrative Measures can be found in document WT/GC/M/102. In 2009, the Committee on Budget, Finance and Administration established a working group to review these measures and the Group recommended that the Secretariat ensure their full implementation. The measures regarding provision of training and technical assistance were therefore being implemented in full as of 1 September 2011.

CHAPTER THREE

PARTICIPATION IN REGULAR WORK – CHAIRMANSHIPS

1. Introduction

Based on the institutional structure of the WTO, there are 78 WTO bodies – regular, interim and ad hoc (see Figure 6).

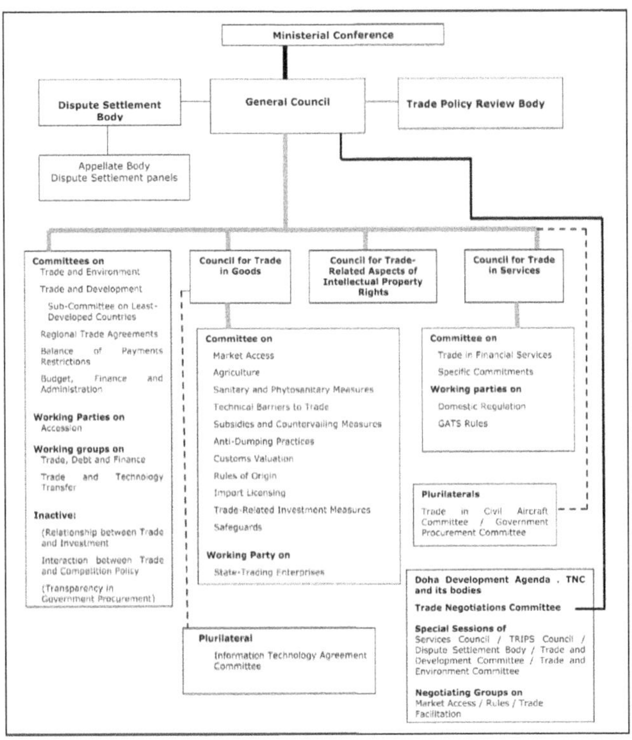

Figure 6. WTO institutional structure.[1]

[1] Source, WTO website www.wto.org.

Core WTO substantive technical work is generated mainly in limited group informal consultations. However, the share of chairmanships held by Members in the formal process, from different regions, is reflective of the level of participation and engagement and their ability to steer the system. It is also a rough indicator, approximating effectiveness levels in formal participation in the rules-based system.

In the period 1995–2010, the data collected and analysed showed that the share of chairmanships held by African Members was minimal, in many cases nominal and ceremonial, although there were specific instances of individual effectiveness and technical competence. For the first six WTO Ministerial Conferences (1996–2005), when individual Members volunteered to host ministerial conferences, there was no African volunteer. As a consequence, no African Trade Minister hosted and chaired any of the first six conferences. For the rotating chairmanships of principal bodies,[2] 16 per cent of these were chaired by African representatives. This low level of chairmanships of WTO bodies was reflected virtually across the board:

- Goods Council (11 per cent);
- Services Council (11 per cent);
- TRIPS Council (12 per cent);
- Subsidiary bodies of the Goods Council (15.5 per cent);
- Subsidiary bodies of the Services Council (5 per cent);
- Other subsidiary bodies reporting directly to the General Council (26.8 per cent); and,
- Plurilateral committees (3.3 per cent)

In using the chairmanships of formal bodies as a measure of level of participation/engagement in the WTO, including in regular bodies, care must be exercised. Preponderant technical work that lays the foundation for building consensus on the rules is situated in informal consultations in various formats and configurations. This is a systemic *acquis*. In these situations, in many instances the chairman of a formal regular body may be minimally or, in some cases, uninvolved in reconciling Members' positions and text-based consensus building. The most obvious example is the fact that the Director-General *ex-officio* by custom "chairs" green room meetings that *inter alia*, prepare some items on the General Council's agenda over which a Member presides as chairman. Examples are legion. This situation is similarly replicated in the negotiating arena (chapter 4). Furthermore, in some instances where the issues are broad and complex or where the technical ability of the chairman is questionable, or where "regional perspectives" are implicitly required, groups of Members designate a friend or friends of the Chair to manage the core technical negotiations to maturity, in an informal setting, before wider formal consideration and decision making in the formal regular body setting. African Members have repeatedly made a case for a correction to their low level of participation in the "involved" informal processes. This position acknowledges their low level of engagement/participation in informal consultations where substantive work is initiated and advanced.

What factors account for this low level of participation/engagement in regular bodies as reflected in chairmanships by African Members in the period reviewed? These

[2] General Council, Dispute Settlement Body, Trade Policy Review Body.

revolved around several reasons: capacity constraints, technical expertise, mission size, financial resources, concrete commercial and systemic interests, and WTO internal rules on the appointment of officers to regular bodies. In this connection, one of the factors was the continuing insistence by Members on the Guidelines for Appointment of Officers to WTO Bodies in particular:

- Paragraph 1.2: "The choice of a chairperson should primarily reflect the capacity of that person to undertake the special responsibilities required of such post in the WTO system"; and,
- Paragraph 1.3: "Appointments must be acceptable to the membership as a whole and not only to regions or groupings that may have proposed them"
- Paragraph 4.1: For bodies under Group 1 and 2 chairpersons should be appointed from among Geneva-based Heads of Delegations. In the case of Groups 4, 5, 6 and 8, chairpersons should be Heads of Delegations or officials of delegations of Members of the WTO in Geneva. Non-residents may be appointed in exceptional circumstances where the necessary expertise can only be found in capitals.
- Paragraph 1.1: "Chairpersons must be representatives of Members. Representatives of Members in financial arrears for over one full year cannot be considered for appointment."[3]

Inside knowledge of the process for the selection of individuals to chair WTO bodies provided evidence, confirming that key Members of the Organisation, in coordination with the Secretariat, have set a strict standard of technical competence and expert capacity for candidates to chair substantive-oriented regular bodies. Many African ambassadors/delegates, with the exception of a few, have not passed this test. Furthermore, although unstated, by custom in a very conservative rules-based system, key Members and the Secretariat are keenly watchful to ascertain the professionalism and personal commitment of candidate chairs for professional consistency and established views that reinforce and ensure systemic stability.[4] Dark horses tend to be passed over in the unstated rule for the systemic selection of chairpersons.

The work programme of the WTO is extensive. It encompasses the rules contained in 29 Agreements, 30 accession Working Parties,[5] specialized sessions of regular bodies and negotiating groups in the Doha Work Programme and an ever-expanding raft of informal negotiating groups and constituency coalitions. The work load is heavy and still expanding. The ability of Members to cope requires a combination of well-staffed and resourced delegations in real time coordination with capital authorities. African Members have been lacking in both. Many of the bodies in figure 6 meet on a frequent basis. The work load is heavy, particularly for those with small sized missions and low-levels of real time coordination with their capitals.

In 2009 for instance, there were 322 formal meetings; 237 informal multilateral and plurilateral meetings; and, 6536 private meetings (appellate body, panels, chair consultations, bilateral meetings). These totalled 7,095 (half-day meetings).[6]

---

3 WTO, Guidelines for Appointment of Officers to WTO Bodies, WT/L/31.
4 The author is a staff member of the WTO Secretariat. This is the author's personal view.
5 With the accession of six new Members as of March 2013, 26 Accession Working Parties remain.
6 WTO Secretariat Conference Office.

2. Chairs of Ministerial Conferences

Rule 12 of the Rules of Procedure for Meetings of WTO Bodies provides that during the course of each regular session of a Ministerial Conference, a chairperson and three vice-chairpersons should be elected from among the Members. They would hold office from the end of that session until the end of the next regular session.

The practice has been that the host country of a ministerial conference chairs the conference.[7] In the period researched, no African WTO Member had hosted a WTO ministerial conference. As a consequence, no African WTO Member had chaired a ministerial conference.[8] However, there tended to be regional balance in that vice-chairs were selected from other regions not chairing a conference. For all seven conferences, although generally the position has tended to be purely ceremonial, there was a vice-chair from Africa. (Figure 7).

Ministerial Conference	Chair	Vice-Chairs
1st Ministerial Conference (Singapore, 1996)	Singapore	Ireland; Uruguay; Tunisia
2nd Ministerial Conference (Geneva, 1998)	Switzerland	Guatemala; Korea; Zimbabwe
3rd Ministerial Conference (Seattle, 1999)	United States	Colombia; Burkina Faso; Pakistan
4th Ministerial Conference (Doha, 2001)	Qatar	Botswana; Finland; Costa Rica
5th Ministerial Conference (Cancun, 2003)	Mexico	Egypt; Netherlands; Bangladesh
6th Ministerial Conference (Hong Kong, 2005)	Hong Kong China	Austria; Barbados; Nigeria
7th Ministerial Conference (Geneva, 2009)	Chile[9]	Switzerland; Egypt; Indonesia

Figure 7. Chairs and vice-chairs of WTO ministerial conferences held in the period 1995 to 2010.

[7] At the seventh Ministerial Conference held in Geneva (WTO Headquarters) Members agreed that without setting a precedent, the country providing the Chairman of the General Council would provide the Chair of the Ministerial Conference, as no Member had undertaken to host the conference.

[8] The Eight WTO Ministerial Conference in Geneva from 15 to 17 December 2011 was chaired by H.E. Mr Olusegun Olutoyin Aganga of Nigeria.

[9] See footnote 7.

(a) *The Role of the Chair*

The role of the chair of a ministerial conference is largely procedural. According to Rule 17 of the Rules of Procedure for Ministerial Conferences, these include declaring the opening and closing of each meeting; directing the discussions; according the right to speak; submitting questions for decision; announcing decisions; ruling on points of order and having complete control of the proceedings. Other roles include drawing up the provisional agenda of the meeting in consultation with the Secretariat.

However, at ministerial conferences involving negotiations, chairs have sometimes, but not always, played an influential role. Keenly sensitive to selecting chairs of proven systemic technical competence, the first seven Ministerial Conferences showed a swing of the pendulum in who chairs informal working sessions/green rooms, between the Director-General *ex-officio* (as guardian of the system) and the host of a Ministerial Conference, depending on where Members judged competence existed. The critical point is that Members and the Secretariat are in close and constant coordination to ensure that technical ability, competence and knowledge of the issues prevail in respect of the individual Member/delegate that chairs working sessions.

The roles of vice-chairs have been largely ceremonial and limited to assisting in conducting plenary sessions of ministerial conferences, were general statements are delivered and no real negotiations take place or serving as a friend of the chair on specific issues.

3. Chairs of Principal WTO Bodies – General Council, Dispute Settlement Body and Trade Policy Review Body

Institutionally, the General Council, the Trade Policy Review Body and the Dispute Settlement Body are hierarchically the same with different mandates. Figures 8, 9, 10 and 11 show the distribution of chairs of these three principal bodies by region between 1995 and 2010.

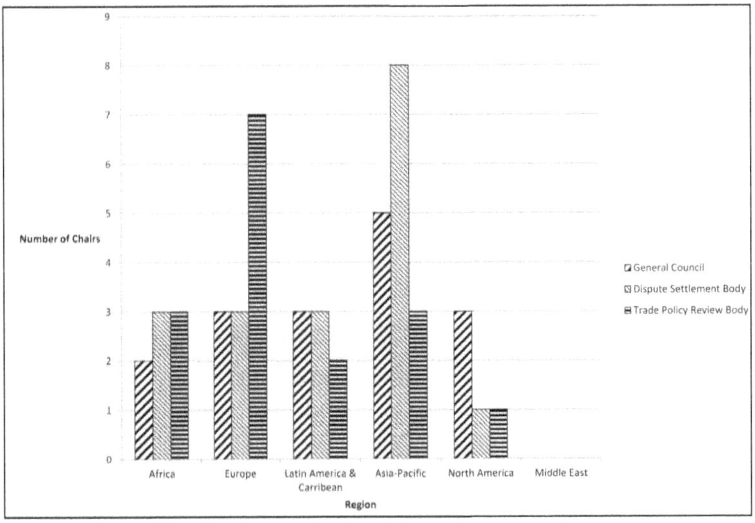

Figure 8. Chairs of WTO principal bodies (1995–2010).

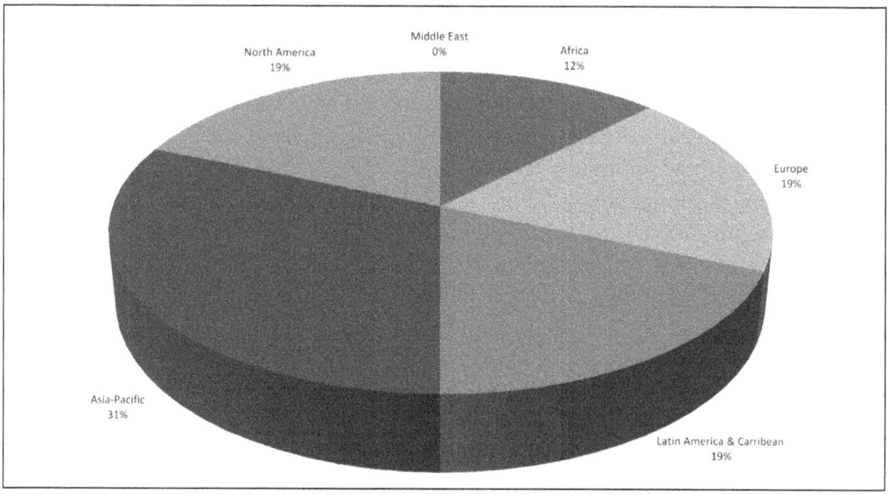

Figure 9. Chairs of the General Council (1995–2010).

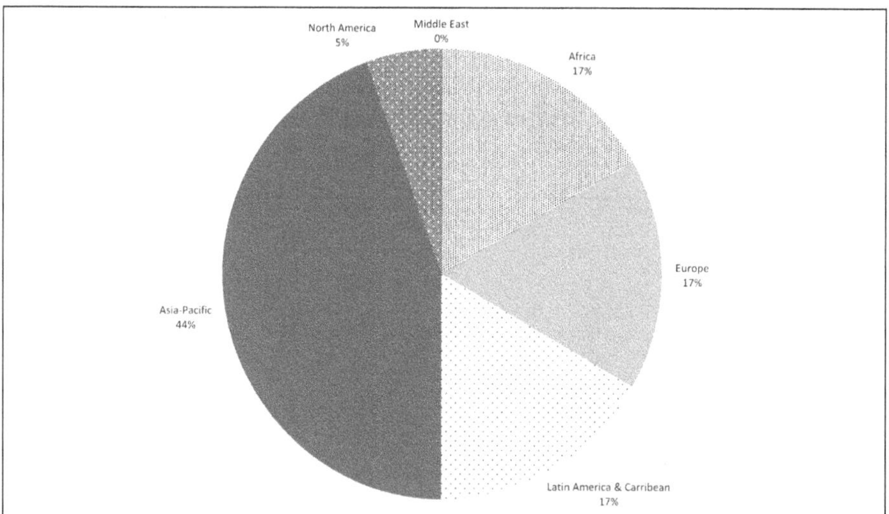

Figure 10. Chairs dispute settlement body (1995–2010).

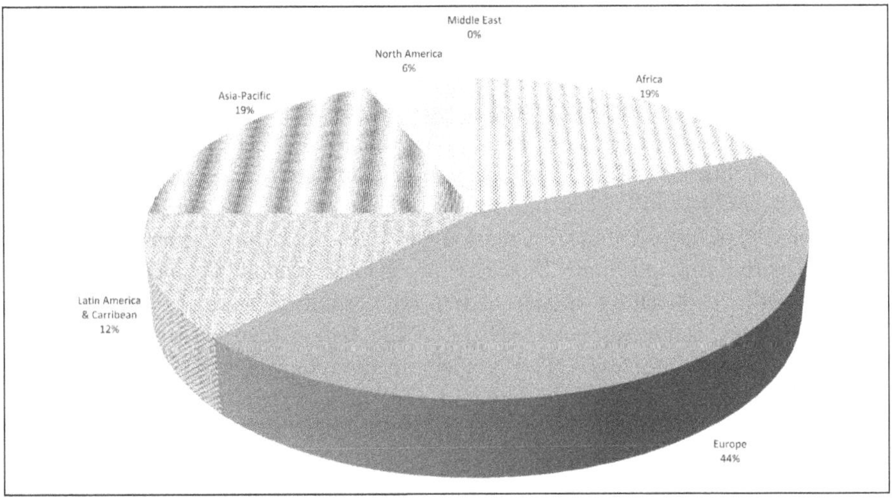

Figure 11. Chairs trade policy review body (1995–2010).

Figure 8 shows that the Asia Pacific region had had the highest overall percentage share of chairs of principal WTO bodies – (31 per cent – General Council; 44 per cent – DSB; 19 per cent –TPRB). Europe followed: (19 per cent – General Council; 17 per cent – DSB; and, 44 per TPRB). Latin America and Caribbean region had had (19 per cent – General Council; 17 per cent – DSB; and, 12 per cent – TPRB). Africa had had (12 per cent – General Council; 17 per cent – DSB and 19 per cent – TPRB). North America had had (19 per cent –General Council; 5 per cent – DSB; and, 6 per cent – TPRB). In the period researched, the Middle East had so far not chaired any of these bodies.

Although the chairmanship share of African WTO Members of principal bodies was low, in relative terms it was better than that of North America and the Middle East.[10] Detailed Africa WTO Members' analysis showed that only 9 per cent of African WTO Members – four of 42 Members – had dominated these chairmanships – Kenya, Tanzania, Tunisia and Nigeria. Over 90 per cent of African WTO Members had not been involved and not chaired principal WTO bodies. As of 2010, Kenya was the only African WTO Member to have chaired all three bodies.[11] Direct observation of the facts and of the personalities involved provide evidence of well-trained Kenyan and Nigerian professionals, technically expert with a high level of Geneva/Nairobi/Abuja (i.e. capital) coordination and a long tradition of diplomacy and foreign policy.

10 With the exception of the Middle East, Africa's larger share of chairmanships relative to North America is not a significant point. For the purpose of this study, the North American region was composed of the United States and Canada. Because of its economic and political weight, the US tends not to seek to chairs of WTO bodies, presumably, to avoid perceptions of being overbearing. The United States also presumably tends to avoid chairmanships in order not to constrain the liberty of its policy positions.

11 Nigeria was the other African WTO Member to have chaired all three principal WTO bodies, following the election of its Ambassador in 2011 to chair the General Council.

The explanations for the low level of individual African WTO Member share of chairmanships go beyond professional and competency reasons, or Geneva-capital coordination. There were also the factors underpinning the Guidelines for Appointment of Officers to WTO Bodies. The financial guidelines were strictly applied. They stipulate that Members in financial arrears over one full year cannot hold office. About 35 per cent – one third – of African WTO Members have been in arrears, at different times, and classified in categories I to IV.[12] This rule has had a limiting effect. However caution needs to be exercised in the use of the "financial arrears" factor as a "limiting factor" of Africa's share of chairmanship positions. This factor needs to be carefully weighed for plausibility against other explanatory variables. For instance, some of the African countries that have been in financial arrears such as Nigeria, Chad, Gabon, Cameroon, are significantly endowed countries with "cash". The problem, in the inquiry for this study, is related to inter-departmental domestic coordination and bureaucracy. There is the example of Nigeria paying its outstanding arrears one week before the 2005 Hong Kong Ministerial Conference to qualify for appointment as the vice-chairman for the Africa region.

The "capacity deficit" remains a constant and credible explanatory factor in combination with other factors. Although several African WTO Members currently have Geneva-based missions, their sizes remain very small – on average three to four officials including Heads of Missions. Considering the demanding workload of chairs of principal WTO bodies and the high frequency of meetings and informal private consultations with Members, human resource capacity constraints have made it less likely for many small African delegations to take up "additional" roles. Capacity constraints in terms of size of missions and quality of officials have not been fully addressed. These choices and decisions impact on deployment of adequate and competent officials to WTO missions; investing in training officials which in turn impacts knowledge and experience, including in diplomacy and building trust of other Members to be entrusted with office.

However, large needs/increasing demands in relation to limited resources entail rational choices to maximize supply of resource to need/demand. There is greater scope for rational choice making by African WTO Members, with regard to the deployment and participation of African negotiators in WTO meetings for greater effectiveness. Interviews, observations and knowledge of the operation of the vast majority of these missions, frequently indicated irrational considerations at play. The "rationality assumption" requires qualification to indicate that "irrationality" is also at play. The end/means goal-oriented "rationality" is not evident. Furthermore, this specific "rationality" assumption operates

---

[12] The administrative measures for Members classified in categories one to four with regard to chairmanships of WTO bodies is that such Members cannot be nominated to preside over such bodies – see Revised Administrative Measures for Members in Arrears – in minutes of the General Council in WT/GC/M/102. Category IV members have mainly been from the African region. As of December 2010, some of these included – Burundi; Chad; D.R. Congo; Djibouti, Dominica; Gambia; Guinea; Guinea-Bissau; Mauritania; Nicaragua; Niger; Sierra Leone and Togo. Some of these Members engaged in payment plans aimed at liquidating their arrears over an agreed time period, in exchange of suspension of administrative measures against them. Clearly financial constraints persist coupled by heavy financial requirements for those who were previously non-resident to open up missions in Geneva and domestic budget cycles that affect meeting of agreed timelines (case of Togo) – see WT/GC/M/127.

at two levels, not only in Geneva but also in capitals. Both levels are interlinked. The facts suggested that there were neither consistent rational (end/means) capital choices in the deployment of negotiators to Geneva missions nor consistent rational (end/means) capital choices in determining the appropriate staffing level between negotiators to cover the WTO and other multilateral institutions and diplomatic missions across Members' diplomatic arena. Furthermore, for decisions in Geneva, it would also be rational for individual African Missions to seek key chairmanships because they would provide efficient vantage points for effective systemic participation. Interviews and observation in the participation of African delegations still indicated minimal overriding "rationality", and continued randomness, reflective of "muddling through" and default outcomes.

4. Chairs of Sectoral Councils – Goods, Services and TRIPS Councils

Three subsidiary Councils on Goods, Services and Intellectual Property Rights operate under the guidance of the General Council. Figures 12, 13, 14 and 15 show the distribution of chairs of sectoral councils by region from 1995–2010.

In the period analysed, the distribution of sectoral chairmanships by region was as follows:

- Asia-pacific, 34 per cent overall average (CTG-33%; CTS-22%; TRIPS-47%);
- Europe, 28 per cent overall average (CTG-39%; CTS-39%; TRIPS-6%);
- Latin America and the Caribbean, 24.6 per cent overall average (CTG-17%; CTS-22%; TRIPS-35% and,
- Africa, 11.3 per cent overall average (CTG-11%; CTS-11%; TRIPS-12%).
- North America had chaired the Services Council once accounting for 6 per cent and an overall average of 2 per cent for sectoral chairmanships;
- The Middle East has not chaired any sectoral council.

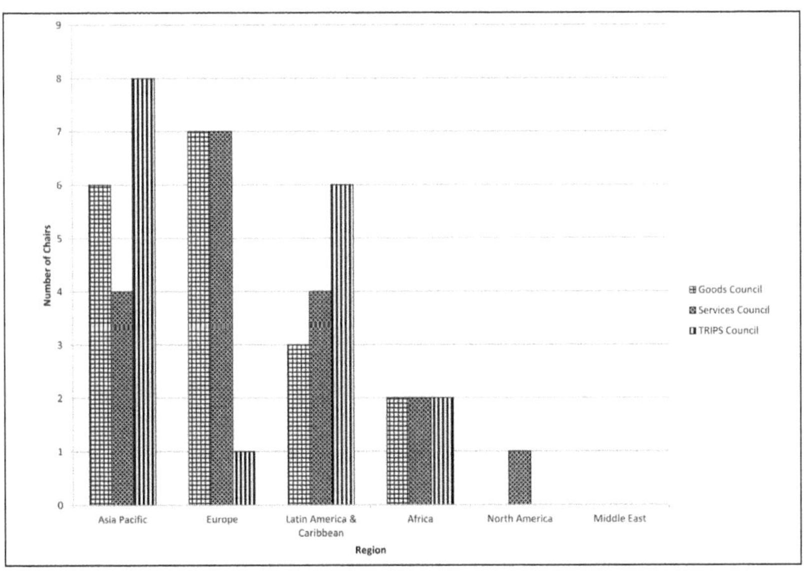

Figure 12. Chairs of Sectoral Councils (1995–2010).

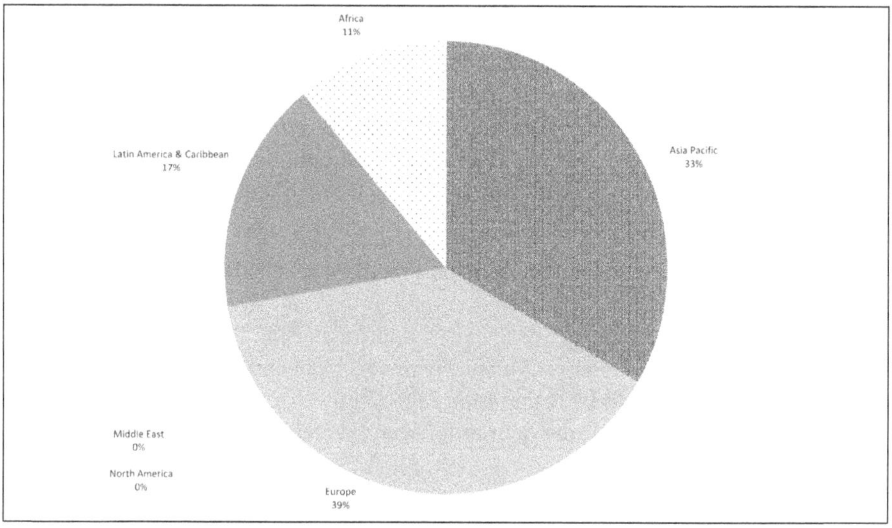

Figure 13. Chairs of the Goods Council (1995–2010).

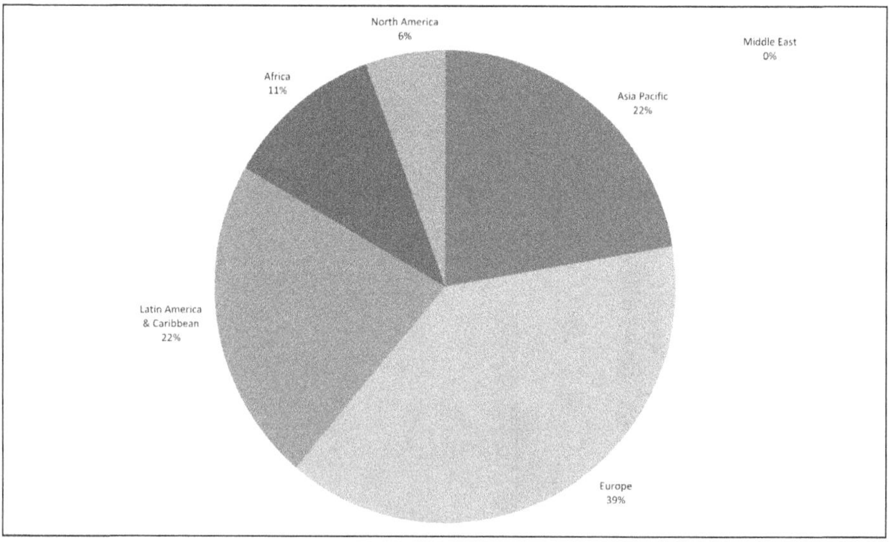

Figure 14. Chairs of the Services Council (1995–2010).

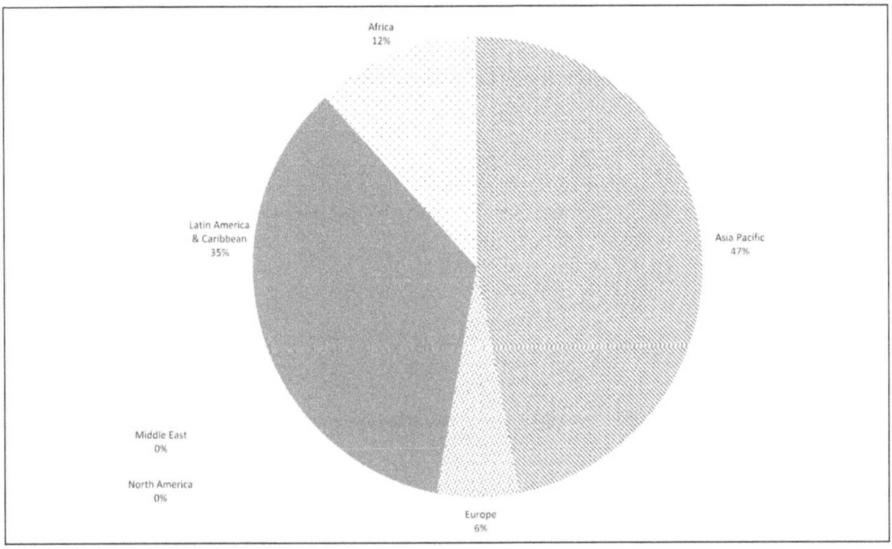

Figure 15. Chairs of the TRIPS Council (1995–2010).

In the share of these chairmanships, the Asia-Pacific region measured higher and participated more effectively than Africa and other regions. Although the focus of this study is on Africa, there are useful lessons that could be drawn. Higher capacity levels, a wider range of individual technical expertise, rising trade shares in more competitive emergent economies and tighter Geneva/capital coordination provide plausible explanations for comparatively higher levels of participation/engagement. Furthermore, there was a point to be made about the greater mixture of developed and developing countries in this region. With the informal understanding of rotational allocation of chairs of principal WTO bodies between developed and developing countries, this in part was a supplementing explanation.

Africa's share of the chairmanships of sectoral councils was low, only better than the Middle East, which was lower and also minimally participatory, and North America, which was nominally low presumably because of the avoidance of the perception of being overbearing and to ensure its degree of policy freedom. One African WTO Member – Nigeria had chaired all sectoral councils. This was partly because it had an Ambassador specifically accredited to the WTO and a dedicated WTO commercial office. This was not the case for several African WTO Members. Therefore, because of relatively better capacity and internal organisation in its mission, African WTO Members such as Nigeria could afford to prioritise and devote time and resources and actively engage in the activities of the organisation.

5. Chairs of Subsidiary Bodies under the Goods Council

Figure 16 shows the distribution of chairmanships of subsidiary bodies under the Goods Council as follows:

- Asia Pacific, overall average of 29.6 per cent;
- Europe, overall average of 28.1 per cent;
- Latin American and Caribbean, overall average of 18.9 per cent;
- Africa, overall average of 15.5 per cent;
- North America, 5.8 per cent overall average;
- Middle East regions 1.9 per cent.

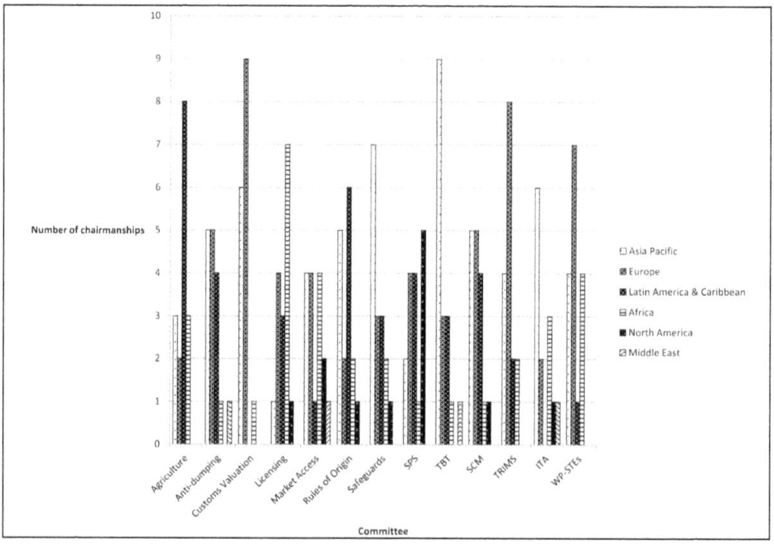

Figure 16. Share of Chairmanships of Subsidiary Bodies of the Goods Council.

Figure 17 shows the distribution of chairmanships of for the *Committee on Agriculture.*

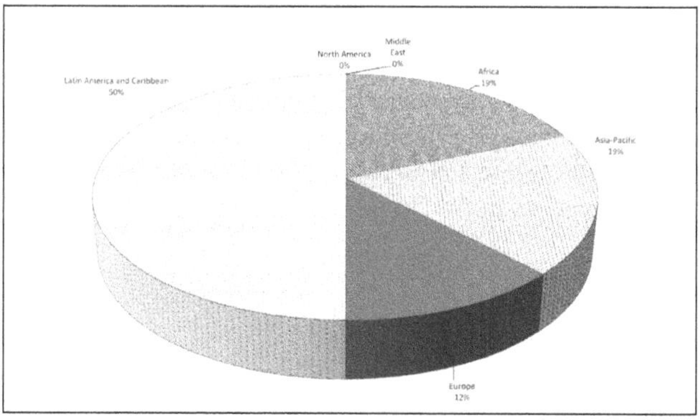

Figure 17. Chairs of the Committee on Agriculture (1995–2010).

The 18.7 per cent share for Africa in chairing the Committee on Agriculture was low, only better than the Middle East and North America. The only African exception was Egypt whose delegate had chaired this committee. The Egyptian delegate in question was a highly experienced individual, technically competent, with a long history in Egyptian trade missions. There was also relatively tight Geneva-Cairo coordination. Like Nigeria for sectoral councils, Egypt is an exception. Furthermore, Egypt had demonstrated unremitting focus in WTO agriculture negotiations and committee work because of its sensitive interests as a net food importing developing country. In addition, Egypt was one of the few WTO African Members to have a dedicated commercial office for WTO work. As such, it could unlike other African Member that were resource constrained, devote the time and resources of its officials to work that it deemed beneficial to the country's overall trade/commercial interests.

Figure 18 shows the distribution of chairmanships for the *Anti-dumping Practices Committee.* Africa's share was low at 6.25 per cent, at the same level with the Middle East and only better than North America. This trade remedy body requires specialised technical ability. The Asia Pacific region tied with Europe at 31.2 per cent, over Latin America and the Caribbean at 25 per cent. Israel's chairmanship accounted for the 6.25 per cent share of the Middle East, with Egypt accounting for Africa's 6.25 per cent. For the period analysed, data showed that only two of the 42 (or 4.76 per cent) African WTO Members had initiated anti-dumping investigations (Egypt and South Africa). In addition, only 5 African WTO Members had been the subject of anti-dumping investigations (Malawi, Mozambique, Nigeria, South Africa and Zimbabwe). The number of investigations against these countries ranged from 1 to 59. Most investigations had been against South Africa, but it had also been one of the main initiators (EU is the other) of investigations against its African trading partners.

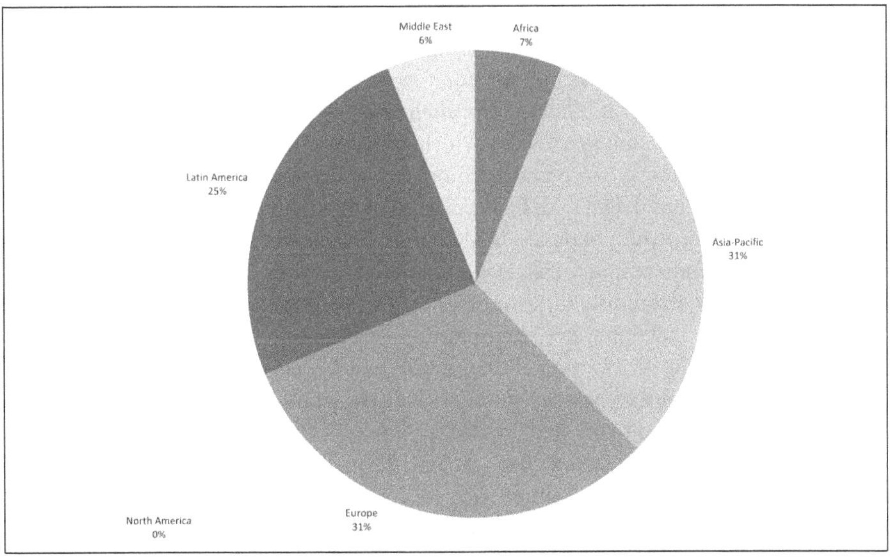

Figure 18. Chairs of the Anti-Dumping Committee (1995–2010).

Egypt and South Africa have been the most active African WTO Members in the area of trade remedies. Only Egypt had chaired the Anti-dumping Committee. Infrequent use of trade remedies and therefore, possibly lack of experience with use of the instrument and the process involved; lack of national legislation and trade remedies authorities in many African countries; and, the complexity of the subject matter were some factors explaining the very low participation of African WTO Members in the work of this Committee, including chairmanships.

Figure 19 shows the distribution of chairmanships for the *Customs Valuation Committee.*

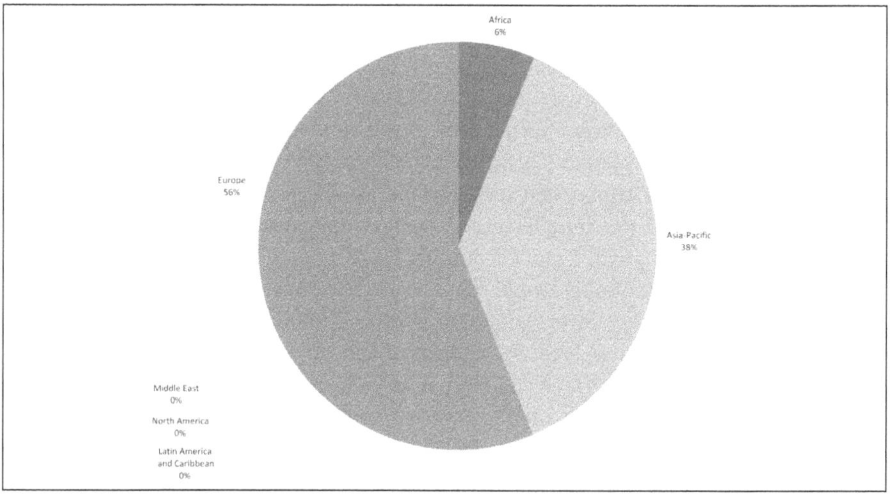

Figure 19. Chairs of the Customs Valuation Committee (1995–2010).

In the period studied, Morocco was the only African country that had chaired the Customs Valuation Committee accounting for the 6.25 per cent share of African chairmanship. The regions that dominated the chairmanship of the Committee on Customs Valuation were Europe and Asia Pacific, which are very actively engaged in world trade. Several countries in these two regions are ranked as leading world traders. They more frequently encounter and deal with huge volumes of merchandise that have to be valued and thus have extensive experience in this area. The issues involved in the committee are technical and complex. This is compounded by capacity problems of technical knowledge and understanding the requirements of the Agreement in a number African Members probably explaining low chairmanship levels.

Figure 20 shows the distribution of Chairs of *Import Licensing Committee.* In this Committee, Africa had had the majority share of chairmanships at 43.7 per cent, accounted for by Zimbabwe, Côte d'Ivoire and Tanzania. Although these African delegations were relatively active, specific reasons also applied. The delegate of Zimbabwe, who first chaired the Import Licensing Committee, was technically competent. The succeeding participation of the delegate of Côte d'Ivoire waned as the level of democratic governance in Côte d'Ivoire diminished. The long tenure in Geneva of the delegate of Tanzania led to a three year consecutive term as Chair. Interviewed African delegations in Geneva suggested in their responses that the chairmanship of Import Licensing Committee had primarily been allocated to African delegates, because of low level of interest – "not so important committees or uninteresting ones" and because of failure to find candidates from other regions. The delegations interviewed therefore believed that some of these "uninteresting committees" were allocated to African delegates simply to meet the regional balance required in the guidelines on appointment of officers to WTO bodies. Regardless of the perceptions and the sentiments, the Import Licensing Committee is at a lower level of technical complexity than other committees. But, even so, the evident facts showed that the delegations that accounted for the chairmanships, when they did, were active, competent, and originated from democracies, at the time.

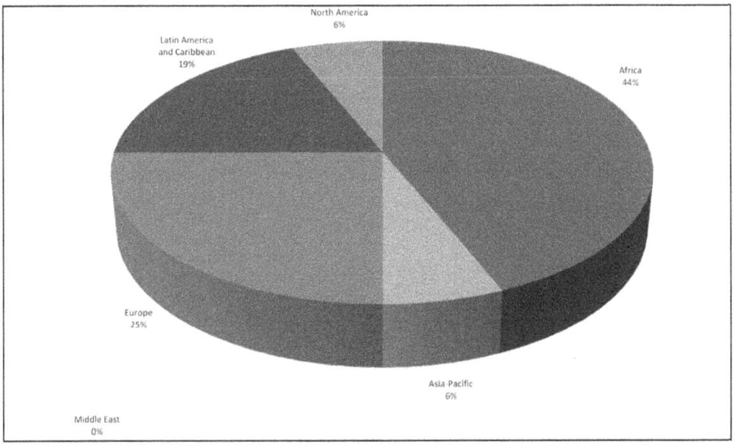

Figure 20. Chairs of the Import Licensing Committee (1995–2010).

Figure 21 shows the distribution of chairmanship of the *Committee on Market Access.*

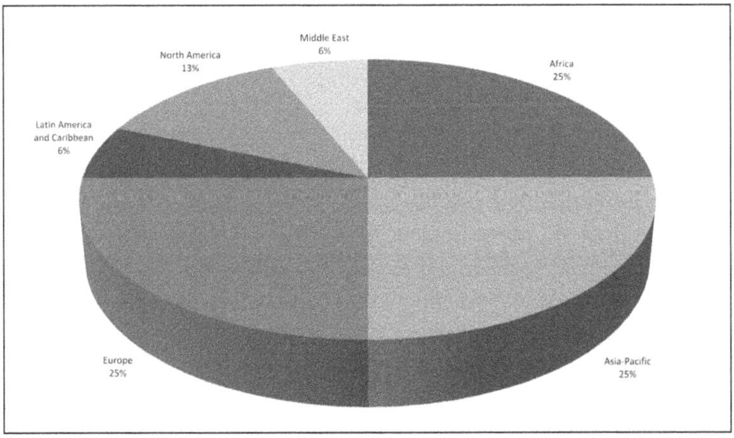

Figure 21. Chairs of the Committee on Market Access (1995–2010).

Four African countries, drawn from the same limited universe of active African delegations, accounted for the African chairmanship of the Committee on Market Access. These were Morocco, Lesotho, Egypt and Kenya. Analysis of the four delegations involved reveal particular active individual professionals: experienced, with high exposure and previous service in other diplomatic missions prior to Geneva.

Figure 22 shows the distribution of chairmanship of the *Committee on Rules of Origin.* Nigeria was the only African Member to have chaired this committee in two consecutive years by the same delegate. It is recalled that rule 5.1 of the guidelines of appointment of officers to WTO bodies provides that for bodies falling under group 6 (subsidiary bodies of the CTG, CTS and TRIPS Council), the incumbent chairperson may be considered for reappointment whenever this is found to be in the interest of the efficient functioning of the body. From the Latin American and Caribbean region, Brazil had chaired this body for six consecutive terms. The case of Brazil suggested that a relatively lower rate of turnover of delegates in Geneva (which is not the case with many African delegates) the higher the chances for reappointment to chairmanships.

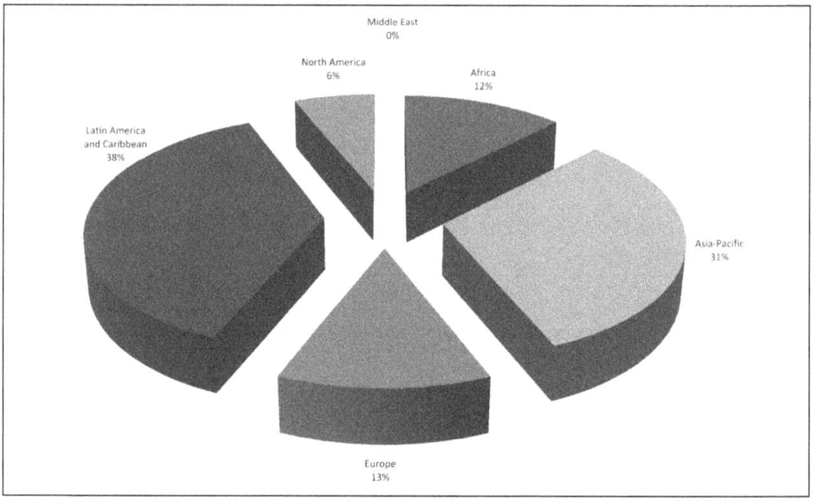

Figure 22. Chairs of the Rules of Origin Committee (1995–2010).

The figure 23 shows the distribution of chairmanship of the *Safeguards Committee.* African delegates accounted for 12.5 per cent of the chairmanship of the Safeguards Committee. This was lower than the Asia-Pacific at 43.75 per cent and Latin America and the Caribbean and Europe, respectively, at 18.75 per cent, but more than North America at 6.25 per cent. The Middle East had not chaired this committee. As of 2010, Lesotho and Mauritius were the two African Members that had chaired the Safeguards Committee. The reasons for low level of chairmanship by African Members as highlighted in the Anti-dumping Committee to a great extent apply to this Committee.

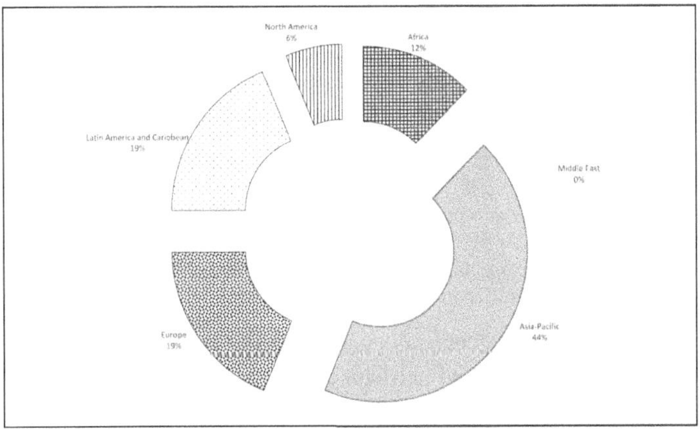

Figure 23. Chairs of the Safeguards Committee (1995–2010).

Figure 24 shows the distribution of chairmanship of the *SPS Committee.* In the SPS Committee, North America had had a relatively significant percentage share (31 per cent) of chairmanships in comparison to other regions. The United States chaired this body four times and Canada, once. Europe and Latin America and Caribbean followed with 25 per cent each; with Asia-Pacific accounting for 12.5 per cent; and Africa, 6.25 per cent. Developed Members in particular have consistently attached high priority to sanitary and phytosanitary matters. Domestic populations in these Members have exhibited acute sensitivity to health and food safety matters associated with the sanitary and phytosanitary environments in agricultural exporters. These concerns, in many instances, have been reflected into electoral behaviour. This could account for the evident insistence and tradition by the developed Members in chairing the SPS Committee. Developing Members, on the other hand, associate SPS measures and issues as aspects of increase in non-tariff barriers by developed Members. The management of this committee is not routine. Africa (South Africa) chaired this Committee once. The Middle East had not chaired this committee.

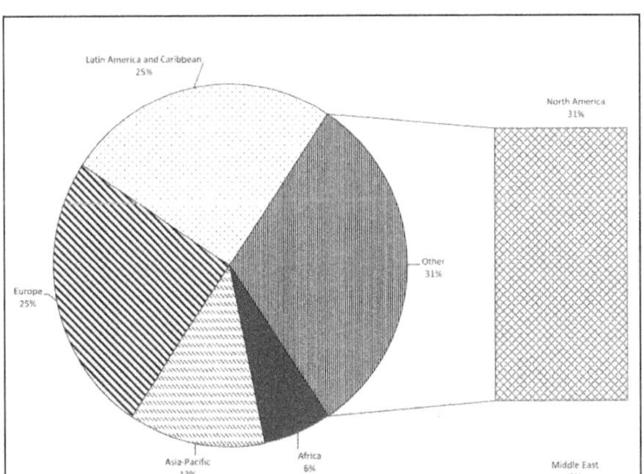

Figure 24. Chairs of the SPS Committee (1995–2010).

Although the percentage share by African Members in the chairmanship of the SPS Committee was low, this stands in sharp contrast to the level of activity and the seriousness of SPS issues brought to the Committee by some African Members. There were a number of examples that underlined this point:[13]

- Tanzania (concerns/complaints against EC SPS measures in relation to fruit, vegetables and fish products),
- Cote d'Ivoire (concerns/complaints against EC maximum residue levels for pesticides in fruits and vegetables);
- South Africa (concern/complaint against the EC's directive on foot and mouth disease)
- Egypt (concern/complaint against the EC measures on import of Egyptian potatoes)

This situation was illustrative of instances where chairmanships were not reliable predictors of the level of engagement and participation.

The figure 25 shows the distribution of chairmanship of the *Committee on Technical Barriers to Trade*. In the TBT Committee, Lesotho was the only African country that had chaired the Committee once. Although Lesotho is a small country, its delegates have been professionally active and well trained including from a number of donor aid capacity building programmes. The individual delegate concerned was also active with prior experience from other diplomatic missions before Geneva.

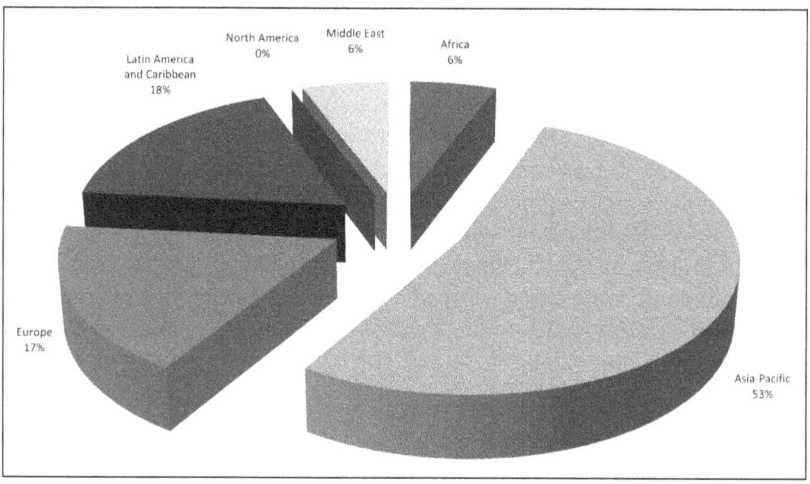

Figure 25. Chairs of the TBT Committee (1995–2010).

Similar to the situation in the SPS Committee, although the percentage share by African Members in the chairmanship of the TBT Committee was low, this stood in sharp

[13] These specific SPS cases and others to which African WTO Members gave support are treated in chapter five and listed in Annex XIII:2.

contrast to the level of activity and the seriousness of TBT issues brought to the Committee by African Members. A number of examples underlined this point:[14]

- Burundi, Kenya, Malawi, Mozambique, Zimbabwe, Uganda, Egypt, Tanzania and Zambia (Canada-Bill C32 Amendment to Tobacco Act)
- Botswana, Egypt, South Africa (EC-Regulation on the Registration, Evaluation and Authorization of Chemicals – REACH).

This situation was illustrative of instances where chairmanships are not reliable predictors of the level of engagement and participation.

Figure 26 shows the distribution of chairmanship of the *SCM Committee*. Africa's share was low at 6.25 per cent, at the same level with North America and only better than the Middle East with zero per cent chairmanship share. Comparable to the Antidumping Committee, this trade remedy body requires specialised technical ability and knowledge *inter alia* of data bases and the collection and maintenance of data over long periods. Europe and the Asia Pacific regions accounted for most chairmanships tying at 31.5 per cent, with Latin America and the Caribbean at 25 per cent. As of 2010, Mauritius was the only African Member to have chaired the SCM Committee.

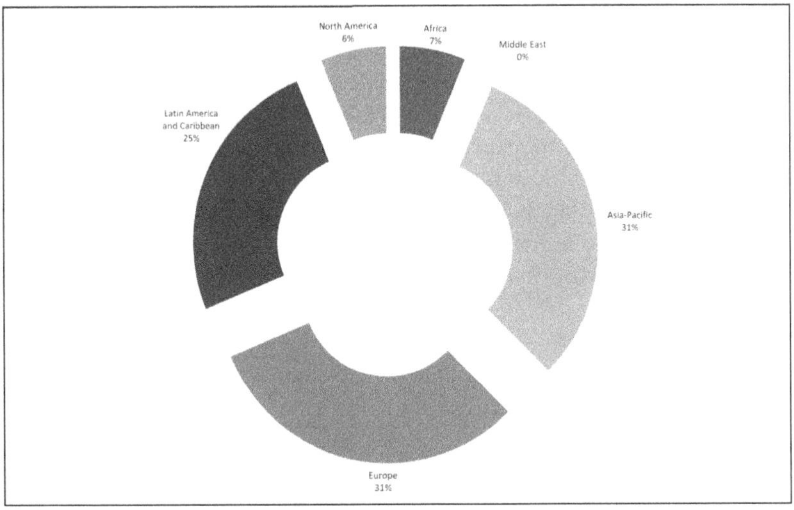

Figure 26. Chairs of the SCM Committee (1995–2010).

Figure 27 shows the distribution of chairmanship of the *TRIMS Committee*. Africa's share was low at 12.5 per cent and tied with Latin America and the Caribbean. Both were better than North America and the Middle East with zero per cent share of chairmanships. Europe accounted for the most chairmanships at 50 per cent followed by Asia Pacific at 25 per cent.

[14] These specific TBT cases and others to which African WTO Members gave support are treated in chapter five and listed in Annex XI:2.

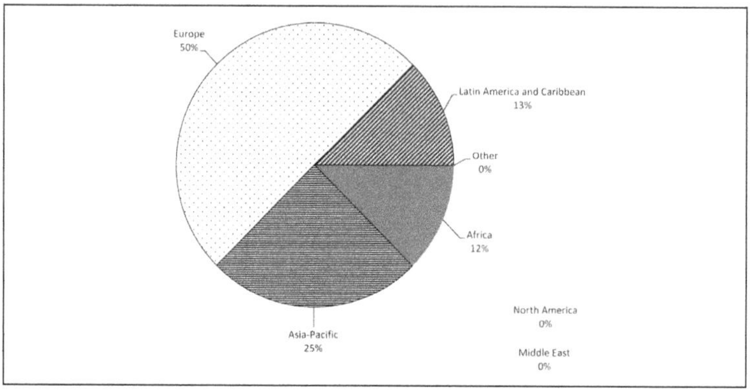

Figure 27. Chairs of the TRIMS Committee (1995–2010).

As of 2010, Mauritius was the only African country to have twice chaired this committee. Mauritius has traditionally been one of the few active African delegations in the WTO. There is a range of explanatory factors. Domestically, it has a competitive economy, high growth rates and is considered internationally competitive with real commercial interests. The Mauritian delegation in Geneva has been relatively better resourced than most African delegations. Therefore, capacity factors (financial, human and technical resources) have been less constraining compared to other African Members. As a consequence, it has been able to devote its officials to the work of the WTO and actively engaged, including in chairing bodies. The Mauritian delegation has been a frequent coordinator of the WTO African Group and the African, Caribbean and Pacific Group. The delegation has a reputation of professionalism, diplomacy and sustained hard work. In addition, some of its delegates have had longer tenures in Geneva.

Figure 28 shows the distribution of chairmanships of the *Information Technology Agreement Committee.*

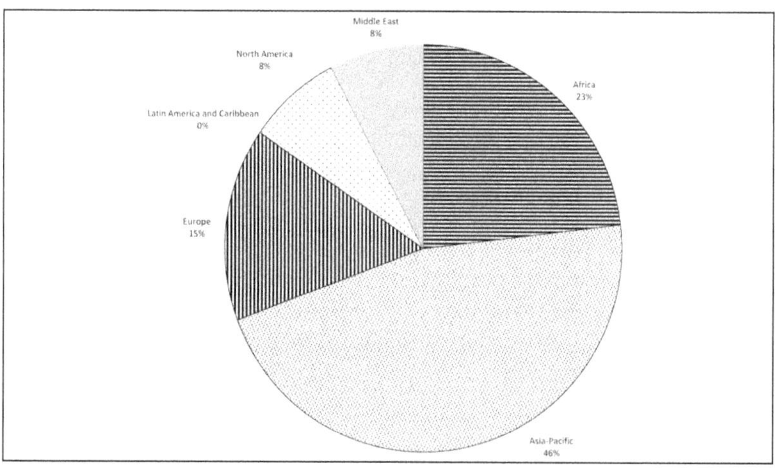

Figure 28. Chairs of the ITA Committee.

Africa's share of chairmanships of the ITA Committee stood at 23 per cent, below the Asia Pacific region at 46 per cent and better than Europe at 15 per cent. North America and the Middle East were tied at 8 per cent, with the Latin America and the Caribbean at zero per cent. In the period reviewed, there were three African Members of the ITA (Egypt; Mauritius; and, Morocco). The level of participation and engagement in this sectoral agreement is in direct relationship to real commercial interest. Egypt was the only African Member of the three African participants to have chaired the ITA Committee thrice.

Figure 29 shows the distribution of chairmanship of the *Working Party on State Trading Enterprises*.

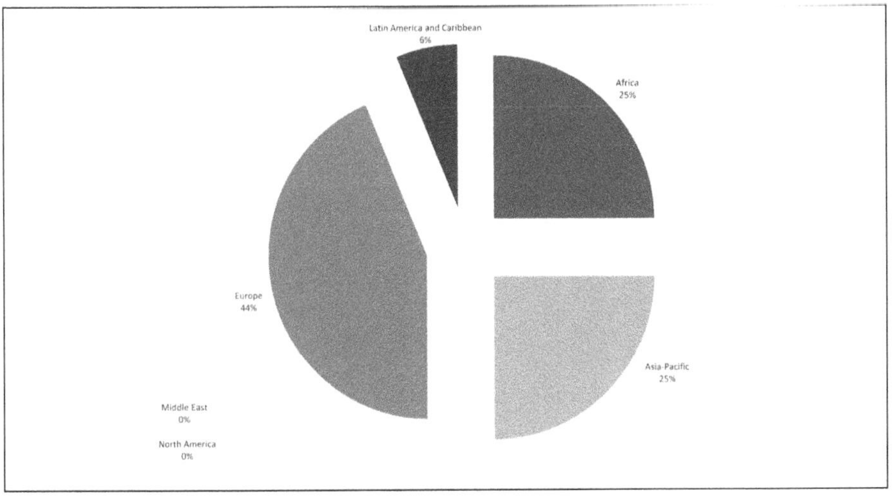

Figure 29. Chairs of the Working Party on STEs.

Africa's share of chairmanships of the STE Working Party was relatively high and effective. It tied with the Asia Pacific to account for 25 per cent share each of chairmanships, both only less than Europe at 44 per cent, and better than Latin America and the Caribbean at 6 per cent and, North America and the Middle East with zero per cent share of chairmanships. Nigeria, Lesotho and Namibia chaired the Working Party. The individual African chairs reflected African WTO Members with large-sized industry (Nigeria and Namibia), with the three Members having higher levels of technical trade capacity relative to other African Members.

6. Chairs of Subsidiary Bodies of the Services Council

Four subsidiary bodies report to the Services Council. These are: the Committee on Financial Services; Committee on Specific Commitments, Working Party on GATS Rules and Working Party on Domestic Regulation.

Figure 30 shows the overall distribution of chairmanships of subsidiary bodies as follows:

- Asia Pacific, 45 per cent;
- Europe, 23.3 per cent;
- Latin America and the Caribbean, 18.3 per cent
- North America, 8.3 per cent
- Africa, 5 per cent
- Middle East, 0 per cent

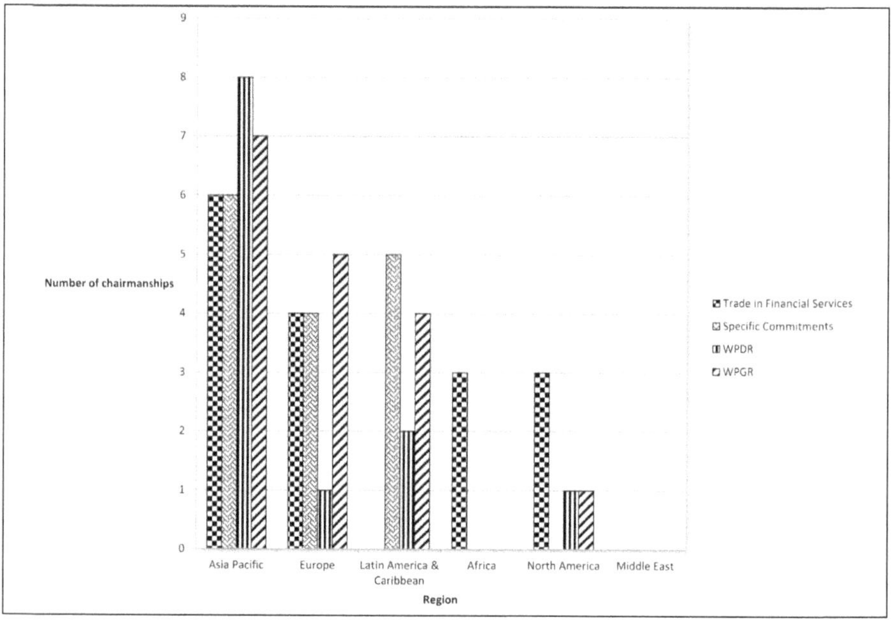

Figure 30. Share of Chairmanships of Subsidiary Bodies of the Services Council.

In these subsidiary bodies, Africa's share of chairmanship was low at 5 per cent, below Asia Pacific, Europe and Latin America and the Caribbean and North America and only better than the Middle East at zero per cent. Egypt and South Africa were the African Members that have chaired the Committee on Financial Services. The individual delegates were well trained and from economies with relatively well-developed financial services sector, relative to other African Members.

Figure 31 shows the distribution of chairmanships of the *Committee on Trade in Financial Services.*

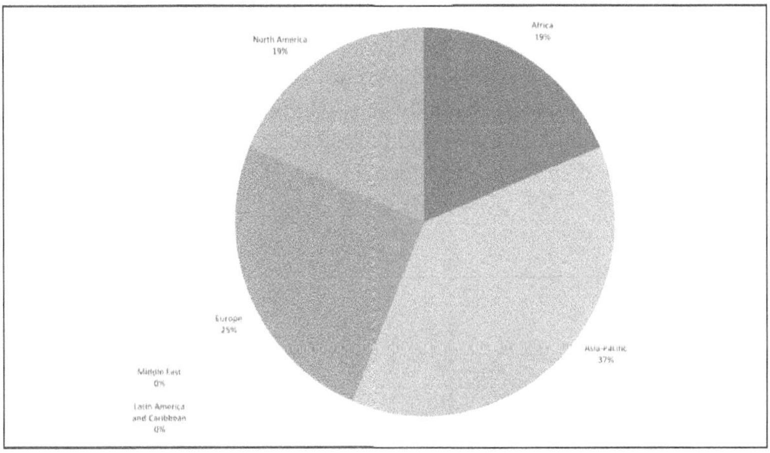

Figure 31. Chairs of the Committee on Trade in Financial Services.

The percentage share of chairmanships reflected in part commercial interest in trade in financial services. Africa's share of 18.75 per cent of the chairmanships was low, below Asia Pacific, Europe but tied with North America. Africa's share was better than Latin America and Caribbean, albeit with considerable interest and stake in trade in financial services. The limited interest in chairmanships by the Middle East region was reflected in its zero per cent share.

Figure 32 shows the distribution of chairmanships of the *Committee on Specific Commitments*.

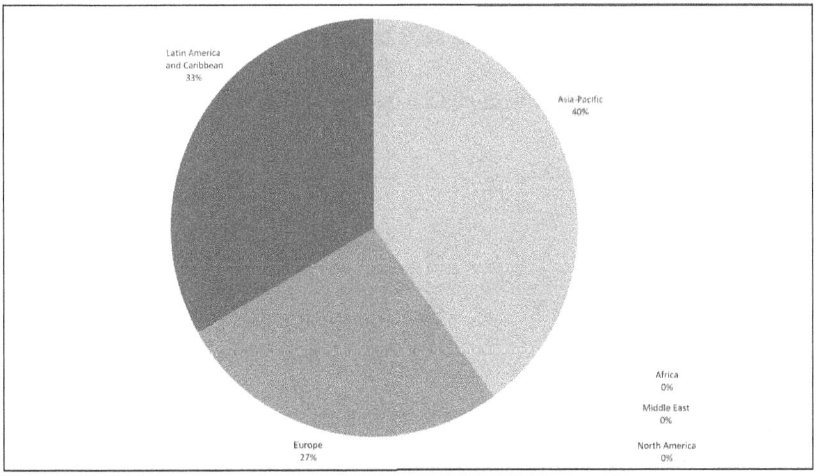

Figure 32. Chairs of the Committee on Specific Commitments.

In the period studied, Africa had not chaired this Committee. With a number of African Members having undertaken limited specific commitments, there has been limited interest in the work of this specialised subsidiary body of the Services Council. Asia Pacific accounted for the largest share of chairmanships at almost 40 per cent, followed by Latin America and Caribbean at 33 per cent and Europe at 27 per cent.

Figure 33 shows the distribution of chairmanships of the *Working Party on Domestic Regulation.*

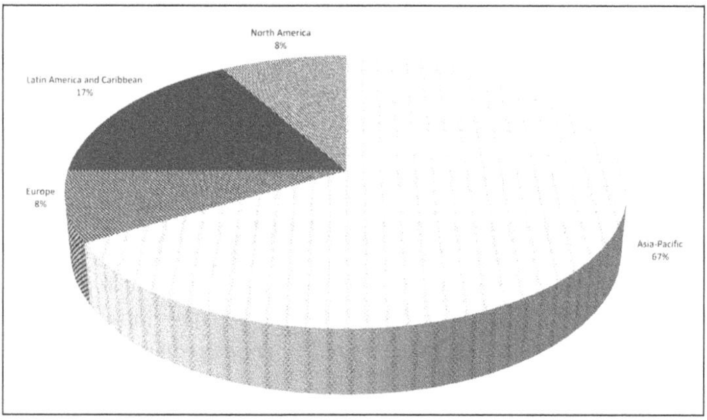

Figure 33. Chairs of the Working Party on Domestic Regulation.

In the period studied, Africa had not chaired this Committee. Its Members had expressed limited interest in the work of this specialised subsidiary body of the Services Council. Asia Pacific region accounted for the largest share of chairmanships at 67 per cent, followed by Latin America and Caribbean at 17 per cent, with Europe and North America tied at 8 per cent.

Figure 34 shows the distribution of chairmanships of the *Working Party on GATS Rules.*

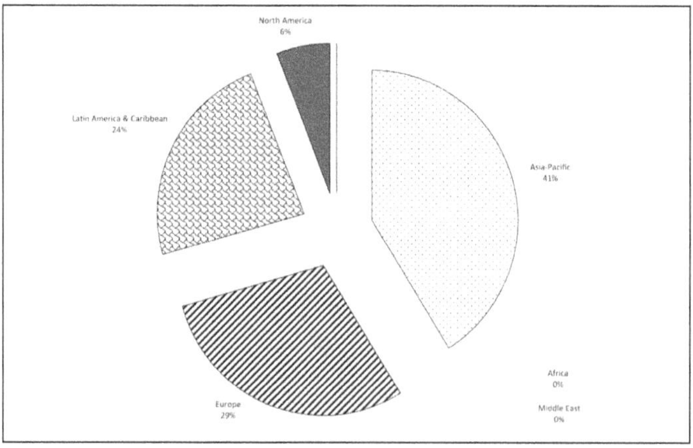

Figure 34. Chairs of the Working Party on GATS Rules.

In the period studied, African Members had not chaired this Committee. Its Members had expressed limited interest in the work of this specialised subsidiary body of the Services Council. Asia Pacific region accounted for the largest share of chairmanships at 41 per cent, followed by Europe at 29 per cent, Latin America and Caribbean at 24 per cent and North America at 6 per cent. Similar to Africa, the Middle East had not chaired this Committee.

7. Chairs of Other Subsidiary Bodies Reporting to the General Council

Seven committees directly report to the General Council in addition to accession working parties. The seven are:

- Committee on Trade and Development;
- Committee on Budget Finance and Administration;
- Committee on Regional Trade Agreements;
- Committee on Trade and Environment;
- Committee on Balance of Payment Restrictions;
- Working Group on Trade, Debt and Finance; and
- Working Group Trade and Transfer of Technology.

Figure 35 shows the overall distribution of chairmanships of the other bodies reporting to the General Council as follows:

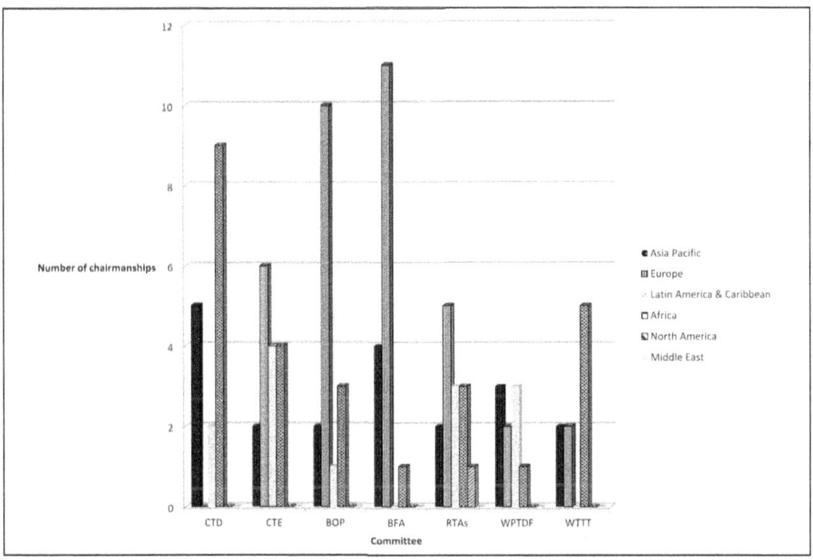

Figure 35. Share of Chairmanships of other bodies reporting directly to the General Council.

- Europe, 37 per cent
- Africa, 27 per cent
- Asia Pacific, 21 per cent
- Latin America and Caribbean, 13 per cent
- North America, 2 per cent
- Middle East, 0 per cent

Taken together, Africa accounted for 27 per cent of the chairmanships of these bodies. Only Europe ranked higher at 37 per cent, principally because of its long term chairmanship of the Committee on Budget Finance and Administration, where several African countries were in outstanding arrears. The Asia Pacific region accounted for 21 per cent, below Africa, and better than Latin America and the Caribbean at 13 per cent, North America, at 2 per cent with no interest by the Middle East region at 0 per cent.

Figure 36 shows the distribution of chairmanships of the *Committee on Trade and Development.*

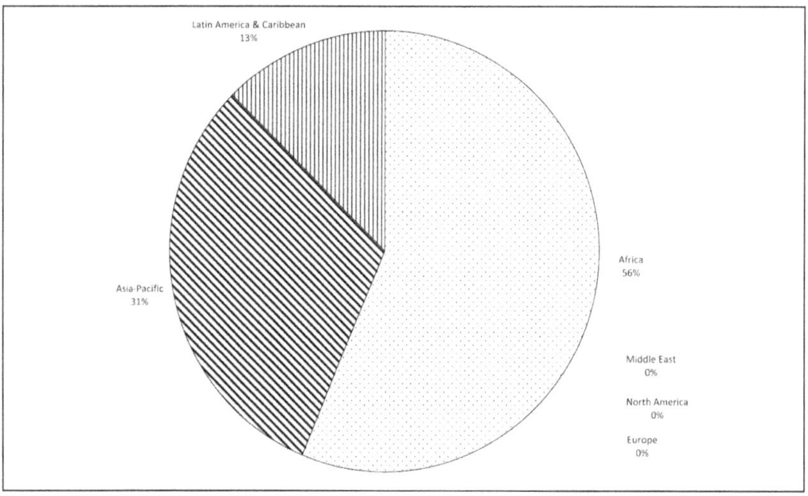

Figure 36. Chairs of the Committee on Trade and Development.

The Committee on Trade and Development is one of the committees to which WTO African Members have accorded very high priority, although it has limited scope for rule-making. This committee is a forum for statements, consensus-building on trade development issues with negotiations for "guidelines" (soft law) in the multilateral trading system. In the period reviewed, the African region had a high and the most share of chairmanship of the CTD at 60 per cent. It was followed by the Asia-Pacific region accounting for 27 per cent, Latin America and Caribbean at 13 per cent with Europe, North America and the Middle East having never chaired the CTD. Amongst WTO Members the tradition has taken hold that the CTD is chaired by developing countries. In the period studied, the African Members that had chaired the CTD were: Morocco, Mauritius, Senegal, Uganda, Tunisia and South Africa.

Figure 37 shows the distribution of chairmanship of the *Committee on Trade and Environment.*

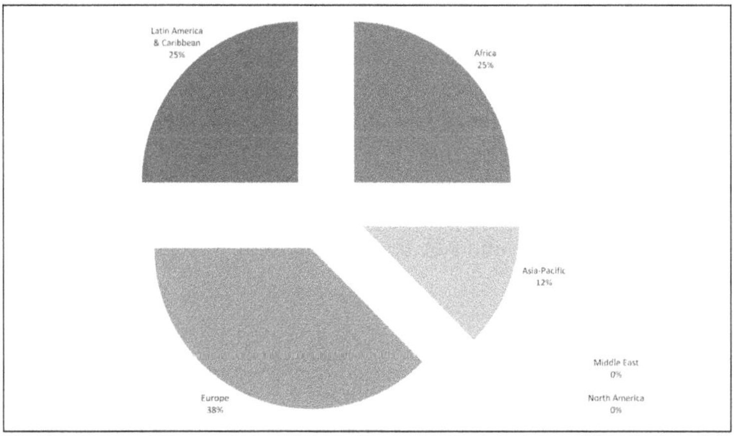

Figure 37. Chairs of the Committee on Trade and Environment.

The content of discussions in the Committee on Trade and Environment is intellectually sophisticated, involving complex and evolving relationships between domestic law, regulation multilateral environment rules and multilateral trade rules. Traditionally, this committee has been of high policy and rule relevance for Europe. For developing countries, including Africa, the overall position has been that trade and environment rules must not negatively impede development growth rates. Europe accounted for the most shares of chairmanships at 37 per cent, followed by Latin America and the Caribbean and Africa tied at 25 per cent each. Asia Pacific was below, accounting for 12 per cent with North America and the Middle East having never held chairmanship of this Committee. Egypt, Mauritius and Gabon were the African Member that chaired the CTE.

Figure 38, shows the distribution of the *Committee on Balance of Payments Restrictions*.

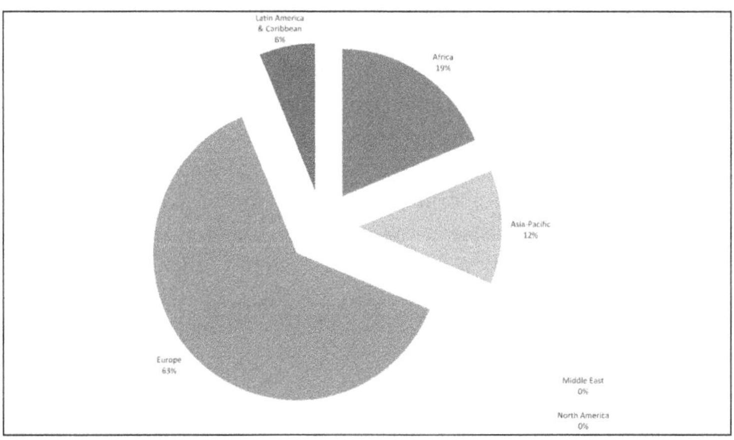

Figure 38. Chairs of the BOP Committee.

The Committee on Balance of Payments Restrictions is technical. In the period studied, Europe accounted for 63 per cent share of chairmanship of this Committee, followed by Africa with 18.75 per cent and the Asia Pacific region, accounting for 12.5 per cent of the chairmanships. Latin America and the Caribbean followed with 6.25 per cent of the chairmanship. North America and the Middle East reflected a zero per cent share. The ability to manage this Committee requires competent technical knowledge. Uganda, Zambia and Zimbabwe were the African countries that had chaired this committee.[15]

Figure 39 show the distribution of the chairmanship of the *Committee on Budget Finance and Administration.*

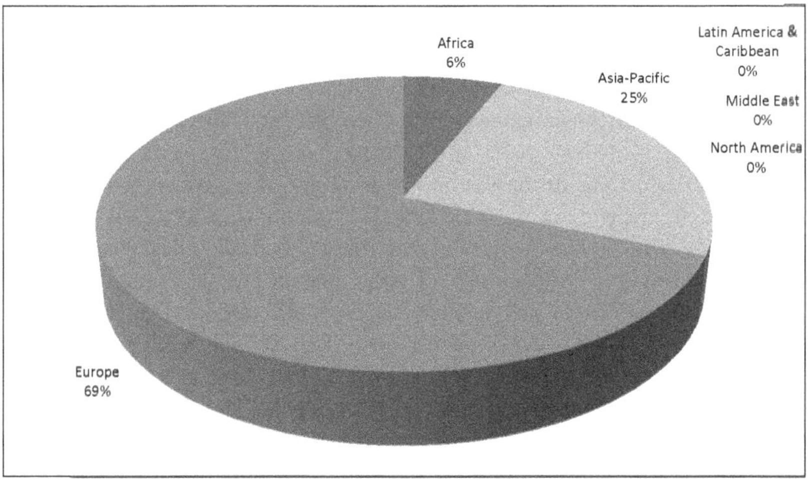

Figure 39. Chairs of the BFA Committee.

The Committee on Budget Finance and Administration is systemic and vital. In the BFA Committee, the contributions of individual Members are assessed and those in arrears over a period of time are placed in an inactive category. A number of African WTO Members have on several occasions been in arrears with regard to their membership contributions. Africa's share of chairmanships of this committee was low at 6.25 per cent. It ranked below the share of chairmanships of Europe and the Asia Pacific regions. Africa's share of chairmanships was better than Latin America and the Caribbean, North America and the Middle East, all accounting for zero per cent share of the chairmanship. Tunisia chaired the BFA Committee in 1997.

Figure 40 shows the distribution of the chairmanships of the Committee *on Regional Trade Agreements.*

15 The Zambian Chairman (2010) was a lawyer and the Ugandan a trained economist, with previous consultancy for the World Bank.

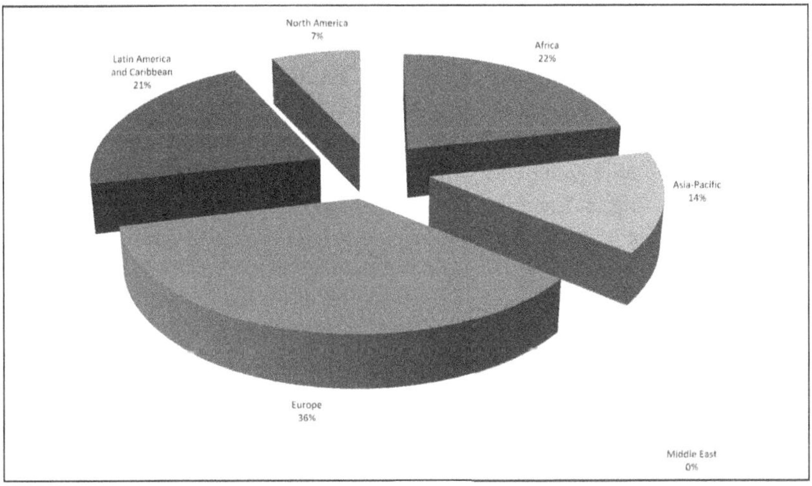

Figure 40. Chairs of the CRTA.

The Committee on Regional Trade Agreements is vital and systemic. Europe accounted for the highest percentage share of chairmanship at 36 per cent, followed by Africa at 22 per cent and Latin America and Caribbean at 21 per cent. Asia Pacific had a 14 percentage share, while North America had 7 per cent share of chairmanship. The Middle East region had never chaired this committee. WTO African Members have demonstrated a keen and sensitive interest in the RTA Committee and GATT Article XXIV matters. Zimbabwe, Mauritius and Senegal were the African countries that had chaired this Committee.

Figure 41 shows the distribution of chairmanships of the Working *Group on Trade Debt and Finance.*

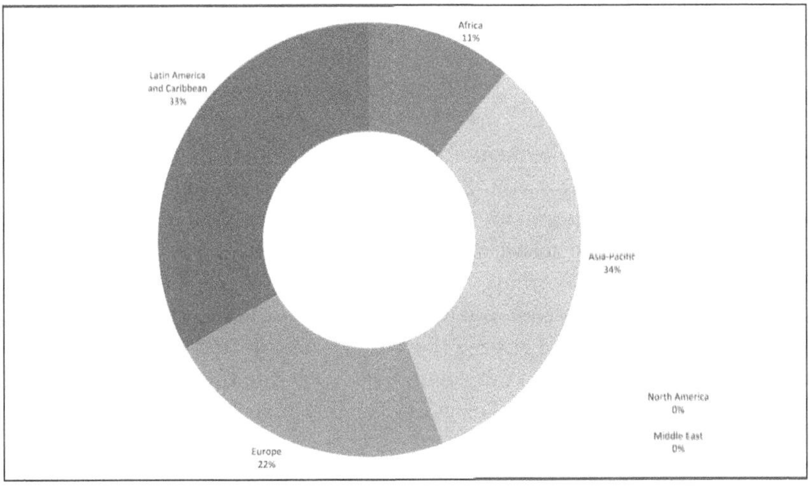

Figure 41. Chairs of the Working Group on Trade, Debt and Finance.

This Working Group is development-oriented, mandated by the 2001 Doha Ministerial Declaration. It was part of the "Positive Agenda" around which developing countries worked together in the negotiations that led to the launch of the Doha negotiations. Although it has minimal to zero scope for rule-making, African WTO Members attach high priority to this working group. African Members considered that this Working Group had scored a major gain in the July 2005 G8 Gleneagles Agreement, that cancelled the debt of several Highly Indebted Poor Countries (HIPC), many African, before the December Hong Kong Ministerial Conference. However, their share of the chairmanship of this working group was low at 11 per cent. Uganda was the only African country that chaired this working group. Africa's share was only better than North America and the Middle East with a zero per cent share and behind Europe and the Latin America and Caribbean region. The Asia-Pacific region had the most share of the chairmanship of this working group at 34 per cent.

Figure 42 shows the distribution of the chairmanship of the Working *Group on Trade and Transfer of Technology.*

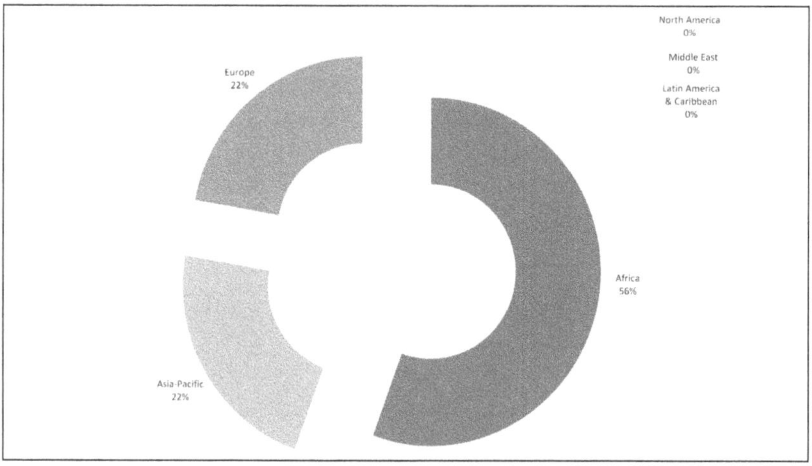

Figure 42. Chairs of the Working Group on Trade and Transfer of Technology.

This working group is development-oriented, mandated by the 2001 Doha Ministerial Declaration. It was part of the "Positive Agenda" around which developing countries came together in the negotiations that led to the launch of the Doha negotiations. Although it has minimal to zero scope for rule-making, African WTO Members attach high priority to this working group. Africa had the most share of the chairmanship of this working group at 56 per cent. Ghana, Mauritius, Zimbabwe, Kenya and Egypt were the African Members that had chaired the WGTTT. Europe and Asia Pacific tied at 22 per cent each of chairmanship of this committee. North America, Latin America and the Caribbean and the Middle East had each a zero per cent share.

8. Chairs of Plurilateral Committees

Two plurilateral committees – Government Procurement and Trade in Civil Aircraft – report directly to the General Council. Figure 43 shows the distribution of chairs across regions and amongst Members that are signatory to these Agreements as follows:

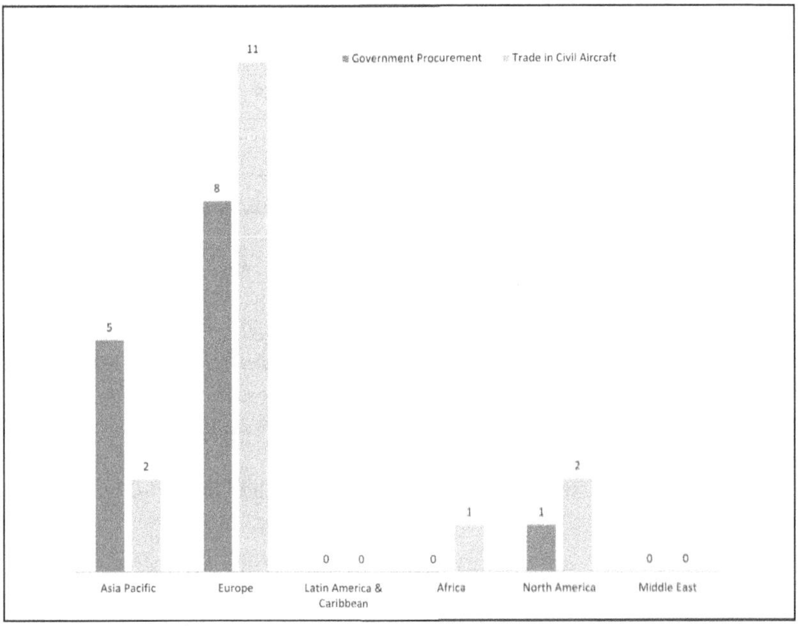

Figure 43. Share of Chairmanships of Plurilateral Committees.

- Europe, 63 per cent
- Asia-Pacific, 23 per cent;
- North America 10.5 per cent,
- Africa 3.3 per cent
- Latin America and the Caribbean, 0 per cent,
- Middle East, 0 per cent

Plurilateral bodies reflect highly specialised sectoral commercial areas with high market access content. Africa's share of the chairmanship was low, at 3.3 per cent, only better than Latin America and Caribbean and the Middle East both tied at zero per cent. Egypt was the only African WTO Member that had chaired any of the plurilateral bodies. Europe accounted for the highest percentage share of chairmanships at 63 per cent better than the Asia Pacific region at 23 per cent and North America at 10.5 per cent.

Figure 44 shows the distribution of the chairmanship of the *Committee on Government Procurement.*

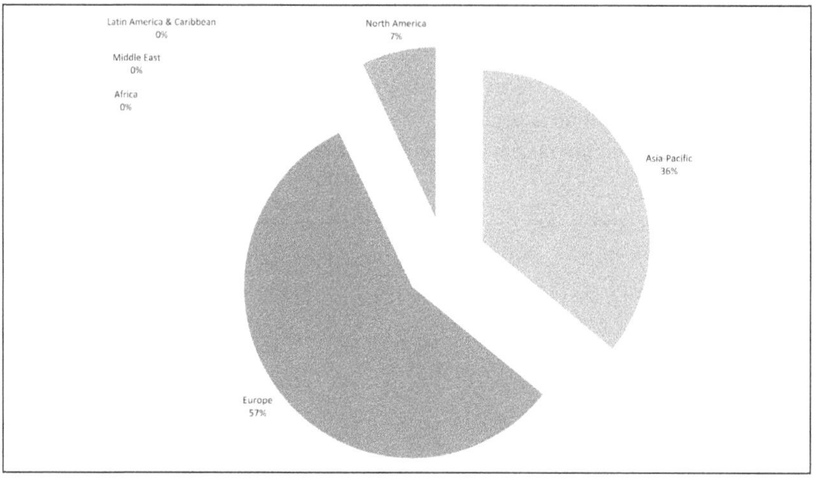

Figure 44. Chairs of the Government Procurement Committee.

In the period reviewed, no African Member had ever chaired this committee because no African WTO Member was party to the GPA. Only Members that are party to the Agreement are eligible to chair the committee. Africa was tied with the Middle East and Latin America and Caribbean at zero per cent.

Figure 45 shows the distribution of chairmanships of the *Committee on Trade in Civil Aircraft.*

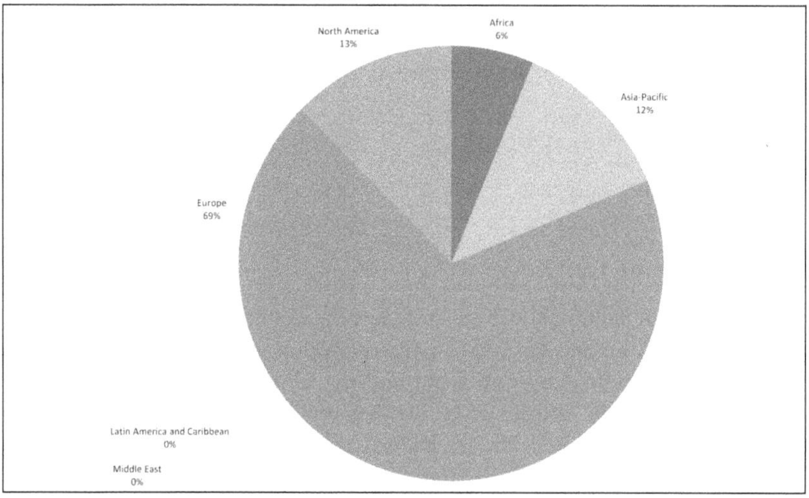

Figure 45. Chairs of the Committee on Trade in Civil Aircraft.

Africa's share of the chairmanship of the Committee on Trade in Civil Aircraft was low at 6.25 per cent, but better than the Middle East and Latin American and Caribbean regions at zero per cent. Europe accounted for the most chairmanships at 68.75 per cent. North America and the Asia pacific regions tied at 12.5 per cent share. Egypt was first chair of this Committee.

9. Overall Assessment of the Participation of African Members as Chairs of WTO Bodies

The purpose of this chapter was to examine "chairmanship shares of regular bodies" to ascertain if they accounted in part for the explanation of the level of Africa's engagement/participation in the WTO. The results of data gathered, analysed and interpreted suggested an improvement from a very low base between 1995 and 2005. However, systemically, this level remained low.

The data collected for this chapter show that 19[16] African WTO Members out of a total of 42 (i.e. 40 per cent) had chaired WTO regular bodies, although 92.8 per cent of African WTO Members are Geneva resident. No non-resident African Member had thus far held a chairmanship. The data analysed showed that although the share of regular-body chairmanships accounted for by Africa had gradually risen from 1995 to its current level, it remained low in relation to the number of African WTO Members. The data analysed showed that Africa's share of chairmanships had only been better than for the Middle East on competitive grounds and better also than North America, but only because of the latter's conscious policy to be minimalist in taking chairmanships. The Asia Pacific region had performed better, followed by Europe and Latin America and the Caribbean.

Chairmanships have several advantages in both regular bodies and DDA negotiating groups. They range from the substantive to the trivial. The chairmanship position at the core is a vantage point for the management, understanding and obtaining inside knowledge of the operation of the rules-based multilateral trading system. The role of the chair is strictly limited to brokerage and consensus building, where possible, (because sometimes brokerage and consensus building are carried out, not by the chairperson, if weak or constrained, but by "friends of the chairperson"). The role of chairs in the rule-making system which is Member-driven is constrained. Apart from gavelled decisions, the critical process of drafting and building consensus for rules are in informal formats of regular bodies. Yet, there is also value in profile and ceremony which carry a degree of influence for the wider public and constituencies in Member countries. Normally, chairs do not make statements, except of an introductory nature, or in the rare and exceptional circumstances where their "statement" constitutes a requirement in an agreement by Members as was the case in the TRIPS Agreement amendment in 2005.

The question, therefore, is not whether African WTO Members, or for that matter any Member, should make a choice either in favour of struggling for and holding

[16] Botswana, Burkina Faso; Cote d'Ivoire; Egypt; Gabon; Ghana; Kenya; Lesotho; Mauritius; Morocco; Namibia; Nigeria; Senegal; South Africa, Tanzania; Tunisia; Uganda; Zambia; Zimbabwe.

chairmanships, on the one hand, or attending as many meetings as possible, on the other hand. Both and all must be done. The decisions that need to be made are in a better, more rational allocation of resources, evenly distributed across the three areas of core work. The biggest bang for the buck emerges from rational allocation of resources evenly distributed.

The data analysed suggested a range of factors to explain the share of chairmanships by African WTO Members. As analysed, various factors were at play in different bodies. Primarily, operative factors typically included capacity constraints, technical expertise and specialization, commercial and systemic interests; internal organisational rules in the appointment of officers to regular bodies, particularly the strict standard of technical competence, and, Geneva/capital coordination which significantly influenced chairmanship shares. Financial resources, as part of Organizational rules on appointments, exercised considerable influence because otherwise eligible candidates could be disqualified if their country was in financial arrears for a given period.

In addition, interviews conducted, to plumb the data analysed, revealed the importance of Geneva/capital coordination as well as the "unwritten custom of parcelling out specific bodies to particular regions". There was an "immeasurable" political factor of parcelling out chairmanship of particular regular bodies, such as the EU's "tradition" of chairing the BFA Committee. Similarly Africa, exercised preponderant chairmanship of the CTD because of the committee's core position of the mutual supportiveness of trade and development.

The questions for African policy makers are what are the solutions and how could the level of engagement/participation with regard to chairmanships be improved? There are several solutions, revolving around better Geneva-capital coordination, tenure and quality of delegations.

First, an observation made evident by the combination of analysed data and individual interviews suggested that the level of participation and share of chairmanships could be enhanced by stronger Geneva/capital coordination. Second, there was evidence of technically competent individuals with specialised knowledge, but the numbers were low and there was considerable discontinuity in tenure. The evidence indicated that up to a point in time, longer tenures in Geneva, to cover the WTO, increased the quality of participation and effectiveness. African WTO Members should be well served by this recommendation. Longer tenures, generally, are consistent with deeper specialization and knowledge, more familiarity with procedures, better peer recognition and more stable networks that enhance effectiveness. However, it is also the case, as suggested by the evidence, that beyond a certain threshold in time, complacency, fatigue and cynicism are likely to set in, requiring a vital rotation of the negotiator and "refresh" of the Member. Third, one of the findings observed in analysing the data was that the more technical, specialised, experienced professionally motivated the delegates (in a delegation), the higher the share of chairmanships. This was obvious in the pattern that had emerged from the limited universe of African WTO Members that repeatedly account for the largest share of chairmanships within the African Group. Specifically, the more technical and specialized individuals in this limited universe of African countries had been systemically accepted to chair perceived "complex" regular bodies such as trade remedies bodies, trade in financial services, regional trade agreements, and, trade in civil aircraft.

CHAPTER FOUR

PARTICIPATION – NEGOTIATING ENGAGEMENT

1. Introduction: The "Hang-Over" from the Uruguay Round

What was the *level of African negotiating engagement/participation in the Doha Round* in the period 2002–2010? In what *structural settings* were African WTO Members operative? How did their *negotiating behaviour manifest* in the various negotiating settings? What were their priority areas of focus? This chapter examines the participation of African WTO Members in relation to other Members in the Trade Negotiations Committee (TNC) and its subsidiary bodies. It assesses their level of engagement/participation by examining the number of chairmanships held, priority areas for African countries in the DDA negotiations, and the quantity and quality[1] of submissions/proposals made. Based on reviewed data, the analysis in this chapter primarily compares the level of African WTO Members' engagement/participation to Members from other regional groups. In addition, a comparison is made with participation in the two other core areas namely, regular committee work and the dispute settlement system. How did African Members' participation in the Doha Round negotiations compare to their level of engagement in regular committee work and dispute settlement?

The participation of African Members in the Uruguay Round, under the GATT, was very low to non-existent. The vast majority of African countries were essentially "absent" and non-participatory in the Uruguay Round negotiations. At the coming into force of the WTO in 1995, African WTO Members were confronted with the "implementation challenge" of the substantive legal results of the Uruguay Round to which they were bound regardless of their level of engagement and whether they had fully understood those commitments. The common position of the African Group, more strongly elaborated in individual statements, was best summarized in the Abuja Ministerial Declaration, before the launch of the Doha Round in 2001. While they reaffirmed their commitment to the rules-based multilateral trading system, they concluded that the WTO and its Members

[1] There is a "quality" question in contrast to the "quantity" of tabled proposals. The answer to this important question revolves around the factors of substantive content, attraction of consensus, and, eventual results at the *dénouement* of the Doha Round. Preliminary assessments are suggested in this chapter in the contrast drawn between quantity and quality of proposals.

needed to "respond in a manner that supports Africa's *development and integration into the MTS*." They also concluded that, "... there is an urgent need for *development issues* to be put at the centre-stage at the WTO ... *addressing asymmetries in existing Agreements*; ... The objective should be the achievement of global growth and development for all Members, while decisively *addressing the present inequities in the MTS*."[2] (Emphasis added by author). Some African trade negotiators have alluded to these issues of imbalance and lack of fairness. (Ismail, Faizel, 2009)

Individual statements went further. The position was taken that the results of the eighth Round of multilateral trade negotiations were "unfair and unbalanced". It was considered that international trade trends made evident their loss of trade share, "marginalization" and that the trading system needed to better respond to their development objectives. Some African trade negotiators have alluded to and summarized the various references characterizing the results of the Uruguay Round as unbalanced and against the interests of developing countries. Their writings also refer to lack of equity. (Ismail, Faizel, 2009).

With the background of a very low participation and engagement level in the Uruguay Round, African WTO Members sought to play a more active, engaged and participatory role in the Doha Round. Substantively, the broad, all-encompassing positions of African WTO Members have evolved in the course of the Round since 2001. They have adopted many declarations/decisions, which do not fully reveal individual African WTO Member differences. However, the Kigali (2004)[3] Cairo (2005)[4] and Addis Ababa (2009)[5] Declarations best capture the common African Group positions in the Doha Round.

This chapter analyses the data to ascertain whether this objective for an activist engagement in the Doha Round has been achieved. The indices identified to objectively assess the level of engagement/participation were the following:

- number of DDA chairmanships,
- number and quality of individual and co-sponsored written proposals/submissions,
- number and quality of individual, co-sponsored and group written proposals/submissions
- interventions/oral statements[6]

A set of explanatory variables emerged from the analysis to suggest, and in some cases decisively, why the level of African WTO Members' engagement/participation was either

---

[2] World Trade Organization, *Organization of African Unity/African Economic Community, Fourth Ordinary Session of the Committee on Trade, Customs and Immigration, 19–23 September, 2001, Abuja, Nigeria*, Communication from Zimbabwe, WT/L/423, 18 October 2001.

[3] World Trade Organization, *Kigali Declaration and Kigali Consensus, Kigali, Rwanda, 27–28 May 2004*, Communication from Mauritius, WT/L/572.

[4] World Trade Organization, *Cairo Declaration and Road Map on the Doha Work Programme, Cairo, Egypt, 5–9 June 2005*, Communication from Rwanda, WT/L/612

[5] World Trade Organization, *AU Conference of Ministers of Trade, 5th Ordinary Session Addis Ababa, Ethiopia, 20 March 2009*, Communication from Egypt, WT/L/751.

[6] This was only done for the TNC and not for its subsidiary bodies. From about 2007 the work in most negotiating bodies took place mainly in informal modes where no official records are kept.

low or relatively higher than a starting low base. These variables revolved around the continuing inertia of special and differential treatment; Geneva-capital coordination; the rationality of allocation of African trade negotiators across different negotiating bodies; capacity for complex trade policy questions; and, the levels of personal commitment and professional engagement of individual negotiators. Variables that also figured, in this mix, included trade and GDP shares; and, the competitiveness rankings of particular individual African economies. No less important was the nature of the domestic governance systems from which African negotiators emerged. Sometimes, it made a huge difference as to whether a negotiator emerged from a system accustomed to democratic practices, the rule of law and the experience of foreign and trade policy advocacy. The picture is a complex one, not amenable to simple mono-causal analysis. Overall, the conclusion from the analysis of the data, to which these variables were applied, including through regression analysis, was that the level of African participation/engagement in the Doha Round negotiations, although low, was relatively higher than in the other two core areas of regular committee work and dispute settlement. The negotiations generated excitement as the most seductive area of work. It was seen as an opportunity to correct perceived imbalances from the Uruguay Round results. To a large extent for many of the African newcomers to the rules-based system, the negotiations became synonymous with the regular work of the Organization. However, with an on-going negotiation of over ten years, the question is whether this relatively, activist higher level of engagement will be sustained if the Doha Round survives. It also raises the broader more systemic question as to where African WTO Members would be best served in investing their efforts and allocating their resources amongst the three core areas. These questions are addressed with recommendations in chapter 7.

2. The Doha Development Agenda Negotiations

At the fourth Ministerial Conference in Doha, Qatar, in November 2001, WTO Member governments agreed to launch a new trade negotiation as part of the broader Doha Development Agenda (DDA). In launching the Round, Ministers agreed to seek to place the "needs and interests" of developing countries at the heart of the work programme. Ministers agreed to make positive efforts designed to ensure that developing countries, particularly the least developed of them, secured a share in growth of world trade, commensurate with the needs of their economic development. To achieve these objectives, Ministers in their Declaration underlined the vital roles to be played by enhanced market access, balanced rules, and well-targeted, sustainably financed technical assistance.[7]

The Doha negotiations take place in the Trade Negotiations Committee (TNC) and its nine subsidiary bodies. (Figure 46)

[7] WT/MIN(01)/DEC/1, 20 November 2001, the Doha Ministerial Declaration.

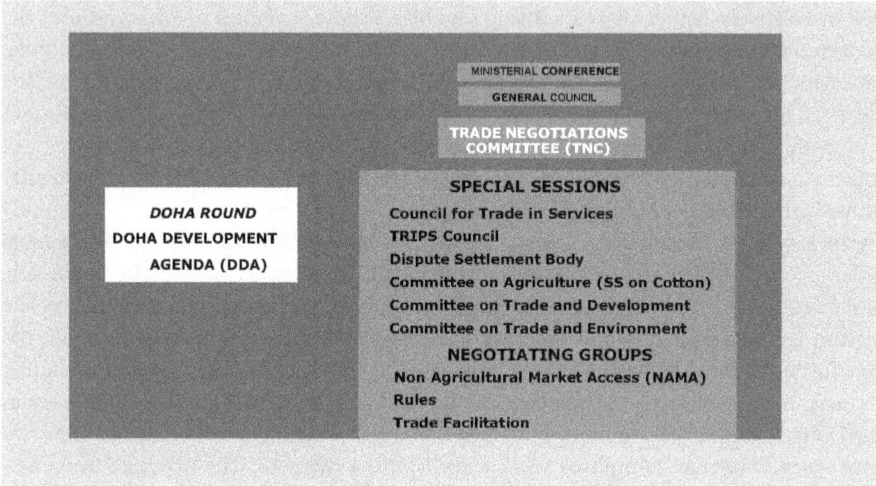

Figure 46. Doha development agenda.

3. Chairs of Subsidiary Bodies of the Trade Negotiations Committee

Chairpersons of individual negotiating bodies are appointed following consultations by the Chairman of the General Council. At its first meeting, the TNC agreed to appoint chairs of its subsidiary bodies until the fifth session of the Ministerial Conference in Cancun in 2003. The practice since then has been that chairs are appointed until "the next session of a Ministerial Conference" and in most cases their appointment has been rolled over to the following Ministerial session or lapse with departure from Geneva.

In the period studied, twenty five (25) WTO Members had chaired the nine TNC subsidiary bodies. Figure 47 shows the regional distribution of negotiating group chairs. The data showed that the Asia Pacific region accounted for 40 per cent of these chairmanships. It was followed by Latin America and the Caribbean region at 32 per cent. These two regions encompass several of the emerging dynamic developing economies. Africa's share was relatively low at 12 per cent. Europe accounted for 12 per cent share of chairmanships with North America accounting for 4 per cent. The Middle East region had not chaired any negotiating group.

In the period 2002–2010, the details of the Members that have chaired negotiating bodies were as follows:

- The Special Session of the Committee on Agriculture / Sub-Committee on Cotton – Hong Kong China, and New Zealand (Asia-pacific region)
- Negotiating Group on Market Access – Switzerland, Iceland and Canada (Europe and North America)
- Special Session of the Council for Services – Chile and Mexico (Latin America and Caribbean).
- Negotiating Group on Trade Facilitation – Guatemala, Hong Kong China and Malaysia (Asia-pacific and Latin American regions).
- The Negotiating Group on Rules – New Zealand, Uruguay and Trinidad and Tobago (Asia Pacific and the Latin America and Caribbean regions)

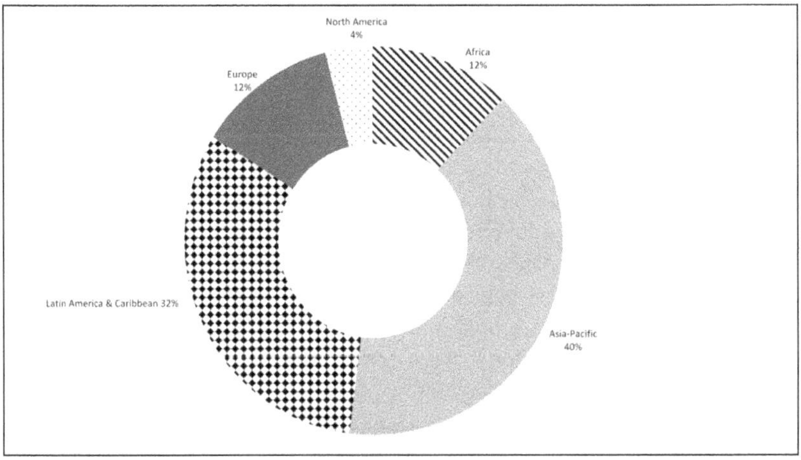

Figure 47. Distribution of Chairs of Negotiating Bodies by Region 2002–2010.

- The Special Session of the Council for TRIPS – Korea, Pakistan, Barbados, Singapore and Zambia (Asia-pacific, Latin America and Caribbean and Africa regions)
- The Special Session of the Committee on Trade and Environment – Gabon, Bangladesh, Chile and Philippines (Africa, Asia-Pacific and Latin America and Caribbean).
- The Special Session of the Committee on Trade and Development – Jamaica, South Africa, Singapore and Thailand (Latin America and Caribbean, Africa and Asia-pacific).
- The Special Session of the Dispute Settlement Body – Hungary, Australia and Costa Rica (Europe, Asia Pacific and Latin America).

There has been regional and group interest in chairmanships of negotiating bodies. However, actual allocation revolves around several of the variables previously identified as operative in the allocation of chairmanships of regular bodies. Chairpersons must be acceptable to the entire membership. Premium is accorded to technical competence, combined with proven ability to build consensus, on the basis of textual work. Only a limited universe of chairpersons emerged in the 8 year period of the Doha Round studied and there was near-unanimous reluctance to depart from the crop of chairpersons. The evidence showed, different from chairmanships of the regular bodies, that there was less politicization with chairpersons of negotiating bodies who exercised a higher level of care and diligence. In the period studied, three African Members (Gabon, South Africa, and Zambia) had chaired negotiating bodies in the areas of Trade and Environment, Development and TRIPS.[8] Participation as chairs of negotiating bodies also guaranteed African presence in small group consultative processes that were not open to all 153 WTO members. This included access to green-room meetings; invitation to mini-ministerial meetings and private consultations convened particularly by the more advanced countries and lead-traders – including the so-called G5/G6/G-7/G11/G23 plus, breakfast group processes etc., over the years. Furthermore, the role of chairpersons could also be

[8] In 2012, Nigeria was appointed as Chair of the Special Session of the TRIPS Council following the departure of the Zambian Chair.

critical in the rare and exceptional circumstances where their "statement" constitutes a requirement in an agreement by Members.[9]

4. Forms of African Negotiating Engagement

African engagement in the Doha Round negotiations has been manifested in specific forms. Although there was a limited degree of robust individual activity by some in the small universe of active African WTO Members,[10] the principal form of negotiating engagement was in coalitional behaviour. African WTO Members operated in a wide range of intra-regional, inter-regional and issue-specific coalitions to compensate for their individual weakness. This form of engagement was more effective than their individual activity in relation to their negotiating objectives.

Figure 48 in Annex VII shows the principal coalitions in which African negotiating engagement manifested. There are several observations. First, African Members were operative and worked through 18 basic coalitions in the Doha Round negotiations. Second, most of African Member engagement was through the African Group, LDCs' Consultative Group and the ACP Group to which most belonged. Third, these coalitions ranged across priority areas of interests for African Members. These areas included development, special development needs of LDCs, special development needs of non-LDC vulnerable Members (special and differential treatment), targeted reform and liberalization position (RAMs), agriculture, cotton, NAMA, flexibility and protection for development purposes, trade facilitation, and intellectual property. These coalitions included both those that were unique and some traditional, long-standing coalitions that had been re-adjusted to the DDA negotiations.

5. African Participation in Negotiating Bodies

The negotiating behaviour of African WTO Members manifested variously, across the different negotiating bodies, in the form of oral statements and tabled proposals/submissions.

(a) *The Trade Negotiations Committee (TNC)*

The Doha Ministerial Declaration established the mandate for the negotiations. The TNC established nine negotiating bodies. It supervises the overall conduct of the negotiations under the authority of the General Council.

---

[9] For example, the Chairman's statement on the Amendment to the TRIPS Agreement.

[10] Benin, Burkina Faso, Chad, Cote d'Ivoire, Egypt, Gabon, Ghana, Kenya, Lesotho, Mauritius, Morocco, Namibia, Nigeria, Senegal, Tanzania, Tunisia, Uganda, Zambia, and, Zimbabwe.

(i) Oral Statements at the TNC[11]

Figure 49 shows the number of individual oral statements, in the period 2002–2010, by Members in different regions, in the TNC. The data shows that Latin America and Caribbean region made the most oral statements in the TNC. It was notable that 100 per cent i.e. all countries in this region had intervened orally at least once. Similarly, all countries in the North American region had intervened. Europe followed with 98 per cent of members in the region intervening. 82 per cent of members in the Asia Pacific region intervened with 315 statements. 42 per cent or less than half, of African WTO Members expressed individual negotiating positions on the Doha Round in the TNC. The African Members that intervened correspond to the same limited universe of active African WTO Members.[12] The Middle East was the region with least expressed positions on the Doha Round in the TNC at 37 per cent of its members intervening.

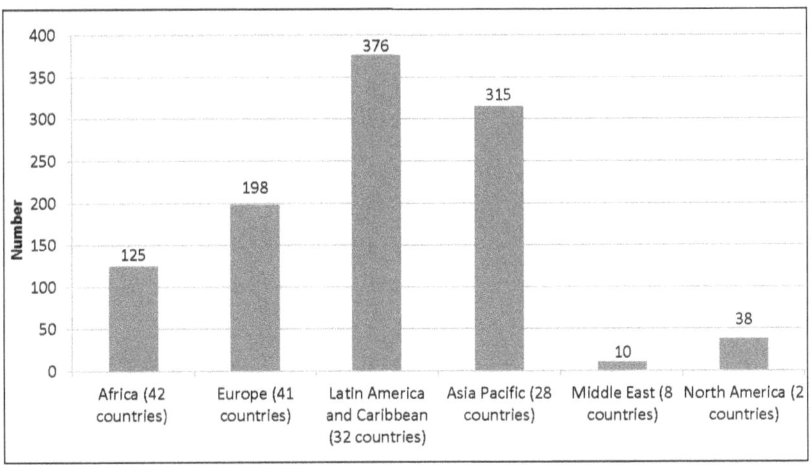

Figure 49. Individual statements in the TNC (2002–2010).

Disaggregated, the data collected showed that the most statements had been made by India (33); European Union (32); Cuba (29); Chile (28); Colombia (28), China (27), Brazil (27), and, Argentina (26). Other Members with over 20 statements included Pakistan, Mexico, Bulgaria, United States, Japan, Korea, Costa Rica, Switzerland, the Philippines and Thailand. Most of these countries are either leading trading Members or "emerging" developing economies. They are active participants in the TNC for their offensive

11 Minutes of the Trade Negotiations Committee TN/C/M/1 to 30. This analysis reflected only the formal meetings of the TNC. Informal TNC meetings were not factored into this analysis as formal records are not kept.

12 African Members that made individual statements in the TNC from 2002–2010: Benin, Botswana, Chad, Cote d'Ivoire, Djibouti, Egypt, Gabon, Ghana, Guinea, Kenya, Lesotho, Mali, Mauritania, Mauritius, Morocco, Nigeria, Rwanda, Senegal, South Africa, Tanzania, Tunisia, Uganda, Zambia, Zimbabwe.

and defensive commercial interests as well as systemic concerns such as transparency, inclusiveness or the development mandate of the negotiations.

Amongst WTO African Members Kenya made the most statements (19). Other countries with a relatively high number of statements included Nigeria (13); South Africa (13); Uganda (12), Egypt (10), and, Morocco (10). These African Members not only form part of the limited universe of active African WTO Members, but some of them are principal economies on the African continent. South Africa, Nigeria and Egypt are the top three economies in Africa. In addition, some of these active African Members have WTO dedicated missions with delegate compositions that combine trade policy specialists and Foreign Service personnel.

In the period 2002–2010, figure 50 shows the number of group oral statements, in the TNC. It confirms one of the propositions in this chapter that the principal form of negotiating engagement was in coalitional behaviour. African WTO Members operated in a wide range of intra-regional, inter-regional and issue-specific coalitions to compensate for their individual weakness.

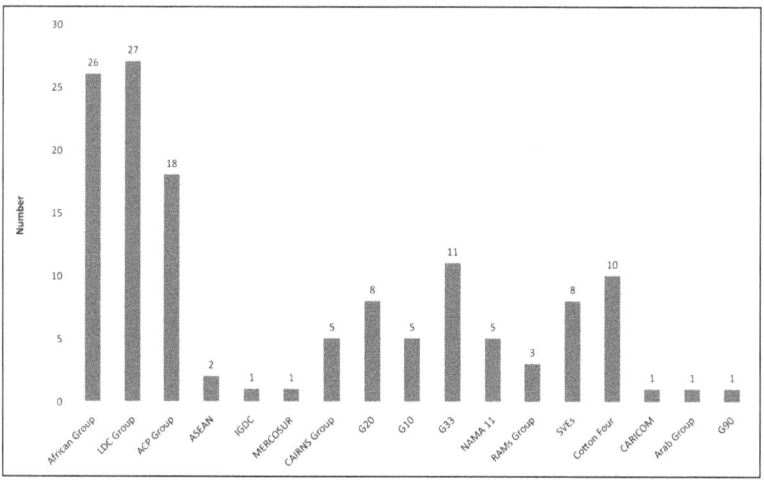

Figure 50. Group Statements at the TNC (2002–2010).

The statement behaviour of African WTO Members was higher within the African and the Least Developed Countries Consultative Groups. Data also showed that the "weaker" groups made the most statements in the TNC.

(b) *Special Session of the Committee on Agriculture*

Beyond their common group positions on the agriculture negotiations in the Doha Round, African Members reflect real negotiating diversity. Most African countries are net food importers. Twenty five (25) African WTO Members are LDCs and most African countries depend on preferential market access. The broad agricultural negotiating platform as agreed by African Trade Ministers, in several Declarations, was that account should be taken of the need for appropriate policy space that would allow African countries to pursue agricultural policies that are supportive of their development goals, poverty reduction strategies, food security and livelihood concerns, while ensuring improved market access for the agricultural products of African countries, both in primary and processed forms. In reality, the negotiating diversity and overlapping membership of African Members in the Doha Round Agriculture negotiations fell in five broad categories. First, ambition led by South Africa as a member of the Cairns Group. The Cotton-Four that seek the elimination of trade distortions in cotton also fell into this category. Second, the combination of ambition and development represented by Egypt, Nigeria, South Africa, and, Tanzania, as G20 members. Third, the policy space position was represented by a number of African countries that belonged to the G33 (Benin, Botswana, Congo, Côte d'Ivoire, Kenya, Madagascar, Mauritius, Mozambique, Nigeria, Senegal, Tanzania, Uganda, Zambia and Zimbabwe). Fourth, protection was represented by Mauritius, a member of the G10 with strong defensive interests in agriculture. Finally, there were the African Net Food Importers.

(i) Individual and Co-Sponsored (Non-Group) Written Proposals

Figure 51 shows the number of individual Member and co-sponsored (non-group) written proposals, in different regions, in the Special Session of the Committee on Agriculture and its Sub-Committee on Cotton in the period 2002–2010. The level of African negotiating engagement was relatively high at 100 individual and co-sponsored proposal, but lower than 198 for Latin America and the Caribbean, 126 for Europe, and, 107 for Asia Pacific. However, it was higher than, 42 for North America and 1 for the Middle East. The explanation laid in the fact that agriculture, cotton and associated special and differential treatment considerations constituted areas of priority negotiating interest for the African WTO Members. However, this relatively high level of engagement was more pronounced at a group platform.

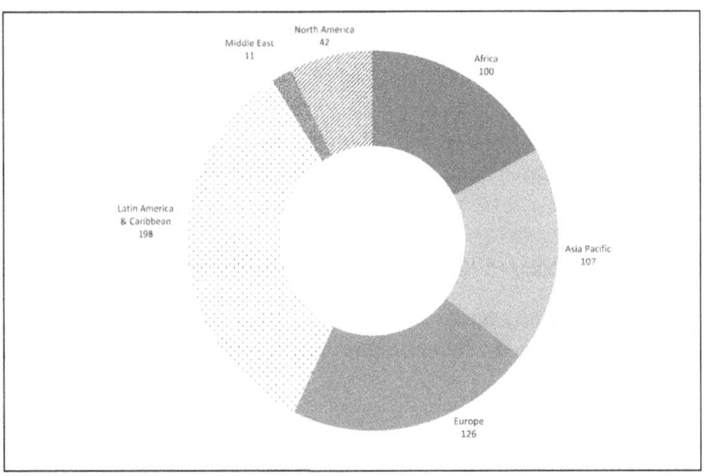

Figure 51. Individual and co-sponsored agriculture proposals by region (2000–2010).

Disaggregated, the data collected showed that the most individual and co-sponsored proposals in the agriculture negotiations had been tabled by the United States (25); Argentina (25); European Union (23); Canada (17); Uruguay (15) and Japan (14). These are leading trading nations and emerging economies with high offensive and defensive interests in the agricultural negotiations. They have real commercial, systemic and in some cases protectionist interests as reflected in the content of proposals tabled. However, it is vital to stress that the level of engagement is not uniquely influenced by commercial interests *per se* (i.e. trade/GDP shares), but also and in some cases more critically the rules *qua* rules that accompany market access and associated commercial interests. In addition, all these Members had resident and sizeable missions in Geneva and have reliable and quick capital-based support in these negotiations, with which they were in real time coordination. They were generally less constrained both on the human resource and technical knowledge fronts.

Two African countries (Burkina Faso and Kenya) had tabled at least 10 proposals. Burkina Faso had tabled the highest number of proposals totalling 11. These proposals related to cotton, the offensive interest of the Cotton-Four (Benin, Chad and Mali) coordinated by Burkina Faso. African countries with more than five proposals were Zimbabwe, Nigeria and Mauritius. These Members had offensive interests in this area. It is recalled that Zimbabwe was once referred to "the bread basket of Africa"; Nigeria is one of the largest economy on the continent and Mauritius has been the leading competitive African economy with regard to domestic reforms.

Although African countries were relatively active in the Doha Round, compared to previous rounds, where their participation ranged between minimal and non-existent, they tabled the fewest individual proposals, relative to all other regions with the exception of the Middle East, despite significant membership share and agro-based economies. It is observed that the draft agriculture modalities of December 2008 would exempt several African WTO Members from undertaking commitments in market access, domestic support and export competition for a number of reasons including status as LDCs or SVEs or NFIDCs – an illustration of continued inertia with an SDT exemption orientation. Yet, they have been very active in the agriculture negotiations, where they have overcome typical capacity constraints because of assistance received from other multilateral institutions such as UNCTAD and the South Centre and from civil society, such as IDEAS on cotton. This intelligent compensation for capacity weakness of African WTO Members contributed significantly in explaining how they overcome this handicap and as a consequence augmented their level of negotiating engagement in the Doha Round agriculture negotiations.

(ii) Individual, Co-Sponsored (Non-Group) and Group Proposals

Figure 52 shows that for all regions in this study, the number of tabled agriculture proposals substantially increased when group proposals were taken into account.

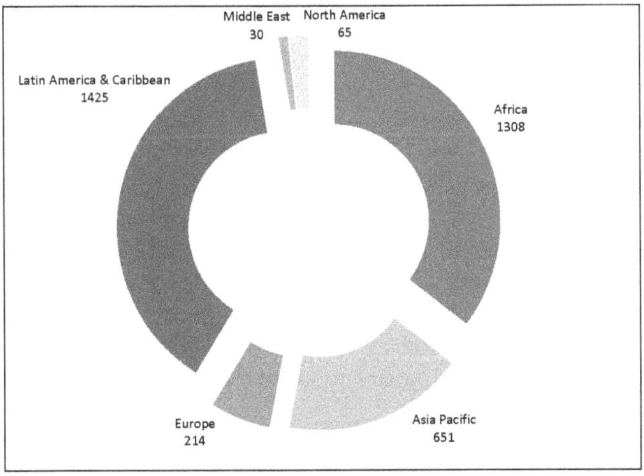

Figure 52. Individual, co-sponsored and group agriculture proposals by region (2000–2010).

This distribution confirms the proposition that the weaker Members were more coalitional which produced the effect of a larger number of submissions and proposals. The data for the combined total of individual plus co-sponsored and group proposals showed that Africa registered 1305 proposals, only below Latin America and Caribbean with 1425 proposals and greater than the number of proposals from Europe, North America and the Middle East combined. However, "volume" is not necessarily a good predictor of the "quality" and does not indicate the likelihood of "consensus" and "passage". Furthermore, it was obvious that the higher volume of proposals was "nominalism" and not necessarily related to quality.

What explained this relatively higher level of African Members' participation/ engagement? Part of the reason is the fact that this was one of the key aspects *of their* response to their conclusions about "imbalances, asymmetries, and inequities" resulting from the Uruguay Round. Agriculture was and remains one of the "battle grounds" between developed and developing including Africa countries in the Doha Round. In over ten years of the Doha Round "other battle grounds" have emerged for example in sectorals in NAMA and in services. Furthermore, the higher volume of proposals was "nominalism" considering the significant membership share of African WTO Members coupled with the fact that they belonged to 11 groups in the agricultural negotiations.

Disaggregated, the data collected showed that up to 2010, Bolivia (84); Guatemala[13] (80); Philippines (81); Pakistan (78) and Indonesia (72) had tabled the most proposals overall.[14] There was a significant percentage increase in the number of proposals tabled by individual Members as they signed-on to and co-sponsored proposals in different

13 Methodologically, a proposal was attributed to each member of a group. For example, one proposal from the African Group was counted as 42 (the number of members in the group).

14 The five countries in each region with the most proposals were: **Africa** (Zimbabwe; Nigeria; Tanzania; South Africa; Kenya); **Europe** (Turkey; EU; Norway; Switzerland; Iceland); **Latin America and Caribbean** (Bolivia; Guatemala; Peru; Argentina; Cuba); Asia Pacific (Philippines;

groupings. As shown by the data in the agriculture negotiations, the number of proposals to which African Members associated increased by 1208 per cent, in relation to Latin America & Caribbean with 619 per cent and with respect to the Asia Pacific region with 508 per cent.

In the agriculture negotiations, African WTO Members operated on the group platforms of the African Group; ACP Group; LDC Group; RAMS; Cairns Group; G10; G20; G33; G90; SVEs; and, Cotton-four. Disaggregated data showed for example that, Tanzania which had co-sponsored one proposal, registered a 6500 per cent increase in the number of proposals to which it was associated through other agricultural groups. Tanzania belonged to the ACP, African Group, G90, LDCs, G20 and G33 groups in the agriculture negotiations. There are questions about the mutually supportiveness, policy and negotiating positional consistency of so many proposals to which an individual member has signed on to.

Figure 53 shows that overall, in the context of groups, the proposals tabled by African countries significantly increased. All African WTO Members had ten or more proposals tabled, compared to the situation where only individual and/or co-sponsored proposals were analysed. Again, top performers in terms of tabling of proposals were those countries that not only had an offensive interest in agriculture, but were leading economies in Africa and had the resources to devote to actively engage in these negotiations including Nigeria; South Africa; Kenya and Zimbabwe.

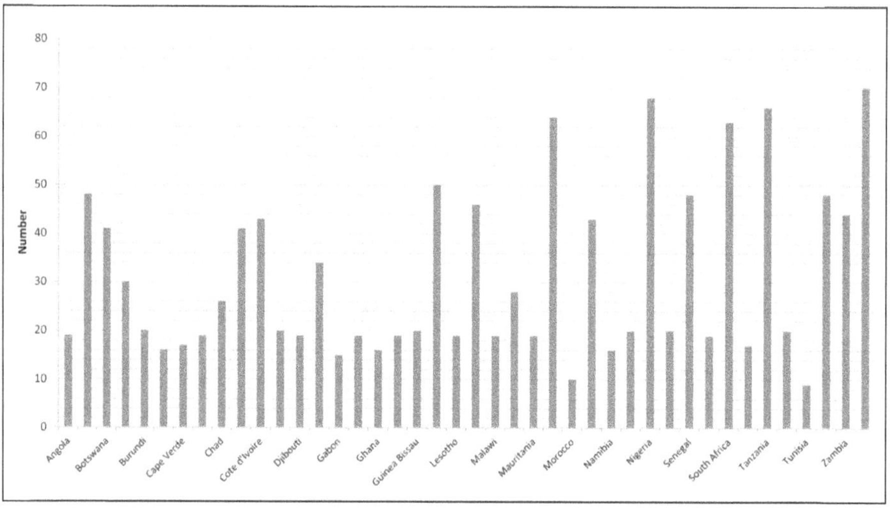

Figure 53. Group, joint, individual agriculture proposals by African countries (2000–2010).

Pakistan; Indonesia; India; China); **Middle East** (Israel, Jordan, Oman, Saudi Arabia, Bahrain); **North America** (Canada; United States).

However, as already noted above, a number of countries "participated" better by virtue of belonging to several groups – a case in point was Tanzania. There is a positive relationship between *increased capacity building* (training, TA, and compensated capacity from support groups and pro-bono legal services support) and *participation*. Tanzania is a case in point that demonstrates a relationship between increased capacity building and engagement. For instance, the technical assistance that it had benefitted from increased by 22.5 per cent, from 31 in 2002 to 38 in 2010; cumulatively between 2002 to 2010, Tanzania benefitted from a grand total of 314 technical assistance activities.[15] This excluded assistance it received from many other non-WTO sources. It also demonstrated more effective engagement and a higher level of participation resulting from its membership to a range of other negotiating groups. This enabled it to punch above its weight. Yet, other variables influenced the effectiveness of participation. These included: individual professional behaviour, priority areas of commercial and systemic interest and linkage between Geneva and capital rationality assumptions.

(c) *Negotiating Group on Market Access (NAMA)*

The connectors in the common position of the African Group in the NAMA negotiations revolved around policy space; special and differential treatment conditioned on less-than-full-reciprocity; flexibility on binding coverage commensurate with development objectives; separation of flexibilities and ambition levels; a WTO mechanism for addressing preference erosion and non-tariff measures; LDCs' exemption from tariff reduction commitments; and, opposition to sectorals. In summary, with exception of the NTB negotiations, the Group position lacked ambition and was based on S&D and exemptions for LDCs. African WTO Members in the Doha Round NAMA negotiations fell largely into three mutually supportive categories. First, a defensive orientation, led by South Africa as the coordinator of the NAMA 11. The "development-oriented" position of the NAMA 11 is to minimize further de-industrialization and achieve policies such as diversification, employment and other trade-development objectives. Second, the "paragraph-6" countries' grouping, averse to 100 per cent binding coverage for so-called policy flexibility reasons, in which are, Cameroon, Congo, Côte d'Ivoire, Ghana, Kenya, Nigeria and Zimbabwe. Third, the LDC exemption category.

(i) Individual and Co-Sponsored (Non-Group) Written Proposals

Figure 54 shows the number of individual Member and co-sponsored (non-group) proposals in NAMA, in different regions in the period 2002–2010. The level of African negotiating engagement was low at 83 individual and co-sponsored (non-group) NAMA proposals, that is 7.2% of the total, compared to Asia Pacific region (440), Europe (222), North America (199), Latin America and Caribbean (178), only higher than the Middle East at 30 individual and co-sponsored proposals.

15 See Annex VI.

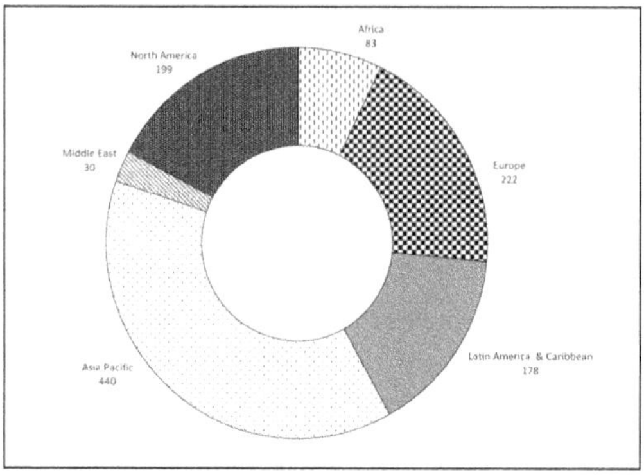

Figure 54. Individual and co-sponsored NAMA proposals (2002–2010).

Disaggregated data showed that most individual and co-sponsored proposals were generated by the developed countries. In rank order, the United States (146), European Union (84), Japan (80), Singapore (53), and, Switzerland (50) had made the most statements. This reflected the significant interest of these developed Members in the Doha negotiations in non-agricultural market access, where they have a strong export interest.

Figure 55 below shows that despite significantly high nominal membership share, the number of proposals individually tabled by African Members and co-sponsored with others in non-group settings was low. Eighteen (18) African countries tabled individual and co-sponsored proposals. Mauritius tabled the most (18) followed by Egypt (12), South Africa (10), Namibia and Tunisia tied at 7, Kenya at 5 and others below. In the circumstance of the NAMA negotiations, Mauritius as the African Member with the most individually tabled/co-sponsored proposals focused the content of its proposals on special and differential treatment (in a defensive orientation). South Africa, as the coordinator for the NAMA 11 with the second most individual/co-sponsored NAMA proposals in Africa, was also defensively oriented. Similarly, Egypt, Tunisia, Nigeria, Ghana and others had defensive orientation in the proposals tabled in the industrial products negotiations.

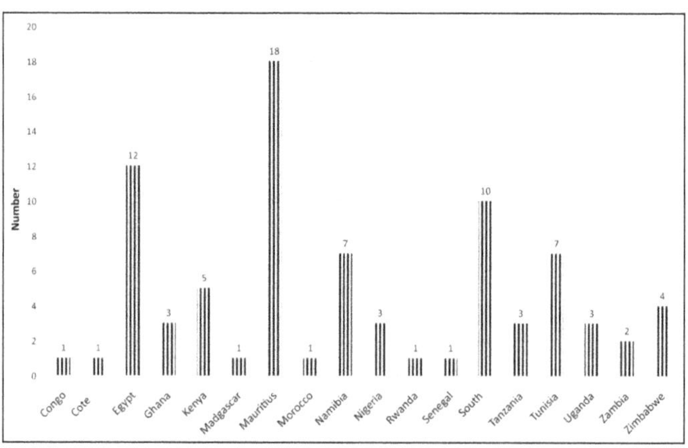

Figure 55. Individual and/joint NAMA proposals by African countries.

These African Members held a defensive line on Doha Round liberalization in manufactured products because of their expressed concerns about the possibility of increased "de-industrialization", unemployment, or revenue loss from tariff reductions. They also wished to ensure a level of harmonization of commitments assumed" in light of the customs unions to which they belonged.

(ii) Individual, Co-Sponsored (Non-Group) and Group Proposals

Figure 56 shows that for all regions in this study, the number of tabled NAMA proposals substantially increased when group proposals were taken into account.

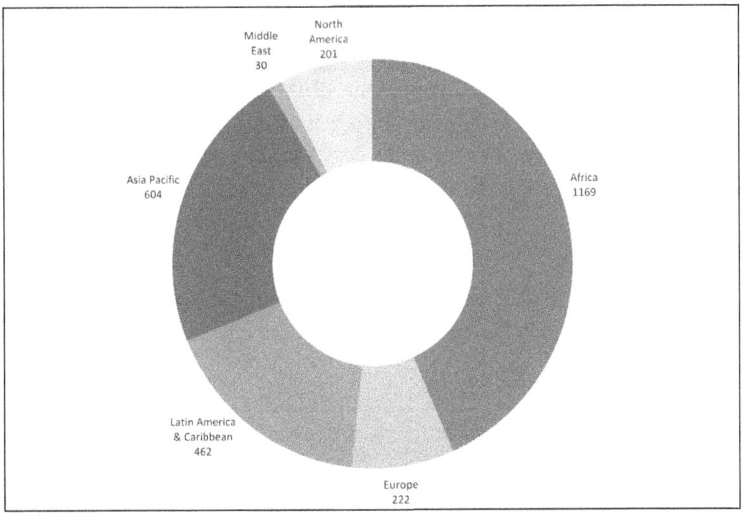

Figure 56. Individual, co-sponsored and group proposals in the NAMA negotiations (2002–2010).

Similar to agriculture, this distribution of proposals in the NAMA negotiations confirmed the proposition that the weaker Members exhibited greater coalitional behaviour, which had produced the effect of a larger number of written submissions and proposals. The data for the combined total of individual plus co-sponsored and group proposals showed that African countries registered the highest number of proposal at 1169. Asia pacific followed with 604 proposals, Latin America and Caribbean, with 462 proposals, Europe, 222 proposals and North America, 201 proposals. The Middle East registered the least number of combined proposals at 30. However, similar to the case of agriculture, greater "volume" was not necessarily a predictor of better "quality" and did not indicate the likelihood of "consensus" and "passage". Furthermore, it is obvious that the higher volume of proposals was "nominalism", from which quality did not necessarily follow.

As shown by the data in the NAMA negotiations, the number of proposals to which African Members associated increased by 1308 per cent, in relation to Latin America & Caribbean with 159 per cent and the Asia Pacific region with 37 per cent. There were minimal or no increases in the number of proposals from North America; the Middle East and Europe. African countries participated in the most groups in the NAMA negotiations.

These were: the African Caribbean and Pacific (ACP) Group; the Least Developed Countries' Consultative Group; the "Paragraph-6 countries" Group; Small Vulnerable Economies (SVEs) Group; Group of Recently Acceded Members (RAMs); and, the NAMA 11 group of developing countries, coordinated by South Africa.

(d) *Special Session of the Council for Trade in Services*

The overarching African position in the services negotiation was marked by ambition in Mode 4 (movement of natural persons to supply services), a defensive orientation that African countries had undertaken extensive commitments in liberalizing their services sectors and that credit should be accorded to this autonomous liberalization, and, the full implementation of the LDCs special modalities. Ambition in the Group's position was also linked by the request for the effective implementation of Article IV[16] of the GATS. African Members essentially operated within the African Group and the Least-developed Countries Consultative Group. One of the findings in this study is that the likelihood for consensus submissions/proposals is higher when the proponents secure co-sponsors beyond their groups and much less when they operate solely within their groupings. The exception seems to apply to LDCs.

(i) Individual and Co-Sponsored (Non-Group) Proposals

Figure 57 shows the number of individual Member and co-sponsored (non-group) proposals, in different regions, in the services negotiations in the period 2002–2010.

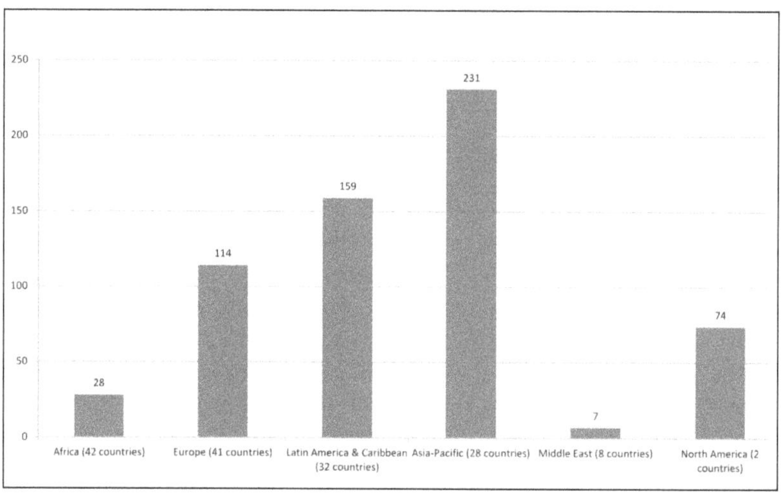

Figure 57. Individual and/joint proposals in the services negotiations (2000–2010).

[16] "Increasing participation of developing countries". This paragraph provides for the increased participation of developing country Members in world services trade through "negotiated specific commitments, by different Members"; and, establishment of contact points by developed

The level of African negotiating engagement in the services negotiations was low at 28 individual and co-sponsored (non-group) proposals (bench marked to agriculture and NAMA) and compared to proposals from the Asia Pacific region (231), Latin America and Caribbean (159), Europe (114), North America (74), only higher than the Middle East at 7 individual and co-sponsored proposals. Disaggregated data showed that the highest numbers of individual proposals had been submitted by the European Union, Australia, United States, Canada, Switzerland and Japan. These are developed, OECD countries, which have an offensive interest in the services negotiations and have been keen to see deeper liberalization in an area where they have a comparative advantage and seek more access to markets particularly in emerging economies. Similarly, a relatively high number of proposals – over 10 each – were tabled by emerging economies and other developing countries in the Asia-Pacific and Latin American regions.

For the 11 African Members that had tabled individual or co-sponsored proposals – Djibouti; Egypt; Gambia, Kenya, Mauritius, Nigeria, Senegal, Tanzania, Uganda, Zambia, Zimbabwe – the number of proposals were very low, ranging between 1 and 4. In addition, unlike proposals from Members in other regions that had focused on a wide range of sectors, modes of supply and horizontal issues, with the exception of the co-sponsored proposals on logistics services (Mauritius and Djibouti) and on maritime transport (Gambia), the proposals by African Members reflected a continuation of the quest for special and differential treatment in the form of lower obligations as a result of autonomous liberalization undertaken. They sought preferential and more favourable treatment as a result of economic status, either as small economies or least developed countries, and sought technical assistance or invested energy on process-related issues, such as how negotiating guidelines ought to be implemented. This special and differential treatment and exemption-seeking orientation behaviour is explained by the insistence by African WTO Members that their services industries were too weak to compete and should be shielded; or that they had undertaken autonomous liberalization or liberalization within the framework of structural adjustment programmes of international financial institutions and therefore credit should be given for this. Some had argued that domestic prudential regulations were either non-existent or too weak to compete. Only one individual proposal was tabled by one African WTO Member after the 2005 Hong Kong Ministerial Decision which exempted LDCs from undertaking additional commitments. The focus of LDCs seems now to obtain preferential market access treatment by obtaining a waiver from the most favoured nation obligation for this purpose.[17]

country Members, within two years of the entry into force of the WTO Agreement, to facilitate the access of developing country Members' services suppliers to information related to their respective markets. This article provides that special priority shall be accorded to LDCs.

17 Trade Ministers at the 8th WTO Ministerial Conference in Geneva on 17 December 2011, adopted a waiver to enable developing and developed-country Members to provide preferential treatment to services and service suppliers of least-developed country (LDC) Members. LDCS now seek implementation of this Decision.

(ii) Individual, Co-Sponsored (Non-Group) and Group Proposals

Figure 58 shows that in the period 2002–2010, with the exception of the Middle East and Europe, for all other regions in this study, the number of individual, co-sponsored and group services proposals substantially increased.

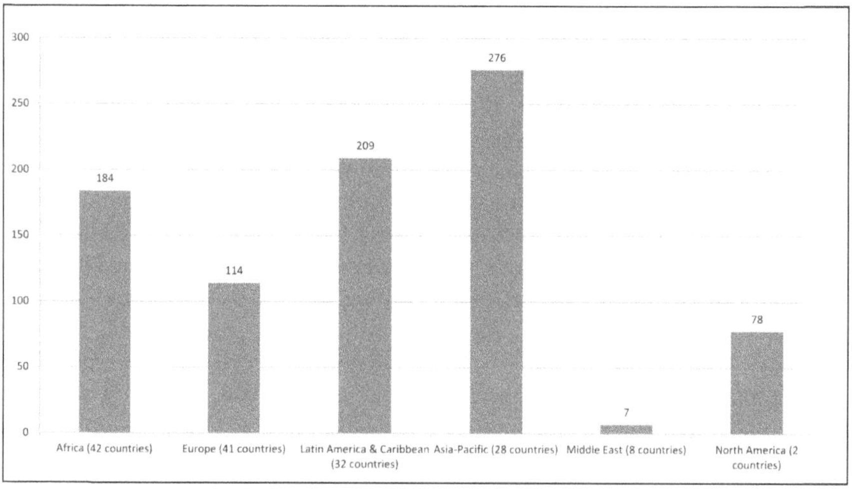

Figure 58. Individual, joint and group proposals in the services negotiations (2000–2010).

The changed distribution of individual plus co-sponsored (non-group) and group proposals showed an increase in the number of proposals associated with individual Members. The increase occurred as coalitional behaviour increased, confirming the proposition that as individual Members co-sponsored more proposals and operated in more groups, the number of proposals, with which they were associated, increased. The data showed that African Members registered a relatively higher number of proposal at 184, lower than Asia Pacific at 276 and Latin America and Caribbean at 209, but higher than Europe at 114 and North America at 78. Adhering to the pattern across the board, the Middle East registered the least number of combined proposals at 7. Similar to the situation in other negotiating groups, "volume" is not necessarily a good predictor of the "quality" and does not indicate the likelihood of "consensus" and "passage". Furthermore, it was obvious that the higher volume of proposals was suggestive of "nominalism" and not necessarily related to quality. African Members had tabled group proposals in the services negotiations within the Africa Group and the LDCs' Group. The thread in the four proposals tabled was to seek lower obligations in the form of special and differential treatment as a result of autonomous liberalization undertaken, seek preferential and more favourable treatment as a result of economic status (least-developed), and technical assistance. This was in contrast to group proposals from non-African Members where the focus had been on seeking enhanced market access in common interest sectors or modes of supply as illustrated in proposals tabled by APEC; CARICOM; ANDEAN; and, MERCOSUR WTO members.

(e) *Negotiating Group on Rules*

The position adopted by African WTO Members in the Rules negotiations was defensively-oriented, linked to development. African WTO Members sought the "need to avoid the introduction of more complex rules and disciplines under the Anti-Dumping Agreement and the Agreement on Subsidies and Countervailing Measures".[18] The position was taken that the Doha mandated "clarification and improvement of disciplines" relating to RTAs should not reopen the Enabling Clause (S&D); and, that negotiations on systemic issues must address the Doha principle of "less than full reciprocity", asymmetry in market access, and Africa's development concerns with regard to regional trade agreements with developed countries, pursuant to GATT 1994, Article XXIV and GATS Article V.

(i) Individual and Co-Sponsored Proposals

Figure 59 shows the number of individual Member and co-sponsored (non-group) proposals, from different regions, in the Rules negotiations in the period 2002–2010.

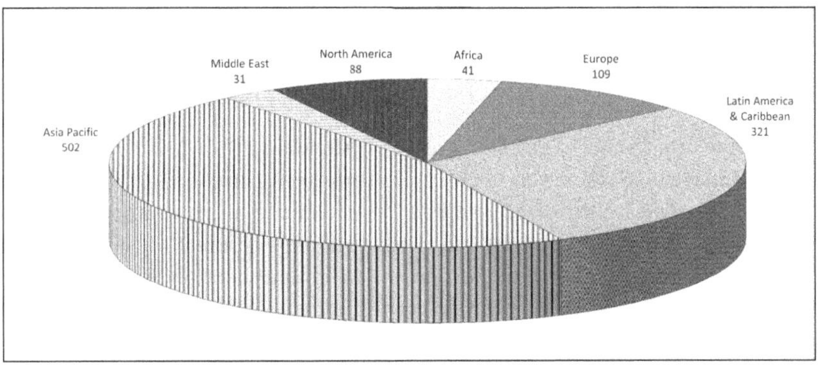

Figure 59. Individual and co-sponsored rules proposals 2002–2010.

The level of African negotiating engagement was low at 41 individual and co-sponsored (non-group) proposals, compared to Asia Pacific region (502), Latin America and Caribbean (321), Europe (109), North America (88), only higher than the Middle East at 31 individual and co-sponsored proposals.

Five African Members had tabled 41 proposals: Egypt (30 proposals); South Africa (4); Mauritius (3); Kenya and Morocco (2 each). With the exception of South Africa and Egypt, interest, use and experience with trade remedy instruments was limited. The greater use and experience with trade remedy instruments by Egypt was reflected in its tabling of 30 proposals in this relatively complex area of trade policy. The low overall number of proposals also corresponded to the low trade shares and level of trade by African Members with other countries. Africa's total merchandise export to the world

[18] Cairo Declaration, paragraph 16.

was 0.4 per cent. The low number of proposals similarly corresponded to the low level of intra-African trade which was 11.7% of Africa's overall trade.[19] Furthermore, very few African countries had been the target of trade remedy measures – anti-dumping or countervailing measures. Exports from eight (8) African countries had been the subject of anti-dumping initiations by other countries in the period 1995–2010. The exports were from Algeria, Egypt, Libyan Arab Jamahiriya;[20] Malawi; Mozambique; Nigeria; South Africa; and, Zimbabwe. Finally, the low number of tabled proposals by African WTO Members also confirmed the proposition that there was an inverse relationship between the degree of complexity and specialization, on the one hand and tabled proposals on the other. The more complex and specialized the negotiating area, the lower the number of tabled proposals. This tended to be more adversely felt by regions/delegations with limited technical competencies.

Overall, WTO Members from the Asia-Pacific, Latin America, Europe and North America had tabled the most individual/ co-sponsored proposals. In the Middle East, all proposals had originated from Israel. Most proposals in the Rules negotiations had been tabled by members belonging to two informal coalitions. The "Friends of Anti-dumping Negotiations"[21] who seeks tighter, clarified and improved disciplines on the use of anti-dumping measures. The "Friends of Fish" who seek a significant reduction in fisheries subsidies.[22]

(ii) Individual, Co-Sponsored (Non-Group) and Group Proposals

Figure 60 shows that with the exception of North America and the Middle East, the number of individual, co-sponsored (non-group) and group proposals increased in the period 2002–2010. The data for the combined total of individual plus co-sponsored and group proposals showed that Africa registered a relatively high number of proposals at 201, lower than Asia Pacific at 535 and Latin America and Caribbean at 381, but higher than Europe at 112 proposals and North America at 88 proposals. The Middle East registered the least number of combined proposals at 31. This higher number of tabled proposals by African Members confirmed the proposition, that there tended to be significant percentage increases in the number of proposals tabled by individual Members as they signed-on to and co-sponsored proposals from different groupings.

---

[19] WTO International Trade Statistics, 2010: Table 1.4, Intra and Inter regional merchandise trade, 2009, pg. 13.

[20] For Libya and Algeria, anti-dumping initiations against these two non-Members appear to be routed in the use of dual-pricing, which subsidize through lower domestic gas and energy pricing distinct from higher global market prices for gas and energy. In this instance, the initiation of anti-dumping action appears to be the pattern against oil and gas exporting economies that engage in dual pricing to the advantage of domestic manufacturers that produce downstream products for exports.

[21] Brazil; Chile; Colombia; Costa Rica; Hong Kong China; Israel; Japan; Korea; Mexico; Norway, Singapore; Switzerland; Chinese Taipei; Thailand; Turkey.

[22] Argentina, Australia, Chile, Colombia, Ecuador, Iceland, New Zealand, Norway, Pakistan, Peru, US.

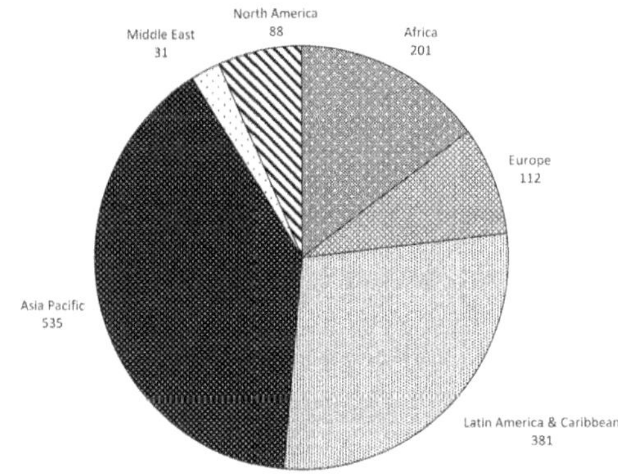

Figure 60. Individual, joint and group rules proposals 2002–2010.

As shown by the data in the Rules negotiations, the number of proposals to which African Members associated increased by 390 per cent. Proposals by African Members, on the platform of group sponsorship, in the Rules negotiations were tabled by the African Group, the ACP Group, the Commonwealth Group of Developing Countries and small vulnerable economies.[23] There was a question as to the correspondence between quantity and quality. The majority of proposals tabled by the African Members focused on special and differential treatment either in trade remedies imposed against developing countries or in the new disciplines to be developed in the area of fisheries subsidies to take into account their special situations and concerns. Concerns have been expressed in negotiations by other Members as to whether the content/quality of these proposals will achieve the mandate of clarifying and improving the rules.

(f) *Special Session of the Council for TRIPS*

The common African position was to push for the amendment of Article 31 of the TRIPS Agreement. This position was achieved in December 2005 with the Decision by Members.[24] However, in the period studied only five (or 11.9 per cent) of the 42 African Members had so far ratified their acceptance of the Protocol amending Article 31.[25] This was a low level of engagement for an amendment to which all African WTO Members vigorously sought. Although the focus of the work of the Special Session of the TRIPS

[23] Mauritius is the only African country in the SVEs Rules Group. Other members of this group are Barbados, Cuba, Dominica, Dominican Rep, El Salvador, Fiji, Honduras, Jamaica, Mauritius, Nicaragua, Papua New Guinea, St. Lucia, St Vincent & the Grenadines, and, Tonga.

[24] Decision on Amendment of the TRIPS Agreement, 6 December 2005, WT/L/641.

[25] Mauritius (16 April 2008), Egypt (18 April 2008), Morocco (2 December 2008), Zambia (10 August 2009), and, Uganda (12 July 2010). Since 2011, Senegal (18 January 2011); Rwanda (12 December 2011) and Togo (13 March 2012) notified their acceptance of the Protocol amending the TRIPS Agreement. Thirty four WTO African Members are yet to notify acceptance of the Protocol.

Council is on the establishment of a multilateral system for the registration and notification of geographical indications for wines and spirits, Members have discussed other TRIPS issues notably the relationship between the TRIPS Agreement and the Convention on Biological Diversity and the extension of the higher level of geographical indications accorded to wines and spirits to other products.[26]

(i) Individual and Co-Sponsored Written Proposals

Overall, in the period reviewed, the number of written proposals tabled in the TRIPS negotiations was low, across the board, compared to other areas. Figure 61 shows the number of individual Member and co-sponsored (non-group) proposals, in different regions, in the TRIPS negotiations in the period 1998–2010.

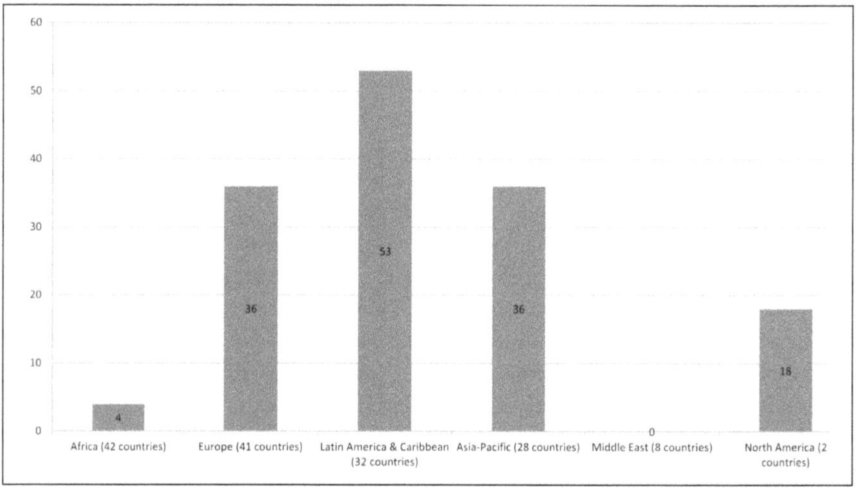

Figure 61. Individual and/joint register proposals 1998–2010.

The level of African negotiating engagement was very low. African WTO Members had tabled four proposals. This number contrasted to the huge volume of oral statements by African Members on the TRIPS and Public Health debate in the period 2001–2003. Namibia, Nigeria, Mauritius and South Africa were the four Members that had tabled proposals. The United States and the European Union tabled the most proposals. These two Members have strong defensive and offensive interests in these negotiations. Other countries that have strong interests in these negotiations and tabled individual or co-sponsored proposals included Chile, Australia, New Zealand, Canada and Argentina.

[26] These latter two issues have been discussed in informal consultations by the Director-General. Some Members have tended to link the three TRIPS issues of GI extension, TRIPS/CBD and establishment of the Register.

(ii) Individual, Co-Sponsored (Non-Group) and Group Proposals

Figure 62 shows an increase in the number of individual, co-sponsored (non-group) and group proposals for Africa, Latin America and Caribbean and Asia Pacific in the period 1998–2010.

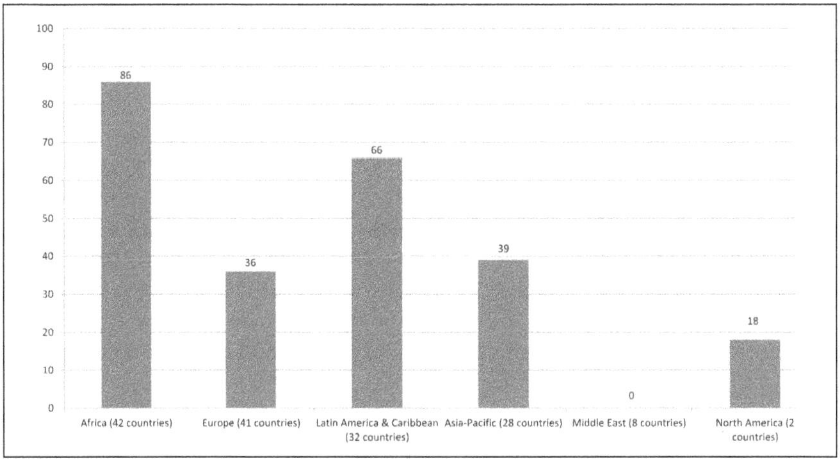

Figure 62. Individual, joint and group register proposals (1998–2010).

Several Members from Africa, Latin America and the Caribbean and Asia Pacific belong to the two main groupings in the TRIPS negotiations – the "W52 Group" and the "Joint Proposal" Group.[27] The data showed that Africa registered the highest number of proposals at 86, greater than Latin America and Caribbean at 66, Asia Pacific at 39, Europe at 36 and North America at 18. The Middle East had no proposals in the TRIPS negotiations partly because of less interest on this issue and also possibly because of cultural and religious reasons. This higher number of tabled proposals by African Members confirmed the proposition, that there tended to be significant percentage increases in the number of proposals tabled by individual Members as they signed-on to and co-sponsored proposals in different groupings. As also argued in this study, all WTO Members, but Africa more so, have used co-sponsored proposals and associated themselves with proposals on their regional platforms to increase their bargaining positions, compensate for weaknesses and raise the likelihood of achieving their objectives in the Doha negotiations.

(g) *Special Session of the Committee on Trade and Environment*

With the exception that the negotiations should take account of concerns of developing countries, there was no formulated common African Group position on the complex, contemporary and substantive inter-relationship on trade and environment. In this area

[27] The description of these groups is provided in Annex VII.

of the negotiations, the level of engagement/participation by individual African WTO Members was very low to non-existent.

(i) Individual and Co-sponsored Proposals

Figure 63 shows the distribution of individual and co-sponsored (non-group) proposals in the Trade and Environment negotiations in the period 2002–2010. As of 2010, no individual or co-sponsored (non-group) proposal had been tabled by any African WTO Member. As observed and argued in chapter three, the substance of negotiations in the Special Session of the Committee on Trade and Environment is profoundly intellectual, involving complex, evolving relationships between domestic law and policy and multilateral trade rules in the two areas of trade and environment. Furthermore, the complexity is increased by overlapping and "unresolved" issues in multilateral negotiations in two different arena, namely in the area of Multilateral Environmental Agreements (MEAs)[28] and the WTO Doha negotiations. In addition to the technical and intellectual complexity of negotiating issues in the two different arenas, African WTO negotiators have been handicapped by minimal to non-existing levels of domestic coordination amongst line ministries and departments in this complex and rapidly evolving area of multilateral negotiations.

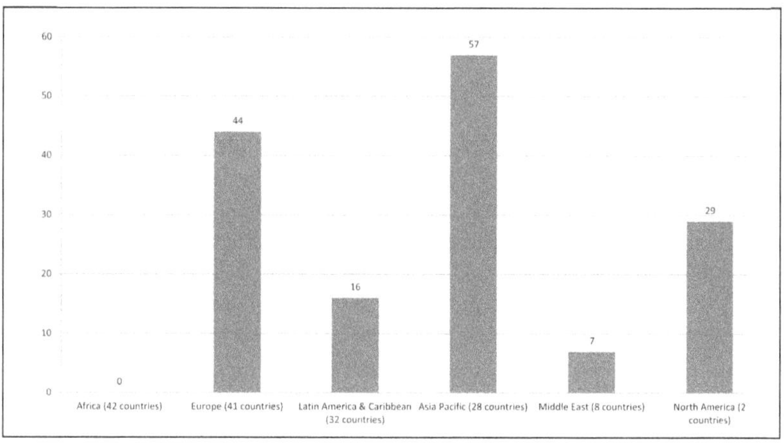

Figure 63. Individual and joint environment proposals 2002–2010.

[28] Climate change negotiations and the successor to the Kyoto Protocol and the Secretariats of other MEAs. The WTO has in different formats maintained co-operation and information exchange with UNEP and other MEAs and a document produced by the Secretariat on this co-operation has assisted in the discussions in the CTESS on the information exchange component of Doha Declaration paragraph 31(ii) mandate. See, Committee on Trade and Environment, Special Session, *Existing Forms of Co-operation and Information Exchange between UNEP/MEAs and the WTO,* TN/TE/S/2/Rev.2. At its meeting of 12–13 February 2003, agreement was reached in the CTE Special Session to invite a number of organizations on an ad hoc, meeting-by-meeting basis. These organizations include UNEP and the following seven MEAs: the Basel Convention, the CBD, CITES, the Montreal Protocol, the Rotterdam Convention, the Stockholm Convention, and the UNFCCC.

Most proposals originated from the Asia-Pacific region, tabled by 10 Members mainly by New Zealand and Japan and covering all three pillars of the mandate.[29] In Europe, proposals were tabled by the European Union, Norway and Switzerland. Six Members in the Latin American region had tabled proposals – Argentina, Brazil, Colombia, Cuba, Peru and Uruguay, while only two Members – Qatar and Saudi Arabia – had tabled the proposals from the Middle East region. All countries in the North America region had tabled over 10 proposals each. The European Union, United States, New Zealand, Japan and Canada had so far tabled the most individual proposals in these negotiations. These countries have been offensive in the negotiations and believe that that the trade and environment negotiations can be a win-win-win for trade, the environment and development.

(ii) Individual, Co-Sponsored and Group Proposals

Figure 64 shows the distribution of individual, co-sponsored and group proposals by region in the period 2002–2010.

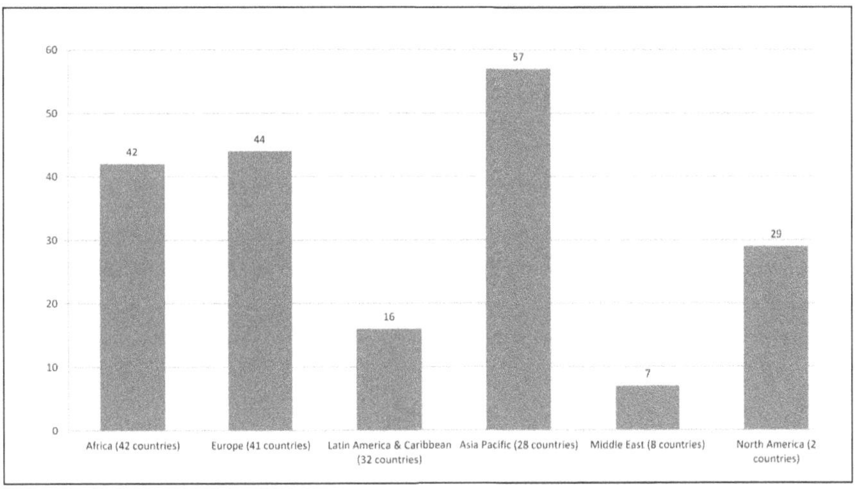

Figure 64. Individual, joint and group environment proposals 2002–2010.

Data showed that when group proposals were taken into account, the participation of African countries in tabling written proposals increased by 100 per cent. All African WTO Members were registered as having tabled a proposal. This was represented by the sole African Group proposal on paragraph 31 (i) of the negotiations. The figures for Members in all other regions remained constant as none of them had been involved in coalitional behaviour by tabling group proposals in the trade and environment negotiations.

29 Australia, China, Hong Kong, China, India, Korea, Malaysia, Philippines, Singapore and Chinese Taipei also tabled individual proposals.

The only African Group proposal in the trade and environment negotiations paragraph 31(i) proposes the establishment of a group of experts to assist Members in implementing specific trade obligations under multilateral environment agreements. The African Group suggested that the establishment of such a group, a trade related technical assistance and capacity building mechanism would be a concrete outcome in strengthening the relationship between WTO agreements and MEAs.[30] The content of the African Group proposal raises the question of "quantity" in contrast to "quality" that addresses the substance of mandate of negotiations. This example in the CTESS is illustrative.

(h) *Special Session of the Committee on Trade and Development*

The position of African WTO Members on trade and development was all encompassing. It was configured around policy space and flexibility; special and differential treatment; trade solutions that address preference erosion; trade rules that accommodate poverty reduction strategies, livelihood concerns, and takes into account the needs of net food importing countries and commodity producers. The development dimension was also based on the concept of differentiation of countries in the trading system. Technical assistance, training and capacity building and Aid for Trade are the supply-side dimensions of the development aspects of the Round for African WTO Members. Finally, the amendment of the TRIPS Agreement to address public health crises in LDCs and African countries in particular was part of the broader development aspects of the Doha Round for African countries.

(i) *Individual, Co-Sponsored and Group Proposals Tabled in the CTD SS*

Figure 65 shows distribution of individual, co-sponsored and group proposals tabled in the Special Session of the Committee on Trade and Development in the period 2002–2010.

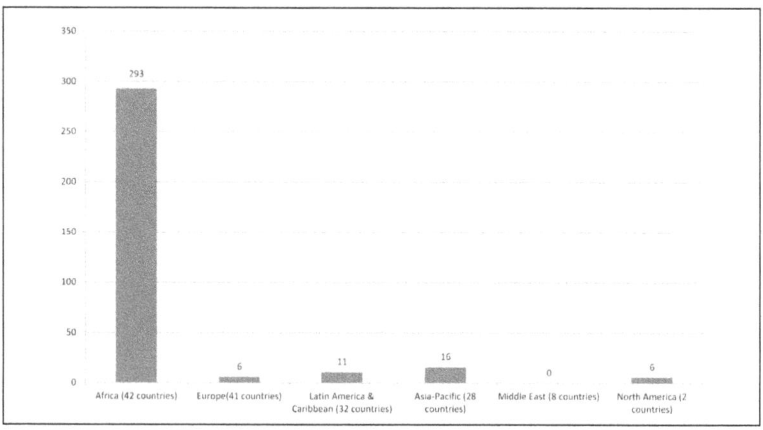

Figure 65. SDT proposals tabled in the CTD special session (2002–2010).

[30] African Group – Proposal for the Establishment of a Group of Experts on Trade and Environment, JOB (08)/38.

As the main *demandeurs* for strengthening and making special and differential treatment provisions in WTO Agreements more precise, operational and effective, the African Group and LDC Group tabled the most proposals. Their proposals covered the GATT and several multilateral agreements on trade in goods; GATS; TRIPS; and, DSU. Proposals also sought deeper, better and more secure preferential market access and requests for mobilization for more development assistance funding to improve supply capacity. A number of individual or co-sponsored proposals were also tabled by Members originating from other regions. Egypt, Kenya, Mauritius, Tanzania and Zimbabwe co-sponsored proposals with other developing countries belonging to the Like-Minded Group of Developing Countries.[31]

African Members and least developed countries consider that they have already achieved a degree of progress from their proposals, even at this stage of the negotiations. They refer to the adoption by Ministers at the 2005 Hong Kong Ministerial Conference of the Decisions in Annex F, containing five LDC-specific proposals, including the Decision improving preferential market access for LDCs through Duty Free, Quota Free (DFQF) market access.[32] They also refer to the agreement at the Hong Kong Ministerial Conference to enhance the Integrated Framework for trade related assistance for LDCs and for Aid for Trade for developing countries and a "Doha Round for free" as LDCs are exempt from undertaking any new market access commitments.

(i) Negotiating Group on Trade Facilitation

The common position of African WTO Members is premised on the benefits that would accrue from trade facilitation measures for enhanced competitiveness in African economies and the promotion of intra-Africa trade. The common position links the "the potential benefits" with associated trade facilitation costs and proposes the balancing of the "level of commitments", associated costs and the availability of financial and technical resources for capacity building to implement outcomes. The "need" has been restated for S&DT provisions, policy space and flexibility for African countries. Trade Facilitation is an area in the Doha negotiations that has been the least divisive, attracted the most consensual submissions, and where African WTO Members have joined in building consensus. Yet participation has been low across the indices examined. Individual African WTO Members compensated for the weaknesses of individual positions through their participation in the Trade Facilitation negotiating group known as the "Core Group of Developing Countries".

(i) Individual and Co-Sponsored Proposals

Figure 66 shows the distribution of individual and co-sponsored proposals in the Trade Facilitation negotiations in the period 2004–2010.

---

[31] Cuba, Dominican Republic, Honduras, India, Indonesia, Pakistan, Sri Lanka.

[32] The 2005 Hong Kong Declaration set the implementation of this Decision at the conclusion of the Doha Round under the Single Undertaking principle. Several preference granting Members have stated that they are already implementing the substance of the Hong Kong Ministerial Decision.

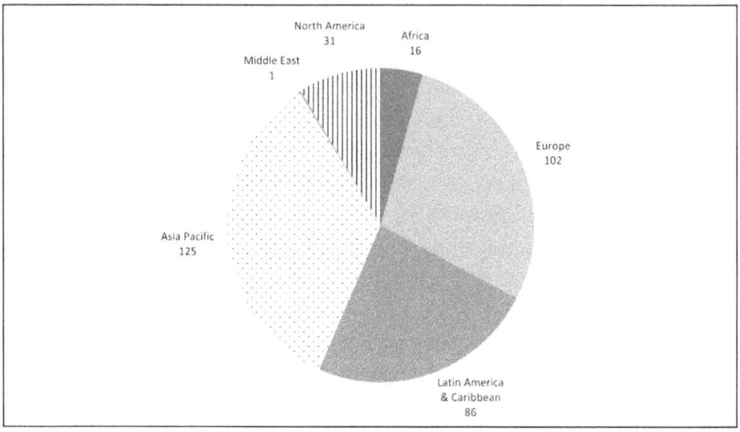

Figure 66. Individual and/or joint proposals in trade facilitation negotiations 2005–2010.

In relation to the declared position of African Members in this area of the Doha negotiations, their level of negotiating engagement was low with 16 individual and co-sponsored (non-group) proposals by Benin (1); Egypt (3); Morocco (1); Namibia (1); Nigeria (1); Rwanda (3); South Africa (2); Swaziland (1); and Uganda (3). This low level of engagement was in contrast to relatively higher levels of engagement by other regions: Asia pacific (125), Europe (102), Latin America and Caribbean (86), North America (31).[33] Africa's level of engagement was only higher than the Middle East with one individual and co-sponsored proposal. The trade facilitation negotiations are generally viewed as a win-win for all WTO Members, particularly for low income and land-locked countries. Whilst African WTO Members acknowledge the relationship between efficient trade infrastructure and the growth of their economies, substantive proposals have been low. Although a relatively non-complex area of the negotiations, the low level of proposals tabled by African Members was to a greater extent accounted for by a low level of domestic and regional/sub-regional coordination.

The WTO Secretariat has invested resources and time to compensate for the coordination deficit of African Members in this area by the organisation of regional technical assistance activities on Aid for Trade, followed up with annual reviews.[34] In addition, the WTO Secretariat, together with the World Bank, African Development Bank, World

[33] In the post-2010 period, trade facilitation is one of the areas that Members have identified for focused attention with a view for possible earlier harvest. An additional number of African Members have therefore been engaged in tabling textual proposals in areas of interest such as on pre-shipment inspection; customs brokers; transit; consularization fees or special and differential treatment, technical assistance and capacity building to implement a Trade Facilitation Agreement. These additional players include: Angola, Ghana, Sierra Leone, Comoros, Mali, Zimbabwe, Cote d'Ivoire, Tanzania and Nigeria. The African Group, ACP Group and LDC Group have also increased their activity level and participation in the trade facilitation negotiations in the post-2010 period.

[34] First annual Global Aid for Trade Review, 19–21 November 2007. Second annual Global Aid for Trade Review, 6–7 July 2009. Third Annual Global Aid for Trade Review: 18–19 July 2011. The

Customs Organisation and other regional bodies have assisted African WTO Members in undertaking needs assistance on trade facilitation. Furthermore, to improve the participation of capital-based experts in the negotiations, specific funding has been earmarked. In spite of these efforts, the level of African engagement was low. This was mainly because the "coordination challenge" amongst African countries had not been fully solved.

In relation to Members from other regions, disaggregated data showed that the Members which tabled proposals had been better coordinated and actively involved in trade facilitation at a regional/national level. These were Members from the regions of APEC countries, Europe and North America. The other Members that had been actively involved in tabling proposals were land-locked developing countries, with an interest in transit rights and facilitated movements and for the clearance of goods. In the period studied, the Members with the most proposals in rank order were Switzerland, European Union, Korea and Chinese Taipei, Mongolia and the United States.

(i) Individual, Co-Sponsored and Group Proposals

Figure 67 show the distribution of individual, co-sponsored and group proposals, in the trade facilitation negotiations in the period 2005–2010.

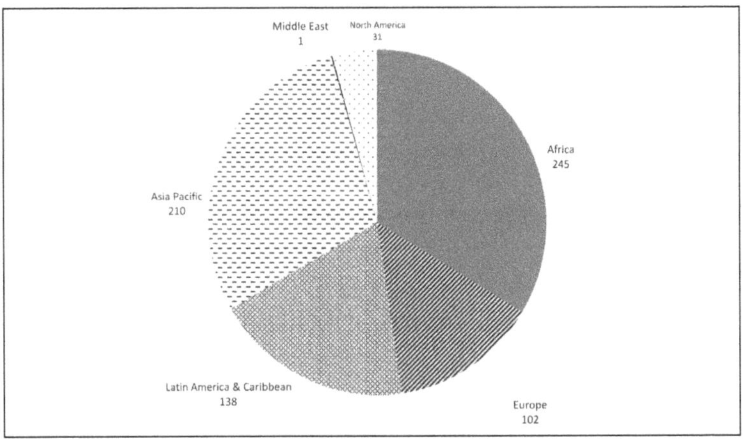

Figure 67. Individual, joint and group trade facilitation proposals (2005–2010).

The level of African negotiating engagement was higher than for all regions at 245 proposals. Asia pacific followed with 210, Latin America and Caribbean, 138, Europe, 102, North America 31 and the Middle East, one proposal. The increase occurred as coalitional behaviour increased, confirming the proposition that as individual Members co-sponsored more proposals and operated in more groups, the number of proposals, with

Fourth Global Review of Aid for Trade, "Connecting to Value Chains", is scheduled from 8–10 July 2013.

which they were associated, in that negotiating area increased. The main groups through which African Members expressed their positions and tabled their proposals were the African Group, ACP Group, LDCs Group and the Core Group of Developing Countries.

When group proposals were taken into account, Africa recorded the highest increased number of 245 proposals, or a 1431 percentage increase from individual/co-sponsored proposals tabled. The top performing countries in Africa in terms of submission of proposals were mainly LDCs: Uganda (14 proposals); Rwanda (13); Tanzania (11); Zambia (11) and Benin (10). Most of these countries are land-locked and experience transit problems which they are keen to overcome in order to boost their economic development. As a consequence, they have offensive interests in the trade facilitation negotiations. These countries have devoted required resources and time to the preparation of proposals despite human and financial resources or their trade and GDP levels. They have made best use of the fund created at the WTO to enable experts from capitals to fully participate in the negotiations, so as to obtain concrete results in a key area of real commercial interest for them. Studies indicate that historically land-locked countries have been poorer than littoral states. They have sought to overcome this disability through bilateral trade and cooperation agreements. The present reality is that land-locked countries inevitably, out of reality, are trading countries. This is a policy evolving away from their historical inward looking position. The current reality is reflected in the Doha negotiations in trade facilitation, where land-locked African countries have originated the most proposals and are at the forefront of African Trade Facilitation negotiations. Their experience has driven them to seek reforms.[35] Uganda is illustrative. It registered the highest number of trade facilitation proposals from Africa (14). However, the tabling of proposals by African countries in this area of negotiations still reflects capacity constraints; a horizontal problem for African WTO Members in the Doha negotiations.

(k) *Special Session of the Dispute Settlement Body*

The common Group position was elaborated to improve the participation of African WTO Members in the WTO dispute settlement system through enhanced affordability and accessibility. It was also predicated on the effective enforcement of the recommendations

[35] In the post-2010 period, trade facilitation is one of the areas that Members have identified for focused attention with a view for possible earlier "harvest". An additional number of African Members have therefore been engaged in tabling textual proposals in areas of interest such as on pre-shipment inspection; customs brokers; transit; consularization fees or special and differential treatment, technical assistance and capacity building to implement a Trade Facilitation Agreement. These additional players have included: Angola, Ghana, Sierra Leone, Comoros, Mali, Zimbabwe, Cote d'Ivoire, Tanzania and Nigeria. The African Group, ACP Group and LDC Group have also increased their activity level and participation in the trade facilitation negotiations in the post-2010 period including by tabling proposals or draft negotiating textual language. In addition, a number of African Members have engaged or are undertaking trade facilitation country needs assessments. These have included Angola, Benin, Botswana, Burkina Faso, Burundi, Cameroon, Cape Verde, Central African Republic, Chad, Congo (Brazzaville). Democratic Republic of the Congo, Egypt, Gabon, The Gambia, Ghana, Kenya, Lesotho, Mauritius, Mozambique, Namibia, Nigeria, Rwanda, Sudan, Swaziland, Tanzania, Togo, Uganda, Zambia and Zimbabwe.

and rulings of the Dispute Settlement Body. More specifically, a "Fund on Dispute Settlement", has been proposed to achieve the aim of increased accessibility and affordability of the System. On effective enforcement of recommendations and rulings, it has been proposed that, "where it is demonstrated that the suspension of concessions or obligations would have negative consequences on the economy of a Member that is a developing or least-developed country, the DSB may, upon request authorise a Member or a group of Members to suspend concessions on behalf of the affected Member."[36] In spite of common position, the level of engagement/participation has been very low on the indices examined.

(i) Individual and Co-Sponsored Proposals

The figure 68 shows the distribution by region, of individual and co-sponsored proposals in the dispute settlement negotiations in the period 2002–2010.

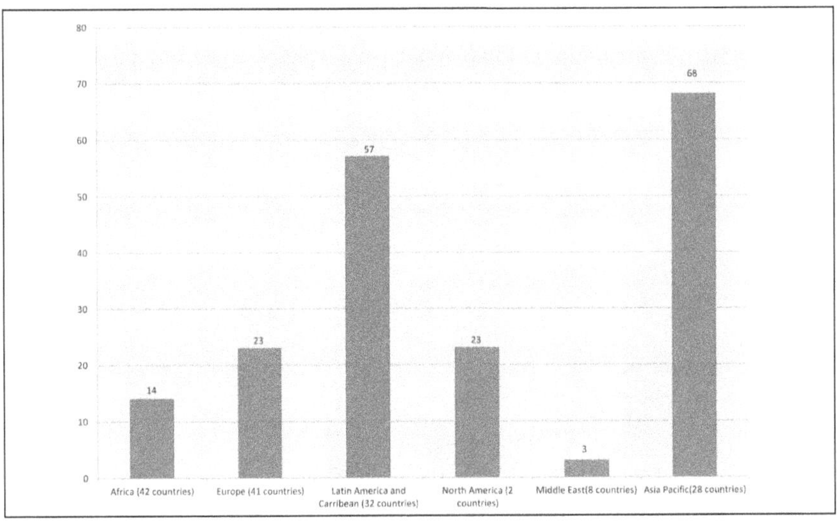

Figure 68. Individual and/co-sponsored proposals in the DSB negotiations (2000–2010).

The dispute settlement negotiations are less a function of commercial interest and largely about systemic considerations in which all Members regardless of trade shares and commercial interests, should engage in maximally. The number of proposals tabled by African Members was very low, higher only than the Middle East, whose participation has been typically low. Most proposals originated from the Asia-Pacific, Latin America and Caribbean, Europe and North America regions. The number of proposals from these regions reflected to a large degree the trend in participation in regular WTO dispute

36 TN/DS/W/92: *Text for the African Group Proposals on Dispute Settlement Understanding Negotiations, Communication from Côte d'Ivoire, 5* March 2008.

settlement. Members that had been involved in WTO dispute settlement, either as complainants, respondents or third parties, had submitted more proposals for its improvement. They had drawn on established expertise and experience, compared to the African and Middle East regions, with limited use of the dispute settlement system so far.

No African WTO Member had tabled an individual proposal in the DSU review negotiations. This low level was accounted for by a low level of expertise and minimal experience with the System. Egypt, Tanzania and Zimbabwe had co-sponsored proposals with other Like-Minded Group of developing countries. One of the key findings from the results of the regression analysis was that the level of engagement/participation in the dispute settlement system was not necessarily related to trade and GDP shares in particular with regard to third-party participation. Whether trade or GDP shares were high, medium or low did not matter for third-party participation. This was an interesting finding which confirmed the value of the practice of systemic engagement/participation, regardless of the value of trade/GDP shares.

(ii) Individual, Co-Sponsored and Group Proposals

Figure 69 shows the distribution of individual, co-sponsored and group proposals.

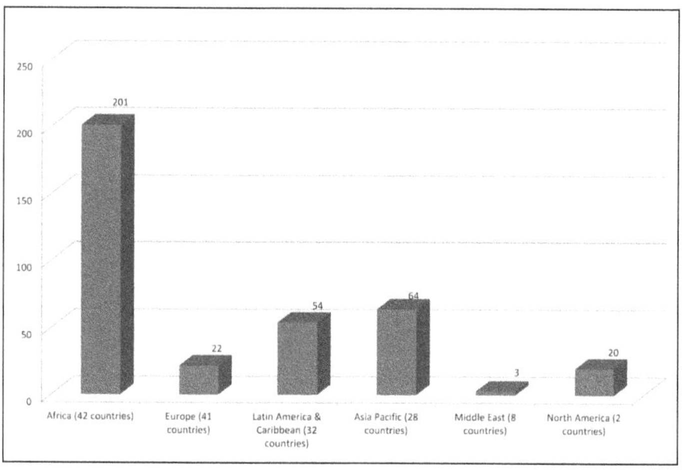

Figure 69. Individual, joint and group DS proposals 2002–2010.

The increases in individual, co-sponsored and group proposals were for Africa, Asia Pacific and the Latin America and Caribbean regions. Africa had originated the most proposals at 201. These increases had occurred as coalitional behaviour expanded, confirming the proposition that as individual Members co-sponsored more proposals and operated in more groups, the number of proposals, with which they were associated, increased. Proposals tabled by the African and LDC Groups had covered most stages of the WTO dispute settlement system – consultations, panels, appellate review and implementation and surveillance. Proposals had also covered the structural difficulties that these groups had highlighted as hindering them from fully accessing the dispute settlement system. Although there were evident expertise and experience limitations, African

Members in the DSU review negotiations acknowledged their limited participation and related reasons in a particular way. As stated:

> African Members, many of them being least-developed country Members, have not been active participants in the WTO dispute settlement system (DS). This diminutive participation is not because they have never had occasion to want to enforce their rights, or the obligations of other Members, but due to structural difficulties of the system.[37]

The issues in the proposals of African WTO Members included: (i) complexity of the dispute settlement system; (ii) high cost (iii) unsatisfactory enforcement mechanisms (iv) scope for a development dimension, including inadequacy of special and differential treatment provisions; (v) unbalanced and inequitable geographical distribution of panel and AB members.

The underutilisation of the dispute settlement system, by African WTO Members, also explained in part the low level of individual/group engagement in the negotiations. The level of engagement further reduced as the negotiations advanced, became more text-based and required more in-depth technical competence on matters of law and policy. It was also observed that the participation of African countries had been marked by reactions rather than a constructive, systematic and consistent engagement with all aspects of the negotiation process. Coupled with their lack of participation in the "litigation" process, African countries had had little impact on the structure of the process and the resulting jurisprudence (Mosoti, Victor 2006).

African WTO Members have tried to correct and compensate for their weaknesses in various ways. First, advice has been sought from the Advisory Centre on WTO Law. The Centre has provided advice both open and private in several areas. Second, the WTO legal internship system has increased opportunity and space for Africans. Third, several civil society organisations have provided policy and quasi-legal advice on the negotiations including in cases such as on cotton. An example is IDEAS. Fourth, although African WTO Members are yet to fully seize the opportunities, more Geneva-based firms have offered pro bono services. Finally, Article 27 of the DSU, *inter alia* provides for WTO Secretariat assistance to provide additional legal advice and assistance in respect of dispute settlement to developing country Members (paragraph 2); and, conduct special training courses for Members a propos on dispute settlement procedures and practices so as to enable Members' experts to be better informed (paragraph 3). It is argued in this study that more would have to be done to increase supply of legal training from providers, but even greater more coordinated efforts are required by African consumers of the legal supply of training and advice to ensure sustained cumulation for expert application.

6. Summary: African WTO Members' Negotiating Engagement

Several findings and conclusions were drawn from the combination of data analysed and interviews for this chapter. First, in relation to the three areas of analysis in this study

[37] See TN/DS/W/15, *Negotiations on the Dispute Settlement Understanding – Proposal by the African Group*, 25 September 2002.

namely, WTO regular work, the Doha Round negotiations and dispute settlement, the data collected and analysed for negotiating engagement showed that the engagement level by African WTO Members was at a relatively higher level in relation to the other two areas. But even so, the data analysed still showed low levels of individual African engagement. The same limited universe of African Members remained active in the negotiations (similar to their activity levels in WTO regular work).[38]

Is there a right amount of participation expected or ideal? Obviously, not. There is no "right amount of participation" *ex ante* on a normative question, either for African WTO Members or Members from any other region. The question is *neither purely statistical* nor can the answer be *purely judgemental*. The "expectation" on participation is linked to "effectiveness", the "optimization" of the number of African WTO Members and "maximization" of available resources in regular work, negotiations and dispute settlement in relation to the common positions established by the Group. To compensate for weaknesses, recommendations are made. These include, compensated capacity from support in civil society and think-tank groups, *pro-bono* legal services support from law firms, policy advice from academia, better Geneva-capital coordination, coalition behaviour, stricter more disciplined individual professional behaviour, reduced "irrational" interference and greater "rationality" (means and ends) in the deployment of negotiators and maximization of limited professional resources.

Second, although the data showed robust individual activity of a small universe of active African WTO Members, the principal form of negotiating engagement was in coalitional behaviour. African WTO Members had operated in a wide range of intra-regional, inter-regional and issue-specific coalitions to compensate for their individual weakness because of inter-alia low trade share levels. This form of engagement was more effective than their individual activity in relation to their negotiating objectives.

Third, the number of proposals tabled and statements made point to the priority areas of interest for African WTO Members. The data suggested a pattern of higher levels of African-related proposals on negotiating issues associated with development, scope for flexibility and special and differential treatment and technical assistance. It is argued that African WTO Members would increase their organisational effectiveness by departing from the undiscriminating positions for special and differential treatment, except in the most necessary of transitional movement to implementing the core rules of the System. Their effectiveness would be enhanced if they invested their energies in reinforcing the system of balance of rights and obligations.

Analysis of the data on the proposals also suggests that the number of proposals tended to decrease with greater technical complexity in the negotiating area and narrower scope for differentiated treatment. Analysis of the proposals in the DSU review negotiations, Rules and Trade and Environment negotiations were illustrative. The engagement of African Members in the Doha negotiations still revealed considerable weaknesses in technical expertise, trade policy experience and Geneva/capital coordination deficits. Corrections are still required to address these weaknesses as African Members seek to enhance their level of engagement both in the Doha negotiations and regular work.

[38] Benin, Burkina Faso, Chad, Cote d'Ivoire, Egypt, Gabon, Ghana, Kenya, Lesotho, Mauritius, Morocco, Namibia, Nigeria, Senegal, Tanzania, Tunisia, Uganda, Zambia, and, Zimbabwe.

Remedial action would be required through consistent, cumulative training, rational deployment of professional resources, accepting the offer of *pro bono* legal services by Geneva-based law firms, with more disciplined self-improvement by African trade negotiators and better Geneva-capital coordination. Ministerial and Senior-Officials involvement in the negotiations and more direct Ministerial contacts with trade negotiators are desperate necessities. While multilateral institutions and civil society have a role to play in the supply of legal advice, African trade negotiators and their senior officials from capitals Ministers must exercise primary and final ownership.

Fourth, because coalitional behaviour was the primary and largest form of WTO African engagement in the Doha negotiations, there was a significant percentage increase in the number of proposals tabled by individual Members as they signed-on to and co-sponsored proposals in different groupings.

Fifth, there was an evident issue of "quantity" verses "quality" in the number of proposals and the area of negotiations. Areas of negotiations where African Members tabled the most proposals – quantitatively – were in negotiating areas associated with development, S&D, preferences, and technical assistance and where their proposals had been mutually reinforced with many oral statements as bargaining manoeuvres to counteract or block others, or advocate. Cotton was an exception.

Finally, the data analysed in this chapter indicates that all WTO Members, but Africa more so, co-sponsored proposals and associated themselves with proposals on their regional platforms to increase their bargaining positions, compensate for weaknesses and raise the likelihood of achieving their objectives in the Doha negotiations.

CHAPTER FIVE

PARTICIPATION IN REGULAR WORK—COMMITTEE-SPECIFIC WORK

1. Introduction

The regular work of the WTO is principally embodied and provided for in Article III of the Marrakesh Agreement Establishing the WTO. This Article provides that the WTO shall facilitate the implementation, administration and operation and further the objectives of the Covered Agreements (paragraph 1); provide the forum for negotiations amongst Members (paragraph 2); administer the DSU (paragraph 3); administer the Trade Policy Review Mechanism (paragraph 4), and, cooperate, as appropriate with the IMF and the World Bank (paragraph 5).

This chapter examined the *level of African participation/engagement in WTO regular bodies (see figure 6)*, in the period 1995–2010, across variables as follows:

- number of oral statements in WTO bodies;
- number of written submissions/proposals;
- compliance with notification (transparency) requirements,
- number of discussants in trade policy reviews; and,
- action on identified priority areas of interests and engagement (including in selected subsidiary bodies of vital interest to African WTO Members). Beyond these, additional specific variables were analyzed, depending on the subject matter and mandate of a committee.

This chapter examined the performance of African WTO Members in relation to other Members with regard to these specific variables. Ministerial Conferences were not examined.[1] Finally, as in the analysis of African engagement in the Doha negotiations (Chapter 4), the *structural forms* of the engagement of African WTO Members in the regular work of the Organization were examined. The analysis identified behavioural patterns of African WTO Members in regular committee work in the Organization.

[1] The Ministerial Conference is the supreme organ of the WTO. It is mandated to meet at least once every two years. In light of the political and ceremonial nature of meetings of the Ministerial Conference, coupled with the long frequency of scheduled meetings, this study did not address participation in Ministerial Conferences.

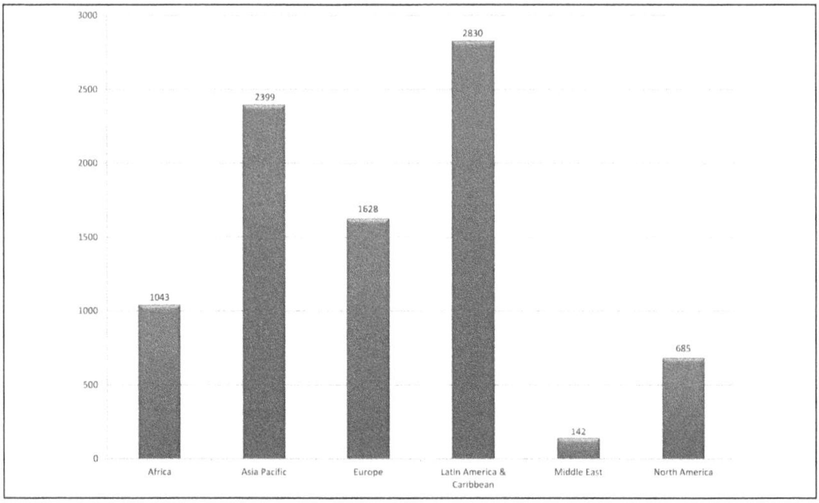

Figure 70. Individual Statements in the General Council (1995–2010).

2. The General Council

The General Council carries out the functions of the Ministerial Conference in intervals between meetings of the Ministerial Conference. It meets about five times a year on the average. It is responsible for the day-to-day management of the WTO and oversees the regular work of all WTO Councils and Committees. The General Council uses both formal and informal processes to conduct the business of the WTO. It is the vital organ for binding decision-making for WTO Members. Participation in the General Council provides a strategic vantage point for an understanding of the overall functioning of the Organization. Participation is therefore essential.

The participation of African WTO Members in the General Council was analysed, compared to Members from other regions, with regard to oral statements made and written submissions/proposals.

(a) *Individual Statements in the General Council*

Figure 70 shows the distribution of individual statements by Members in different regions in the General Council in the period 1995–2010.[2]

As measured by the "number of statements made", the level of African engagement/participation in the General Council was relatively high. African WTO Members engaged in this central decision-making body of the Organization. Individual oral statements by African Members totalled 1043. This number was close to the 2830 statements by Members from the Latin America region; 2399 by Members from the Asia Pacific region, and 1628 from Members from Europe. Total number of African statements was higher than

[2] Minutes of the General Council, WT/GC/M/1 to 129.

statements from North America at 685 and the Middle East at 142 statements. Latin America and the Caribbean was the most active region in the General Council.

Disaggregated data showed that in rank order, the most statements in the General Council in the period analysed were made by the US (454), EU(396), India (366), Japan (308), Pakistan (283), Mexico (250), Brazil (249), Cuba (237), Canada (231), and, Egypt (218).

Figure 70(b) shows the distribution of individual oral statements by African Members in the General Council in the period 1995–2010. With the exception of Central African Republic, Chad, Gambia, Malawi, Niger and Sierra Leone, all African WTO Members had made at least an individual statement in the General Council. Three of the African Members that had not made individual statements are non-resident in Geneva.[3] Of the Geneva resident African Members, most statements were made by Egypt (218), Morocco (104), Kenya (91), Nigeria (65), Mauritius (62), Uganda (60), Zambia (53), Senegal (36), Zimbabwe (34), and, Djibouti (34). Most of these countries constitute the limited universe of active African WTO Members. Egypt and Nigeria had commercial offices in Geneva dedicated to WTO work, while Kenya and Nigeria had Ambassadors specifically accredited to the WTO. Despite capacity constraints in many African Missions in Geneva, this universe of active African Members had a pool of professionals that had displayed personal commitment, professionalism and capacity for sustained hard work explaining in part, their relatively better participation levels.

Overall, many African Members had made more individual statements in the General Council. Djibouti was a case in point. In the period reviewed, its mission had an average of one delegate, but, it made 34 individual interventions in the General Council between 1995–2010.

Content examination of the statements, showed that African Members intervened on a variety of subject areas. These included: (i) administrative matters such as appointment of WTO Director-Generals, and, WTO staff salaries and pensions; (ii) process-related issues such as: preparatory work for WTO Ministerial Conferences, internal transparency and effective participation of all Members and WTO observership matters; (iii) substantive issues such as: Balance of Payments consultations; LDC issues; accession matters; Doha negotiations; textiles and clothing matters including those relating to the expired Agreement on Textiles and Clothing; outstanding implementation issues under Uruguay Round Agreements; TRIPS and Public Health; and, cotton (iv) SDT and development-related issues such as: waivers under Article IX of the WTO Agreement; Aid for Trade; LDC matters; and, training and technical assistance.

(b) *Group Statements in the General Council*

Figure 71 shows the distribution of group/coalition statements by Members in the General Council in the period 1995–2010.

The foregoing data revealed several useful facts and observations. First, groups and coalitions had been operative and very active in the General Council, more than in other regular WTO bodies. Second, the activity of these groups reflected a mixture of technical

[3] The Gambia; Malawi; and, Sierra Leone.

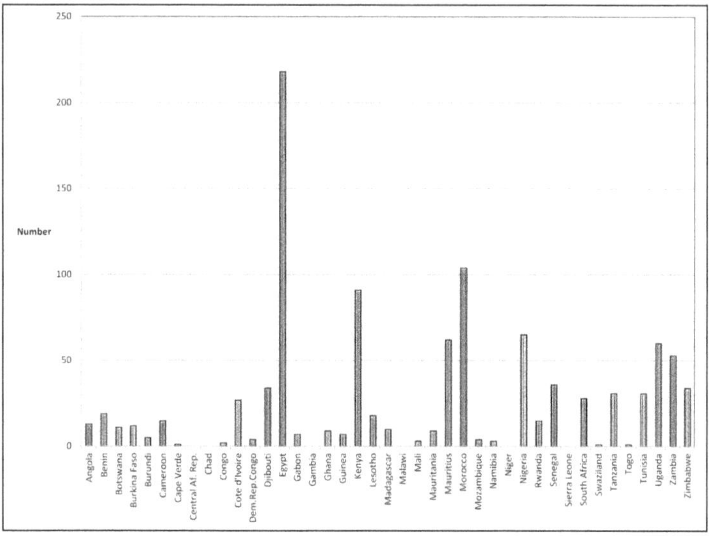

Figure 70(b). Individual Statements by African Members in the General Council 1995–2010.

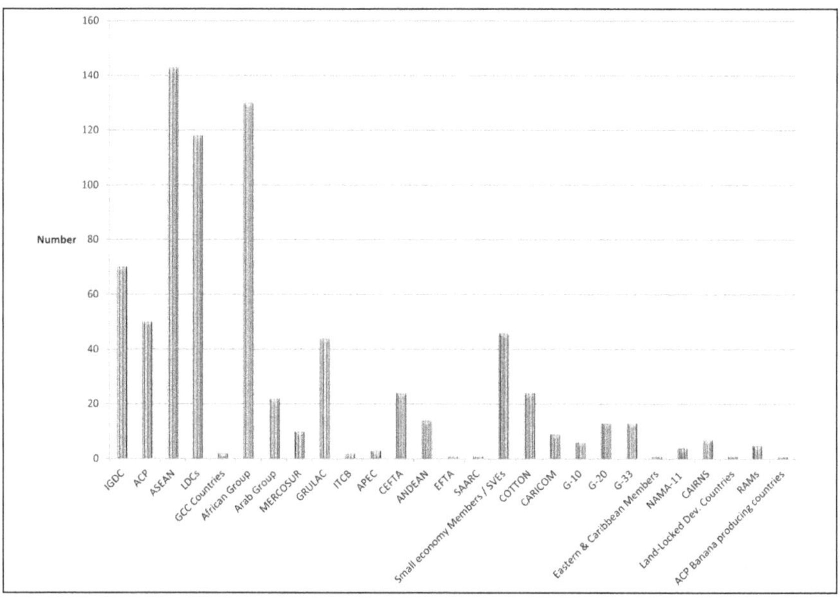

Figure 71. Group Statements in the General Council (1995–2010).

substance with trade policy positions and politics that converged in the General Council. Third, a content examination of the statements indicated intervention in areas of high sensitivity for the coalitions. Fourth, the rank order of the number of statements by these coalitions and groups indicated that developing country coalitions were in the top eight positions. Fifth, coalitional behaviour and the content of statements in the General Council largely reflected differences between developed and developing countries.

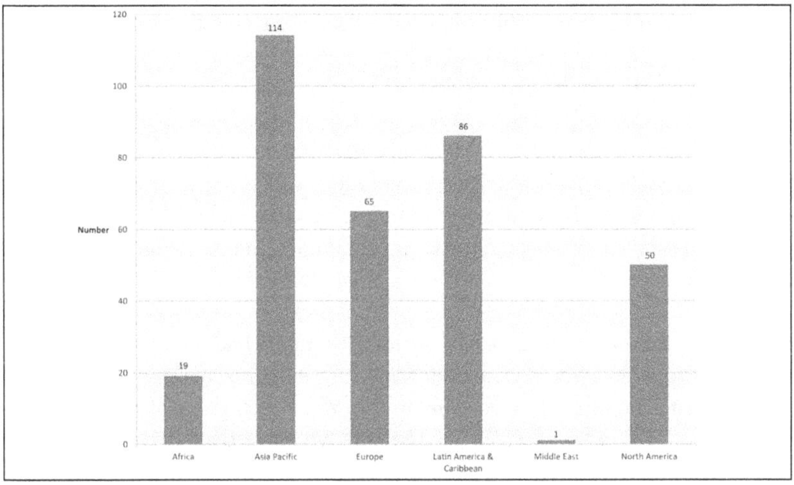

Figure 72. Proposals and Submissions to the General Council (1995–2010).

Finally, the statements in the General Council clearly showed that significant increase in coalition intervention in the General Council was related to the Doha negotiations under the item introduced on the agenda of the Council, in 2002, entitled: "Report by the Chairman of the TNC".[4]

The high level of individual African WTO Members intervention in the General Council was equally sustained at the level of group interventions. African WTO Members had made group statements through 16 of the 25 groups that had intervened in the General Council.[5] Similar to the situation on negotiating engagement, coalitional behaviour had been one of the primary forms of WTO African engagement in the General Council including in statement making. This had compensated for individual weaknesses because of *inter alia* low trade share levels. In the General Council, it was evident that the content of individual and group statements had been mutually supportive.

(c) *Individual Written Proposals/Submissions to the General Council*

Figure 72 shows the distribution of individual written submissions/proposals by Members in different regions in the General Council in the period 1995–2010.[6]

In contrast to statement-making, the level of engagement/participation of African WTO Members fell and was low in the number of tabled proposals/submissions. The total count of the latter was 19 which was low, compared to 114 submissions from the Asia Pacific region, 86 from the Latin American region, 65 from Europe, 50 from North America, but only higher than the Middle East, with one submission and whose participation had typically been very low.

4 The author is staff of the WTO Secretariat.

5 African Group; LDC Group; Informal Group of Developing Countries; ACP Group; SVEs Group; Cotton Four; WTO Arab Group; G20; G33; Cairns Group; G10; RAMs Group; NAMA 11; ITCB; Land Locked Developing Countries Group; ACP Banana Producers Group.

6 WT/GC/W/1 to 628.

Africa's participation in the tabling of proposals in the General Council was accounted for by 10 out of 42 African Members of which 39 were resident in Geneva.[7] These were: Cameroon(1), Cape Verde (2), Cote d'Ivoire (2), Egypt (2), Madagascar (2), Mauritius (1), Senegal (5), Sierra Leone (2), Tanzania (1), and, Uganda(1). These countries were part of the limited universe of African WTO Members that are relatively active in the work of the WTO. The individual number of written submissions was low, ranging between one and two proposals/submissions. Members in other regions had had relatively higher number of written proposals/submissions to the General Council. In rank order, the highest numbers had originated from the EU (41), US (36), Japan (20), Colombia (18), Canada (14), and China (13).

Fifteen of the total 19 submissions by African Members had focused on seeking waivers from obligations that would arise under WTO Agreements, mainly the Customs Valuation Agreement. The other proposals related to the phasing out of the Agreement on Textiles and Clothing and related post-adjustment concerns that African textiles producers or beneficiaries of preferential treatment related to textiles trade would face. This trend reflects an inertia for special and differential treatment in the form of waivers from obligations or safeguarding preferential trade benefits from erosion through MFN trade liberalization. It also reflected the capacity constraints that African WTO Members faced in implementing their obligations which included considerable weakness in technical expertise (as appears to be the case for the Customs Valuation Agreement) and the slow process for adjustment and reform at the domestic level to comply with required WTO rules and procedures.

The proposals/submissions from Members in the other regions spanned a wider scope reflecting offensive and defensive commercial and systemic interest and capacity to generate proposals. For example, countries with higher trade shares or higher GDP levels (EU and its Members; US, Japan, Australia, Switzerland, Canada) and rapidly growing trading economies (China, Korea, Brazil) had tabled the most proposals. These submissions included applications for waivers to grant preferential trading treatment to certain categories of Members (EU for the ACP, Bosnia & Herzegovina, Western Balkan States; US for AGOA, CBERA, ANDEAN countries; Canada for CARIBCAN). Recipients of these preferential regimes had either tabled proposals or made oral interventions to support the grant or extension of these waivers. Most proposals from a number of Central American Countries in the General Council had focused on questioning and opposing the grant of or extension of waivers to ACP countries by the EU. African WTO Members, particularly within the framework of the ACP remained strong advocates of waivers for preferential market access.

Other areas included the extension of the transition period under the Agreement on the Trade-Related Investment Measures (TRIMS was another area of sensitive engagement and request for waivers). A group of advanced Members had posed questions to developing countries who had sought to extend transition periods. These questions had

[7] Sierra Leone, a non-resident African WTO Member, had co-sponsored two proposals on the Kimberley Process Certification Scheme for Rough Diamonds. This suggests that non-residency is not necessarily a bar to active engagement. African participation was low in circumstances where a limited universe participated through tabling of proposals.

been posed to better understand the rationale for further exemptions, in light of the objective to limit continuation of restrictive and distortive effects of investment measures and facilitate investment across international frontiers. Questions and concerns had also been raised about the trade policy decisions of certain Members which were perceived as potentially trade restricting. There were also questions in the context of the mandated China Transitional Review Mechanism under its Protocol of Accession.[8] Other areas where proposals had been tabled included, trade facilitation, e-commerce and textiles and clothing.

In the General Council, proposals or submissions by African Members (but also by those in other regions) were only at an individual level and not through coalitions or groups, in contrast to their behaviour in negotiating engagement. Submissions/proposals had focused on the particular situation of a specific Member raising/tabling the proposal. However, African Members had in their oral interventions supported the views expressed in proposals of other African Members.

A question that stands out is why the inverse relationship between a high number of oral statements and a low number of written proposals/submissions in the General Council? Several factors appear to be in play. The preparation of oral statements is technically easier than the preparation of written proposals/submissions which *inter alia* requires consensus building for adoption. More work and greater efforts are required for the latter than the former. Furthermore, the General Council is seen as a wider political arena where the attention of the international trade community is focused. This is an opportunity not to be missed; and therefore more oral statements. Finally, it is also the case that substantively, African WTO Members have a lesser need for proposals/submissions because of exemptions or S&D that they enjoy compared to Members from other regions that require specific proposals/submissions to articulate specific situations. Finally, in this connection, the General Council is not a principal forum for substantive work or the primary forum for considering proposals. These tend to come from subsidiary bodies.

3. The Trade Policy Review Body

The objective of the Trade Policy Review Mechanism (Annex III of the Marrakesh Agreement) is to contribute to improved adherence by all Members to rules, disciplines and commitments made under the Multilateral Trade Agreements and the plurilateral trade agreements where applicable and hence to the smoother functioning of the multilateral trading system through greater transparency and understanding of the trade policies and practices of Members. (Annex III (i)). This assessment is carried out in the context of the wider economic and developmental needs, policies and objective of the Member and its external environment. In this regard, Annex III clearly states that "the function of the review mechanism is to examine the impact of a Member's trade policies and practices on the multilateral trading system. The Trade Policy Review Mechanism (TPRM) is not intended to serve as a basis for enforcement of obligations or for the settlement of disputes.

[8] It is observed that the mandated review expired in December 2011.

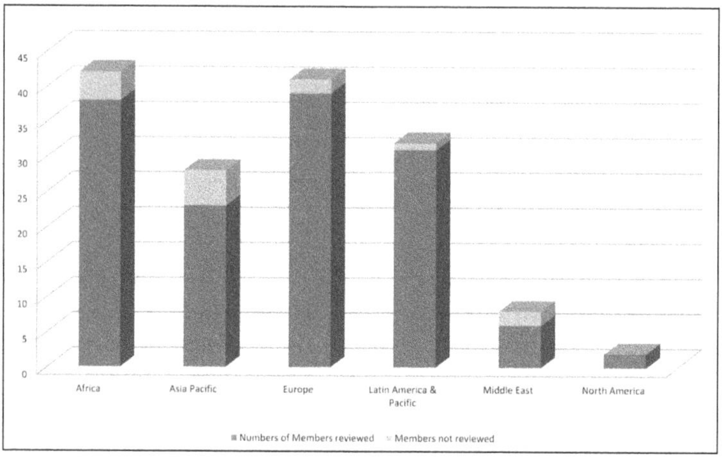

Figure 73. Members reviewed by region 1995–2010.

The frequency of reviews depends on a Member's share of world trade. The top four are examined every two years, the next sixteen, every four years, and the rest every six years with the possibility for longer time periods for least developed countries. Two reports form the basis of a review. A full report prepared by the government being reviewed and a report by the WTO Secretariat on its own responsibility, taking into account information provided by the Member being reviewed. These reports and the minutes of the discussion are published after the review.

The participation of African WTO Members in the Trade Policy Review Body was analysed based on the following indices:

- number of Members reviewed;
- number of advance written questions posed in preparation for reviews;
- oral statements made at reviews; and,
- participation as discussants in reviews.

(a) *Members Reviewed*

Figure 73 shows the distribution of Members reviewed by region in the period 1995–2010.

Most Members in all regions in this study had undergone a review of their trade policy at least once in the period reviewed.

Thirty-nine (39) Members in Africa or 92.8% had undergone a trade policy review, once. This was a high number of review and therefore participation in the Trade Policy Review Mechanism. The North America region, however, had a higher review percentage at the maximum of 100 per cent. For the Latin American and Caribbean region, 96.8 per cent of Members had been reviewed at least once in the period reviewed; again a high percentage. Cuba was the only Member in the Latin America and Caribbean region that had not undergone a trade policy review, possibly because of its political-economic relationship with the United States. In Africa, the three countries that had not been reviewed in the period analysed were Cape Verde, Guinea Bissau, and, Zimbabwe. Cape Verde had recently acceded to the WTO and was a least developed country at accession, thereby benefiting from longer time period before review. Guinea Bissau and Zimbabwe shared the common characteristic of domestic difficulties making difficult the collection of data and meeting with officials.[9]

Africa's performance in terms of Members reviewed was better than Europe, Asia Pacific and Middle East regions where respectively 92.6, 82 and 75 per cent of Members in those regions had been reviewed at least once. In Europe, the three countries that had not yet been reviewed were FYR Macedonia, Moldova and Ukraine which had all recently acceded to the WTO. Five countries in the Asia-Pacific region had not yet undergone a trade policy review: Cambodia, Myanmar, Nepal, Tonga and Vietnam. Four of these were recently acceded to the WTO (Cambodia, Nepal, Tonga and Vietnam). Myanmar is an LDC and domestic difficulties could have impacted accomplishment of its reviews. In the Middle East, Kuwait and Saudi Arabia were the two countries that had not yet undergone a review. Saudi Arabia was a recently acceded country. Kuwait is an original WTO Member that had not been keen on a review.[10]

Table 1 in Annex VIII shows the overall number of times each Member had undergone trade policy reviews in the period studied. With the exception of the first four ranked Members with two year review cycles and those that follow with four-year review cycles, a number of countries had undergone three or five reviews as should have been the case by 2010.

(b) *Participation/Engagement in Reviews of Other Members: Advance Written Questions*

The Rules of Procedure for meetings of the Trade Policy Review Body provide that Members should submit written questions to the Member under review at least two weeks before the review meeting, to allow time to prepare replies.[11] This section analyses participation/engagement in the TPRB by counting the number of advance question submitted prior to review meetings of Members. Figure 74, shows the distribution of advance questions submitted by Members in different regions in the period 1995–2010.[12]

African WTO Members' participation/engagement in the submission of advance written questions in the TPR process was low, compared to the number of times other regions had submitted "advance questions" and low with regard to the fact that only 6[13] (or 14 per cent) out of 42 African Members had "submitted questions". Time and effort, based on the understanding of the substance of the reports of the Member under

---

9 D.R. Congo was reviewed for the first time towards the end of the period analysed – 24 and 26 November 2010. Zimbabwe was first reviewed in 1994 under the auspices of the GATT where coverage did not include trade in services and intellectually property. Zimbabwe's "first" review under the WTO took place in October 2011.

10 The State of Kuwait underwent its first trade policy review on 7 and 9 February 2012.

11 WT/TPR/6/Rev.2.

12 Minutes of meetings of TPRB, WT/TPR/M/1 to 235, Annexes.

13 Egypt (twice); Kenya (five times); Mauritius (thrice); Nigeria (once); South Africa (four times); Zambia (once).

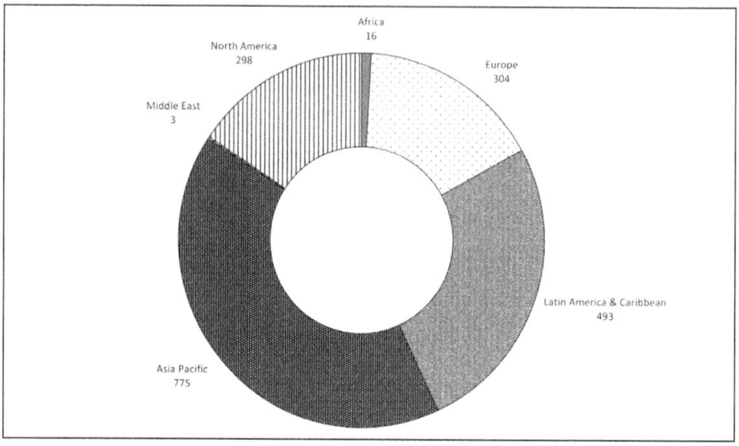

Figure 74. Advance written questions for member reviews 1995–2010.

review are required for the precise formulation of questions. In other words, more work is required than for the drafting of statements. Kenya had submitted the highest number, five times.

In the Asia-pacific region, 64 per cent of Members had submitted questions, at least once. Japan and Hong Kong, China had each submitted questions for more than 100 reviews. Other countries in this region that had submitted advance questions for more than 50 reviews included Korea, Australia, Chinese Taipei, India and New Zealand. In the Latin America and the Caribbean region, 59 per cent of Members had submitted advance written question at least once. Brazil was the only country to have submitted questions for more than 100 reviews. Other countries that had submitted advance questions for more than 50 reviews included Argentina, Colombia, Chile and Mexico. In the Caribbean region, only Trinidad and Tobago had submitted advance written questions, twice. All other Caribbean countries had not submitted advance written questions. Seventy-six per cent (76%) of Members in Europe had submitted advance questions at least once. Switzerland, Norway and Turkey had each submitted questions for more than 40 reviews. All countries in this region had submitted at least one advance written question. North America had submitted questions 298 times. Canada and the United States had each submitted questions for more than 100 reviews. 25 per cent of Members in the Middle East had submitted advance written questions, at least once.

Participation in the TPR process is demanding and knowledge-based. Specialized expertise, knowledge and resources are required with diligent Geneva-capital coordination, the latter amongst government ministries and departments. This seemed to be weak for many African WTO Members. As a consequence, participation in the "submission of advance questions" for TPRs was low. In Africa, the six countries that had submitted advance questions at least once in the period analysed were better equipped in terms of human and financial resources, technical and analytical capacity, domestic coordination, and, capital/Geneva coordination. TPR reports, particularly those of advanced economies, are voluminous and complicated. This situation was compounded by the rules of procedure, which provide that Members have only two weeks to read the government and Secretariat reports and prepare and submit advance written questions. In practice, however, Members with an interest in an economy are expected to track and monitor developments in an economy in between reviews. This situation underlines that this area of regular work is resource intensive with a requirement for enhanced Geneva-capital coordination and an institutional capacity of the part of a Member to track and monitor trade policy developments in trading partners in between trade policy reviews.

There were notable observations in the approach of African WTO Members to TPRs. First, although real trade policy developments seemed to underline the trade policy friction amongst neighbouring African countries, the pattern showed that very few African Members had posed questions to other African Members being reviewed. This was in contrast to the pattern in other regions where Members posed questions to Members being reviewed in their regions. The exceptions were the US, EU, Japan and Canada which posed questions to almost all Members being reviewed, regardless of region of origin. Oral statements by African WTO Members in the trade policy review of other African Members were of a "solidarity nature". This might not be completely "healthy" for deeper African trade integration and could also explain in part the low level of intra-African trade at 11.7%. Africa's trend in "non-intra-regional" questioning was partly a reflection of the low-rate of intra-African trade compared to the level of intra-regional trade in other regions.[14] In addition, questions posed by African Members were very few, on average five (5), compared to over 50–100 questions posed by Members in other regions.

Second, questions posed to African Members originated mainly from the United States, Japan, Canada and the European Union but also from Argentina, Brazil, India, Switzerland and Norway. These were countries that either provided preferential trading schemes or were donors to African countries or had historical, cultural and colonial ties to African countries. In addition, the evidence showed that the number of questions posed to African countries had been the lowest, a reflection of the low level of non-preferential trade between African Members and the rest of the world.

Third, the low number of questions posed to African Members partly reflected low trade shares. It is useful to note that in contrast however, in accession negotiations, even least developed countries had had a very high number of questions put to them, as high and in some cases higher, than number of questions for non-LDC acceding governments. This contrast is important in underlining the observation, if not the fact, that Members are driven not only by commercial/trade share and GDP considerations, but also by rules-related considerations and by the degree of importance they attach to a WTO regular body. The contrast in the seriousness accorded accession working parties (which are regular bodies) to other regular bodies underlines this point. WTO Members are sensitive about ensuring that trade measures by Members are pursuant to rules of the system in this peer review process, regardless of level of economic development.

14 According to the International Trade Statistics 2010, the share of regional trade flows of Africa in total merchandise exports was 38.8% with Europe, 22.2% with Asia, 17.1% with North America, and, 11.7% with Africa.

It is recommended that African WTO Members take a more organized and systemic approach to the TPR process on this particular aspect. The assessment in this study was that so far this had not been the case.

Fourth, the emergence of the Trade Policy Reviews of African WTO Members on the platform of Regional Economic Communities (RECs) is a welcome and more serious approach. In the period studied, reviews had been held for the East African Community (EAC) Members;[15] and, the Southern African Custom Union (SACU). A review is also scheduled under the CEMAC configuration.[16] It is recommended that African WTO Members henceforth organize their trade policy reviews on the platforms of the RECs in order to make it more worthwhile for other Members, but more importantly to create a wider economic space for improving Africa's intra-regional trade.

Fifth, responses by some African Members to questions that had been posed by other Members during their reviews tended to be general and not sufficiently specific in response to Members posing the questions. In a number of cases, African Members requested deferring their responses until after the review.

Sixth, although there was the perennial challenge of capacity constraints, a more rational assignment of resources, prioritization and linkage of means and ends should improve Africa's participation in the TPR process.

Finally, and on balance, it is useful to observe that across the board, since 2003, several Members had focused their attention and resources on the Doha negotiations and not paid equal attention to other areas of WTO work. It is argued in this study that in a system of balanced rights and obligations, the luxury of choice does not exist in a "menu selection". Members, at every level of development, have a duty to respect their obligations and exercise their rights, if the system is to yield any benefits for their membership.

(c) *Participation/Engagement in Reviews of Other Members: Oral Statements at TPRB Meetings*

Figure 75 shows the distribution of individual oral statements made in the TPRB by Members in different regions in the period 1995–2010.[17]

Lesser time and effort and a lower level of technical expertise are required for drafting oral statements than for formulating questions, proposals and submissions. With regard to the volume of statements prepared and delivered by African WTO Members, although it was relatively higher than the number of advance questions, it was still low in relation to the number of African WTO Members and in comparison to the statements from Members in the other regions. Figure 76 shows that 32 African WTO Members (or 76 per cent) had made 483 statements. Although apparently high, this was a low percentage for the least demanding type of engagement/participation. Ten[18] African

[15] Kenya, Uganda and Tanzania. Burundi and Rwanda recently acceded to the EAC.

[16] SACU (Botswana, Namibia, Lesotho, Swaziland and South Africa), CEMAC (Cameroon, Central African Republic, Chad, Republic of Congo, Gabon and Equatorial Guinea).

[17] WT/TPR/M/1 to M235 and addenda.

[18] Cape Verde, Central African Republic; Gambia; Ghana; Guinea Bissau; Malawi; Niger, Sierra Leone, Swaziland and Togo.

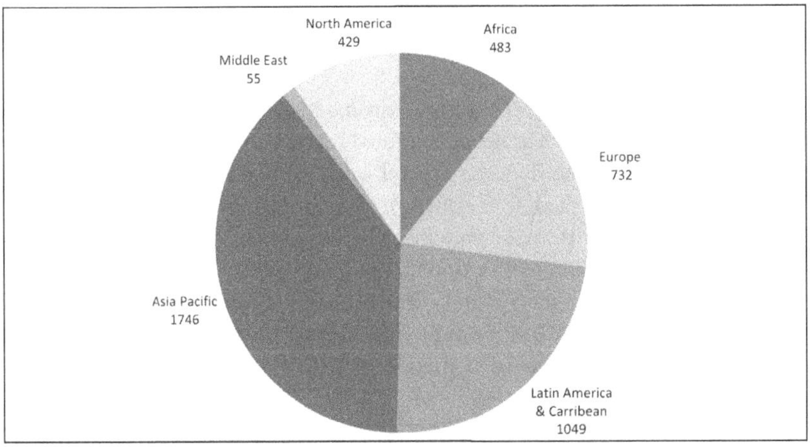

Figure 75. Statements at TPRB meetings per region: 1995–2010.

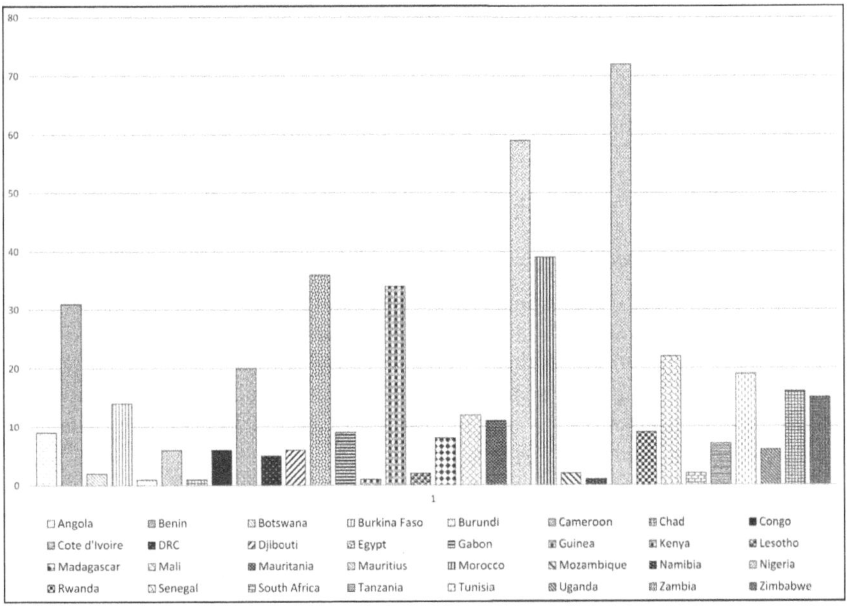

Figure 76. Statements by African members in the TPRB 1995–2010.

Members, including those had been reviewed, had not yet made individual statements in review meetings of other Members. As to whether they should, it is consistently argued in this study that in a system of balanced rights and obligations, the luxury of choice does not exist in a "menu selection". Members, at every level of development, have a duty to respect their obligations and exercise their rights, if the system is to yield any benefits for their membership.

Nigeria, Mauritius, Morocco, Egypt, Kenya and Benin had made the most statements – ranging between 60 and 30. This was low in comparison to the top performers in the other regions, whose statements were over 100.

Analysis of the data indicated that statements made by African Members were usually short (ranging between 1–5 standard paragraphs) relative to those made by Members in other regions. These statements were general, addressing issues such as regional integration (including intra-Africa); infrastructure, governance; peace and security and aid. Observed was the pattern to make statements at reviews of other African countries.[19] In relation to other regions, the 483 statements made by African WTO Members were less that the Asia Pacific region (1746); Latin America and Caribbean region (1049) and, Europe (732). The two North American Members made a high proportion of 429 statements. The level of engagement/participation by the Middle East in total number and proportion was low at 55 statements.

The content of statements by Members in other regions was not only "diverse" in terms of composition of Members, but also tended to be substantively focused on specific issues of trade policy and practices of Members being reviewed. African Members tended to make "solidarity" statements mostly in reviews of other African Members or in reviews of those with whom there exist historical, cultural, donor-aid, and/or political ties.[20] Statements were also sub-region specific. These statements were made to encourage and "praise neighbours" (North Africa, South Africa, West Africa, and East Africa). Evidence suggested that countries that had coordinated the African Group tended to make relatively more statements in reviews of other members.[21]

Some of the challenges to the level of engagement/participation in reviews of other Members by African Members emerged from the questionnaire responses. These revolved around limited analytical capacity, minimal instructions from capitals; limited human resource capacity to assign to coverage of TPRs and schedule conflicts with other equally important meetings for African Members. Similar to the recommendations for addressing and overcoming the challenges in preparing advance questions for the TPR process, several recommendations are made. A more rational assignment of resources, prioritization and linkage of means and ends are recommended. In addition, it is recommended that African WTO Members take a more organized, regional and systemic approach to the TPR process.

(d) *Participation as Discussants in TPRs*

The TPRM provides that in consultation with the Member or Members under review, the Chairman may choose discussants who, acting in their personal capacity, shall introduce the discussions in the TPRB. In practice, the choice of discussants is made by the Secretariat and, over time, the Secretariat has used the selection and appointment of

19 However, countries such as Nigeria, Mauritius, Egypt, and Kenya spoke at reviews meetings of Members from other regions as well.

20 These countries included the US, EU, China, Japan, Canada, India, Brazil, Norway and also countries that belong to the WTO Arab Group; LDC Group or ACP Group.

21 These included Benin, Egypt, Kenya and Nigeria when delivering statements on behalf of the African Group.

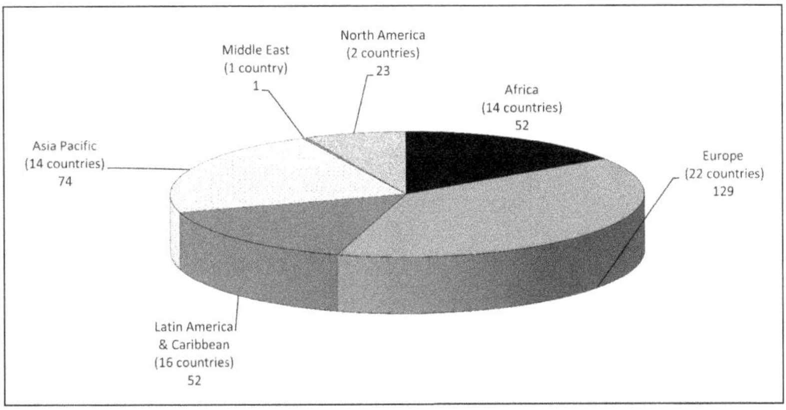

Figure 77. Distribution of discussants by region 1995–2010.

discussants to "develop trade policy capacity" in developing countries. This accounts for the moderately decent level of African participation as discussants to lead off the trade policy review of Members. Although the precise and final contents of the statements by discussants are decided by the discussants, they are drafted by the Secretariat.

Figure 77 shows the distribution of discussants in the TPRB by region in the period 1995–2010.[22]

In the period reviewed, there were 52 African discussants in the review of Members' trade policies in the TPRB. It was neither low nor minimal, but moderately decent. The relationship between African WTO Members and the WTO Secretariat is a healthy one. The result of this specific relationship in the TPR process has enormously contributed to deepening desperately urgent specialized trade policy capacity in African countries. The relationship between the WTO Secretariat and African Members over the selection of trade policy discussants is one good example. Building on this, from 2002, WTO technical co-operation initiated the practice of combining trade policy review missions by the Secretariat to low income Members including African countries and LDCs with Secretariat staff from the Institute of Training and Technical Cooperation to assess technical assistance and capacity building needs to enhance capacity. It is recommended in this study, as elaborated in chapter 7 that continued wide scope remains to reduce Africa's capacity constraints in the WTO through significantly scaled-up mutual reinforcement of trade policy reviews and Secretariat trade capacity building.

In general, a trend that was evident was that a selected discussant was usually from the same region as the country being reviewed. However, for the case of African trade policy reviews, discussants originated mostly from countries with historical, cultural, colonial, economic and political links. Most times from a Member speaking the same language as

[22] Arrangements for Review Meetings – WT/TRP/1 to 210; Communication from discussants, WT/TRP/D/1 to 183.

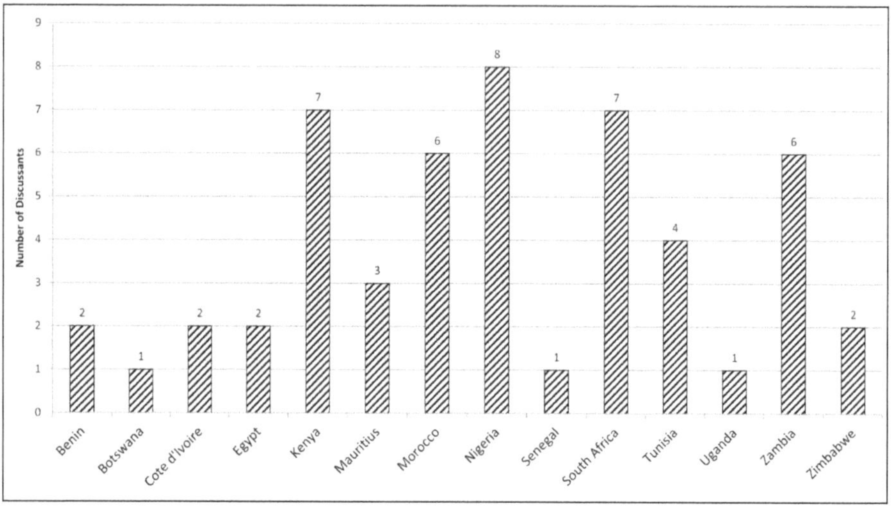

Figure 78. African participation as discussants in the TPRB 1995–2010.

the African Member being reviewed – French, English, Arabic or Portuguese;[23] or having "donor/aid" links.[24]

Figure 78 show that 14 African Members (or 33.3 %) accounted for the 52 African discussants. Although moderately decent in the specific context of discussants in the TPR process, this number was low with regard to the 42 African WTO Members and there is scope for improvement.

The African countries from which discussants had originated were from the same universe of active African Members in the work of the WTO. Some are leading traders on the continent (South Africa, Nigeria, Egypt, Kenya, and Morocco) and generally have greater systemic/commercial stake in reviews of other Members. However, some are classified as least developed countries (Zambia, Uganda, Senegal and Benin). These African countries tended to be "more-organised" in their Geneva missions and had regular capital support. Officials from these Members had demonstrated personal commitment and professionalism to the work of the WTO despite capacity constraints.

Most African discussants had performed this function mainly at reviews of fellow African Members. However, some exceptions existed: Kenya in the case of the United States, South Africa for the European Union and for Switzerland, and, Nigeria for Korea and Malaysia. In these cases, the personality, diplomacy and experience of the individuals that undertook discussant roles in these particular reviews, played a role in their being selected. On average, the Members in Africa that had provided discussants had done so three times. This was very low in comparison with discussants from other regions. For instance, in North America, discussants had on average been provided 10 times by the countries in that region. The choice of discussants is illustrative of another area of regular

23 The official WTO languages are English, French and Spanish.

24 Sweden, Denmark, Norway, Luxembourg, UK, France, Switzerland, Japan have for instance provided discussants for reviews of African countries.

work where the variable of the level of trade/GDP shares does not provide an explanation, but rather the professionalism of the individual that is chosen as a discussant.

Overall, the results showed improved but still low levels of participation of African countries as discussants in reviews of other members. The constraints advanced in relation to submission of advance written statements and making of statements at review meetings equally applies to participation as discussants in TPR meetings.

4. The Council for Trade in Goods

Article IV.5 of the Marrakesh Agreement established the Council for Trade in Goods (CTG). It is charged with overseeing the functioning of the Multilateral Trade Agreements in Annex 1A of the Marrakesh Agreement. The CTG oversees the activities of 12 WTO subsidiary bodies.[25] Several of these subsidiary bodies, over the years, have emerged to be of key systemic and commercial interest for African WTO Members. These bodies have addressed several of the priority interest areas for African WTO Members such as agriculture, customs valuation, SPS, TBT and TRIMS. In the CTG, Members discuss agenda items, consider draft decisions, including proposals by Members, pursuant to the Covered Agreements under Annex 1A. CTG draft decisions require action by the General Council.

The level of participation/engagement of African WTO Members in the CTG was analysed and compared to Members from other regions, on the basis of the following indices:

- Oral statements made; and,
- subject matter of submissions/proposals.

(a) *Oral Statements in the CTG*

Figure 79 shows the distribution of oral statements in the CTG by Members in different regions in the period 1995–2010.[26]

In the period analysed, a total of 2,724 oral statements were made in the CTG; disaggregated as in figure 79. African WTO Members made a total of 412 statements, or 15 per cent of the total number of statements. Of the 42 African WTO Members, only 15, or 35 per cent intervened with individual statements. These were Benin, Botswana, Burkina Faso, Gabon, Egypt, Mauritius, Madagascar, Morocco, Nigeria, Tunisia, Kenya, Senegal, Uganda, Zimbabwe, and Zambia. This was a low level of engagement/participation with scope for improvement.

25 Committee on Agriculture; Committee on Anti-dumping Practices; Committee on Customs Valuation; Committee on Import Licensing; Committee on Market Access; Committee on Rules of Origin; Committee on Safeguards; Committee on Sanitary and Phytosanitary Measures; Committee on Subsidies and Countervailing Measures; Committee on Technical Barriers to Trade; Committee on Trade Related Investment Measures; and, the Working Party on State Trading Enterprises.

26 Minutes of the Council for Trade in Goods, G/C/M/1 to 104.

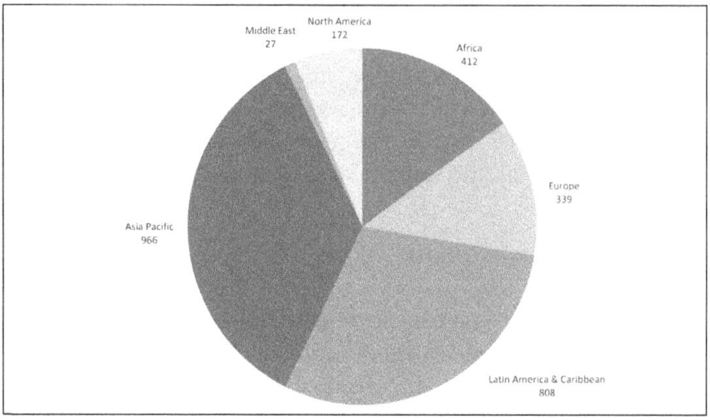

Figure 79. Total number of Interventions in CTG by region (1995–2010).

Data gathered and analysed and interviews with African negotiators indicated very low interventions prior to 2000. Relatively, however, most statements by African Group Members were made after the year 2000. Several factors contributed to understanding and explaining this situation. First, was the spike in engagement in the regular work of the Organization, linked to the launch of the Doha Round in 2001. The launch of the Round focused the attention of developing countries, including in Africa, on the urgent necessity to increase resources for engagement in the WTO, as they analysed it, so as to correct the imbalances from previous rounds of trade negotiation. As a consequence, increase in resources by African Members for Doha Round negotiations also benefitted African Members' participation in the regular work of the Organization. Between 1995 and 2010, for example, the number of negotiators in African WTO missions increased by 125 per cent.

Second, with the passage of time, knowledge and experience increased the level of participation/engagement in the institutional functioning of the rules-based multilateral trading system. African WTO Members were simply getting better at "working the system". Whereas they claimed that they had not understood what they signed at the conclusion of the Uruguay Round in 1994 and that their participation had been low, unpredictable and nominal at the establishment of the WTO in 1995, by the launch of the Doha Round, their level of participation/engagement, in relative terms, had started to improve.

Third, essential improvements in the quantum and quality of WTO specific delivered technical assistance were producing improved participatory effects. Data gathered and analysed (Annex VI) showed a steady increase in technical assistance activities delivered, from the year 2000 (one year before the launch of the Doha Round) to 2010. Technical assistance delivered to the 42 WTO African countries increased by 360 per cent from 2000 to 2010. Quality also significantly improved based on annual audits of WTO delivered technical assistance.

Furthermore, no less important, was the confirmation that several aspects of the work of the Organization, such as technical co-operation and capacity building, transitional periods, etc., were core elements of the development dimension of the Multilateral Trading System.[27] These were of vital importance for African Members from 2000 onwards. Development aspects of the trading system, of significant importance for African countries, were also "accommodated" within the rules for exceptions. These included negotiations amongst Members in the CTG on the draft decisions for the Marrakesh Agreement Article IX waivers for preferences granted to eligible African WTO Members by the EU under the Cotonou Agreement and by the US under African Growth and Opportunity Act (AGOA).

(b) *Subject Areas of Intervention by African Members in the CTG*

The agenda of the CTG is varied. The 15 African Members that individually intervened did so in the context of waiver requests to preserve existing preferential trading systems, or extend country-specific waivers relating to their individual commitments under WTO Agreements e.g. Malawi, Senegal, Zambia, Cameroon, Madagascar, Cote d'Ivoire, and Cape Verde. Most interventions were in support of waiver requests by preference-granting Members, for preference schemes to which African Members were beneficiaries. The examples included the United States AGOA scheme and the Cotonou Agreement within the framework of which the European Union granted preferences to ACP countries.

Egypt, Uganda, Kenya, Zimbabwe, Mauritius and Cote d'Ivoire intervened on the subject of trade in textiles, as ITCB members and in the context of post-ATC-related issues and cotton. The European Union raised concerns against Nigeria with regard to certain trade restrictive measures. No African country raised a trade concern against any WTO Member.

The level of notification of Free Trade Agreements (FTAs) by African countries in the CTG was low. This low level of notification reflected low levels of conclusion of FTAs amongst African countries themselves and with countries from other regions. Countries in North Africa (Egypt, Morocco, and Tunisia) and Southern Africa have been the most active in negotiation and conclusion of FTAs. However, under GATT Article XXIV – two Economic Partnerships Agreements (EPAs) between the EU and two African Members, (Côte d'Ivoire and Cameroon) were notified.

5. The Council for Trade in Services

Article IV.5 of the Marrakesh Agreement establishes the Council for Trade in Services (CTS). The CTS is charged with overseeing the functioning of the General Agreement on Trade in Services (GATS) and carrying out such other functions as may be assigned to it to facilitate the operation of the Agreement and further its objectives. (Article XXIV of the GATS). The CTS is also responsible for a technical review of the GATS under Article XX.2 provisions; waivers from specific commitments pursuant to paragraphs 3 and 4 of Article IX of the Marrakesh Agreement; periodic review of developments in the air

27 WT/MIN (01)/DEC/1: Ministerial Conference, Fourth Session, Doha, 9 to 14 November (paragraph 38).

transport sector; the transitional review mechanism under China's Protocol of Accession; and, notification requirements under the GATS.

In the period reviewed, Africa's level of engagement/participation in the regular work of the CTS had not matched the increasing share of the GDP of African countries accounted for by trade in commercial services. In 1995 trade in commercial services as a percentage of Africa's GDP stood at 11.8 per cent. It increased to 12.9 per cent by the launch of the Doha Round in 2001, and further increased to 14.7 per cent in 2008 before the onset of the global financial and economic crisis. (See Annex XV) Overall, WTO Secretariat statistics clearly showed the trend that services trade demonstrated the most rapid growth from which there were significant dynamic gains from global trade. The data reviewed in this research indicated that African WTO Members had not sufficiently accorded priority to this area of regular work.

The level of participation/engagement of African WTO Members in the CTS was analysed and compared to Members from other regions with regard to the following indices:

- oral statements made in the Council;
- written submissions/proposals; and,
- notification count.

(a) *Oral Statements in the Council for Services*

Figure 80 shows the distribution of statements in the CTS in the period 1995–2010 by Members in different regions.[28]

In the period analysed, a total of 2,951 statements were made in the CTS; disaggregated as in figure 80. African WTO Members made a total of 96 statements, or 3.2 per cent of the total number of statements made in the CTS. Eleven (or 26 per cent of) African Members intervened in the CTS with individual statements. These were: Côte d'Ivoire, Djibouti, Egypt, Ghana, Kenya, Mauritius, Morocco, Nigeria, Senegal, South Africa, and, Tunisia. (Figure 81). This was a low level of engagement/participation with wide scope for improvement. This was also a low level of engagement *per se*, compared to other regular bodies particularly the General Council, the Council for TRIPS and in Doha negotiations. In the period reviewed, Africa had the most number of Members that had not intervened in the CTS, totalling, 31 countries.[29]

The number of interventions by the African WTO Members that had intervened the most was low in comparison to Members from other region. Most interventions were made by Egypt (34); Morocco (16); South Africa (13); Mauritius (9) and Tunisia (5).[30]

---

28 Minutes of the Council for Services, S/C/M/1 to 101.

29 Angola, Benin, Botswana, Burkina Faso, Burundi, Cameroon, Cape Verde, Central African Republic, Chad, Congo, D. R. Congo, Gabon, Gambia, Guinea, Guinea Bissau, Lesotho, Madagascar, Mali, Malawi, Mauritania, Niger, Rwanda, Sierra Leone, Swaziland, Tanzania, Togo, Uganda, Zambia, Zimbabwe.

30 These four African Members feature on the list of the 40 leading exporters of commercial services. Egypt is ranked 20th with a 0.9% share in exports; Morocco is ranked 26th with a 0.5% share; South Africa is ranked 28th with a 0.5% share, and Tunisia is ranked 40th with a 0.2% share, *Leading exporters and Importers in World Trade in Commercial Services (excluding intra-EU (27) trade), 2009, Table I.11*, International Trade Statistics, 2010, pg. 16.

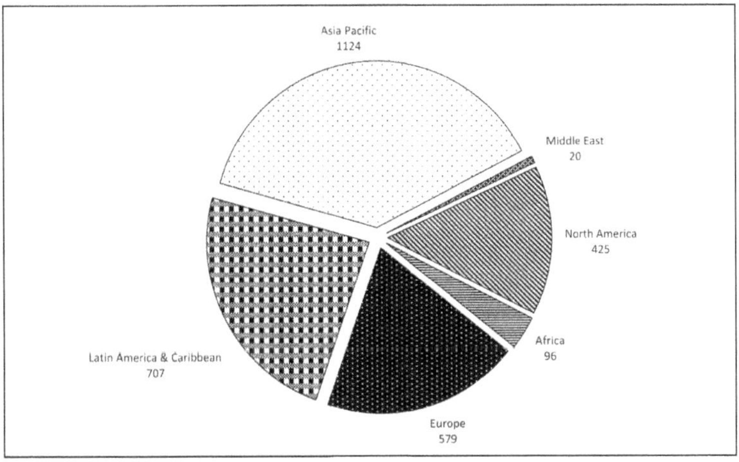

Figure 80. Statements in the CTS by region (1995–2010).

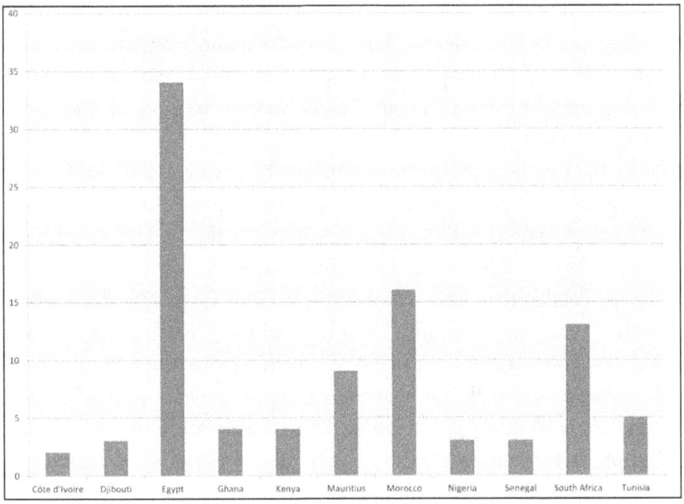

Figure 81. Interventions by African WTO members in the CTS (1995–2010).

Compared to other regions, in Europe for instance, the top five Members that intervened the most were the European Union (281); Switzerland (122); Norway (41); and Turkey (34). In the Latin America and Caribbean region, Brazil topped with 131 interventions. Others included, Mexico (114); Argentina (70); Chile (66); and, Uruguay (55) interventions. The interventions by the Middle East region were also relatively low – Israel (9); Jordan (6); Kuwait and Oman (2 respectively).

The top five Members active in the CTS were the United States; European Union; Japan; Hong Kong China; Australia and Brazil (Figure 82). These Members are leading world

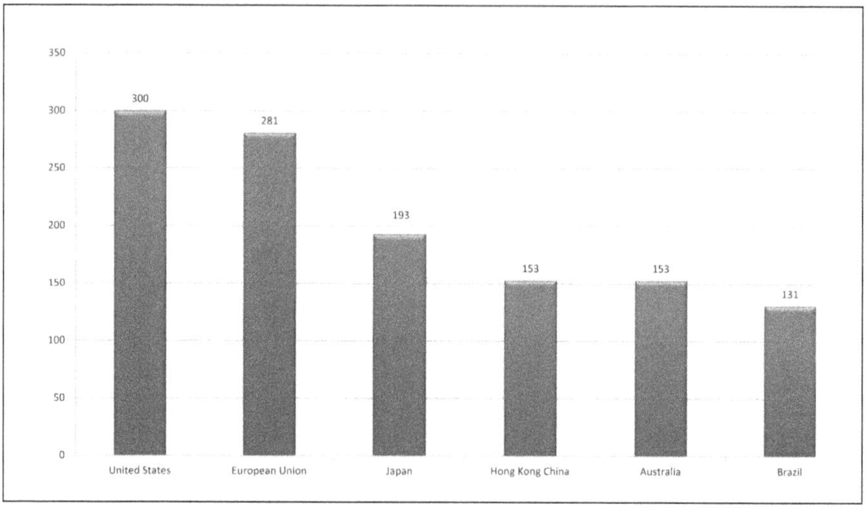

Figure 82. Members with the most statements overall in the CTS (1995–2010).

traders and net exporters of services.[31] Their prevalent contribution to the discussions in the CTS is explained by their preponderant share of global trade in services. They have an offensive commercial interest in trade in services and an equal interest in the rules underpinning trade in services.

What explains the low number of interventions by African WTO Members? There are several factors. Trade in services for most African countries constitutes a low proportion of overall trade compared to merchandise trade, with the exception of countries such as Morocco, Egypt, South Africa, Tunisia, Djibouti, and, Kenya. Trade in services has required greater specialization and was a latter area of focus for African trade negotiators, whose initial focus was on goods. Their level of participation/engagement reflected *inter alia* minimal understanding of the GATS. Furthermore, the dynamic effects of trade in services for growth were little understood in the early years of the WTO. Finally, services trade statistics have been of low quality, unreliable and in many cases absent.

The initial approach to engagement in the regular work of the Organization on trade in services reflected Africa's impediments to services trade *per se*. In the early 1990s, while Members from other regions generally intervened on most subject areas of the agenda of the CTS, the interventions by African Members revolved around efforts to re-open particular protocols (on financial services and, on basic telecommunications) for acceptance beyond the time-limits for ratification. Delays in domestic ratification processes, weak administrative structures, technical deficiencies and limited understanding

[31] The EU is ranked number 1, with a share of 26.3% in world commercial services exports; US ranked 2nd with 19.2% share; Japan ranked 4th with 5.1% share; Hong Kong China ranked 7th with 3.5% share; Australia, ranked 11th with 1.7% share, and Brazil, ranked 18th with 1.1% share, *Leading Exporters and Importers in World Trade in Commercial Services (Excluding intra-EU 27 trade), 2009, Table I.11,* International Trade Statistics, 2010, pg. 16.

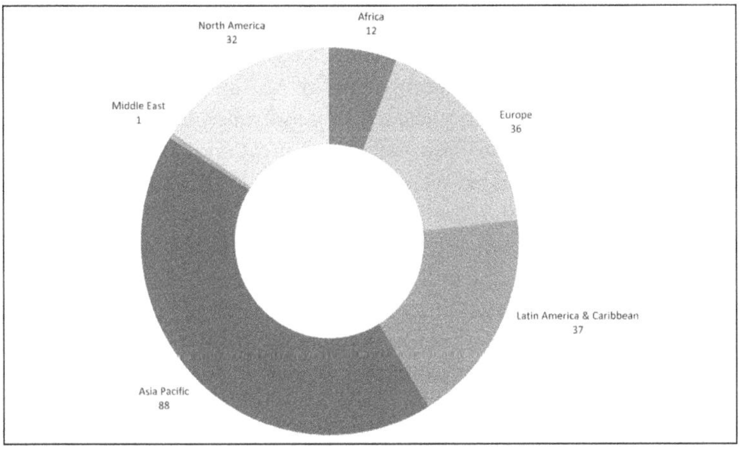

Figure 83. Submissions/proposals to the CTS (1995–2010).

of the GATS were some of the reasons that impeded participation and minimised the participation of African WTO Members in the CTS. However, some African Members, notably Egypt, Morocco, Tunisia and Kenya, with *inter alia*, relatively better developed services industries, substantively intervened on CTS agenda items such as electronic commerce, franchising, emergency safeguard measures and in sectoral discussions to which they attached commercial or systemic interest.

(b) *Written Proposals/Submissions in the CTS*[32]

In the period analysed, a total of 196 proposals/submissions were made in the CTS; disaggregated as in figure 83. African WTO Members made a total of 12 proposals/submissions, or 6.1 per cent of the total number of proposals/submissions made. Only two African Members (South Africa and Morocco) or 4.7 per cent of African WTO membership submitted individual proposals. This low level of proposals submitted corresponds to the low number of oral statements and low level of engagement overall by African Members in the CTS. This level of engagement was in contrast to the rising level of trade in services as a share of the GDP of African countries,[33] particularly for such African countries like Egypt, Djibouti, Morocco, South Africa and Tunisia.

Data analysed showed that the level of engagement/participation of African WTO Members in submission of proposals in the CTS ranked below Asia Pacific, Latin America and Caribbean, Europe, and North America and was only better than the Middle East with one proposal. This was a low level of engagement/participation with wide scope for improvement.

---

32 Council for Trade in Services, S/C/W/1 to 329.

33 In 1995 trade in commercial services (exports and imports) as a percentage of GDP for Africa was 11.8%. This increased to 12.9% in 2001 and to 13.5% in 2010. Source: WTO estimates and IMF, WEO database for GDP.

Explanations for the low level of participation (submission of proposals) correspond to the same factors with regard to the low level of statements made.

The priority focus of proposals/submissions by African WTO Members in the CTS related mainly to mandatory certification work on individual schedules of commitments and acceptance of protocols on basic telecommunications and/or financial services. In addition, proposals were tabled on GATS Article II MFN exemptions (South Africa and Morocco). South Africa and Morocco are the two African WTO Members actively engaged in trade in services on the Continent, but also with countries outside Africa.[34] It is also notable that Morocco is the only African country that has concluded an FTA with a services component.[35] These two African WTO Members have demonstrated their real commercial interests in the services sector in the multilateral trading system as reflected in their level of substantive participation/engagement in the CTS compared to other African WTO Members.

(c) *Notifications Pursuant to GATS Articles III.3; V.7; and, XXII*

(i) Notification Requirements are the Foundation for GATT/WTO Transparency Obligations

Article III: 3 of the GATS requires Members to notify to the CTS the introduction of any new laws or any changes to existing laws, regulations or administrative guidelines which significantly affect trade in services covered by its specific commitments under the GATS. As of mid-June 2010, 404 notifications had been received from 53 Members (counting European Union Members individually).[36] Six African Members (or 14.2 per cent) had notified under this provision since 1995. These were Central African Republic, Egypt, Madagascar, Niger, Nigeria, and, Senegal. This number of notified laws and regulations was low compared to those notified by Members from other regions and ranged between 1 and 4. This was an added indicator of the low level of engagement by Africa in regular work on trade in services. It was also indicative of the low level of services regulation in African countries and of specific commitments bound.

Article V: 7 (a) of the GATS requires any Member which is party to an economic integration agreement to notify such agreement to the Council. In the period reviewed, ninety-two (92) such notifications had been made. One notification was made by Morocco, which was the only African Member that had concluded an FTA with a services component. In general, African countries have shied away from participating in FTAs involving services.

Article VII: 4 of GATS requires each Member to inform the CTS of its existing recognition measures within 12 months from the date on which the WTO Agreement takes effect

[34] According to the 2010, International Trade Statistics, Morocco is ranked 26th with a 0.5 % share in world services exports while and South Africa is ranked 28th with a 0.5 % share in world services exporters., International Trade Statistics, 2010.

[35] US-Morocco, Free Trade Agreement and Economic Integration Agreement.

[36] Council for Trade in Services, *Overview of Notifications made under relevant GATS provisions, Informal Note by WTO Secretariat*, 21 June 2010, JOB(09)/10/Rev.2.

for it. As of June 2010, 50 notifications had been made to the CTS from 35 Members, counting EU members individually.[37] The data showed no African country had notified under this provision. This in part is a reflection of the low state of conclusion of mutual recognition agreements amongst African countries, but also with other WTO Members.

The level of engagement/participation in WTO regular work on services is a clear weak link for Africa at the WTO. Although the domestic services sector of a number of African economies is relatively open, Africa's participation in international trade in services is low and data is unreliable. Specialized expertise on the GATS is still being developed in a number of African WTO Members and has not attained a critical mass that can make a decisive contribution to influence the work of the CTS. The problem is compounded by weak coordination between government line Ministries, services regulators and the Geneva frontline. The focus of African delegations, reflecting *perceived* priority areas of interest, has tilted more towards development, S&D and selected Goods issues including agriculture. General statements by African Members in the area of services broadly refer to "natural advantages/competitiveness" in services sectors such as tourism and mode 4.

6. The Council for TRIPS

The Agreement on Trade-Related Aspects of Intellectual Property Rights (TRIPS Agreement), lays down minimum standards for the protection of intellectual property as well as the procedures and remedies for their enforcement. It establishes a mechanism for consultations and surveillance at the international level – the Council for TRIPS – to ensure compliance with these standards by Members at the national level. The TRIPS Council also undertakes specific tasks assigned to it by the General Council. (Annex 1 C of the WTO Agreement).

The level of participation/engagement of African WTO Members in the TRIPS Council was analysed and compared to Members from other regions with regard to the following indices:

- Oral statements made;
- Written submissions/proposals; and,
- Notification count.

(a) *Oral Statements in the Council for TRIPS*[38]

In the period 1995–2010, a total of 6232 statements were made in the TRIPS Council; disaggregated as in figure 84. African WTO Members made a total of 430 statements, or 6.8 per cent of the grand total number of statements made. These statements were made by 27 (or 64 per cent) of African WTO Members, as in figure 85.

---

[37] Ibid.

[38] Minutes of the Council for TRIPS, IP/C/M/1 to 64.

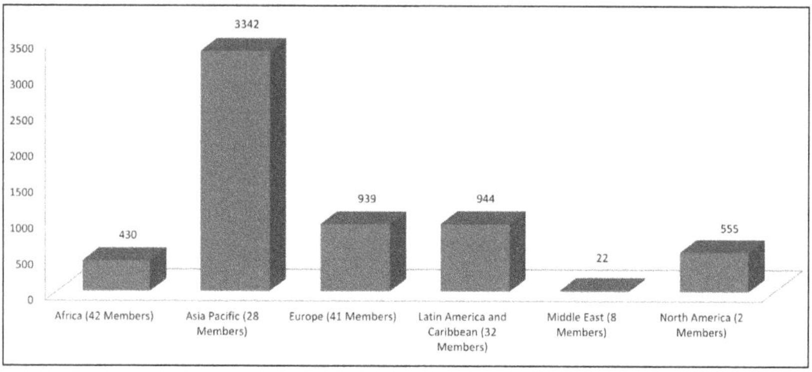

Figure 84. Statements in the TRIPS Council (1995–2010).

Most statements by African Members were made by Egypt (104), Kenya (67), Mauritius (38), South Africa (38) and to a lesser extent by Zambia (22), Zimbabwe (21), Nigeria (20), Uganda (19); and, Angola (18).

Although only 27 African WTO Members or 64 per cent intervened with oral statements, the substantive engagement was intensive and robust. They focused on specific areas in the regular work on TRIPS. In the TRIPS Council, several African Members intervened in the context of the review of their TRIPS implementing legislation (either to introduce or explain legislation or to respond to questions posed by other Members).[39] There was robust African participation in the review of Articles 23 and 24 concerning *geographical indications* (Morocco, Mauritius, Kenya, Egypt); *E-commerce* (Egypt); *transfer of technology* (Zambia, Senegal, LDC Group); *technical assistance and capacity building* (Zambia, Djibouti, LDC Group, African Group); and the *extension of transition period for LDCs* (Senegal, Zambia, LDC Group). They also intervened in the *review of Article 27.3(B) of the TRIPS Agreements*, addressing issues such as bio-piracy, traditional knowledge and folklore, patenting of life forms, and the overall relationship between the TRIPS Agreement and the Convention on Biological Diversity (African Group, ACP Group, LDC Group, Kenya, Egypt, and South Africa). Attracting intensive engagement also were the areas of *non-violation and situation complaints* (Nigeria, Egypt); *observer status*, including of regional IP bodies in Africa (Egypt, African Group) and, *priority needs for technical assistance and financial assistance for LDCs* pursuant to the November 2005 Decision of the TRIPS Council.[40] (Sierra Leone, Uganda, Rwanda, Tanzania).

The pattern in the subject-areas of intervention by African countries highlighted a mixture of national, development, social and morality concerns(TRIPS and Public Health

[39] These countries included Botswana, Cameroon, Congo, Cote d'Ivoire, Egypt, Ghana, Kenya, Mauritius, Morocco, Namibia, Nigeria, Senegal (until it notified the Council that it had fallen to LDC status), South Africa, Swaziland, Tunisia and Zimbabwe. It is observed that African WTO Member LDCs are not required to apply the provisions of the TRIPS Agreement other than Articles 3, 4, 5 until 1 July 2013. As of June 2013, this period was extended by the TRIPS Council to 1 July 2021.

[40] Extension of the Transition Period under Article 66.1 for Least-Developed Country Members, Decision of the Council for TRIPS of 29 November 2005, in document IP/C/40.

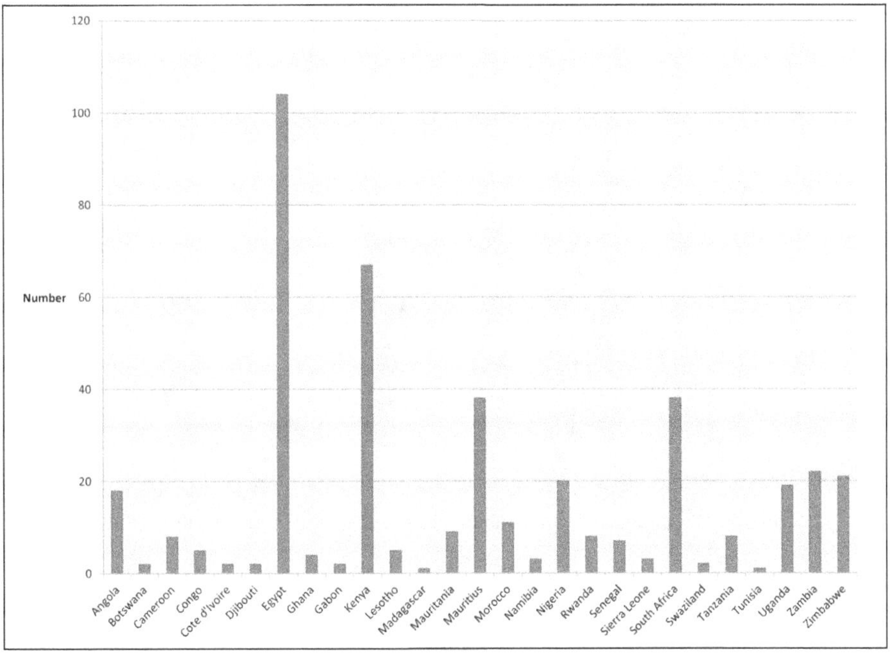

Figure 85. Individual African Statements in the TRIPS Council (1995–2010).

and patenting of life forms), potential commercial interests (e-commerce, geographical indications, traditional knowledge and folklore), technical capacity constraints (transfer of technology, technical assistance and capacity building, extension of transitional period for LDCs, priority needs assessment for LDCs) and systemic interests and coherence concerns (non-violation and situation complaints; and, the relationship between the TRIPS Agreement and the Convention on Biological Diversity).

Why was there such a relatively high level of African WTO Member engagement in the TRIPS Council? Observation of African WTO Members in the TRIPS Council and interviews of several African delegates clearly indicated a deep policy fascination with the substance and the process of engagement on intellectual property negotiations amongst WTO Members. This high level of "excited policy engagement" was attributed to several factors. A primary reason was the support provided by civil society groups in the beginning of substantive work on TRIPS for African delegations. At the beginning, the content of this support from civil society was for African delegations to challenge and resist IP consideration in WTO regular work. This situation however changed as understanding was improved for African delegations and an African Ambassador was appointed to chair the TRIPS Council.[41] As knowledge improved, specialized capacity developed, and African delegations begun to associate themselves with the stability of the system, and utilization of its benefits, the level of engagement/participation markedly improved.

41 Ambassador Guwa Chidyausiku of Zimbabwe.

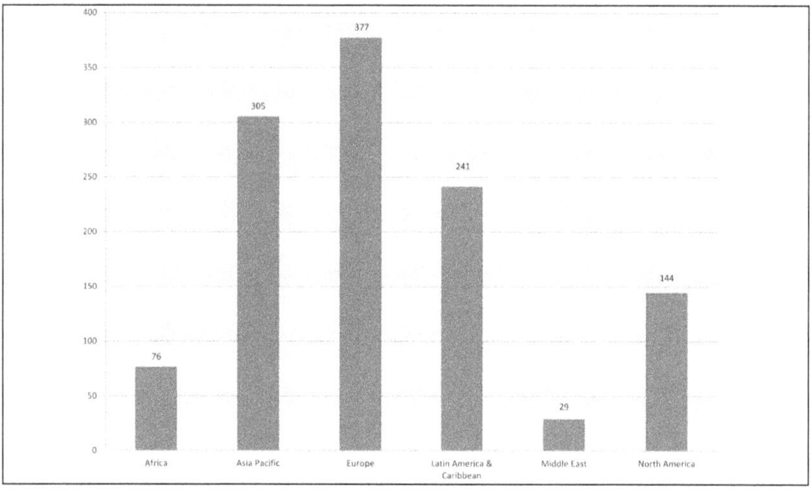

Figure 86. Proposals and other submissions to the TRIPS Council (1995–2010).

(b) *Council for TRIPS: Written Proposals/Submissions*[42]

Figure 86 shows the number of written proposals/submissions in the TRIPS Council in the period 1995–2010 by individual Members and groups in different regions. Over the 15 year period, proposals/submissions by individual African WTO Members, including those in their group framework, totalled 76. In contrast to their relatively high percentage of statements in the TRIPS Council, the number of written proposals/submissions made was low *per se* and low in relation to proposals/submissions by other regions. The number of African proposals/submissions was 76 (or 6.4 per cent) of the total number of proposals/submissions to the TRIPS Council). These proposals were made by 21 (or 50%) of African Members (figure 87); a slightly lower percentage of African Members that intervened in the TRIPS Council. Most of these written submissions were made by Egypt (10); Morocco (10) and, Zambia (6). Proposals and submissions from other African WTO Members ranged between one and three.

In relation to proposals/submissions from other regions, African WTO Members' share of written proposals/submissions in the TRIPS Council was low compared to 377 from European Members; 305 from Asia Pacific Members; 241 from Latin America and Caribbean Members; 144 from North America; and only higher than proposals from Members in the Middle East region at 29 proposals.

Most submissions were responses to questions posed to African WTO Members in the context of the review of TRIPS implementation legislation. Other areas where African WTO Members submitted papers and proposals were (i) review of Article 27.3 (b) of the TRIPS Agreement (African Group, Morocco, South Africa, Zambia, Zimbabwe, Tanzania, Uganda); (ii) non-violation complaints (Egypt, Kenya); (iii) technology transfer (Zambia,

[42] Council for TRIPS, IP/C/W/1 to 553.

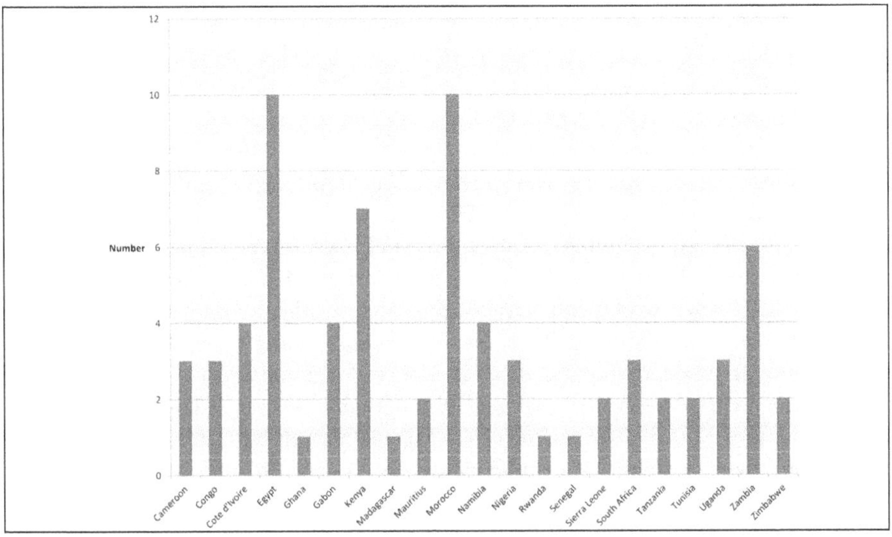

Figure 87. Individual African proposals/submissions to the TRIPS Council (1995–2010).

LDC Group); (iv) geographical indications (Egypt, Mauritius, Nigeria, Kenya); and, (v) priority needs for technical and financial co-operation (Sierra Leone, Uganda, Tanzania, Rwanda). The subject-diversity of proposals/submissions from African WTO Members was limited in comparison to those from Members from other regions (with the exception of the Middle East) on a wider range of subjects discussed in the TRIPS Council.

On the agenda of the TRIPS Council, the total number of submissions and proposals from developed Members was higher. In addition to proposals, which any Member could make, developed Members were required by the TRIPS Council to make specific submissions in the following areas: (i) annual reports on actions taken or planned in pursuance of developed Member commitments under Article 66.2 of the TRIPS Agreement to promote and encourage the transfer of technology to least-developed countries; and, (ii) reports on technical co-operation. In addition, several developed countries actively participated in reviews of legislation of Members by posing questions to Members under review. Developed Members were also active in the China transitional review mechanism exercise, where they posed questions to China.[43] Furthermore, developed Members have had the incentive for increased proposals and submissions because of strong commercial and systemic interest.

The United States and Europe placed the item of TRIPS on the agenda of the Uruguay Round negotitions. At origin for these Members, was a strong commercial/industry-driven agenda. The incentive therefore existed and as a consequence their engagement has been high and constant. To the contrary, developing Members, at the beginning, challenged and resisted TRIPS in the WTO. This was evident for African WTO Members.

[43] United States, Canada, Japan, Australia, New Zealand, EU, Norway, and, Switzerland.

However, the data gathered and analyzed and interviews strongly suggest that the engagement of African WTO Members, starting from a low base, has steadily increased. With greater knowledge from capacity building and support from civil society and non-WTO multilateral institutions (WIPO, UNCTAD, World Bank) and regional institutions (OAPI), the engagement of African Members has progressively evolved from low to higher levels. Greater knowledge has improved the understanding of African WTO Members of opportunities and potential benefits in the TRIPS Agreement.

In summary therefore, limited understanding and low levels of participation have progressively changed. There are useful lessons from African Members' participation in the TRIPS Council regular work that could be applicable to other areas. These lessons, consistent with earlier recommendations, revolve around "greater openess to engagement in the rules-based system"; targetted, specialized training and capacity building; better use by African WTO Members of available resources on offer in multilateral and regional instititions; and, more focused and driven engagement on the part of African delegates.

There are two key factors that explain why Africa's engagement in the area of TRIPS regular work became reinforced. First, was the analytic support that better connected, for Africa, the provisions of the TRIPS Agreement on the one hand, with their domestic interest, on the other. This was exemplified by issues such as biodiversity, geographical indications, patenting of life forms etc. Second, the opportunities in the TRIPS Agreement and the flexibility it provided for addressing the catastrophic public health crisis in Africa. In this latter, negotiations provided impetus to regular work. This observation reinforces one of the arguments in this study that higher levels of negotiations have potential to boost African engagement and participation in the WTO, including in regular work. In otherwords, there can be positive association between the levels of engagement/participation in regular committee work and negotiations through maximazing available resources allocated.

(c) *Notifications Pursuant to the TRIPS Agreement*

The TRIPS Agreement contains a number of notification obligations. Some required notification obligations are applicable at the time when a Member is obliged to start applying a provision of the TRIPS Agreement. Others are required when a Member wishes to avail itself of opportunities provided in the Agreement that relate to substantive obligations. There are also notifications that are not regulated by the TRIPS Agreement. These are as a result of subsequent decisions of the TRIPS Council on particular matters. This section analysed the level of participation/engagement of African Members in fulfilling notification obligations with regard to laws and regulations under Article 63.2 of the TRIPS Agreement, which applies to all WTO Members except LDCs.

Initial notifications for developed countries were due from 1997 and developing countries from 2001. The overall status of initial notifications by developed and developing country Members is considered acceptable. In the period reviewed, all Members required to notify, with the exception of St. Kitts and Nevis, had fulfilled their obligations by notifying all or part of their implementing legislation.[44] Of the 42 African Members:

[44] Council for TRIPS, *Timeliness and Completeness of Notifications and Other Information Flows, Note by the Secretariat*, IP/C/W/543, 22 October 2009.

- Sixteen (16) non-LDC African WTO Members submitted an initial notification (Botswana, Cameroon, Congo, Cote d'Ivoire, Egypt, Gabon, Ghana, Kenya, Mauritius, Morocco, Namibia, Nigeria, South Africa, Swaziland, Tunisia and Zimbabwe), of which nine submitted responses to the checklist on enforcement. Two had not submitted an initial notification. (Angola and Cape Verde)
- 24 African WTO Members are LDCs required to comply with this obligation from 1 July 2013 for all other IP areas and I January 2016 for pharmaceutical products.
  - However, in line with the encouragement to provide advance notifications, six (6) African WTO LDCs' Members had submitted initial notifications. These were: Burkina Faso, Burundi, Chad, Senegal, Uganda and Zambia.
- Cape Verde, a recently acceded Member, was required to notify under the TRIPS Agreement in accordance with its Protocol of Accession. The time period established for Cape Verde was similar to that established for LDCs – 1 July 2013; and 1 January 2016 for pharmaceutical products[45] (although Cape Verde has now graduated from LDC status).

The facts demonstrate a progressively high level of engagement by African WTO Members (both LDCs and non-LDCs) at over 50 per cent. Participation by African WTO Members in TRIPS regular work is acceptable and has progressively increased because of a combination of targeted and specific capacity building and training, support from multilateral, regional institutions and civil society, the link between regular work and negotiations and the link by African WTO Members of the use of the TRIPS Agreement to address TRIPS-related domestic problems (such as developing domestic manufacturing capacities e.g. for pharmaceutical products, and drawing other benefits).

7. The Committee on Trade and Development

The Committee on Trade and Development (CTD) is mandated to:

- serve as a focal point for consideration and coordination of work on development in the WTO and its relationship to development-related activities in other multilateral agencies;
- keep under continuous review the participation of developing country Members in the multilateral trading system and consider measures and initiatives to assist developing country Members, and in particular the least-developed country Members, in the expansion of their trade and investment opportunities, including support for their measures of trade liberalization;
- review periodically, in consultation as appropriate with the relevant bodies of the WTO, the application of special provisions in the Multilateral Trade Agreements and related Ministerial Decisions in favour of developing country Members, and in particular least-developed country Members, and report to the General Council for appropriate action; and,
- consider any questions which may arise with regard to either the application or the use of special provisions in the Multilateral Trade Agreements and related Ministerial Decisions in favour of developing country Members and report to the General Council for appropriate action.[46]

---

45 Protocol of Accession of Cape Verde, WT/L/715, and, paragraph 246 of the Cape Verde's Working Party Report WT/ACC/CPV/30.

46 WTO Committee on Trade and Development, Decision of the General Council on 31 January 1995, WT/L/46.

The level of participation/engagement of African WTO Members in the CTD is analysed and compared to Members from other regions, with regard to:

- oral statements and,
- written submissions/proposals.

(a) *Oral Statements in the CTD*[47]

Figure 88, shows the number of individual statements in the CTD by Members in different regions in the period 1995–2010.

Trade and Development issues are of priority interest for African WTO Members. They made a total of 776 statements. The number of statements by African WTO Members was high, that is, 21 per cent of the total number of statements in the CTD. Thirty-five (35) or 83 per cent of individual African Members had made statements in the CTD. (Figure 89).

The area of trade and development was the highest level of participatory engagement by African WTO Members in the three areas of core WTO work namely: regular work; negotiating engagement; and, dispute settlement. The subject area of intervention by African Members in the CTD included technical assistance and capacity building, review of the results of the Uruguay Round on developing countries and least-developed countries, credit for autonomous liberalization and measures and initiatives to assist and expand trade and investment opportunities in developing countries and least-developed countries. Interventions also reviewed the participation of developing countries in the multilateral trading system and included contributions to the preparation and follow-up to a High Level Meeting on Least-developed Countries. Other areas where African Members intervened were E-commerce, trade facilitation, commodities, concerns and problems of small economies, preferential tariff treatment for LDCs, and, duty free quota free market access for LDCs. The Sub-Committee on LDCs is a subsidiary body of the CTD, accounting for the high levels of African Members engagement on issues of trade and development.

Disaggregated data showed that the highest numbers of interventions in the CTD were made by: United States (364); European Union (313); India (209); Egypt (180), and, Switzerland (137). Other Members with relatively high number of interventions by region were: **Africa** (see figure 92) (Kenya (84), Morocco (78), Zambia (57, Mauritius (46)); **Europe** (Switzerland (137), Norway (80)); **Latin America and Caribbean** (Brazil (95), Cuba (64), Venezuela (55), Mexico (52), Barbados (49)); **Asia Pacific** (Japan (106), Pakistan (97), China (96), Bangladesh (83)); **North America** (Canada (177). Statements by Members in the **Middle East** were low, ranging between 0–10.

However, notwithstanding the very high level of African participation in the CTD, Africa had the highest number of Members in its region, compared to those in other regions, which had not made individual oral statements in the CTD, at 17%. In other words, scope exists for maximizing participation. Data for the other regions showed that

[47] Minutes of the Committee on Trade and Development, WT/COMTD/1 to 80.

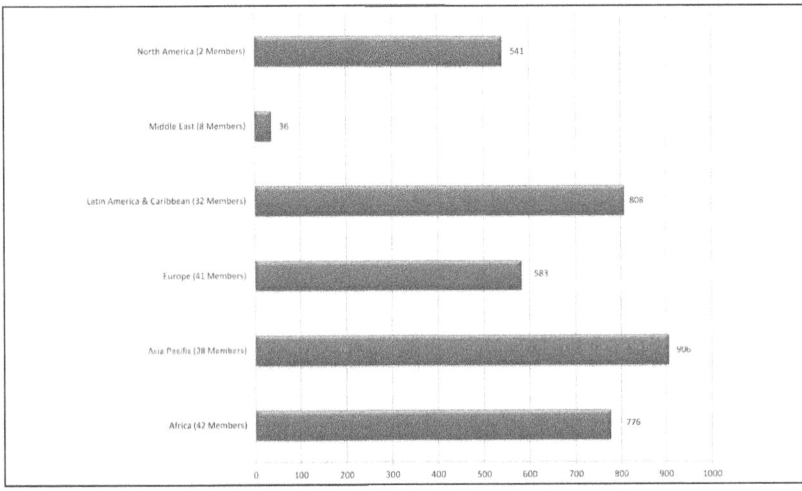

Figure 88. Statements in the CTD (1995–2010).

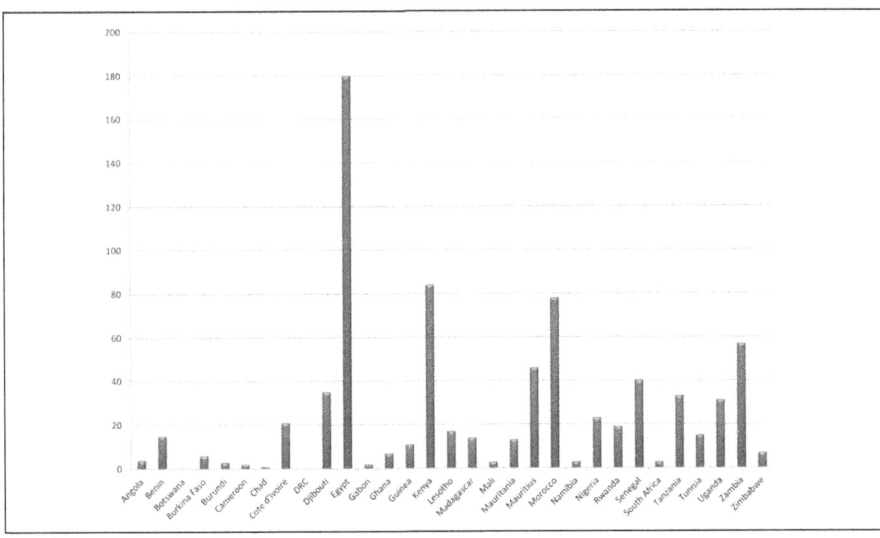

Figure 89. Statements by African members in the CTD (1995–2010).

fewer Members in those regions had not intervened in the CTD: 9% for Latin America & Caribbean; 7.3% for Europe, 7.1 % for Asia Pacific.[48]

48 These Members were: **Africa:** Botswana, Cape Verde, Central African Republic, Congo, D.R. Congo, Mozambique, and Swaziland. **Europe:** Albania, F.Y.R. Macedonia, Ukraine. **Latin America and Caribbean:** Grenada, St. Vincent & the Grenadines, Suriname. **Asia Pacific:** Brunei Darussalam (no individual statements, but has spoken for ASEAN), Macao China.

Intervention by African Members in the CTD was also at the group level, although at a lower level, compared to group activity in the area of negotiating engagement. The groups that intervened in the CTD to which African WTO Members were affiliated included: the Informal Group of Developing Countries (IGDC); African Caribbean and Pacific Group (ACP), the African Group; the WTO Consultative Group on Least-developed Countries, and the WTO Arab Group.[49] In other words, African Members had most intervened individually in the area of trade and development. One of the evident findings was that when African participation in regular work was compared to the negotiations, coalitional behaviour was more manifest in the latter than the former where individual behaviour was evident. In other words, the *"form of participatory behaviour"* was more individual in regular work in relation to more manifest coalitional behaviour in negotiations. This was an interesting finding explaining particular aspects of the behaviour of African Members in the WTO and suggesting how they would be expected to behave in regular WTO work settings as opposed to the negotiating arena. Part of the explanation is that the nature and substance of work although linked, are "different". Work in regular WTO bodies involves the promotion of very specific interests within the context of already established rules in the area of the Agreement being administered by a Committee. Differently, in "negotiations", the dynamics for bargaining are different, strongly linked to the "balance of trade and economic power" and where coalitions are more necessary than usual for negotiating gains.

(b) *CTD: Written Proposals/Submissions*[50]

Figure 90 shows the number of formal written proposals and submissions by Members in different regions to the CTD in the period 1995–2010.

Data shows that overall; the number of written proposals/submissions to the CTD was low, in comparison to the number of proposals/submissions submitted in other WTO Bodies. African countries had a total of 22 proposals/submissions (or 36 per cent) of the total number of proposals/submissions made to the CTD. Although this is the highest number compared to proposals/submissions from the other regions, it was a low proportion in relation to the number of oral statements made; Africa's significant membership share and the high priority accorded to development issues. Eleven (11) African WTO Members accounted for the 22 submissions/proposals. These were: Egypt, Kenya, Lesotho, Mauritius, Morocco, Namibia, South Africa, Tanzania, Uganda, Zambia, and, Zimbabwe. The proposals by African WTO Members spanned a number of areas such as E-commerce; special and differential treatment; concerns and problems of small economies; market access for least-developed countries, commodities, technology transfer, reclaiming development in the Doha Round negotiations; and, notification of FTAs pursuant to the Enabling Clause and/or GATT Article XXIV.

---

[49] Other groups that had intervened in the CTD were ASEAN and the Gulf Co-operation Council (GCC). The Group of Small and Vulnerable Economies (SVEs Group) has intervened on a number of occasions in the meetings of the CTD in dedicated session.

[50] Committee on Trade and Development, WT/COMTD/1 to 176; WT/COMTD 1 to 80.

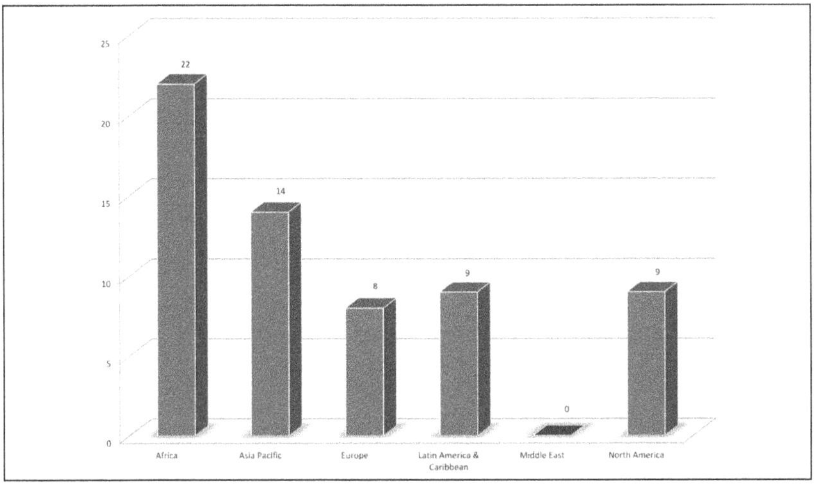

Figure 90. Papers and proposals submitted to CTD (1995–2010).

Participation in Subsidiary Bodies of the Council for Trade in Goods

8. The Committee on Agriculture

The Agreement on Agriculture established a programme for the gradual reform of agricultural trade aimed at establishing a fair and market oriented agricultural trading system. This included substantial progressive reductions in agricultural support and protection, resulting in correcting and preventing restrictions and distortions in world agricultural markets. The Committee on Agriculture (CoA) is charged with overseeing the implementation of the Agreement and related commitments. It affords Members the opportunity of consulting on any matter relating to the implementation of the provisions of the Agreement.[51]

Regular WTO work in the area of agriculture is one to which African WTO Members have attached priority. Traditionally, agriculture has constituted the backbone of most African economies. It is the largest contributor to GNI and the biggest source of foreign exchange. The agricultural sector is the main generator of savings and tax revenue in several African countries. In addition, agriculture plays an important role in achieving the poverty targets of the MDGs in Africa with nearly 80% of the population living in rural areas of which 70% are dependent on food production through farming or livestock keeping for most of their livelihood. African exports have been directly affected by agricultural policies of other Members particularly trade distorting domestic support

[51] WTO Committee on Agriculture, Decision of the General Council, 31 January 1995, WT/L/43. Upon adoption of the Terms of Reference, the General Council took note of the accompanying statement or understanding referred to in paragraph 40 of the Report of the Preparatory Committee contained in document PC/R.

measures, export subsidies, and other market access limiting policies (including SPS measures), with specific impacts on the livelihood and well-being of African agricultural exporters. For instance, the Cotton-Four countries (Benin, Chad, Burkina Faso, and, Mali) tabled a proposal on cotton in the Doha negotiations for market access improvement and to address the situation of trade distorting domestic support in the cotton sector. Agriculture is therefore an area of WTO regular work where their specific trade interests have been affected and market realities have strongly influenced the engagement of African WTO Members.

Against this background, the level of engagement/ participation of African WTO Members in the CoA was analysed and compared to Members from other regions with regard to the following indices:

- Oral statements;
- Written submissions/proposals; and,
- Notification compliance.

(a) *Oral Statements in the CoA (1995–2010)*[52]

Figure 91 shows the distribution of oral statements in the CoA by Members in different regions in the period 1995–2010.

In spite of the priority attached to this area of regular work, African Members' oral interventions in the CoA were paradoxically low at 170 (or 3 per cent) of the total number of statements in the CoA. Their statements were also low *per se* as a proportion of statements by Members from other regions, with the exception of the Middle East. Twelve African Members (or 28 per cent) accounted for these statements. These were: Côte d'Ivoire (1); Egypt (32); Kenya (8); Mauritius (8); Morocco (18); Namibia (4); Nigeria (4); South Africa (55); Swaziland (1); Tanzania (1); Tunisia (34); Zambia (2); Zimbabwe (2). African WTO Members' individual statements were also low in relation to individual statements by Members in other regions. In rank order, the highest numbers of statements in the CoA in the period reviewed were made by the US (811); Australia (756); New Zealand (658); Canada (562); EC (552); Argentina (296); Japan (248); Brazil (117); Thailand (106) and, Switzerland (105). These countries have strong offensive and defensive interests in the area of agriculture, either as leading agricultural exporters or as net food importing countries.

Nonetheless, a point that could be highlighted is that although the level of African participation in the CoA was low, as measured by the oral statement count, this was mitigated by the high level of activity in the area of cotton in the Doha agriculture negotiations. Yet, even this higher level of activity in line with the Doha agriculture negotiations needs to be qualified by the fact that only four African Members (Benin, Burkina Faso, Chad and Mali) have been actively engaged, although a total of 36 African WTO Members produce and trade cotton and were present at the 2004 Cotonou African Regional Workshop on Cotton that produced the basis for the Cotton mandate in the 1 August 2004 General Council Framework Decision. The other African Members, including cotton producers, have not so engaged. It is also interesting that the high level of Cotton-Four

[52] Summary Records of the Meetings of the Committee on Agriculture, G/AG/R/1-60.

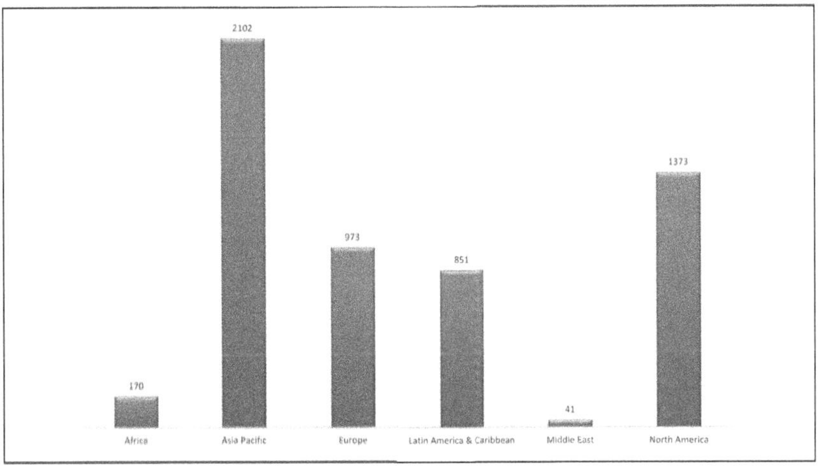

Figure 91. Statements in the CoA (1995–2010).

engagement has been supported by civil society and other multilateral institutions. This situation is similar to other identified areas where African participation has been higher than usual, with the support of think tanks, civil society and multilateral institutions. It strongly reinforces the recommendation that greater targeted African engagement with such institutions has positive knock on effects for increasing their level of participation in various areas of WTO work. This recommendation will need to be actively followed-up by African WTO Members.

Content analysis of the proposals showed that African WTO Members had intervened in the CoA in the context of the discussions of the implementation of the Marrakesh Decision on Net Food Importing Developing Countries and the related questions of food aid. They had also intervened under the Committee's standing agenda item, "Matters related to the Implementation of Commitments under the Reform Programme", in Article 18.6 of the Agreement on Agriculture. In this regard, they have responded to questions put to them about agricultural policies that they had initiated, with potential impacts on market access for other Members.[53] In addition, they have supported concerns raised by other Members with a potential impact on their agricultural exports.[54] A few African Members had been active in the review process of agricultural notifications in the CoA. With the exception of South Africa and Mauritius, the participation of African Members that had intervened, had been in the context of review of their own individual notifica-

[53] **Egypt**: Quantitative Restrictions on Poultry and Fowls; Tariff applied to Dairy Products; Duty Rates and Tariff Quota Implementation in Egypt; Restrictions on beef imports; Tariff rates and ban on poultry. **Kenya**: Import Ban on Dairy Products; Domestic production requirements for maize seed; **Tunisia**: Applied Tariff Rates; Establishment of tariff quotas under new tariff regime and new measures restricting beef imports; **Nigeria**: Import prohibition on certain agricultural products and use of reference prices for customs valuation.

[54] Support (by South Africa) for the complaint by Chile about a restriction on *Canned Peaches in the European Communities.*

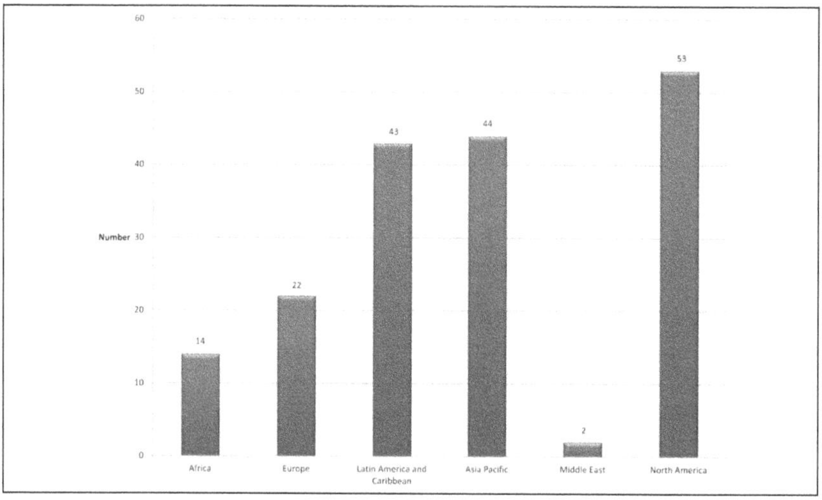

Figure 92. Submissions to the Committee on Agriculture (1995–2010).

tions, and not notifications made by other Members. African participation in the review process of notifications was low mainly because several of them had not frequently complied with their notification obligations. African Members intervened in the CoA to support requests for observer status of organisations to which they belonged, e.g. supporting observership of the ACP. African Members intervened also to inform Members of agricultural-related activities in which they had been involved.

(b) *CoA: Written Proposals/Submissions (1995–2010)*[55]

Figure 92 shows the distribution of written proposals/submissions to the CoA by Members in different regions in the period 1995–2010.

African WTO Members' submissions to the CoA was low at 14 (or 7.8 per cent) of the total number of all written proposals/submissions, only better than the Middle East with two submissions, but lower that North America with 53 submissions, Asia Pacific with 44 submissions and Latin America and Caribbean with 43 submissions. Ten African WTO Members (or 23.8 per cent) of the 42 African Members submitted these proposals. These were Côte d'Ivoire, Egypt, Kenya, Madagascar, Mauritius, Morocco, Senegal, South Africa, Tunisia and Zimbabwe. The number of individual proposals submitted by these countries was very low, on average, 1 Egypt submitted the highest number of submissions at four. The number of proposals was low in contrast to the number of submissions by Members in other regions, with the exception of the Middle East. The United States tabled the most written proposals/submissions at 36, followed by the EU (18) and Canada (17). Other countries with relatively "high" number of submissions included: Argentina (7); New Zealand (7); Brazil (6), Australia (6), India (6); and, Korea (6).

[55] Committee on Agriculture, G/AG/W/1 to 80.

Almost all submissions from African WTO Members to the CoA were in relation to the concerns of Net Food Importing Developing Countries (NFIDCs), including a proposal to create a revolving fund for NFIDCs. Almost all African WTO Members are NFDICs. By contrast the written proposals/submissions by Members from other regions (with the exception of the Middle East) related to dispute settlement consultations or other concerns in agriculture. One of the striking observations in data gathering in the CoA is the tight linkage of the data content to dispute settlement. In addition, proposals from Members in the other regions were made on the three pillars of the Agriculture Agreement, notification matters, initiation of the use of the Special Safeguard (SSG) and in the context of the China Transitional Review Mechanism (TRM).

(c) *Notification Count*[56]

A key function of the CoA is to review progress in the implementation of commitments negotiated under the Uruguay Round reform programme in accordance with the relevant provisions of Article 18 of the Agreement. Pursuant to Article 16:2, the CoA is required to monitor, as appropriate, the follow-up to the Marrakesh Ministerial Decision on Measures Concerning the Possible Negative Effects of the Reform Programme on Least-Developed and Net Food-Importing Developing Countries – the NFIDC Decision. This review process is undertaken on the basis of notifications submitted by Members in the areas of market access, domestic support, and export subsidies and under the provisions of the Agreement relating to export prohibitions and restrictions.

A summary overview of notification requirements under the AoA is provided in Annex IX. This section analyses African Members' level of compliance with regular notification obligations covering domestic support and export subsidies, relative to Members in other regions, during the period 1995–2009.

(i) Domestic Support Notifications (Outstanding)[57] for the 1995–2004 Implementation Years

Figure 93 shows the distribution of *outstanding* domestic support – DS: 1 notifications in the period 1995–2004.

African WTO Members' level of outstanding (yet to be notified) domestic support notifications at 181 was the highest (poorest), in comparison to 87 outstanding notifications from Members in the Latin America and Caribbean region; 52 outstanding notifications from those in the Asia Pacific region; 13 outstanding notifications from Members in Europe; 11 outstanding notifications from Members in the Middle East region and no outstanding notification from Members in the North America region.

---

56 Committee on Agriculture, *Compliance with Notification Obligations, Note by the Secretariat*, G/AG/GEN/86/Rev.4, 17 November 2010.

57 As in the records of the WTO Secretariat, required notifications by Members are recorded and presented as "outstanding" (that is as the balance of) required notifications still to be submitted by a Member for a defined period. In other words, the list of required notifications is presented in a negative and not a positive list form.

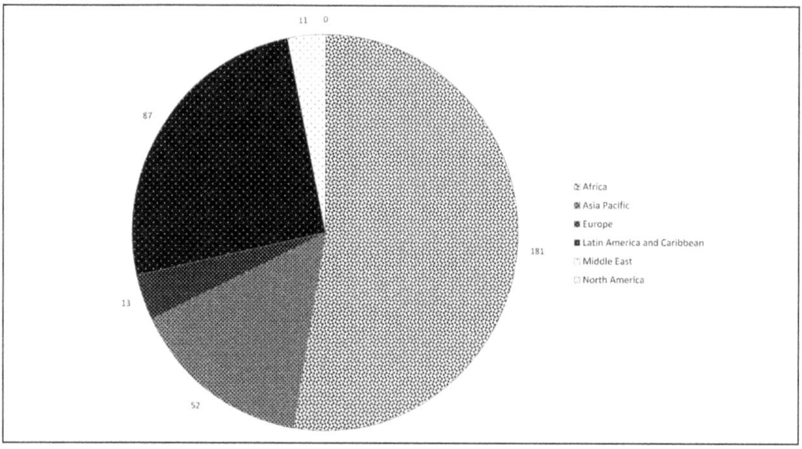

Figure 93. Outstanding DS:1 notifications (1995–2004).

Disaggregated data further showed that, at 78.6 per cent of its membership, Africa had the highest number of Members in its region that had *not* complied with their domestic support notification obligations, in the period 1995–2004. This was compared to no outstanding notifications for the North America region; 10 per cent for Europe; 32 per cent for Asia Pacific; 37.5 per cent for the Middle East, and, 40.7 per cent for the Latin America and Caribbean.

Burkina Faso, Burundi, Gabon, Namibia, Nigeria, South Africa, Tunisia and Uganda had no outstanding domestic support notifications in the period 1995–2004. Some of the African WTO Members that had not submitted domestic support notifications as required in the period 1995–2004 included, Central African Republic, Cote d'Ivoire, Djibouti, Ghana, Guinea, Guinea Bissau, Mauritania, Mauritius, Mozambique, Senegal, Sierra Leone, Swaziland, Tanzania and Togo.

One of the findings in this study is that effective and robust membership is undermined by obligations and commitments not implemented. Un-implemented obligations render a Member vulnerable and, weakens its engagement/participation to *nominalism.* The level of engagement/participation not only includes acts of commission, but also acts of omission.

(ii) Export Subsidies Notifications (Outstanding) for the 1995–2004

Figure 94 shows the distribution of outstanding Export Subsidies – ES: 1 notifications in the period 1995–2004.

African WTO Members' rate of compliance with export subsidy notifications at 244 notifications *outstanding* was highest (poorest), in comparison to 84 outstanding notifications from Members in the Latin America and Caribbean region; 52 outstanding notifications from those in the Asia Pacific region; 24 outstanding notifications from Members in Europe; 16 outstanding notifications from Members in the Middle East region and no outstanding notification from Members in the North America region.

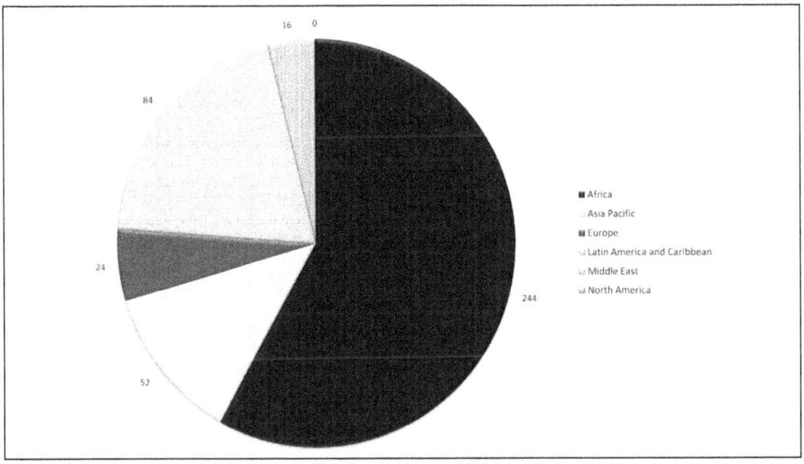

Figure 94. Outstanding ES:1 notifications (1995–2004).

Disaggregated data further showed that, at 88.1 per cent of its membership, Africa had the highest number of Members in its region that had *not* complied with their export subsidy notification obligations, in the period 1995–2004. This compared to no outstanding notifications for North America; 12.2 per cent for Europe; 32 per cent for Asia Pacific region; 37.5 per cent for the Middle East, and, 40.7 per cent for Latin America and Caribbean.

Botswana, Burkina Faso, Burundi, Gabon, Malawi, Namibia, Nigeria, South Africa and Uganda had no outstanding export subsidy notifications in the period 1995–2004. African WTO Members that had not submit export subsidy notifications as required, in the period 1995–2004, included Central African Republic, Cote d'Ivoire, Djibouti, Guinea, Guinea Bissau, Mali, Mauritania, Mauritius, Mozambique, Senegal, Sierra Leone, Swaziland, Tanzania and Togo.

(iii) Domestic Support Notifications (Outstanding): 2005–2009 Implementation Years

Figure 95 shows the distribution of outstanding Domestic Support – DS: 1 notifications, in the period 2005–2009 (period within the Doha negotiations).

With 111 *outstanding* notifications, African WTO Members' level of *compliance with* domestic support notifications for the period 2005–2009 was the poorest, in comparison to 90 outstanding notifications from Members in the Latin America and Caribbean region, 71 outstanding notifications from those in the Asia Pacific region, 40 outstanding notifications from Members in Europe, 18 outstanding notifications from Members in the Middle East region and 5 outstanding notification from Members in the North America region.

Disaggregated data on compliance showed that 78.6 per cent of Members from the African region had *not* complied with DS 1 notifications for the period 2005–2009. This

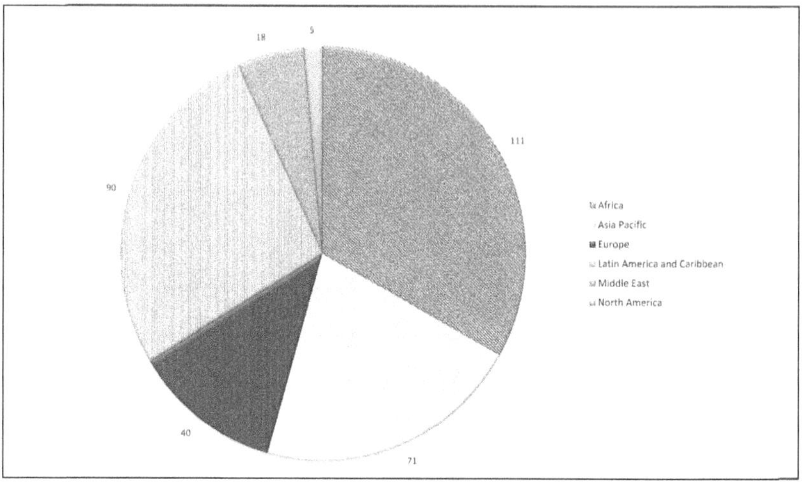

Figure 95. Outstanding DS:1 notifications (2005–2009).

was higher (poorer) than Europe at 29.3 per cent, the Middle East at 75 per cent, and Latin America and Caribbean at 78.2, but, lower (better) than Asia Pacific at 82.13 per cent and North America at 100 per cent.

Burkina Faso, Burundi, Gabon, Namibia and Nigeria were the only African WTO Members with no outstanding domestic support notifications in the period 2005–2009.

(iv) Export Subsidies Notifications (Outstanding): 2005–2009 Implementation Years

Figure 96 shows the distribution of outstanding export subsidies – ES: 1 notifications in the period 2005–2009 (period within the Doha negotiations).

At 165 *outstanding* export subsidy notifications, African WTO Members' level of compliance with export subsidies notifications for the period 2005–2009 was the highest (poorest), in comparison to 83 outstanding notifications from Members in the Latin America and Caribbean region; 56 outstanding notifications from those in the Asia Pacific region; 29 outstanding notifications from Members in Europe; 25 outstanding notifications from Members in the Middle East region and two outstanding notification from Members in the North America region.

Disaggregated data showed that 85.8 per cent of African WTO Members had not complied with their ES:1 notification obligations. This was high compared to 24.4 per cent of Members from Europe; 64.3 per cent from Asia-Pacific; 68.8 per cent from Latin America and Caribbean region; only higher than 87.5 per cent from the Middle East and 100 per cent from North America.

Burkina Faso, Burundi, Gabon, Lesotho, Namibia and Nigeria were the African WTO Members that had no outstanding export subsidy notifications in the period 2005–2009.

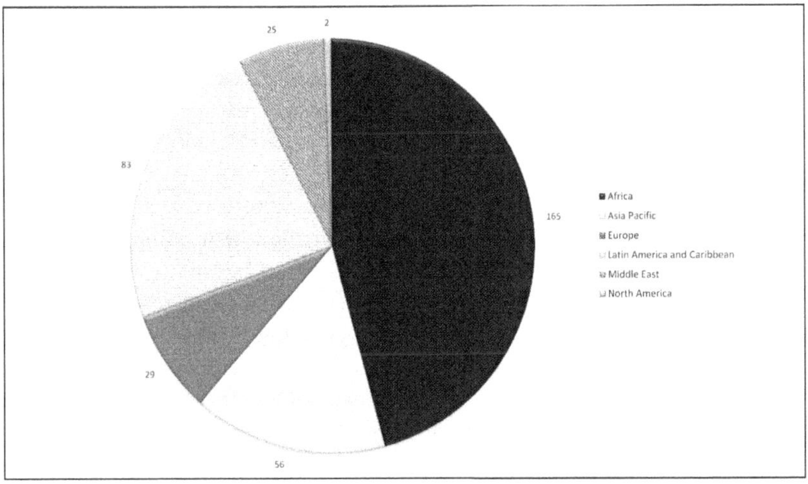

Figure 96. Outstanding ES:1 notifications (2005–2009).

(v) Compliance by African Members with Notification Requirements in the AOA

Overall, compliance with the notification obligations, regular and *ad hoc*, has not been satisfactory.[58] There have been a number of instances where notifications have been incomplete or have not been submitted within the specified timeframes. In some cases notifications due, remained outstanding. Overall, in the period analysed, African WTO Members had the most number of *outstanding* notifications for domestic support and export subsidies.

The typical, pro-forma explanatory factors included level of expertise and limited understanding about notification requirements that are applicable in each pillar/area. Arguments have been made that delegations familiarize themselves with the type of notification that they are required to submit in specific areas. There is the reason frequently advanced of inadequate trained staff with technical and legal skills required to understand, assess and draft required notifications coupled with inadequate human and institutional capacity in Geneva and capitals as constraining factors.

An interview with an official covering work of the Agriculture Committee confirmed that with the exception of South Africa, most African countries were not active in regular work of the Committee. On appearance, their efforts seemed to be concentrated in the work of the special session of the Committee on Agriculture where the agriculture negotiations under the Doha negotiations take place.[59]

Deeper analysis of the data in the two periods of 1995–2004 and 2005–2009 and participant observation of Members' behaviour, suggested other factors at play beyond the routinely invoked reasons of low expert levels, capacity constraints and divided attention.

58 Committee on Agriculture Report on Implementation of the Agriculture Agreement.
59 Interview on 3 September 2009.

The level of notification by African Members in the base period of 1995–2004 was very low. It is argued that there was no obvious reason for this low level of participation. The core factor was simply "the necessity for greater diligence, assiduity and attentiveness". A high level of expertise is not entailed for example in notifying nil returns, except to form the habit of "paying bills on time"; a habit yet to be fully formed on the part of a number of African delegations.

The second period of required notifications (2005–2009), fell within the period of the intense Doha negotiations. The explanation for the low level of notification was more complicated. More broadly, for non-African Members there was probably "conscience negligence" for the low level of notifications as this was linked to "a wait and see" behaviour in relation to domestic support level negotiations in the Round. This situation continued where Members (mainly non-African with the resources for domestic support) tactically preferred to wait and secure agreement for the lowest periods of global agricultural/commodity prices and hence higher levels of domestic support. However, this factor does not explain the high level of outstanding domestic support and export subsidy notifications on the part of African Members most of whom will not operate under the constraint of non-African Members in the Doha Round and the implementation of its results. The argument in this study is thereby sustained for greater reporting and notification diligence on the part of African WTO Members.

9. The Committee on Anti-Dumping Practices

The Agreement on Implementation of Article VI of the General Agreement on Tariffs and Trade 1994 (the Anti-dumping Agreement) lays down rules for determining when a product is considered as being dumped. It authorizes countries to levy compensatory duties on imports of products that are benefiting from unfair trade practices. However, an importing country can only levy such duties if it is established on the basis of investigations carried out by it, that such imports are causing "material injury" to a domestic industry. Article 16 of the Agreement established a Committee on Anti-dumping Practices (AD Committee). The Committee monitors the implementation of the Anti-dumping Agreement and provides a forum for discussion of matters related to the Agreement.

The level of engagement/participation of African WTO Members in the Anti-dumping Committee was analysed and compared to Members from other regions with regard to the following indices:

- Oral statements;
- Written submissions/proposals; and,
- Notification count.

In addition, the trends in the use of this trade remedy by Members in different regions were analysed.

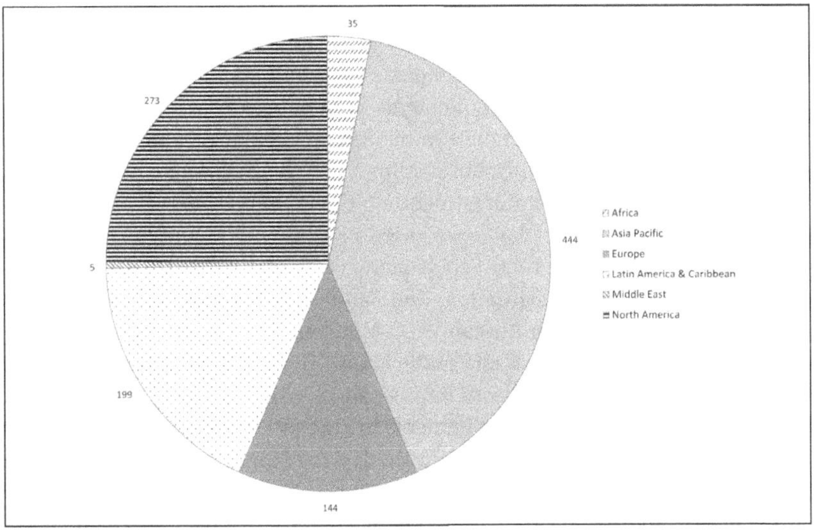

Figure 97. Individual statements made in the AD Committee (1995–2010).

(a) *Oral Statements to the AD Committee (1995–2010)*[60]

Figure 97 shows the distribution of individual-Member oral statements in different regions, in the AD Committee in the period 1995–2010.

Over the 15 year period studied, African WTO Members made a total of 35 statements in the AD Committee that is 3.1 per cent of the total of all statements. These statements were made by three (or 7 per cent) African WTO Members: South Africa (17); Egypt (15) and Côte d'Ivoire (3). These African Members have relatively high trade shares in relation to other African Members. In addition, South Africa and Egypt are large economies in Africa and trade with several partners inside and outside of Africa. Their trade actions are more likely to impact on the economies of other countries, including through the use of the trade remedy of anti-dumping. The facts indicate that they have well established domestic trade infrastructure for the use of trade remedies. The figures indicate that they are users and targets of trade remedy actions. In addition, as illustrated in chapter seven on the level of African participation/engagement in WTO Dispute settlement, the disputes where Egypt and South Africa have been respondents, have mostly related to trade remedies, particularly anti-dumping. These two African Members therefore have systemic and commercial stakes in the discussions in the Anti-dumping Committee.

The substantive content (quality) of oral statements by African WTO Members varied. Several were made in the context of the review of national legislation on anti-dumping; and, to support special and differential treatment for developing countries. Beyond South Africa and Egypt, statements were also made by Côte d'Ivoire and to express concern that

[60] Minutes of the Anti-dumping Committee, G/ADP/M/1 to 39.

questions had been submitted in languages other than French. By contrast, statements by Members in other regions spanned a vast sphere of issues in the Committee.

However, the total number of oral statements made by African WTO Members was low at 3.1 per cent as a proportion of all statements by Members from other regions and low at 7 per cent of statements by members in the African region. Why these low numbers? There are several reasons including, but not limited to the trade share of Africa in global trade, the low level of inexistent infrastructure for trade remedy use in capitals, and, the constantly operative factors of low specialized capacity. As a consequence, Members from other regions with more robust trade activities, better established domestic infrastructure including software (legislation) and hardware (investigative authorities) have participated more actively than African WTO Members with regard to oral statements, written proposals and submissions and notifications. These regions in particular are: Asia Pacific; Latin America and Caribbean, Europe, and North America. Disaggregated data showed that the highest number of statements in rank order were made by the US (234), EU (115), Japan (98), Hong Kong China (59), Mexico (52), China and India (48 each), Brazil (47), Korea (44), Canada (39), Argentina and Australia (34 each). Only the Middle East performed *worse* than Africa, despite Members in the Middle East having relatively higher trade shares than most African Members.

(b) *Written Proposals/Submissions to the AD Committee (1995–2010)*[61]

Figure 98 shows the distribution of individual written proposals/submissions by Members in different regions in the AD Committee in the period 1995–2010. The number of submissions/proposals by African Members at five (5) submissions over the 15 year period studied was very low, relative to proposals by Members in other regions except the Middle East. These five submissions were made by three (3) African Members, or seven (7) per cent of African membership. The three countries were Mauritius;[62] South Africa[63] and Tunisia.[64] Four of the five submissions were written replies to questions posed on their legislation and the other was regarding anti-dumping measures imposed by South Africa on uncoated wood free cut paper from Brazil.

---

61 Committee on Anti-dumping Practices, G/ADP/W/1 to 483.

62 Mauritian trade and economic activities are intensive and growing. Although a small economy, it is ranked as one of the most competitive economies in Africa and the world. Mauritius is ranked at 55 out of 139, with a score of 4.32 in a maximum score of 5 points, in the Global Competitiveness Index 2010–2011 of the World Economic Forum. Only South Africa is more competitive.

63 South Africa, is one of Africa's top economies. This has strong implications for both its use and being a target of trade remedy actions. It was categorized as a developed country economy from the first trade Round to the Uruguay Round concluded in 1994. In the context of the Doha Round, South African trade negotiators have maintained an immovable position that it must be treated as a developing country in terms of commitments it will be expected to assume. It has also argued that account needs to be taken of its situation in the Uruguay Round negotiations.

64 Tunisia's trade and economic activities with the EU are intensive in the context of the 1995 Euro-Med Agreement.

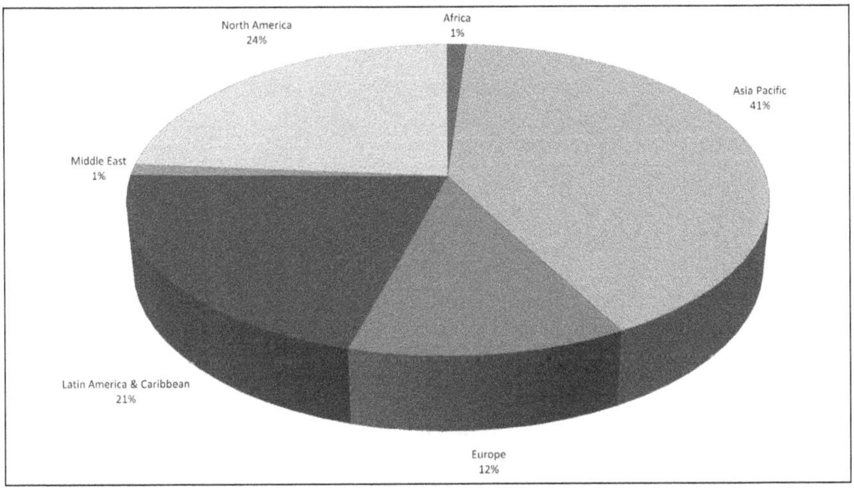

Figure 98. Individual submissions/proposals to the AD Committee (1995–2010).

Disaggregated data showed that in rank order, most written submissions/proposals were made by the US (71), Hong Kong China (60), Australia (42), EU (40), Canada (32), Korea (30); Venezuela (23). Most of these Members have high trade shares and therefore high commercial and systemic interest with regard to anti-dumping legislation or regulation adopted by other WTO Members that could impact their trade. Most submissions by Members in other regions were in the form of questions posed to other Members on laws and regulations on anti-dumping and written responses to questions received. Submissions were also made in the context of the annual review of the Anti-dumping Agreement and China's Transitional Review Mechanism.

(c) *Notification Count (1995–2010)*[65]

(i) National Legislation

In the area of anti-dumping, WTO rules are implemented through Member's national legislation. Pursuant to Article 18.5 of the Anti-dumping Agreement, Members with legislation and/or regulations regarding anti-dumping duty investigations or reviews covered by the Agreement are required to notify the full and integrated text to the Committee. If such legislation and/or regulations do not exist, the Member is required to inform the Committee of this fact, and explain the reasons therefore. Changes in a Member's legislation are also required to be notified.

Figure 99 shows the level of compliance by Members in different regions with notification obligations under Article 18.5 of the Anti-dumping Agreement in the period 1995–2010.

---

65 Report of the Committee on Anti-dumping Practices to the Council for Trade in Goods, G/L/935, 2010.

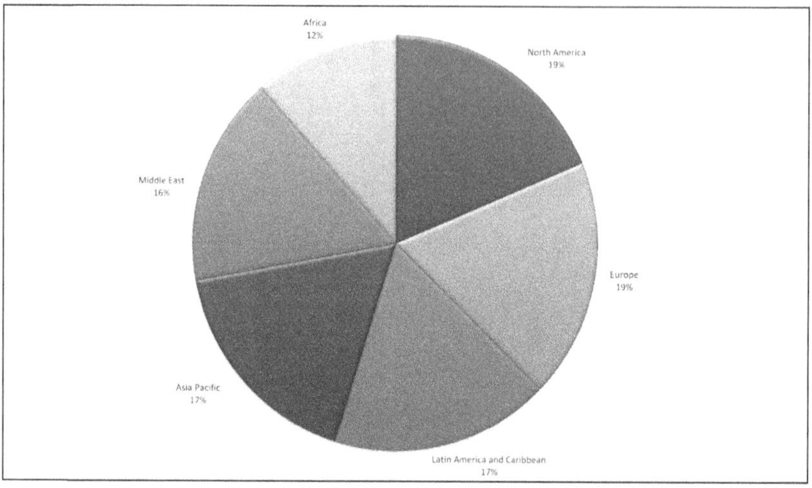

Figure 99. Compliance with Article 18.5 notifications requirements.

Although relatively high, African Members' level of compliance at 62 per cent of membership is lower than that of all other regions. Sixteen (16) African WTO Members had not complied with the obligation to notify the existence or non-existence of AD legislation. These were: Djibouti; Democratic Republic Congo; Congo; Central African Republic; Cape Verde; Cameroon; Mauritania; Lesotho; Guinea Bissau; Gambia; Togo; Tanzania; Sierra Leone; Rwanda; Niger; and, Mozambique. What is required for notification is simple. Members notify existing legislation and provide the text, or notify to indicate the absence of any legislative and/or regulatory software. For those Members that do not have legislation, the notification is in the form of a letter stating the fact of the non-existence of legislation. This does not entail specialized technical knowledge and skills.

Why had 16 African Members not notified? Analysis of the data reviewed and the results of interview indicated low levels of Geneva-capital co-ordination.

(ii) Semi-Annual Reports

Article 16.4 of the Anti-dumping Agreement requires Members to submit reports on a semi-annual basis (July–December and January–June) on anti-dumping duty actions taken within the preceding six months. Members taking no action during a given period are also required to notify the Committee.[66]

To provide an indication of the level of commitment to semi-annual reporting of anti-dumping actions, two specific recent periods were selected for comparative analysis. These were: 1 July to 31 December 2009 and 1 January to 30 June 2010. Figure 100 in

[66] A group of Members opted to make one time notifications. In essence, these one-time notifications have in most cases reported that the country in question has not established an authority competent to initiate and conduct an investigation and therefore has not undertaken any anti-dumping action/s and does not foresee undertaking the same in the near future.

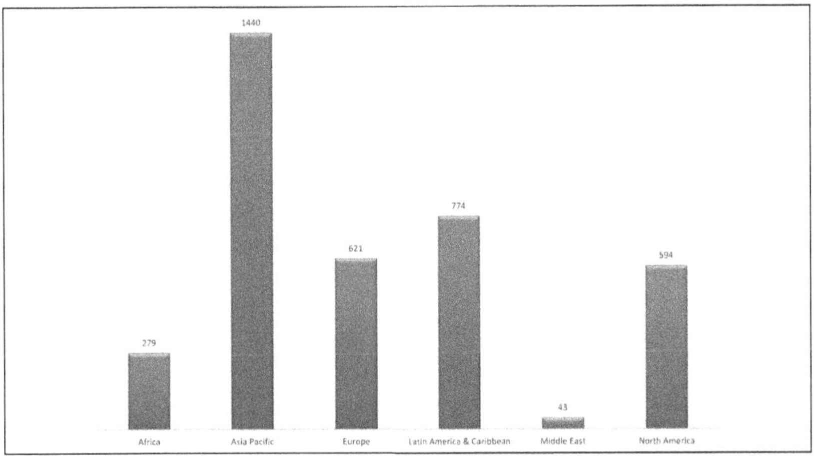

Figure 100. Number of anti-dumping Initiations by region (1/1/1995–30/06/2010).

Annex X shows the level of compliance with the notifications of semi-annual reports by Members in different regions for the selected period.

During the selected period, African WTO Members' level of compliance was low at 38 per cent of its members either submitting a report of action taken or a report of no action or making a one-time notification. Africa's level of compliance was low in comparison with the 100 per cent compliance for North America; 92.6 per cent for Europe; 78.1 for Latin America and Caribbean; 71.4 for Asia Pacific; and, 50 per cent for the Middle East.

Data revealed that the African region had the most number of Members that had not complied with this notification obligation. Twenty-six (26) African WTO Members (or 60 per cent of its membership) had not complied with the obligation for the required periods in 2009/2010. This was the highest (poorest) in comparison to other regions which had Members that had not complied – Middle East, two (2) Members (or 25 per cent); Asia Pacific, eight (8) Members (or 29 per cent); Latin America and Caribbean, seven (7) Members (or 22 per cent); and Europe, three (3) Members (or 7.4 per cent). It is recommended that stricter and higher levels of sustained attention and diligence are urgently required on the part of non-complying African WTO Members.

(d) *Trends in the Use of Anti-Dumping Measures*[67]

(i) Initiations of Anti-Dumping Actions (1 January 1995–30 June 2010)

(a) *Reporting Members*

Overall, a relatively small number of WTO Members – 28 per cent – had been involved in initiation of anti-dumping investigations in the period 1 January 1995 to 30 June 2010 (Figure 101). Figure 100 shows initiations of anti-dumping actions by region.

67 http://www.wto.org/english/tratop_e/adp_e/adp_e.htm.

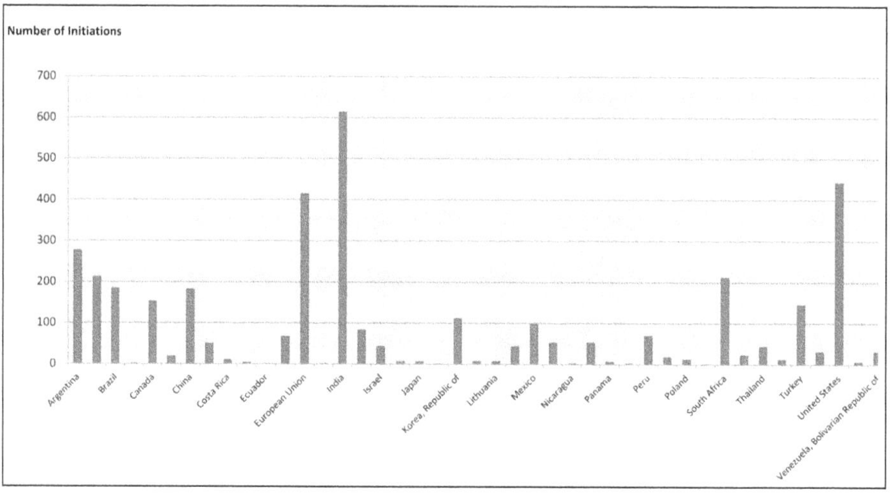

Figure 101. Anti-dumping initiations (1 January 1995–30 June 2010).

African WTO Members initiated a total of 279 anti-dumping actions (or 7.4 per cent of the total number of initiations) in the 15 year period studied. These actions were accounted for two (or 4.7 per cent) of African WTO Members. These were Egypt (67 initiations) and South Africa (212 initiations). With the exception of South Africa which ranked as one of the first five initiators of anti-dumping actions, expectedly, Africa's use of this trade remedy instrument as a trade policy tool was the lowest. In rank order, Members with the highest initiations in the period studied were India (613), the US (442), EU (414), Argentina (277), and, South Africa, tied with Australia at 212.

Why was there a low usage of this trade policy instrument by African Members? It is observed firstly that trade remedy instruments (safeguards, countervailing measures, and anti-dumping measures) are most directly related to trade flows and surges in trade flows in those instances where material injury is caused or potential to a trading partner. African trade as a percentage share of global trade is low and has not yet attained levels where its trade flows either cause material injury or "threaten" manufacturing interest in its trading partners.

Second, with regard to the vast majority of African economies (with the evident exceptions of Egypt and South Africa), infrastructure (legislation and implementing authorities) for trade remedy use in capitals is low to inexistent. Relatedly, specialized capacity is limited with inadequate and in some cases, no, competent authorities to undertake investigations.

Third, cost limitations related to conduct of investigations and maintaining a competent authority have had an effect. Fourth, domestic industries to lobby for "safeguarding" their interests through use of AD are weak, under-developed, or limited. The trade policy reviews of many African countries indicate the use of the blunter instrument of quantitative restrictions which are "easier" to use, over and above trade remedy instruments.

Regardless of these factors, there is the more strategic question of whether this "protectionist route" is a road down which African WTO Members should travel. The excessive and at times abusive use of trade defence measures which can be harmful to overall global trade has led several trade/export-dependent high income developed and developing WTO Members like Japan and South Korea to oppose the use of these measures. To the contrary they have invested negotiating efforts in the Doha Round negotiations to seek to "clarify and improve" trade rules with regard to trade remedy use. It is recommended that African WTO Members do not embark on this trade policy use, except in the most blatant of circumstances of dumping.

(ii) Countries Subject to Initiations

Figure 102 shows the distribution of countries in different regions whose exports have been the subjects of anti-dumping initiations by Members in the period 1 January 1995 to 30 June 2010.

Exports from eight (8) African countries were the subject of anti-dumping initiations by other countries in the period reviewed. The exports were from Algeria, Egypt, Libyan Arab Jamahiriya;[68] Malawi; Mozambique; Nigeria; South Africa; and, Zimbabwe. Expectedly, for reasons already reviewed especially low trade shares and few non-preferential patterns, this was low in comparison to anti-dumping initiations against countries from Europe, Asia-Pacific and Latin America and the Caribbean regions. Overall, China had the highest number of anti-dumping initiations against its exports – 784 initiations. Other countries with relatively high number of initiations included Korea (268); United States (210); Chinese Taipei (201); Indonesia (157), and India (146). However, the number of initiations against the exports of African countries was low ranging from 1 to 59.

Disaggregated data revealed that South Africa initiated at least one antidumping investigation against four (4) of the other seven (7) African countries that had been the subject of antidumping investigations (Egypt, Malawi, Mozambique and Zimbabwe). Most of these Members were from the Southern African region and trade mostly with South Africa. The other initiations against African exports were by the European Union, in the cases of Algeria, Egypt and South Africa. South Africa was the only African country that had over ten (10) countries initiating investigations against its exports.[69] This was not only a reflection of its major trade position on the African continent, but also of its

[68] For Libya and Algeria, anti-dumping initiations against these two non-Members appeared to be rooted in the use of dual-pricing, which subsidize through lower domestic gas and energy pricing distinct from higher global market prices for gas and energy. In this instance, the initiation of anti-dumping action appeared to be the pattern against oil and gas exporting economies that engaged in dual pricing to the advantage of domestic manufacturers that produced downstream products for exports.

[69] These included Argentina, Australia, Brazil, Canada, China, European Union, India, Jordan, New Zealand, Pakistan, Thailand and the United States.

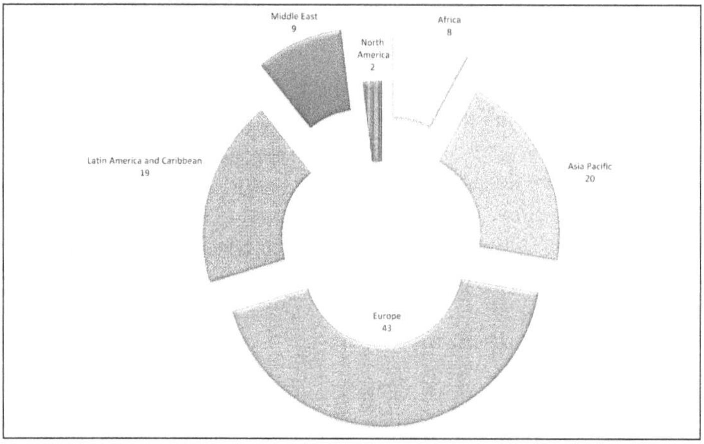

Figure 102. Anti-dumping initiations by exporting countries by region 1/1/1995–30/6/2010.

relatively high trade volume and potential impact on domestic industries of other countries, in comparison to other African countries. It was also a reflection of the diversity of its trading partners and exports destination. It also reflected an active South African industry with special interests.

(iii) Imposition of Anti-Dumping Measures

Data points to the fact that anti-dumping measures are not automatically imposed for all investigations initiated. The number of anti-dumping "initiations" was more than that of "measures imposed". Figure 103 shows the number of anti-dumping measures imposed by Members in different regions.

Positively, with the exception of the Middle East, African WTO Members imposed the lowest number of anti-dumping measures at 180 (or 7.4 of the total number of anti-dumping measures). Egypt (67) and South Africa (212) accounted for these measures. For a range of reasons, Africa is the least "protectionist" region with regard to the use of trade remedies. The same Members that initiated the most investigations imposed the most anti-dumping measures against exports from other countries. These were: India (436), the United States (289), European Union (269), Argentina (190) and China (137). Similarly, those Members most subject to anti-dumping initiations were also the most targeted with anti-dumping measures. South Africa and the European Union were the countries that imposed measures on exports of African countries whose exports had been subject to investigation.

10. The Committee on Customs Valuation

The WTO Agreement on Implementation of Article VII of the General Agreement on Tariffs and Trade (the Customs Valuation Agreement) lays down rules for the valuation of goods for customs purposes. The Agreement's valuation system is based on a simple

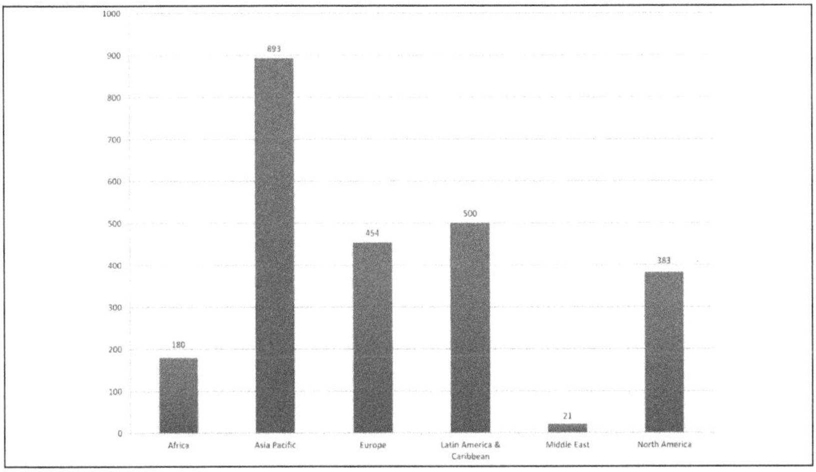

Figure 103. Number of anti-dumping measures by members (01/01/95–30/06/2010).

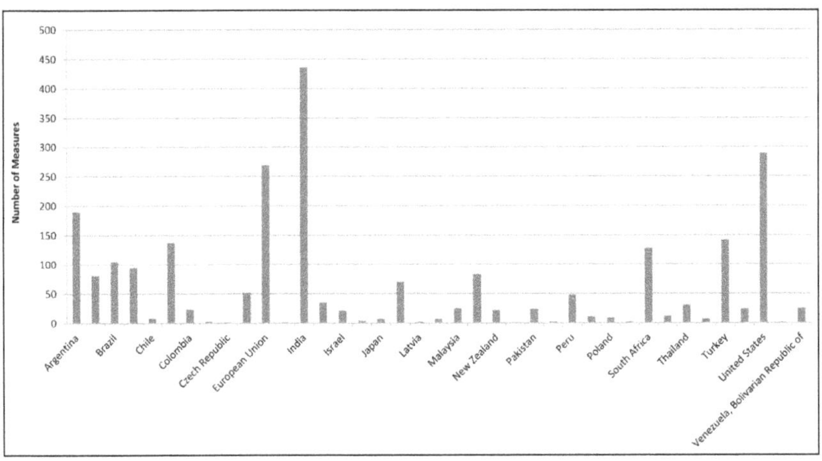

Figure 103 (b). Anti-dumping measures by reporting member 1/1/1995–30/6/2010.

and equity criteria that takes commercial practices into account. The Agreement aims to seek uniformity in Member States in customs valuation by requiring Members to harmonize national legislation with its provisions. Article 18 of the Agreement established a Committee on Customs Valuation. The Committee affords Members the opportunity to consult on matters relating to the administration of the customs valuation system of any Member as it might affect the operation of the Agreement.

The level of participation/engagement of African WTO Members in the Customs Valuation Committee was analysed and compared to Members from other regions with regard to the following indices:

- Oral statements and content analysis;
- Written submissions/proposals; and,
- Notification count.

(a) *Oral Statements in the Customs Valuation Committee (1995–2010)*[70]

Figure 104 shows the distribution of individual oral interventions by region in the Customs Valuation Committee in the period 1995–2010.

The number of individual African oral statements at 68 was low, representing 4.4 per cent of the total of statements in the Customs Valuation Committee. The statements were low in relation to those made by other regions, with the exception of the Middle East. Sixteen (16) African Members or 38 per cent of African WTO membership accounted for the 68 statements. The highest number of statements in the African region, at 14, was made by Egypt. Other African Members that made a relatively high number of statements were Morocco and Senegal each with 11 statements. On average, the interventions of other African Members in the CVA were very low at 2.3 statements. The African Members that intervened were: Burkina Faso (3); Burundi (1); Côte d'Ivoire (4); Gabon (3); Kenya (1); Madagascar (6); Mauritania (3); Mauritius (4), Nigeria (1); Rwanda (1); South Africa (1); Tunisia (2); Zimbabwe (1); and, Gabon (3). Overall, in rank order, the most statements in the CVA Committee were made by US (305); India (238); EC (222); Canada (130); and Brazil (68 equal to the total number of statements by African WTO Members).

The area of customs valuation, similar to that of trade remedies, is strongly associated to trade flows. Members that have higher trade flows, even if relatively, such as Egypt and Morocco, had higher levels of engagement/participation in the area of customs valuation. This would also partly explain a relatively higher level of intervention by these African WTO Members in the Customs Valuation Committee.

Content analysis showed that African WTO Members intervened in the Customs Valuation Committee in the context of the review of national implementing legislation, to seek extension of the delay period for implementation of the Agreement[71] and to register reservations on minimum values or prices. They also highlighted implementation issues and concerns regarding the Agreement and sought technical assistance and capacity building. African Members stated that the CVA dealt with important but technical systemic issues for macroeconomic management. Some African Members intervened on non-substantial issues for instance that all documents issued in the Committee should be simultaneously issued in all three official languages of the WTO (English, French and Spanish) to enable the active participation of all Members.

---

70 Minutes of the Committee on Customs Valuation, WT/VAL/M/1 to 50.

71 G/VAL/M/17, 2001, Burundi for example cited political difficulties it was facing as a reason for seeking extension for the delay period for the application of the Agreement. This is an example where domestic political issues affect the effective engagement and participation of a Member. (see regression results with regard to the explanatory variable of democracy).

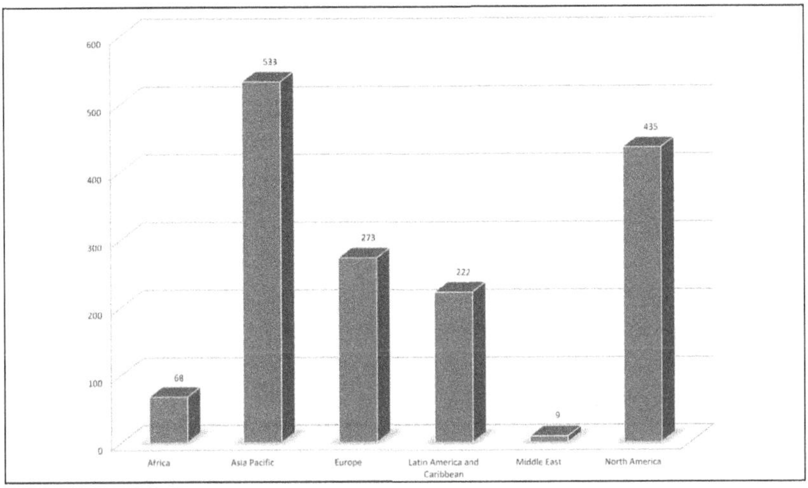

Figure 104. Statements in the CVA (1995–2010).

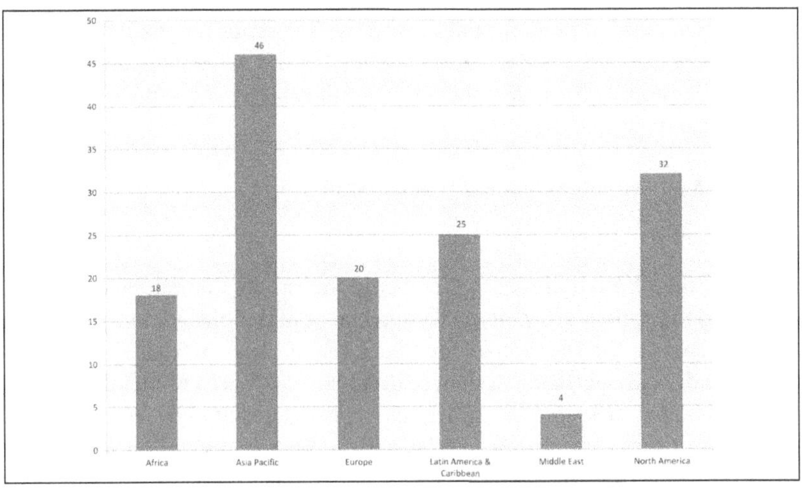

Figure 105. Submissions/proposals to the CVA.

(b) *Written Proposals/Submissions to the Customs Valuation Committee*[72]

Figure 105 shows the distribution of written individual proposals/submissions in the Customs Valuation Committee by region, in the period 1995–2010.

The number of written submissions/proposals made to the Committee was low for all regions, in comparison with submissions/proposals made in other subsidiary bodies

[72] Committee on Customs Valuation, G/VAL/W/1 to 199.

of the Goods Council. Eighteen (or 12 per cent) of submissions/proposals by African Members to the Customs Valuation Committee was lower than that of Members from the Asia Pacific region, North America, Latin America and Caribbean, and Europe. This was only higher than submissions/proposals of Members from the Middle East. The individual proposals/submissions by African Members were very low, ranging between 1 and 4 proposals/submissions. Eleven (11) African Members (or 26 per cent) accounted for the 18 submissions/proposals. These were: Burundi (1); Cameroon (1); Côte d'Ivoire (2); Egypt (4); Gabon (1); Mauritania (1); Morocco (3); Rwanda (1); Senegal (2); Tanzania (1); and, Tunisia (1).

Why was the number of written proposals/submissions low overall? One of the reasons is because the Customs Valuation Agreement was very tightly drafted with little to zero margins for deviation from the established rules. Eleven (11) of the 18 submissions by African WTO Members were to request extension of the five year delay period in the application of the Customs Valuation Agreement (that was, until 2000) in accordance with Annex III, paragraph 1 of the Agreement. This provision had anticipated that the five year delay period, might in practice, be insufficient for certain developing country Members, who upon showing good cause, could have the delay period extended. The other submissions/proposals from African Members were in respect of seeking derogations for minimum values/reference prices for African Members that value goods on the basis of officially established minimum values and providing status reports on adjustment to the transaction value and other valuation methods in the Agreement. Submissions also related to responses by African Members to questions posed about their Customs Valuation laws, regulations and practices.

(c) *Required Notifications Submitted (1995–2009)*[73]

(i) National Legislation

Article 22.2 of the CVA requires each Member to inform the Committee of any changes in its laws and regulations relevant to the Agreement and in the administration of such laws and regulations. The Decision on the Check List of Issues (G/VAL/5) requires Members to respond to 15 questions on their legislation. In the case of Members who were Tokyo Round signatories and whose legislation had already been examined, a communication from those Members could be sent to the Secretariat indicating that their responses to the checklist of issues remained valid under the WTO Customs Valuation Agreement (G/VAL/M/1, paragraph 36–39).

Figure 106 shows the level of compliance by Members in different regions with this notification requirement for the period 1995–2009.

Although the percentage of notification appears to be positive at 52 per cent, (i.e. with twenty two[74] African Members notifying), nonetheless, 20 (or 48 per cent) of

[73] Report of the Committee on Customs Valuation to the Council for Trade in Goods, G/L/942.

[74] Botswana, Burkina Faso, Côte d'Ivoire, Egypt, Gabon, Kenya, Lesotho, Madagascar, Malawi, Mauritius, Morocco, Mozambique, Namibia, Nigeria, Senegal, South Africa, Swaziland, Tanzania, Tunisia, Uganda, Zambia, and, Zimbabwe.

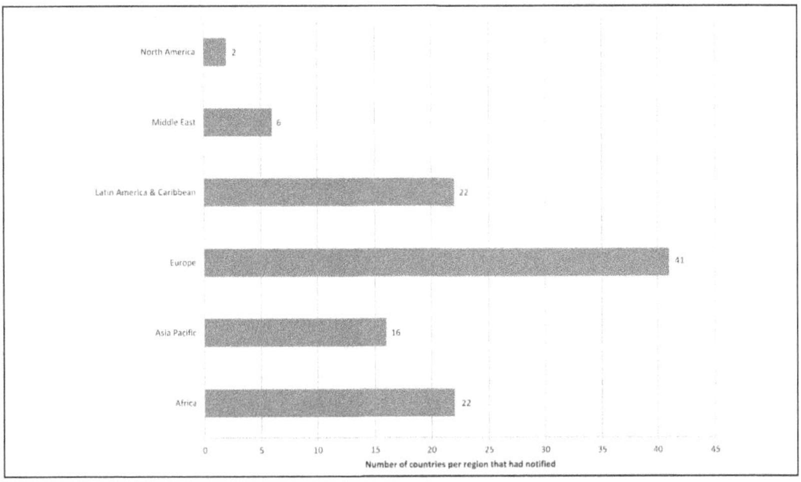

Figure 106. Notification of customs valuation national legislation.

African Members had not notified their legislation. This *per se* was a poor record of compliance.

North America and Europe (the regions whose Members had high compliance levels) have Members very actively engaged in world trade. They more frequently encounter and deal with large volumes of merchandise that have to be valued. They therefore have extensive experience and better infrastructure in the area of customs valuation and high interest in the work of the Customs Valuation Committee. These Members also have high rankings in the Global Competitiveness Index.

Why was engagement in this area of regular work by African WTO Members been low? There is a combination of reasons. Low trade shares, combined with low competitiveness rankings and to a lesser extent, it is in an area prone to red tape and domestic corruption.

11. The Committee on Import Licensing Procedures

The Agreement on Import Licensing recognises that the flow of international trade could be impeded by the inappropriate use of import licensing procedures. The Agreement therefore aims to simplify and bring transparency to the administration and practices used in international trade with regard to import licensing, in order to ensure the fair and equitable application and administration of import licensing procedures. Article 4 of the Agreement on Import Licensing Procedures established a Committee on Import Licensing (ILC) which affords Members the opportunity to consult on any matter relating to the operation of the Agreement or the furtherance of its objectives.

The participation of African WTO Members in the ILC was analysed and compared to Members from other regions with regard to the following indices:

- Oral statements in the Committee;
- Written submissions/proposals;

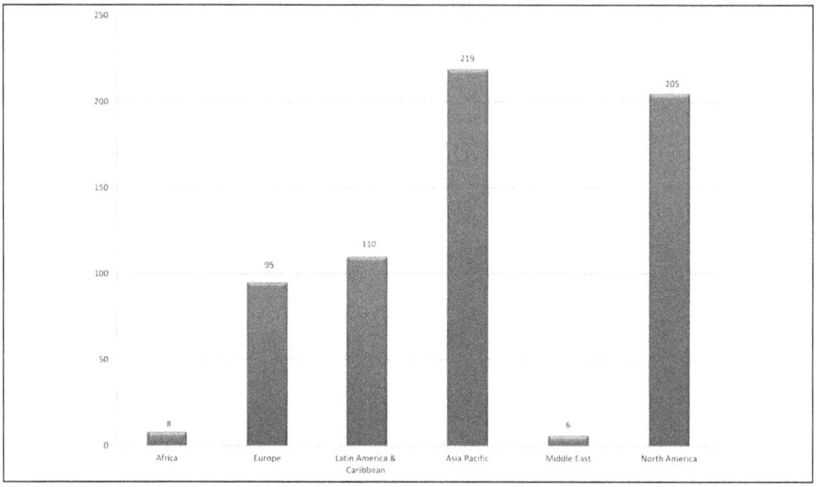

Figure 107. Individual Statements in the Import Licensing Committee.

- Notification count; and,
- participation in the review process of notifications in the Import Licensing Committee: Members posing questions; Members to whom questions were posed

(a) *Oral Statements in the Import Licensing Committee*[75]

Figure 107 shows the distribution of oral statements by Members in the Committee on Import Licensing in different regions in the period 1995–2010.

African Members made a total of eight (8) statements or 2.1 per cent of all oral interventions in the Import Licensing Committee, in the 15 year period studied. This was very low in comparison to statements by Members in all other regions, with the exception of the Middle East. Three (3) African Members (or 7.1 per cent of African WTO membership) accounted for these statements. These Members were: Egypt (6); Djibouti (1); and, Mauritania (1).

In the substance of their interventions, the statements by African Members focused on technical assistance for customs modernization and for compliance with notification obligations. In addition, Egypt posed questions to Turkey regarding its import licensing procedures on rice and to India on its import licensing procedures on marble.

In comparison, most statements in the ILC in rank order were made by the US (180), EU(70), China (59), India (32), Brazil (29), Japan (27), and, Mexico (21). For systemic and commercial considerations, these Members have tended more than other Members, to monitor developments in other trading partners regimes, including on import licensing and as a consequence, been more active in the Committee's work. They have sought clarity and raised concerns, particularly transparency concerns, about Members' procedures.

[75] Minutes of the Committee on Import Licensing, G/LIC/M/1 to 32.

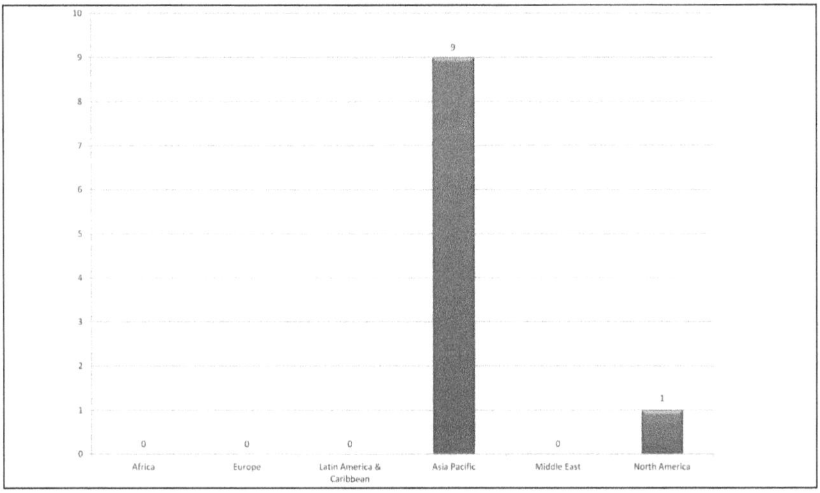

Figure 108. Proposals/submissions to the ILC.

In the data analyzed a question that required a response was why African Members' participation was so low having regard to the fact that: (i) many African Members are users of import licensing as a trade policy instrument; and, (ii)this is a Committee that was chaired mainly by African delegates for essentially half of the 15 year period studied.[76] What requires explanation is that while it has been argued in this study that African WTO participation has improved over time, from the starting point of 1995, in the case of the Committee on Import Licensing, participation had not improved, but remained at its low starting point. Engagement on import licensing subject matter does not entail any specialized expertise. In fact to the contrary, it is a trade policy instrument that many African countries have employed. The analysis of the data and interviews suggested that the low rate of engagement was associated with low levels of professional engagement and diligence. Enthusiasm was minimal with the absence of energetic engagement. Furthermore, overall the Import Licensing Committee is a regular body with low levels of activity. Nevetherless, it is a regular body of relatively greater interest for African Members.

(b) *Written Proposals/Submissions to the Import Licensing Committee*[77]

Figure 108, shows the distribution of written submissions/proposals to the ILC in the period 1995–2010.

Only ten (10) written submissions/proposals were tabled in the ILC in the 15 year period studied. This was the lowest across all subsidiary bodies of the CTG. Most submis-

[76] 1995, 1996 (Zimbabwe); 1998, 1999 (Côte d'Ivoire); and 2007, 2008, 2009 (Tanzania).

[77] Committee on Import Licensing, G/LIC/W/1 to 37. This section reviewed all other submissions to the Committee excluding notifications or questions and responses posed in the review process of notifications in the committee which are addressed in sections c and d respectively.

sions (8) were made by the China in the context of its transitional review. The other submissions were also made in the context of China's Transitional Review Mechanism. There has been a declining trend in the use of import licensing as a trade policy instrument. In commercial practice, import licensing is more used for statistical and administrative purposes and less so for trade/market access restrictions because of the tighter disciplines established in the Agreement.

(c) *Notification Obligations*[78]

In the universe of total WTO membership (153 for the period reviewed), 20 Members had not complied with their notification obligations since joining the WTO. Of these, 12 (over half) were from Africa; two from Latin America and the Caribbean; and six from the Asia-pacific region.[79]

(i) Publications and/or Legislation – Outstanding Notifications (1995–2010)

Paragraph 4(a) of Article 1 of the Agreement on Import Licensing requires Members to publish information for other Members and traders to provide transparency for granting and/or allocating licences. Article 1.4(a) requires Members to notify the Committee of the sources in which the information containing import licensing procedures are published and to make copies of these publications available to the WTO Secretariat.

Article 8.2(a) requires each Member to ensure the conformity of its laws, regulation and administrative procedures with the provisions of the Agreement not later than the date of entry into force of the WTO Agreement for it. Paragraph 2(b) states that each Member shall inform the Committee of any changes in its laws and regulations relevant to the Agreement and in the administration of such laws and regulations.

Since the entry into force of the Agreement, Article 1.4(a) and 8.2(b) notifications were received from 96 Members counting the European Union as one.[80] Figure 109 shows the distribution of outstanding publications and/or legislation notifications by Members in different regions in the period 1995–2010.

Africa WTO Members' level of outstanding (yet to be notified) publications and/or legislation notifications at 17 was the highest (poorest), in comparison to ten (10) outstanding notifications from Members in the Asia Pacific region; two (2) from those in the Latin America and Caribbean region; one from Members in the Middle East region and no outstanding notification from Members in the North America and Europe.

Disaggregated data further showed that at 40 per cent of its membership not having complied with their obligation to notify their publications and /or legislation notification, Africa had the highest rate of non-compliance. This was poor compared to zero per cent

---

[78] Report of the Committee on Import Licensing to the Council for Trade in Goods, G/L/941.

[79] Angola, Belize, Botswana, Cambodia, Central African Republic, Congo, Djibouti, Egypt, Guinea, Guinea Bissau, Mauritania, Mozambique, Myanmar, Nepal, St Vincent & the Grenadines, Sierra Leone, Solomon Islands, Tanzania, Tonga and Vietnam.

[80] Eighth Biennial Review of the Implementation and Operation of the Agreement on Import Licensing Procedures, G/LIC/21, 1 December 2010.

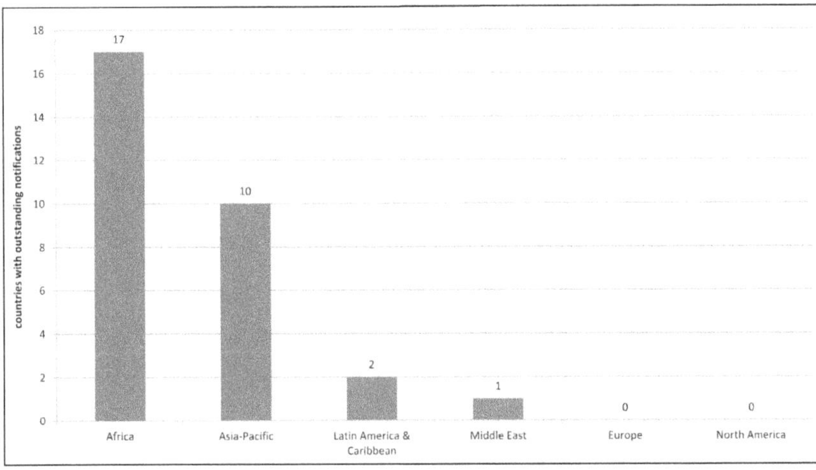

Figure 109. Outstanding Article 1.4(a) and 8.2(b) notifications by region.

for North America and Europe; 6 per cent for the Latin America and Caribbean; 12 per cent for the Middle East; and, 35 per cent for Asia Pacific.

The African WTO Members that had not yet submitted publications and/or legislation notifications as required in the period 1995–2010 were: Angola, Botswana, Cape Verde, Central African Republic, Congo, Djibouti, Egypt, Gambia, Guinea Bissau, Guinea, Lesotho, Mauritania, Mozambique, Rwanda, Sierra Leone, South Africa and Tanzania.[81] Review of the evidence confirmed that the Committee on Import Licensing was an area of regular work of low interest, low activity and waning engagement by Members, particularly African Members.

(ii) Annual Replies to Questionnaire (Outstanding Notifications)

Article 7.3 requires all Members to promptly complete the annual questionnaire on import licensing procedures.[82] As of December 2010, a cumulative total of 98 Members (counting the EU as one) had submitted replies to the questionnaire under Article 7.3 since the entry into force of the WTO Agreement.[83]

Figure 110 shows the distribution of *outstanding* Article 7.3 notifications by Members in different regions in the period 1995 to 2010.

African WTO Members' level of *outstanding* (yet to be notified) annual questionnaire notifications at 15 was the highest (poorest), in comparison to 8 outstanding notifications from Members in the Asia Pacific region; 5 from those in the Latin America and

[81] Outstanding notifications from Members in other regions were: **Latin America and Caribbean:** Belize; and, St Vincent and the Grenadines; **Asia Pacific:** Brunei Darussalam; Cambodia; Malaysia; Maldives, Myanmar; Nepal; Papua New Guinea; Solomon Islands; Tonga; Vietnam; **Middle East:** Saudi Arabia.

[82] The questionnaire is annexed to WTO document G/LIC/3.

[83] Ibid. at footnote 162.

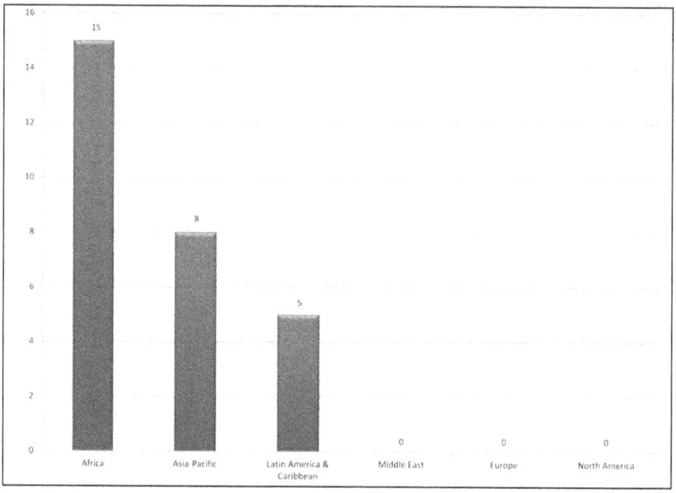

Figure 110. Outstanding Article 7.3 notifications.

Caribbean region; and no outstanding notification from Members in the Middle East, North America and Europe.

In the period 1995–2010, disaggregated data showed that 35 per cent of Africa's WTO membership had not yet complied with annual questionnaire notification obligations. This was the highest number of Members with outstanding annual questionnaire obligation compared to other regions: zero per cent for the Middle East, North America and Europe; 15 per cent for the Latin America and Caribbean; and, 28 per cent for Asia Pacific.

The African WTO Members that had not submitted annual questionnaire notifications as required in the period 1995–2010 were: Angola, Benin, Botswana, Central African Republic, Congo, Djibouti, Egypt, Gabon, Guinea Bissau, Guinea, Lesotho, Mauritania, Mozambique, Sierra Leone, Swaziland and Tanzania.[84]

(d) *Participation in the Review Process of Notifications in the Committee*

The Committee on Import Licensing agreed to review procedures. Under these procedures, questions and comments are made by Members as part of the regular business on the Committee's agenda.[85] In this section, the participation of African WTO Members in the review process is examined by analysing which Members posed questions in the review process and to whom questions were directed.

[84] Outstanding notifications from Members in other regions were: **Latin America and Caribbean:** Belize; and, St Vincent and the Grenadines; El Salvador; Nicaragua; Paraguay **Asia Pacific**: Cambodia; Myanmar; Nepal; Pakistan; Papua New Guinea; Solomon Islands; Tonga; Vietnam.

[85] Committee on Import Licensing, G/LIC/4 on the Understanding reached by the Committee on Procedures for the Review of Notifications.

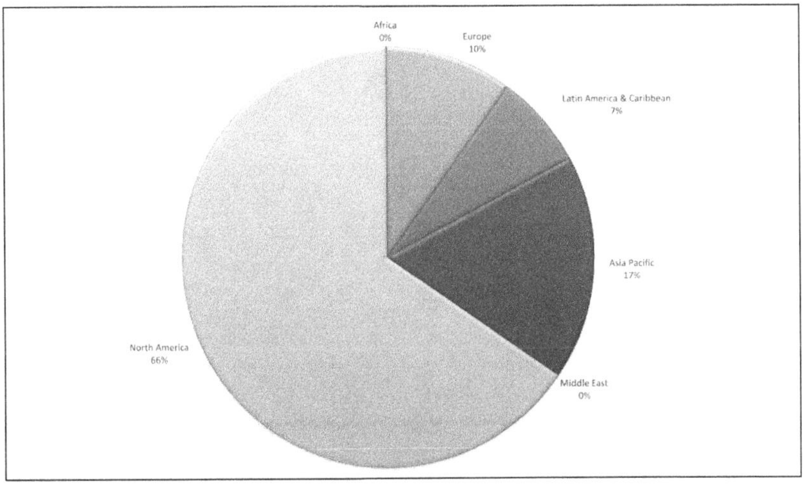

Figure 111. Members posing questions in review process.

(i) Questions by Members (1995–2010)

Figure 111 shows the distribution by origin of questions posed in the ILC by Members in different regions in the period 1995 to 2010.

In the period reviewed, African WTO Members did not pose questions to other Members on notifications submitted on import licensing regimes. Professional diligence for study of the materials to derive and pose questions was lacking. No particular specialized expertise was required. The posing of questions does not necessarily entail commercial interest. The consideration is more systemic. Questions posed have carried implications for systemic interest and the overall functioning of the Organization.

In rank order, most questions were posed by the US (72), Australia (11), EU (10), Canada (5), and, China (4). Other Members that posed written questions about import licensing regimes of other Members included: Mexico, Peru, Chile, New Zealand, Thailand; Chinese Taipei, Korea; and, Turkey. The majority of questions were posed in the context of reviews of national legislation and the China Transitional Review Mechanism.

(ii) Members to Whom Questions Were Posed

Figure 112 shows the distribution of "targets of review questions" in the ILC by region in the period 1995–2010.

Questions were posed to Members from all regions. Five questions were posed to four (or 11 per cent) African WTO members. These were: Ghana, Madagascar, Mauritius and Chad. Questions to these Members originated mostly from the US with regard to their respective legislation. Only Mauritius responded in writing to the questions posed to it. The other African Members did not submit written responses.

Overall, most questions were posed to Members in the Asia Pacific and Latin America and Caribbean regions. Disaggregated data showed that in rank order, most questions were posed to China (23); India 11); Argentina (8); Brazil (8), and EU (7). The US which was the origin of most questions had only one question posed to it. Unlike African WTO

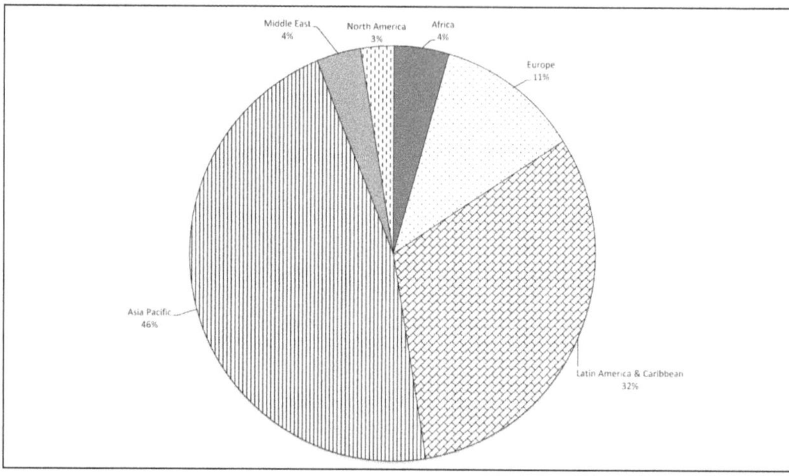

Figure 112. Targets of questions in review process.

Members, the other Members that were most "targeted" are considered emerging economies whose trade policies are of systemic and commercial interest to other trading partners. Their trade shares are relatively high and their decisions are anticipated to have an impact on the trade of other trading partners who sought to clarify issues or raise concerns.

12. The Committee on Market Access

The General Council established a Committee on Market Access (CMA) in 1995. The CMA is mandated to:

- supervise the implementation of concessions and provide a forum for consultations relating to tariffs and non-tariff in relation to market access issues not covered by any other WTO body;
- oversee the application of procedures for modification or withdrawal of tariff concessions;
- ensure that GATT Schedules are up-to-date, and that modifications, including those resulting from changes in tariff nomenclature, are reflected;
- conduct the updating and analysis of the documentation on quantitative restrictions and other non-tariff measures, in accordance with the timetable and procedures agreed by the Members;
- oversee the content and operation of, and access to, the Integrated Data Base; and
- report periodically – and in any case not less than once a year – to the Council for Trade in Goods.[86]

[86] WTO Committee on Market Access, Decision by the General Council of 31 January 1995, WT/L/47.

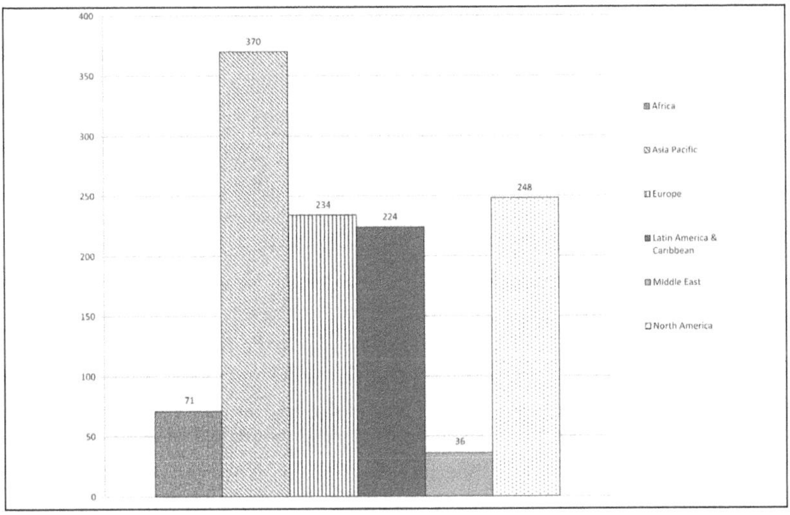

Figure 113. Statements in the Committee on Market Access (1995–2010).

The participation of African WTO Members in the CMA was analysed and compared to Members from other regions with regard to the following indices:

- oral statements in the Committee;
- written submissions/proposals; and,
- notification count.

(a) *Oral Statements in the CMA (1995–2010)*[87]

Figure 113 shows the distribution of oral statements in the CMA by Members in different regions in the period 1995-2010.

In the 15 year period studied, African Members made a total of 71 statements or 6 per cent of all statements in the Committee. This was very low in comparison to statements by Members in all other regions, with the exception of the Middle East. Twelve or (28 per cent) of African WTO membership accounted for these statements. These Members were: Egypt (28), Morocco (20), Côte d'Ivoire (4), Djibouti (1), Kenya (3), Mauritania (1), Nigeria (2), Senegal (3), South Africa (2), Tunisia (2), Zambia (2), and, Zimbabwe (3).

Most statements in the Committee in rank order were made by the US (171), EU (156), Canada (77), Australia (58), India (55), Japan (55), Switzerland (48), New Zealand (44), Mexico (43), and, China (38). Regression analysis conducted for this study indicated that Members with higher trade shares engaged more actively (statements, proposals/submissions) in areas of regular WTO work linked to market access and restrictions. The higher the level of trade shares, the greater the level of WTO engagement in market access and

[87] Minutes of the Committee on Market Access, G/MA/M/1 to 52.

restriction (protection) work. Therefore, for commercial and systemic reasons, these Members tended more than other Members, to monitor developments in other trading partners' regimes.

The subject areas on which African WTO Members intervened related to implementation of Harmonised System (HS) changes or transposition of schedules or renegotiation of their schedules of commitments. African Members cited technical difficulties in the transposition of their schedules and sought waivers and extensions from their obligations. They also sought technical assistance for the transposition exercise. African Members commented on proposals by other Members aimed at further liberalization of industrial market access, including on a sectoral or selective basis. They argued that the focus of the work of the Committee should remain the implementation of Uruguay Round obligations and not a discussion of "new" issues, which they stated "was not the purpose for which the Committee was established".[88] Other areas where African Members intervened in the CMA were discussions on the Integrated Database (IDB); adoption of formats for notifications; concerns raised about their market access practices;[89] concerns over the difficulty in meeting notification obligations; observer requests for intergovernmental organisations; and, technical assistance.

(b) *Written Submissions/Proposals to the CMA*[90]

Figure 114 shows the distribution of written proposals/submissions made to the CMA by Members in different regions in the period 1995–2010.

Africa Members' proposals at 12, (or 5 per cent) of the total number of written submissions/proposals to the CMA was lower than that of Members from the Asia Pacific region, North America, Latin America and Caribbean, and Europe. It was only higher than submissions/proposals of Members from the Middle East. The individual written proposals by African Members were very low, ranging between one and three submissions. Seven (or 16 per cent) of African WTO membership accounted for the 12 submissions/proposals. These were: Egypt (2); Côte d'Ivoire (2); Gabon (1); Mauritius (1); Morocco (1); South Africa (2) and, Tunisia (1). Although the trade shares of these seven countries were low (below one per cent), their shares were high relative to other African Members. As the regression results suggested, Members with higher trade shares and GDP levels have tended to participate more, particularly in areas of regular work more directly linked to market access questions and the use of trade remedy instruments.

The substance of all submissions by African WTO Members was to reserve the right under GATT Article XXVIII.5 to modify their schedules.

---

88 Statement by the representative of Egypt at the meeting of the Committee on Market Access in January 1997, G/MA/M/7.

89 Examples include a concern raised by the US about Egypt's use of specific duties on imports of textiles and clothing items. (see G/MA/M/31, 2002.); a concern raised by the EC with regard to an import ban applied by Nigeria (see G/MA/M/39, 2005).

90 Committee on Market Access, G/MA/W/1 to 104.

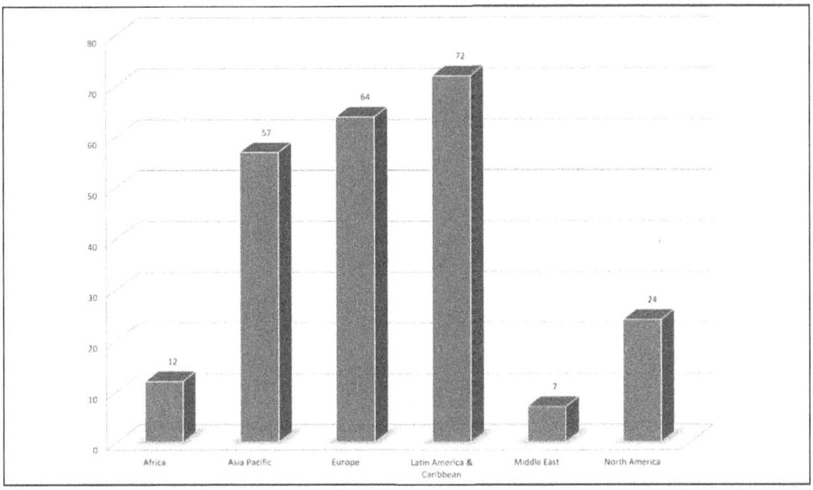

Figure 114. Submissions/proposals to the Market Access Committee (1995–2010).

(c) *Submission of Required Notifications*

The notifications overseen by the Committee on Market Access are mandated by: (i) the Decision on Notification Procedures for Quantitative Restrictions; (ii) the Decision on Reverse Notification of Non-tariff Measures;[91] and, (iii) the Decision on the Supply of Information to the Integrated Database (IDB) for personal computers.[92]

(i) Decision on Notification Procedures for Quantitative Restrictions (QRs) Notifications

A Decision on Notification Procedures for Quantitative Restrictions provides that Members should make complete notifications of quantitative restrictions (QRs) which they maintain by 31 January 1996 and at two-yearly intervals thereafter. Members are required to notify changes to their QRs as and when these changes occur. For the purpose of transparency, Members are encouraged to notify if their governments do not maintain quantitative restrictions. However, such notification is not required by the Decision. The Decision contains a provision for reverse notification.

---

91 Committee on Market Access, *Notifications under the Decision on Reverse Notification of Non-Tariff Measures*, G/MA/NTM/W/3/Rev.1, 23 January 2001.

92 Decision on Notification Procedures for Quantitative Restrictions, adopted by the Council for Trade in Goods, G/L/59; Decision on Reverse Notifications of Non-Tariff Measures, adopted by the Council for Trade in Goods on 1 December 1995, G/L/60; and, Supply of Information to the Integrated Database for personal computers, Decision by the General Council on 16 July 1997, WT/L/225.

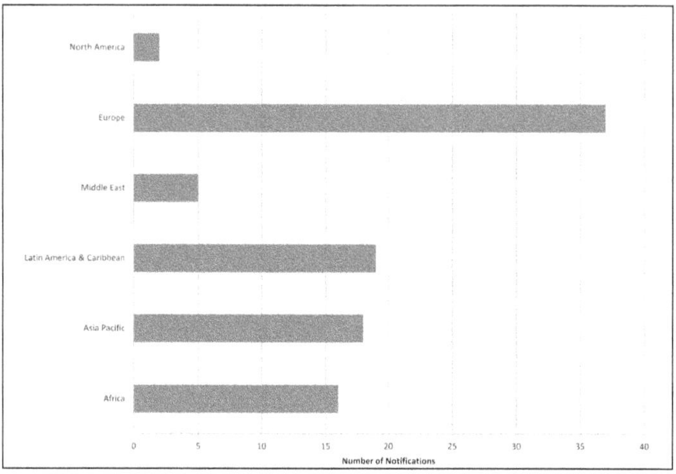

Figure 115. Quantitative restrictions notifications up to March 2009.

Figure 115 shows the level of compliance with notifications of QRs by Members in different regions in the period 1995–to March 2009.[93]

At 38 per cent, Africa had the lowest number of members in its region complying with notification obligations on quantitative restrictions. This was low in relation to the compliance levels in all other regions. African Members accounted for 48 per cent (or 26 out of 54 Members) of WTO Members that had not made a notification under this Decision. Sixteen (16) out of 42 African Members had made a notification. These Members were: Burundi; Central African Republic; DR Congo; Gabon; Gambia; Ghana; Madagascar; Mauritius; Morocco; Namibia; Nigeria; South Africa; Tunisia; Uganda; Zambia; and, Zimbabwe.

Why was the level of compliance low? Geneva-capital coordination remained challenging. There is scope for increased sustained, professional engagement. Specialized expertise is not required for complying with notification obligations. Although it has been argued (internal WTO Secretariat analysis) that there is lack of clarity among Members as to what QRs have to be notified, it is not logical to believe that this situation, even if it existed at the beginning, continues to prevail to the same level, in the 15th year of the Organization's existence.

(ii) Decision on the Supply of Information to the Integrated Database (IDB) for Personal Computers

Submissions to the IDB are required by the General Council Decision of July 1997. In agreeing to this Decision, the General Council noted that it was important to ensure full participation of all WTO Members in the IDB for personal computers. Under the

[93] Committee on Market Access, Timeliness and Completeness of Notifications – Notifications of Quantitative Restrictions, Note by Secretariat, 2 April 2009, JOB (09)/33.

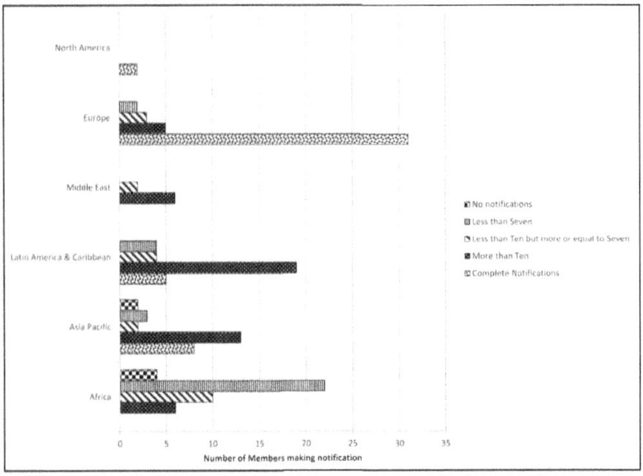

Figure 116. IDB tariff notifications (1996–2010).

Decision, Members are required to supply the Secretariat on an annual basis with information on tariffs and imports.

In quantifying Members' participation in the IDB, the number of submissions was counted since the creation of the database. To be up to date with its notification requirements, a Member should have submitted 15 years of customs duties covering the period 1996–2010 and 14 years of import statistics covering the period 1996–2010.[94]

(iii) IDB Tariff Notification

Figure 116 shows the level of compliance with the IDB tariff notification requirements by Members in different regions in the period 1996–2010.[95]

The data shows that no African Member submitted a complete IDB Tariff notification (i.e. required 15 notifications as of 2010) in the period studied (1996–2010). This level of compliance was low in relation to that of all other regions, where complete notifications were submitted by all members in North America; 73 per cent of those in Europe; 32 per cent of those in Asia Pacific, and, 21 per cent of those in the Latin America and Caribbean region. The only exception was the Middle East.

Data showed that slightly over half of African Members (59 per cent) submitted less than seven (7) notifications, that is, less than half of the total required. In addition, Africa was the only region that had a Member that had not submitted its notification with regard to tariffs (DR. Congo).

---

94 Adjustments would be made for those countries that acceded to the WTO after 1996, i.e., submissions would be less according to the date of accession.

95 Committee on Market Access, *Status of Submissions to the Integrated Database (IDB), Note by the Secretariat*, G/MA/IDB/2/Rev.32, 6 October 2010.

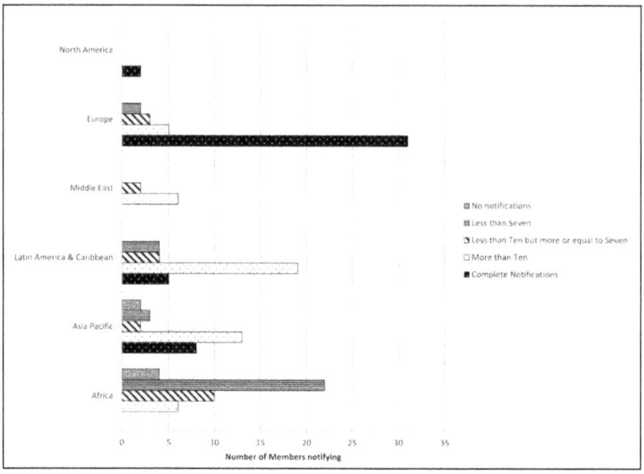

Figure 117. IDB imports notifications (1996–2010).

(iv) IDB Imports Notifications

Figure 117 shows the level of compliance with the IDB Imports notification requirements by Members in different regions in the period 1996–2010.[96]

African WTO Members' record on IDB import data notification in the period studied was abysmal. Only one African Member, Kenya, had submitted a complete IDB import notification (14 notifications) in the period studied (1996–2010). Africa's level of compliance in terms of complete notifications was low in relation to that of all other regions, with the exception of the Middle East. However, it is observed that most Members in the Middle East region submitted more than 10 notifications, that is, more than half of the required number. Regions where complete notifications were submitted were North America (100%); Europe (78%); Asia Pacific (25%), and, Latin America and Caribbean (9.3%).

Data showed that most African Members had submitted between 10 and 7 notifications (by 30 per cent of its membership) and less than seven (7) notifications (by 23 per cent of its membership), that is, less than half of the total required. In addition, Africa had the highest per cent of its membership that had not submitted notification with regard to imports at 28.5%. This was high (poor) in relation to the percentage of Members in other regions that had not submitted their import data. Twelve African Members accounted for the 28.5% of Members that had not submitted import information. These Members were: Angola, Botswana, Burundi, Cameroon, Chad, D.R. Congo, Djibouti, Mozambique, Nigeria, Sierra Leone, Swaziland, and, Uganda.

Overall, the record of notifications under the Decision on the IDB was poor. There were a range of explanatory factors. There are genuine problems of data gaps, absence of data, undeveloped national trade statistical systems and data unreliability. Beyond these, is the long-standing and more challenging problem by Member(s) to delay and/or

[96] Ibid.

not provide trade and tariff information that would place them "under negotiating pressure" in the still lingering "culture" of "concessions" as opposed to" liberalization commitments". This negotiating orientation more or less still characterizes the approach by a number of Members to providing trade and tariff information to the IDB, as a tool for tariff negotiations. Doha Round negotiation pressures have partly mitigated this situation but the problem remains.

With regard to African WTO Members, the applicable explanations related more to the absence of data, poor national trade statistical systems, and data unreliability. The WTO Secretariat Economic Research and Statistics Division has been exceptionally proactive in steps taken to assist African WTO Members. For instance, at a more general level, the WTO Secretariat has proposed a framework to enhance IDB notifications compliance[97] to overcome difficulties of information gaps and lateness in submission of notifications. The proposed framework would give the Secretariat more flexibility to collect data from official national, regional or international sources under certain circumstances with a view to increasing participation in the IDB and easing the reporting burden on Members.

13. The Committee on Rules of Origin

Article 4 of the Agreement on Rules of Origin established a Committee. The purpose of the Agreement is to undertake a Harmonisation Work Programme (HWP) of rules of origin so as to provide greater certainty in the conduct of world trade. The Committee on Rules of Origin (CRO) conducts the HWP. It also carries out other responsibilities assigned to it under the Agreement and by the Council for Trade in Goods.

The level of participation/engagement of African WTO Members compared to Members from other regions was analysed with regard to the following indices:

- Oral statements in the Committee;
- Written submissions/proposals; and,
- Notification count.

The level of engagement/participation of African WTO Members in this relatively complex area of core WTO work was very low. What explained this very low level of African WTO Member engagement?

First, complexity was a factor explaining the low level of engagement. Rules of Origin constitute one of the most complex areas of trade policy, at the intersection of decisions made by national authorities regarding market access, the application of trade remedies, customs valuation and the use of associated trade policy instruments such as tariff rate quotas (TRQs). Complexity is therefore an issue. But this does not mitigate the fact that this is an area where African Members should have developed specialized capacity in light of its implications for market access.

---

97 Committee on Market Access, *Framework to enhance IDB notification compliance – Note by Secretariat*, 2 June 2009, JOB(09)/43/Rev. 1.

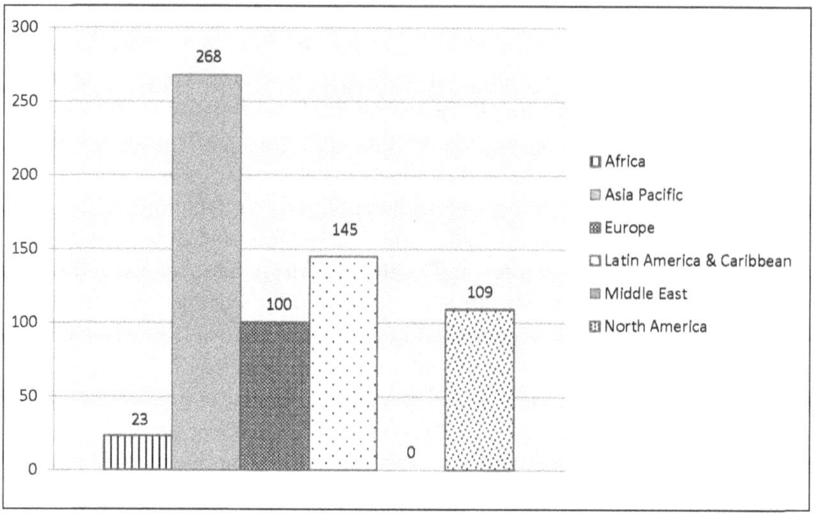

Figure 118. Individual statements in the CRO (1995–2010).

Second, the perennial factor of, professional commitment continues to provide the framework suggesting explanations for the low level of African engagement. The fact that an African WTO Member chaired the Committee on Rules of Origin in the first two years of the Organization (1995–1996) had minimal effect in raising the level of African engagement in this core area of regular work. This calls into question the relationship between chairmanships held on the one hand, and the level of engagement, on the other.

Third, this area continued to reflect the paradox where African WTO Members were not able to thread the needle between an evident area of priority commercial and systemic interest on the one hand, and the commensurate amount of resource and time for engagement. Understanding and resolving this paradox always leads back to the tenuous relationship between the capitals of these African WTO Members and the "Geneva front line".

(a) *Oral Statements in the CRO*[98]

Figure 118 shows the distribution of individual oral statements in the CRO by Members in different regions, in the period 1995–2010.

The number of oral statements by African WTO Member was 23 (or 3.5 per cent) of all statements in the CRO. This level of engagement/participation was low *per se* and also low in relation to statements from all other regions with the exception of the Middle East in typically low engagement. Three (or 7 per cent) of African WTO membership accounted for the 23 statements. These Members were: Egypt (15); Morocco (6); and, Mauritius (2). Rules of origin play a key role in the trade of all African countries, including these three African countries. The majority of African trade/exports are destined for the European market. The rules applied for the conferment of origin have largely influenced

[98] Minutes of the Committee on Rules of Origin, G/RO/M/1 to 55.

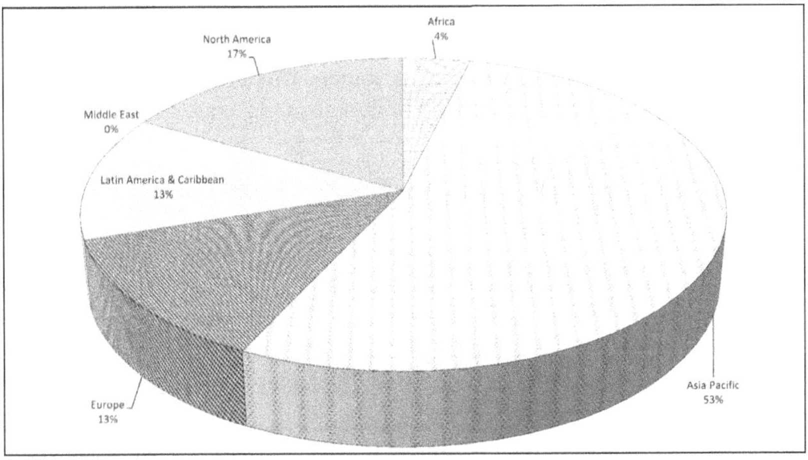

Figure 119. Proposals/submissions to the CRO (1995–2010).

their access of textiles and clothing (Egypt and Mauritius) and fish and fish products (Morocco). These African Members have direct commercial and systemic interests in the Harmonization Work Programme for the rules that would confer origin in the CRO and the potential impact/s for their trading regimes.

Ninety three (93) per cent of African WTO Members did not intervene in the CRO in the 15 year period studied. More scrupulous analytic engagement of this 93 per cent non-participating African WTO Members clearly suggest that they should have been as engaged as Egypt, Morocco and Mauritius because the exports of many of these African countries are governed by preferential access and therefore subject to rules of origin.[99]

(b) *Written Submissions/Proposals to the CRO*[100]

Figure 119 shows the distribution of written proposals/submissions to the CRO by Members in different regions, in the period 1995–2010.

A total of 68 written submissions/proposals were made in the CRO in the 15 year period studied. African Members' submissions/proposals at three (3) accounted for four (4 per cent) of the total number of all submissions/proposals. This was very low *per se*. The same three African WTO Members, that made oral statements in the CRO accounted for these written submissions/proposals. Egypt, Mauritius and Morocco each tabled one written proposal/submission. These submissions related to discussions on the Harmonization Work Programme of non-preferential rules of origin in several product-specific areas of the Harmonised Commodity Description and Coding System (the HS code).

99 Article 1.1 of the Agreement on Rules of Origin excludes the application of parts I to IV to rules of origin covering autonomous trade regimes leading to the granting of tariff preferences (preferential rules of origin). However, Annex II of the Agreement contains a Common Declaration with regard to Preferential Rules of Origin, that inter-alia provides for transparency of these rules and their notification.

100 G/RO/W/1–138.

These were: live animals, animal products; vegetable products, animal or vegetable fats and oil and their cleavage products; prepared foodstuffs, beverages, spirits and vinegar, tobacco and manufactured tobacco products; mineral products, wood and articles from wood, pulp of wood and of other fibrous cellulosic material; and, recovered (waste and scrap) paper or paperboard.

(c) *Submission of Required Notifications*[101]

Article 5.1 of the Agreement on Rules of Origin provides that each Member shall provide to the Secretariat, within 90 days after the date of entry into force of the WTO Agreement for it, its rules of origin (non-preferential), judicial decisions and administrative rulings of general application relating to rules of origin in effect on that date. If by inadvertence a rule of origin has not been provided, the Member concerned shall provide it immediately after this fact becomes known.

In accordance with paragraph 4 of Annex II of the Agreement, Members agreed to provide to the Secretariat promptly their preferential rules of origin including a listing of the preferential arrangements to which they apply, judicial decisions and administrative rules of general application relating to their preferential rules of origin in effect on the date of entry into force of the WTO Agreement for the Member concerned. Furthermore, Members agreed to provide any modifications to their preferential rules of origin or new preferential rules as soon as possible. In both cases – non-preferential and preferential rules of origin – the obligation is of a one-off nature. Changes made are notified on an *ad hoc* basis.

(i) Notification of Non-Preferential Rules

As of October 2010, 38 Members had notified non-preferential rules of origin; 42 had notified that they did not have non-preferential rules of origin, while 46 Members had not notified.

Figure 120 shows the level of compliance with this notification obligation by Members in different regions.

Compared to all regions, African WTO Members compliance was at the bottom. African Members had the lowest level of compliance with the notification of non-preferential rules of origin with 38 per cent of its membership (or 16 African WTO Members) making notifications in the 15 year period studied. Twenty-six (or 62 per cent) of African WTO Members had not submitted notifications with regard to non-preferential rules of origin.[102] This was the poorest in comparison to the percentages of Members in the other regions that had not submitted this notification: 8 Members (or 15 per cent of membership) in the Latin America and Caribbean region; 7 Members (or 15 per cent) in the Asia

---

[101] Sixteenth Annual Review of the Implementation and Operation of the Agreement on Rules of Origin, Note by Secretariat, G/RO/70, 17 December 2010.

[102] Angola, Benin, Botswana, Cameroon, Cape Verde, Central African Rep. ,Congo, Côte d'Ivoire, D.R. Congo, Djibouti, Egypt, Gabon, Gambia, Guinea Bissau, Guinea, Malawi, Mali, Mauritania, Mozambique, Nigeria, Rwanda, Sierra Leone, Swaziland, Tanzania, Togo, Zambia, and, Zimbabwe.

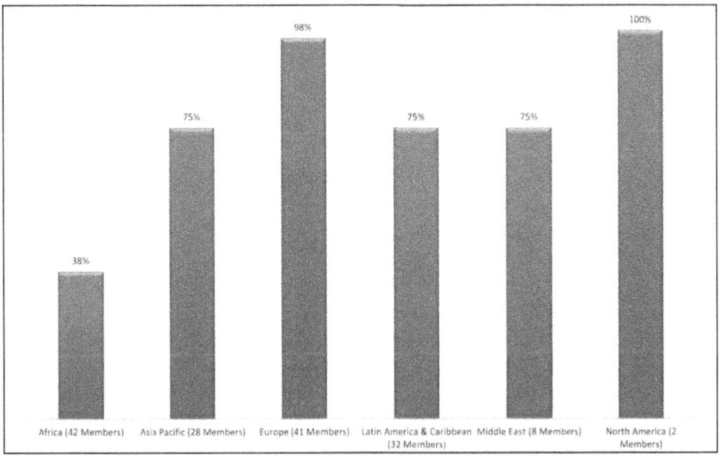

Figure 120. Level of notification of non-preferential rules of origin (1995–2010).

Pacific region; 2 Members (or 15 per cent) in the Middle East; and, 1 Member (or 2 per cent) in Europe.[103]

(ii) Notification of Preferential Rules of Origin

As of October 2010, 84 Members had notified that they had preferential rules of origin; four had notified that they did not have preferential rules of origin; and, 42 Members had not made any notification. There were 37 Members that had notified preferential rules of origin to other WTO bodies. Figure 121 shows the level of compliance with notification of preferential rules of origin by Members in different regions.

As with notifications on non-preferential rules of origin, African WTO Members were at the bottom in fulfilling this requirement in comparison to all other regions. They had the lowest level of compliance with the notification of preferential rules of origin with 47 per cent of African WTO membership (or 20 African WTO Members) making notifications in the 15 year period studied. Twenty-two (or 52 per cent) of African WTO Members had not submitted notifications of their non-preferential rules of origin.[104] This was the poorest in comparison with the numbers of Members in the other regions that had not submitted this notification: 7 Members (or 21 per cent of membership) in the Latin America and Caribbean region; 10 Members (or 35 per cent) in the Asia Pacific region; 3 Members (or 38 per cent) in the Middle East.

---

[103] **Latin America and Caribbean:** Antigua and Barbuda, Barbados, Belize, Ecuador, Grenada, St. Kitts & Nevis, St. Lucia, St. Vincent & Grenadines; **Asia Pacific:** Bangladesh, Cambodia, Myanmar, Nepal, Solomon Islands, Sri Lanka, Tonga, Vietnam; **Middle East:** Bahrain, Kuwait; **Europe:** Kyrgyz Republic.

[104] Angola, Benin, Botswana, Burundi, Cameroon, Cape Verde, Central African Rep., Congo, Djibouti, Egypt, Guinea, Guinea Bissau, Malawi, Mauritania, Mozambique, Nigeria, Rwanda, Sierra Leone, South Africa, Swaziland, Togo.

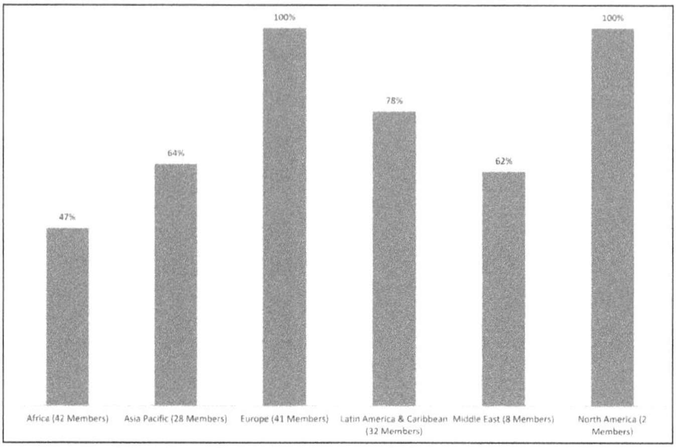

Figure 121. Notification of preferential rules of origin (1995–2010).

The level of African engagement/participation in this vital and complex area of rules of origin is another example where the effectiveness of the participation of African WTO Members has been severely weakened by obligations and commitments not implemented. It reinforces one of the central propositions in this study that unimplemented obligations render any Member or group of Members weak and vulnerable.

(d) *Participation in the Non-Preferential Rules of Origin Harmonization of Work Programme (HWP)*

The participation of African WTO Members in the HWP through contributions to the draft consolidated text was examined for the period 1996–2010.[105] Figure 123 shows the distribution of Members in different regions that had made contributions to the Harmonisation Work Programme through contributions to the draft consolidated text.

The level of participation by African Members in the HWP was low at 9.5 per cent of its membership (or 4 out of 42 African Members) making contributions to the draft consolidated text. Ninety (90) per cent of African membership had not been actively involved in a process linked to their trade policy and commercial interest regardless of trade shares.

Disaggregated data showed that Egypt and Morocco had been the most active African participants in the HWP through the Integrated Negotiating Text. Other countries that had also participated, albeit to a relatively lower degree, in the HWP, were Senegal and Nigeria. The areas of interest for African Members that had participated in the HWP included the product chapters/sectors addressing: animal products (meat, fish, poultry,

[105] See document JOB (01)/52/Rev. 6, Committee on Rules of Origin, *Integrated Negotiating Text for the Harmonisation Work Programme, Technical Issues to be resolved in the Committee, Note by the Secretariat*, 11 April 2007.

Region	Members making contributions to the Integrated Negotiating Text as of 2010.
Africa (4/42)	Egypt, Morocco, Nigeria, Senegal
Asia-Pacific (16/28)	Australia, Fiji, India, Japan, Korea, New Zealand, Thailand, Chinese Taipei, Philippines, Singapore, Malaysia, Sri Lanka, Hong Kong, China, Pakistan, Indonesia, China.
Europe (33/41)	EU, Switzerland, Norway, Iceland, Slovenia, Czech Rep, Turkey.
Latin America & Caribbean (13/32)	Argentina, Mexico, Dominican Rep., Venezuela, Guatemala, Brazil, Honduras, Cuba, Chile, Colombia, Costa Rica, Peru, Ecuador.
Middle East (0/8)	
North America (2/2)	Canada, United States.

Figure 122

and fats); coffee and tea; other beverages; chemical products; textile products, non-ferrous metals, articles of metal; mineral products; and machinery.

14. The Committee on Safeguards

Article 13 of the Safeguards Agreement established a Committee on Safeguards (SG Committee) under the authority of the Council for Trade in Goods. The functions of the Committee are:

- monitoring and reporting annually to the Council for Trade in Goods on, the general implementation of the Agreement and making recommendations towards its improvement;
- finding, upon request of an affected Member, whether or not the procedural requirements of the Agreement have been complied with in connection with a safeguard measure, and report its findings to the Council for Trade in Goods;
- assisting Members, if they so request, in their consultations under the provisions of the Agreement;
- examining measures covered by Article 10 (pre-existing Article XIX measures) and paragraph 1 of Article 11 (prohibition and elimination of certain measures) and monitoring the phase-out of such measures and reporting as appropriate to the Council for Goods;
- reviewing, at the request of a Member taking a safeguard measure, whether proposals to suspend concessions or other obligations are "substantially equivalent", and reporting as appropriate to the Council for Trade in Goods;
- receiving and reviewing all notifications provided for in the Agreement and reporting as appropriate to the Council for Trade in Goods, and;
- performing any other function connected with the Agreement that the Council for Trade in Goods may determine.

The level of participation/engagement of African WTO Members in the Safeguards Committee was analysed and compared to Members from other regions with regard to the following indices:

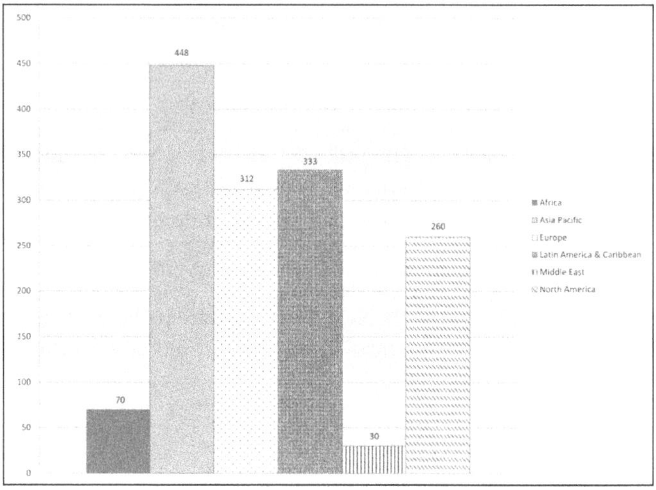

Figure 123. Statements in the Safeguards Committee (1995–2010).

- oral statements in the Committee;
- written submissions/proposals;
- notification count,
- use safeguards.

(a) *Oral Statements in the SG Committee*[106]

Figure 123 shows the distribution of oral statements in the SG Committee by Members in different regions in the period 1995–2010.

African Members' oral statements were low *per se* at a total of 70 (or 4.8 per cent) of the total number of statements in the SG Committee. African Members' statements were also low in relation to statements from Members in all other regions, with the exception of the Middle East. Six African WTO Members (or 14 per cent of African WTO membership) accounted for the 70 statements. These Members were: Egypt (41); Morocco (11); Nigeria (5); South Africa (9); Tunisia (3); and, Zambia (1). These African Members form part of the universe of active African delegations in the Organization's activities. Egypt, Morocco, South Africa and Tunisia were the African WTO Members that had initiated and/or imposed safeguard measures against exports of other Members.

African WTO Members' individual oral statements were low in relation to individual statements by Members in other regions. The low level of African engagement typically reflects the pattern in areas of specialized complexity. With few exceptions the evident pattern was that the more specialized and complex, the lower the level of engagement. Increased technical assistance had not yet been able to mitigate this problem, suggesting that there were other mediating variables that intervened between the level of engagement on a Y axis and capacity building on the X dimension.

106 Minutes of the Committee on Safeguards, G/SG/M/1 to 38.

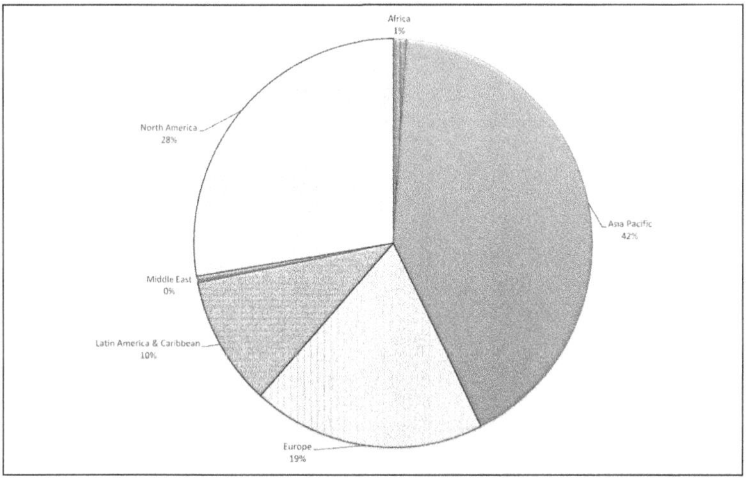

Figure 124. Submissions/Proposals to the Safeguards Committee (1995–2010).

In rank order, the highest numbers of oral statements in the SG Committee were made by: EU (312); US (230); India (67); Brazil (60); Japan (57); Argentina (53); China (52); and, Chile (47). These Members had either initiated or imposed a number of safeguard measures against exports of other Members, or were the targets of safeguard measures by other Members.

African WTO Members intervened in the SG Committee in the context of the discussion of pre-existing Article XIX measures that they maintained. They also intervened in discussions on implementation issues and concerns under the SGA and to voice concern about the manner in which safeguard measures were applied. In this context, some African Members proposed the establishment of a Working Party to discuss and make recommendations on issues concerning the application of the Safeguards Agreement.

(b) *Written Submissions/Proposals to the SG Committee*[107]

Figure 124 shows the distribution of written submissions/proposals in the SG Committee by Members in different regions in the period 1995–2010.

African WTO Members' written proposals/submissions to the SG Committee were very low at two (or 1.08 per cent) of the total number of submissions/proposals in the 15 year period studied. It was low in relation to the number of written proposals/submissions by Members in all other regions, with the exception of the Middle East. Two (or 4.7) African WTO members accounted for these submissions/proposals – South Africa (1) and, Tunisia (1).

[107] Committee on Safeguards, G/SG/W/1 to 215.

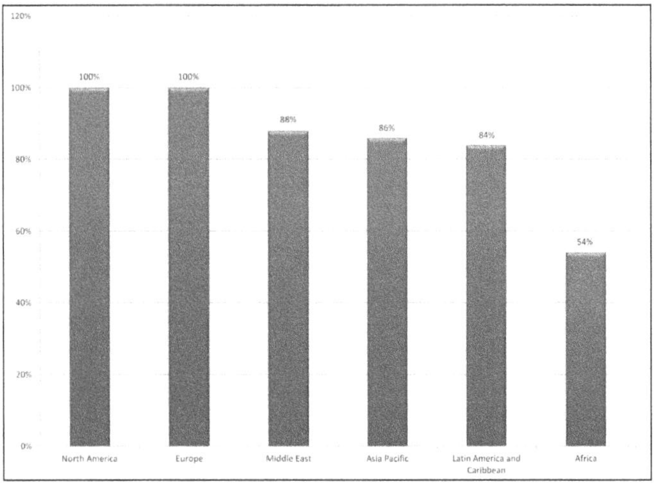

Figure 125. Notification of safeguards legislation (1995–2010).

Submission of Required Notifications to the SG Committee[108]

Article 12.6 requires Members to notify their laws, regulations and administrative procedures, and any changes thereto, to the Committee. For Members that do not have legislation, a notification of this fact has to be made. Figure 125 shows the level of compliance by Members in different regions with the notification of their national legislation, in the period 1995–2010.

African WTO Members' level of compliance was the lowest, at 54 per cent (or 23 of the 42 African WTO Members) submitting a safeguards legislation notification. Africa had the most number of Members in its region, 19, that had not made any notification.[109] This number was the highest (poorest) in relation to other regions with Members that have not made this notification – five for Latin America and Caribbean; four, for Asia Pacific, and, one for the Middle East.

Trend in the Use of Safeguard Measures[110]

(i) Safeguard Initiations

Reporting Members

There were distinct trends in WTO regular work in the use of safeguard measures. Figure 126 shows that in the period studied, the involvement in the highly complex pro-

[108] Report (2010) of the Committee on Safeguards to the Council for Trade in Goods, G/L/936, 29 October 2010.

[109] Angola, Cameroon, Cape Verde, Central African Rep., Congo, D.R. Congo, Djibouti, Gabon, Gambia, Guinea Bissau, Mali, Mauritania, Mozambique, Niger, Rwanda, Sierra Leone, Swaziland, Tanzania, and, Togo.

[110] http://www.wto.org/english/tratop_e/safeg_e/safeg_e.htm

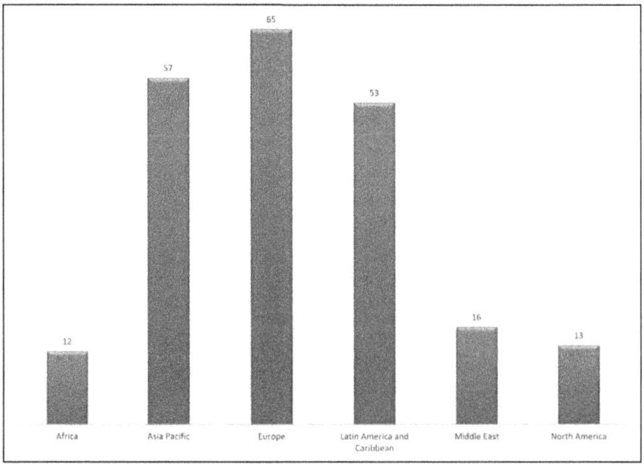

Figure 126. Safeguard initiations: 1995–2010.

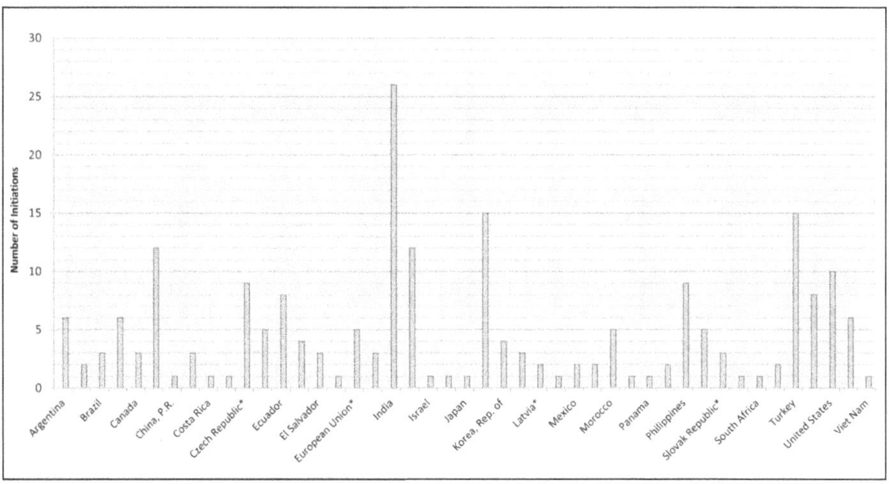

Figure 126 (b). Safeguard initiations 29/03/1995–31/10/2010.

cess of the initiation of safeguard investigations had been limited to only 29 per cent of the entire WTO membership.

Positively, African Members had initiated the least number of safeguard actions at 12, (or 5.5 per cent) of the total number of safeguard initiations in the 15 year period studied. These initiations were accounted for by Egypt (4), Morocco (5), South Africa (1) and Tunisia (2). In rank order, Members with the highest initiations in the period studied were India (26), Turkey (15), Jordan (15), Chile (12); and, Indonesia (12).

(ii) Imposition of Safeguard Measures

Data points to the fact that similar to the case of anti-dumping, safeguard measures were not automatically imposed for all investigations initiated. The number of safeguard

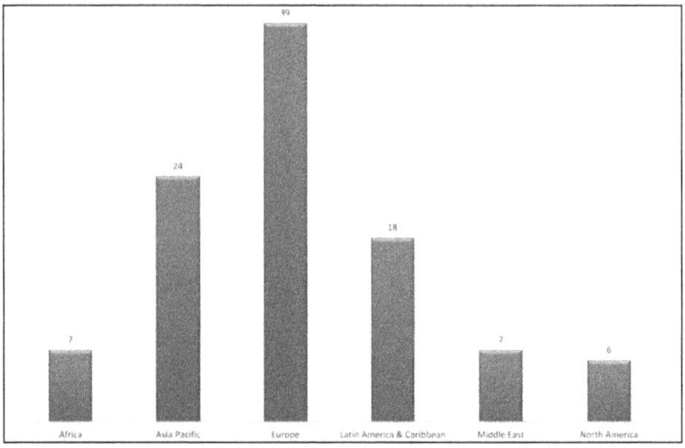

Figure 127. Safeguards measures (29/03/1995–31/10/2010).

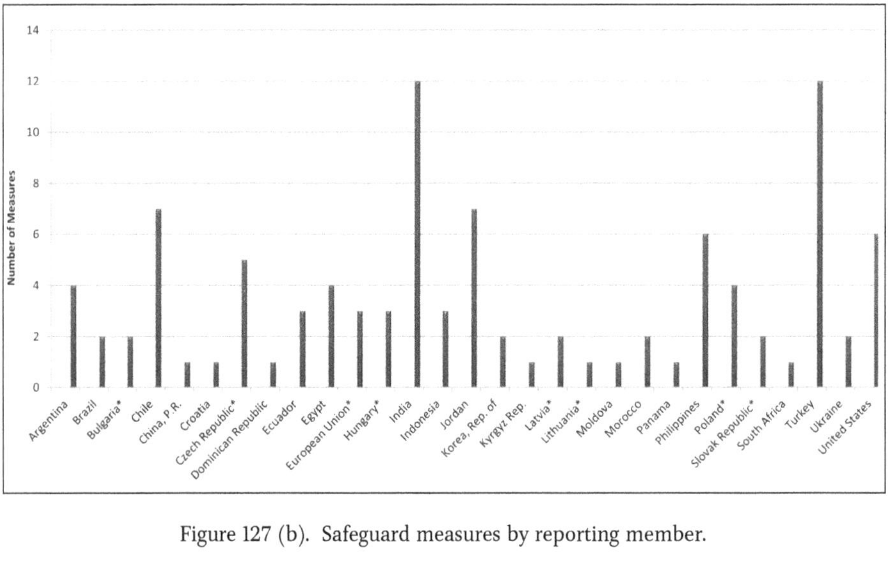

Figure 127 (b). Safeguard measures by reporting member.

initiations was more than that of measures imposed. Twenty nine (29) countries had imposed safeguard measures in the period reviewed. (Figure 127).

In the period 1995 to June 2010, African WTO Members, positively, had imposed the lowest number of safeguard measures – 7 (or 6.9 per cent) of the total number of safeguard measures imposed. Egypt (4), Morocco (2) and South Africa (1) accounted for these measures. For a range of reasons, African Members were the "least protectionist" with specific regard to use of trade remedies. Similar to the situation on initiation of investigations, India (12), Turkey (12), Jordan (7), Chile (7), Philippines (6) and US (6) had imposed the most safeguard measures against exports from other countries.

Why has there been low usage of this trade policy instrument by African Members? The reasons are the same that have applied with regard to the low level of statements, submissions and proposals and notifications in this area of trade remedies. The area of trade remedies use as instruments of trade policy are the most directly related to trade flows and surges. First, African trade as a percentage share of global trade is low. There are few instances of trade flows that either "threaten" or cause material injury to manufacturing interest in target markets. Second, the ability of African countries with the exception of Egypt and South Africa in particular, to use these instruments are limited due to the absence or low level of infrastructure for trade remedy use in capitals. Third, relatedly, specialized capacity is limited with lack of competent authorities to undertake investigations. Fourth, cost limitations related to conduct of investigations and maintaining a competent authority have had an effect. Fifth, domestic industries to lobby for "safeguarding" their interests through use of SG actions are weak, under-developed, or limited.

Regardless of these factors, there is the more strategic question of whether this "protectionist route" is a road down which African WTO Members should travel. It is recommended that African WTO Members do not embark on this trade policy use, except in the most serious of situations where need is warranted.

15. The Committee on Trade Related Investment Measures

Governments sometimes impose conditions to encourage or compel the use of investment measures according to national priorities. WTO Members, including developing countries, have used such measures to promote national priorities, including development objectives. The Agreement on Trade-Related Investment Measures (TRIMS Agreement) recognises that certain investment measures can cause trade-restrictive and distorting effects. It therefore aims to promote the expansion and progressive liberalization of world trade and to facilitate investment across international frontiers so as to increase economic growth of all Members, while ensuring free competition. Article 7 of the TRIMS Agreement established a Committee on Trade-Related Investment Measures. The TRIMS Committee carries out responsibilities assigned to it by the Council for Trade in Goods and affords Members the opportunity to consult on any matters relating to the operation and implementation of the TRIMS Agreement. It also monitors the operation and implementation of the Agreement and reports annually to the Council for Trade in Goods.

The level of participation/engagement of African WTO Members in the TRIMS Committee was analysed and compared to Members from other regions with regard to the following indices:

- Oral statements in the Committee;
- Written submissions/proposals; and,
- Notification count.

(a) *Oral Statements in the TRIMS Committee*[111]

Figure 128 shows the distribution of oral statements by Members in different regions in the TRIMS Committee in the period 1995–2010.

[111] Minutes of the TRIMS Committee, G/TRIMS/M/1 to 30.

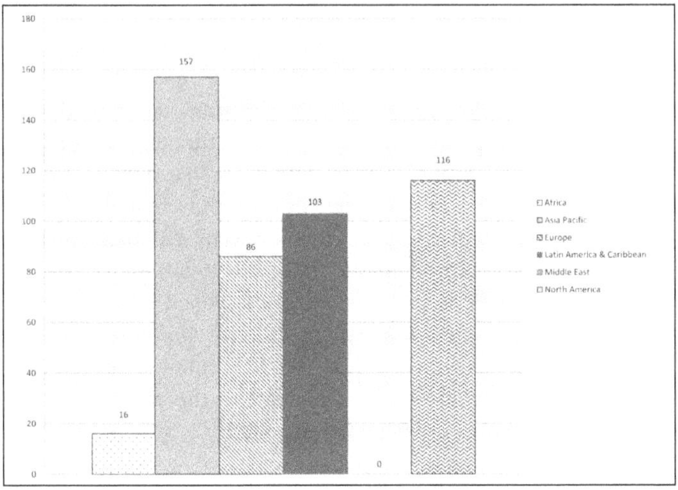

Figure 128. Statements in the TRIMS Committee (1995–2010).

African WTO Members have directly linked the area of regular work governed by the TRIMS Agreement to development gains derivable from the rules-based trading system. The paradox, however, is that their *low level* of engagement (oral statements, written submissions/proposals, notifications) in the TRIMS Committee reflects an inverse relationship to the *high development premium* accorded to trade related investment measures (such as domestic content requirements) for their development.

The low level of engagement was reflected in the number of oral statements by African Members at 16 (or 3.3 per cent) of the total number of statements in the TRIMS Committee in the 15 year period studied. This share was low in relation to statements by Members from all other regions with the exception of the Middle East, whose Members did not made statements in the TRIMS Committee during the 15 year period studied. Six, (or 14 per cent) of African WTO membership accounted for the 16 statements. These were: Egypt (2); Kenya (10); Morocco (1); Nigeria (1); South Africa (1); Zimbabwe (1). The individual number of oral statements by African Members that made statements was low *per se* in comparison to individual statements by Members in other regions. In rank order, most statements in the TRIMS Committee were made by: the US (85); EU (72); Japan (35); Canada (31); India (30); Brazil (28); China (24), and Argentina (19).

What explains this paradox of the low level of participation of African WTO Members in the TRIMS Committee and the high development premium accorded to this area as being important for national priorities? Explaining this paradox is the minimal level of Geneva-capital coordination. In several African countries, legislation either exists or bills are being considered for enactment to require buinesses, both foreign and domestic to use local content inputs. In addition, questions remain about the technical competence, sustained professional commitment and the level of overall policy appreciation of the negotiators deployed to WTO regular work. The TRIMS Committee regular work is not an area of specialized complexity. It is more related to the nexus of trade, investment and development to which African WTO Members in particular and low-income developing countries (such as LDCs) attach priority. Yet, the level of participation was low.

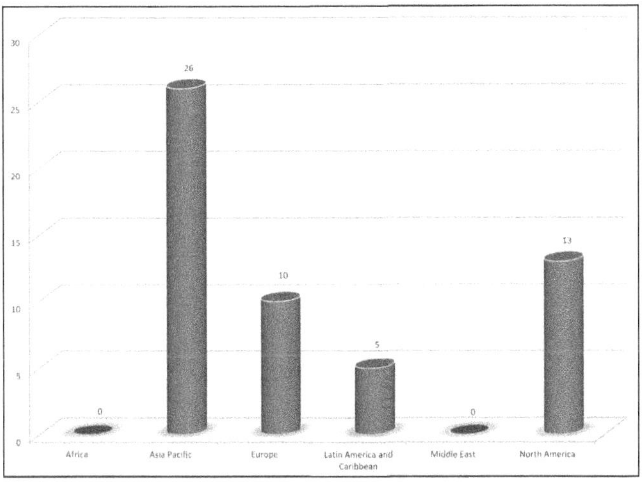

Figure 129. Submissions/proposals to the TRIMS Committee (1995–2010).

The problem of the low level of participation was illustrated in the demand for the extension of the transition period for the elimination of WTO-inconsistent TRIMS notified and, strengthening and making operational special and differential treatment with regard to the TRIMS Agreements . Even with the Decision, in Annex F of the 2005 Hong Kong Ministerial Declaration, to grant an extension for the use of WTO-inconsistent TRIMS, several Members still had not notified the said TRIMS.

The low level of African Members' participation was also evident in submissions to the TRIMS Committee.

(b) *Written Submissions/Proposals in the TRIMS Committee*[112]

Figure 129 shows the distribution of written submissions/proposals to the TRIMS Committee, by Members in different regions, in the period 1995 to 2010.

No African WTO Member had tabled a written submission/proposal to the TRIMS Committee. Although the African Group's views were heavily articulated in the TRIMS Committee meetings, paradoxically, no formal written proposal/submission had been made to the Committee.

(c) *Submission of Required Notifications*

Pursuant to Article 5.1 of the TRIMS Agreement, Members were required to notify any WTO inconsistent TRIMs within 90 days after the entry into force of the WTO Agreement. Article 5.2 allowed for transition periods for the elimination of measures notified under Article 5.1 and which were in existence at least 180 days preceding the entry into force of the WTO Agreement. In April 1995, the General Council decided that governments which had accepted the WTO Agreement after 1 January 1995 had a period of

[112] Committee on Trade Related Investment Measures, G/TRIMS/W/1 to 80.

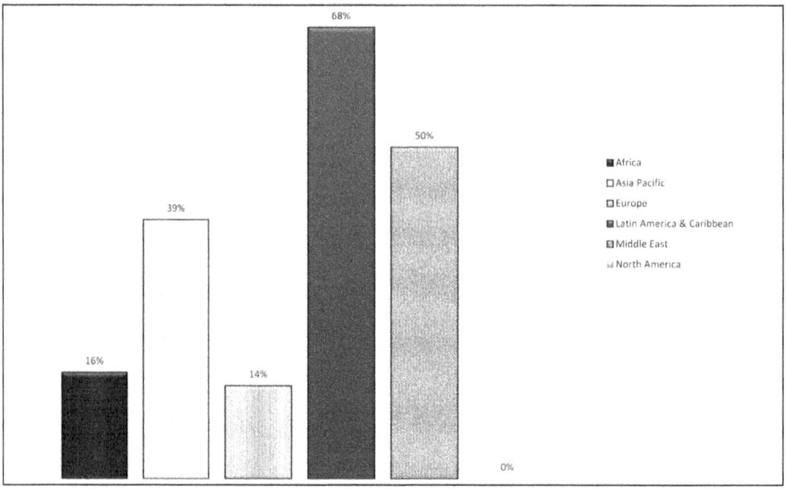

Figure 130. Article 5.1 notifications.

90 days after the date of their acceptance of the Agreement to notify pursuant Article 5.1. The period for the elimination of TRIMS notified under Article 5.1 would be governed by the reference date of the entry into force for them of the WTO Agreement.[113]

(i) Article 5.1 Notifications (WTO-Inconsistent TRIMS)

Figure 130, shows the level of compliance with Article 5.1 notifications by Members in different regions in the period 1995–2010.

The level of compliance by African Members' with TRIMS Article 5.1 notification obligations was low at 16 per cent of its members submitting the notification. This level was low relative to the level of notifications by Members originating from the Latin America and Caribbean, Asia Pacific and Middle East, and only better than the level of compliance of Members from Europe and North America. It was also low *per se*, taking account of the fact that only seven (or 16 per cent) of African WTO membership had complied. The seven African Members were: Egypt, Nigeria, South Africa, Uganda, Mali, Mauritius, and, Zambia. Thirty-five African WTO Members were yet to notify.

(ii) Article 6.2 Notifications of TRIMS Publications

Article 6.2 requires each Member to notify the WTO Secretariat of the names of publications in which TRIMS may be found, including those applied by regional and local governments and authorities within their territories. In case a Member does not maintain any TRIMS which are inconsistent with the Agreement, but maintains TRIMS consistent with the Agreement, that Member has an obligation to report all publications where

[113] Notification under Article 5.1 of the Agreement on Trade Related Investment Measures by States and Separate Customs Territories eligible to become original WTO Members that accept the WTO Agreement after its Entry into Force, WT/L/64, 10 April 1995.

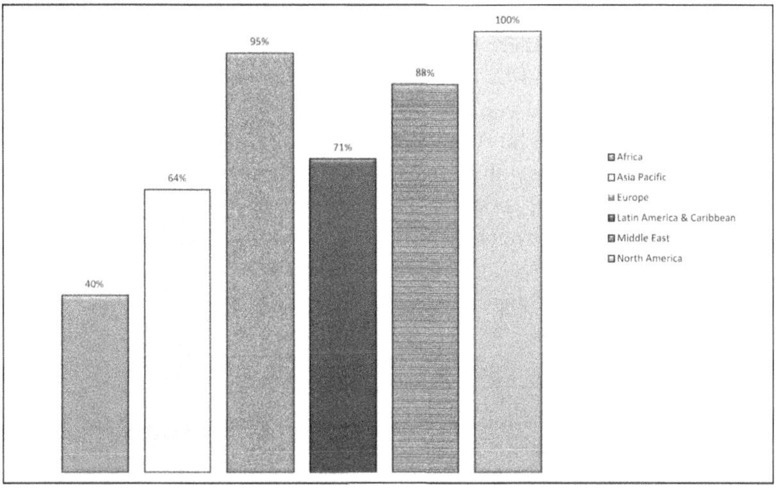

Figure 131. Article 6.2 notifications.

such consistent TRIMS might be found. Figure 131 shows the level of compliance with this notification by Members in different regions, in the period 1995–2010.

African WTO Members' level of compliance was the lowest at 40 per cent (or 17[114] out of 42 African WTO Members) complying with their Article 6.2 TRIMS notifications of publications. This level of compliance was also low in relation to all other regions. Twenty-Four African Members (or 60 per cent) had not complied with this notification obligation. The rate of engagement was associated with low levels of professional engagement and diligence. This notification does not required specialized technical skills, but only communicating and describing existing facts.

(iii) LDC-Specific TRIMS Waivers in the 2005 Hong Kong Ministerial Declaration (Annex F Decisions)

Decision 84 in Annex F of the 2005 Hong Kong Ministerial Declaration allowed LDCs to maintain on a temporary basis existing measures that deviate from their obligations under the TRIMS Agreement.[115] For this purpose, LDCs were required to notify the Council for Trade in Goods of such measures within two years, that is, by 18 January 2008. Data showed that no such notifications were received. The Hong Kong Declaration also allowed least developed countries to introduce new measures that deviate from their obligations under the TRIMS Agreement. These new TRIMS are required to be notified to the Council for Trade in Goods within six months after their adoption. As of 2010, no notifications had been received under this Decision. Again this reflected a paradox. African WTO Members, mostly LDCs, strongly supported this LDC proposal in 2005 at

[114] Angola, Burundi, Cameroon, Chad, Gabon, Ghana, Madagascar, Mali, Mauritius, Namibia, Nigeria, Senegal, South Africa, Tunisia, Uganda, Zambia, and, Zimbabwe.

[115] Hong Kong Ministerial Declaration, WT/MIN (05)/DEC, December 2005.

the Hong Kong Ministerial Conference. After having obtained a Decision on this proposal, vigorously fought for, there has been no follow up. The rational expectation was that African WTO Members/LDCs would have notified more measures under this provision in the TRIMS Agreement consistent with their development priorities. Being host to the majority of LDCs, with 33 African LDCs out of a total of 48, African WTO Members have not taken advantage of this special and differential treatment provision that the LDC Group worked hard to attain. Reinforcing earlier recommendations, African WTO Members need to improve on Geneva-capital coordination, better link their trade, investment and development priorities, and demonstrate keener professional commitment and sustained levels of engagement in WTO regular work.

16. The Committee on Technical Barriers to Trade

Article 13 of the Agreement on Technical Barriers to Trade (TBT Agreement) established a Committee. Fundamentally, the purposes of the TBT Agreement is to ensure that technical regulations and standards including packaging, marking and labelling requirements, and procedures for assessment of conformity with technical regulations and standards do not create unnecessary obstacles to international trade. It recognises that international standards and conformity assessment systems can make important contributions to facilitating the conduct of international trade and improving the efficiency of production. Similar to the SPS Agreement, attaining international standards in these areas are necessary and indispensable for market access. As tariff barriers have declined from previous rounds of trade negotiations, the vital necessity of addressing the trade restrictive effects of TBT and SPS measures has correspondingly increased.

The level of participation of African WTO Members in the TBT Committee was analysed and compared to Members from other regions with regard to the following indices:

- Oral statements in the Committee;
- Written submissions/proposals;
- Notification count; and,
- Participation in specific trade concerns raised in the Committee.

(a) *Oral Statements in the TBT Committee*[116]

Figure 132 shows the distribution of oral statements in the TBT Committee by Members in different regions in the period 1995–2010.

African Members' oral statements in the TBT Committee were low at 193 (or 4.6 per cent) of the total number of statements. Their statements were also low *per se* as a proportion of statements by Members from other regions, with the exception of the Middle East. Nineteen (or 45 per cent) of African WTO membership accounted for the 193 statements.[117] African WTO Members' individual statements were low in relation

---

[116] Minutes of the TBT Committee, G/TBT/M/1 to 51.

[117] Botswana (5), Burundi (1), Central African Republic (1); Djibouti (1); Egypt (126); Ghana (1); Kenya (5); Malawi (1); Mauritius (6); Morocco (4); Mozambique (1); Nigeria (7); Rwanda (1); Senegal (3); South Africa (21); Tanzania (1); Uganda (2); Zambia (1); Zimbabwe (5).

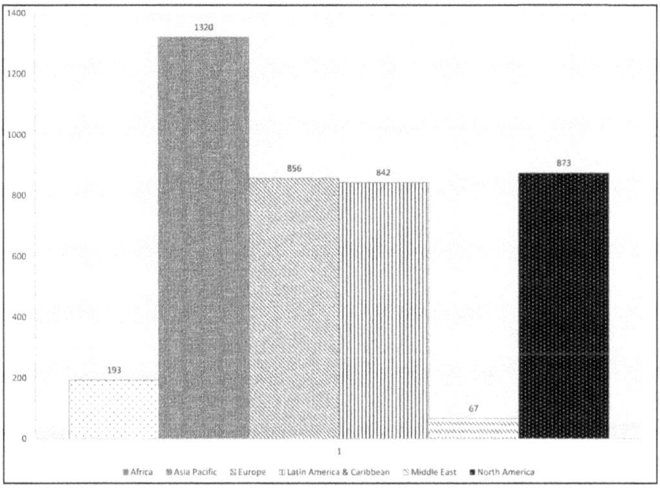

Figure 132. Statements in the TBT Committee (1995–2010).

to individual statements by Members in other regions. Their oral interventions ranged from 1 to 6. In rank order, the highest numbers of statements in the TBT Committee were made by: EU (683); US (557); Canada (316); Japan (282); Mexico (215); China (208); Brazil (164); Australia (143); New Zealand (136); Korea (122).

There was an inverse relationship between the vital importance of this area for African market access on the one hand, with the low level of African participation in the TBT Committee, on the other. Furthermore, a systemic position by African WTO Members makes evident the importance they attach to the use of trade rules and policies to achieve industrialization. In addition, African WTO Members are also Members of international standard setting bodies, such as the International Standards Organization (ISO).

African WTO Members intervened in the TBT Committee in the context of the discussions on specific trade concerns maintained by other Members that impacted on their exports. In this connection, most of their interventions related to measures maintained by Canada (Canada-Bill C-32 Amendment to Tobacco Act) and by the European Union (EC-Regulation on the Registration, Evaluation and Authorization of Chemicals (REACH); and, EC-Dangerous Chemical Substances Directive- ATP 31). African Members expressed concerns that these measures were complex, discriminatory, or unnecessary barriers to trade. In some cases, African Members sought further information, clarification, and time to adapt to these measures.

The African Members that maintained measures that were of concern to other Members intervened to explain their measures, including the objectives, and to respond to questions posed by Members. This was the case for South Africa, Egypt and Tunisia, all three, relatively industrialized African economies, whose measures were deemed as having the potential to impact on the exports of other Members.

The African Members that intervened did so in the discussions of specific topics such as eco-labelling; labelling, equivalence, conformity assessment and proliferation of private standards. They also expressed their views about enhancing transparency on TBT

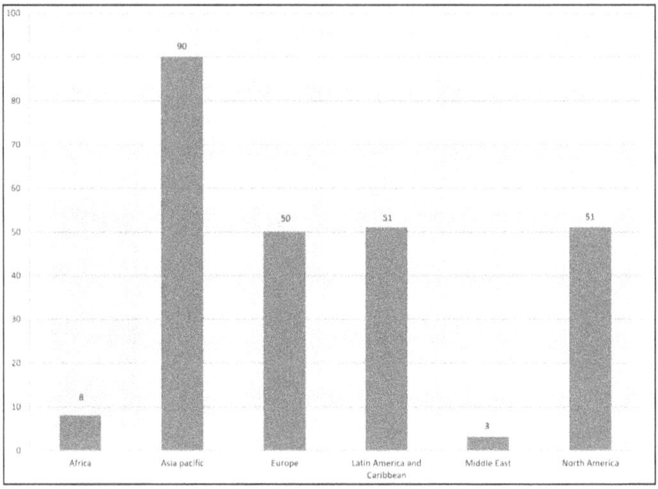

Figure 133. Submissions to the TBT Committee (1995–2010).

matters including by translation of notifications from enquiry points, particularly for the benefit of developing countries and LDCs. African Members expressed concerns about the low level of participation by African countries in international-standards setting work. African Members also intervened to seek observer status for their regional bodies in the TBT Committee, e.g. for SADC. Furthermore, they sought technical assistance and capacity building and operational special and differential treatment to enhance their participation in the work of the Committee.

In response to these requests, the WTO Secretariat has increased its training programmes on TBT matters for African WTO Members, including in collaboration with standards-setting bodies. In addition, some Members have enhanced technical assistance and capacity building programmes for African TBT officials, including by facilitating the participation of Capital-based officials in TBT Committee meetings in Geneva, for example, Sweden for a number of East African countries.

(b) *Written Submissions/Proposals to the TBT Committee*[118]

Figure 133 shows the distribution of written statements in the TBT Committee by Members in different regions in the period 1995–2010.

The number of written submissions/proposals was yet lower than the number of oral statements. As a general overarching technical point, it is to be noted that oral statements seem easier to formulate than the drafting of written submissions and proposals. African WTO Members' proposals/submissions to the TBT Committee were very low at 8 (or 3.1 per cent) of the total number of submissions/proposals, in the 15 year period studied. It was low in relation to the number of proposals/submissions by Members in all other regions,

[118] Committee on Technical Barriers to Trade, G/TBT/W/1–333.

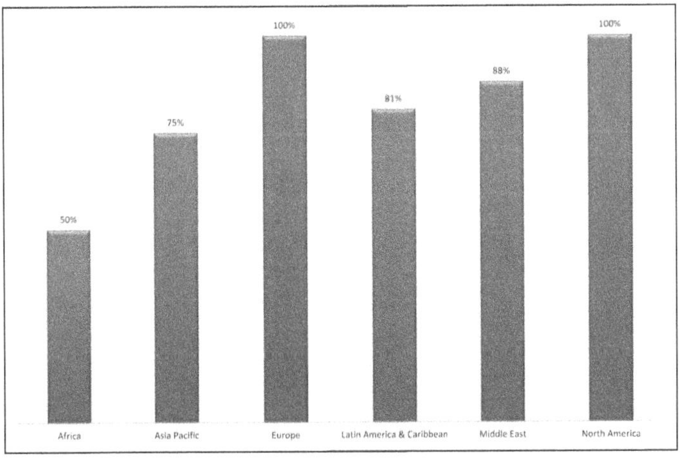

Figure 134. Statements on the implementation & administration of the agreement (Art. 15.).

with the exception of the Middle East. Six African Members (or 14 per cent) accounted for these submissions/proposals. These were Egypt (3); Cameroon (1); Kenya (1); Malawi (1); Tanzania (1), and, Uganda (1). The submissions/proposals related to the triennial reviews of the TBT Agreement. They also included proposals regarding technical assistance. Some of these countries notified technical regulations on specific products. Their submissions also included expressions of concerns on measures maintained by other Members with the potential to impact on their exports. Examples included the effects of Canada's Tobacco Act on Malawi, Kenya, and Uganda; and, the classification in the 31st Adaptation to Technical Progress (ATP) to dangerous substances directive of the EC.

(c) *Submission of Notification Requirements*

(i) Implementation and Administration of the TBT Agreement under Article 15.2

Article 15.2 of the TBT Agreement requires each Member to promptly inform the committee of measures in existence or taken to ensure the implementation and administration of the Agreement after the date on which the WTO Agreement enters into force for it. Any changes of such measures are also supposed to be notified to the committee.

Figure 134 shows the level of compliance with the "notification of statements on the implementation and administration of the TBT Agreement" (Article 15.2), by Members in different regions in the period 1995–2010.

In the period studied, half of African WTO Members had notified a statement on implementation and administration of the TBT Agreement as mandated by Article 15.2 of the TBT Agreement. Twenty-one (or 50 per cent) African WTO Members had not. This was the poorest level of compliance in relation to the other regions that had Members which had not compiled with the notification requirement – 25 per cent of Members in the Asia Pacific region; 18 per cent of Members in the Latin America and Caribbean region; and 12 per cent from the Middle East.

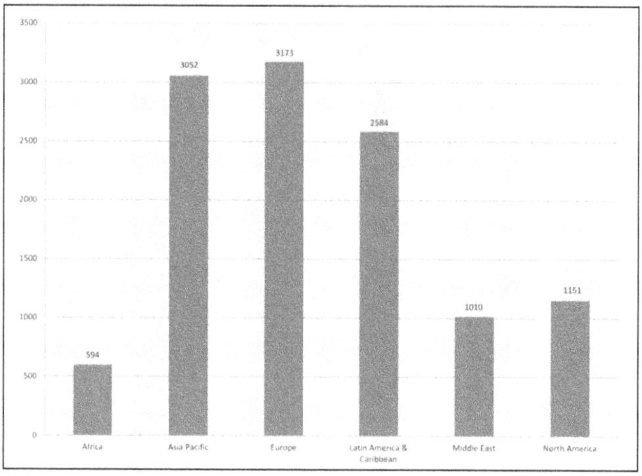

Figure 135. Notification of technical regulations and conformity assessment procedures (1995–2009).

(ii) Notification of Technical Regulations and Conformity Assessment Procedures[119]

In 2009, Members submitted 1490 new notifications (including revisions) of technical regulations and conformity assessment procedures. Between 1995 and 2009, the number of notifications totalled 11,576. These were made by 110 Members.[120] Figure 135 shows the distribution of the number of notifications of technical regulations and conformity assessment procedures by Members in different regions in the period 1995–2009.

African WTO Members notified the least number of technical regulations and conformity assessment procedures at 594 (or 5.1 per cent) of the total number of notifications. This level was the lowest in comparison to all other regions. Sixteen (16) African WTO Members (or 38 per cent) of African membership accounted for the 594 notifications. Most notifications were made by Kenya (199) and South Africa (172). The individual numbers of notifications by other African Members were low *per se*. The other African WTO Members were: Benin (2), Botswana (2), Cameroon (8), Central African Republic (10), Egypt (18), Mauritius (2), Morocco (23), Nigeria (1), Rwanda (8), Senegal (12), Tanzania (16), Uganda (46), and, Zambia (44).

The number of notifications by individual African Members was also low in relation to the number of individual notifications by Members in other regions. In rank order, the most number of notifications of technical regulations and conformity assessment procedures were made by China (723), US (714), Japan (560), Brazil (474), EU (469), Israel (444), Canada (437), Thailand (434), Korea (366),and, Argentina (312). It is observed that

[119] WTO, Committee on Technical Barriers to Trade, *Fifteenth Annual Review of the Implementation and Operation of the TBT Agreement*, Note by the Secretariat, 5 February 2010. The notifications were made pursuant to TBT Agreement Articles 2.9; 2.10; 3.2; 5.6; 5.7; and, 7.2.

[120] Ibid.

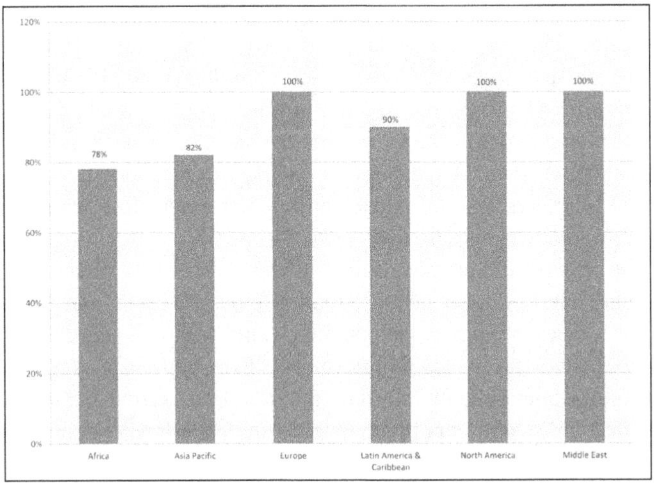

Figure 136. Level of notification of TBT enquiry points (1995–2009).

Members of the EU had a total of 2186 notifications, of which Netherlands (618), Czech Republic (244), Denmark (234), and Belgium (209) had the most notifications.

(iii) WTO TBT Enquiry Points[121]

Articles 10.1 and 10.3 of the TBT Agreement require Members to ensure that an enquiry point exists which is able to answer all reasonable enquiries from other Members and interested parties and provide relevant documents on technical regulations, standards and conformity assessment procedures adopted or proposed within its territory by central, local, non-governmental bodies with legal powers to enforce them or by regional standardizing bodies. Information is also to be provided on membership and participation in international and regional standardizing bodies or conformity assessment systems as well as in bilateral and multilateral arrangements within the scope of the Agreement; location of notices published or provision of information; and, location of enquiry points.

Figure 136 shows the level of compliance with notification of enquiry points by Members in different regions in the period 1995–December 2009.

African WTO Members had the lowest notification level of enquiry points amongst all regions. Seventy eight per cent of the African WTO membership had made the notification in the period studied. Notification of enquiry points is one of the simplest obligation by Members in WTO regular work in the implementation of Agreements. This notification does not require specialized technical skills, but only communicating and describing existing facts, or rectifying the situation if there is a deficiency such as the non-existence

[121] Committee on Technical Barriers to Trade, National Enquiry Points, Note by Secretariat, 5 February 2010, G/TBT/ENQ/36.

of an enquiry point. Nine (9) African Members had not notified their national enquiry points as obligated. These were: Angola, Cape Verde, Chad, Congo, D.R. Congo, Gabon, Mauritania, Senegal and Togo. This level of non-compliance was the highest in relation to other regions with Members that had not notified their national enquiry points: 5 in the Asia Pacific region and 3 in the Latin America and Caribbean region.

As with most other areas of regular WTO work, the recurring question arises: why is African WTO Members' level of participation/engagement low across the indices of statements, submissions/proposals, and notifications?

Although the level of industrialization in Africa is low, this situation still does not explain the relatively low level of participation/engagement in the TBT Committee. Overall analyses suggest a range of factors. First, Geneva-capital coordination is low and as a consequence there has been a failure to provide a common platform that connects African negotiators operating in international standard setting bodies, with capital-based authorities and negotiators in Geneva. Second, the low level of African engagement also typically reflects the pattern in areas of apparent specialized complexity. With few exceptions the evident pattern is that the more specialized and complex, the lower the level of engagement. Third, although there is a need for technical assistance, the technical assistance problem is low on the rung of the explanatory ladder accounting for the low level of participation. A notable feature of technical assistance in the area of TBT (and SPS) is that it is supply driven by technical assistance providers. Developed countries are sensitive and have been on the defensive that they should not use TBT and SPS standards as protectionist measures in response to their domestic constituencies, for "quality imports". In reaction therefore, technical assistance in these areas have been principally supply-driven. Finally, the review of data and interview results continue to highlight the variable of professional diligence and commitment.

However in the period from 2009, the participation of African WTO Members begun to gradually increase in the TBT Committee, with capital-based officials from national standards-setting organization attending meetings. But, the level of their participation was still low relative to all regions in this study. It is recommended, as with other areas of regular WTO work, that African Members must urgently increase Geneva-capital coordination. They need to either establish or make more effective their standing national committees and to enhance government/industry coordination. There is a continuing failure to operate credibly at domestic levels of coordination with relevant, real time stream of instructions to African negotiators at the WTO.

(d) *Specific Trade Concerns Raised in the TBT Committee (January 1995–October 2010)*[122]

Since its first meeting, Members have used the Committee as a forum for discussing issues related to specific measures (technical regulations, standards or conformity assessment procedures) maintained by other Members. The specific trade concerns relate variously either to proposed measures notified to the TBT Committee, in accordance

[122] Committee on Technical Barriers to Trade, *Specific Trade Concerns Raised in the TBT Committee, Note by the Secretariat*, G/TBT/GEN/74/Rev. 6, 19 October 2010.

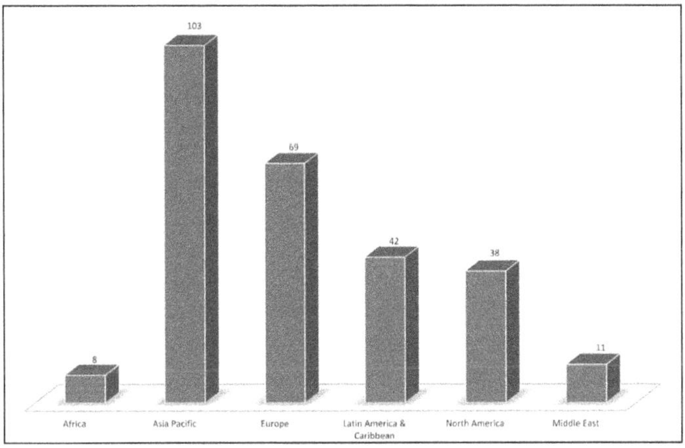

Figure 137. Specific trade concerns by members (1995–October 2010).

with the notification requirements in the Agreement, or to measures currently in force. Committee meetings or informal discussions between Members, held in the margins of such meetings, afford Members opportunity to review trade concerns in a bilateral or multilateral setting and to seek further clarification. Members regularly discuss follow-up in the Committee.

In the period 1995 to October 2010, a total of 271 specific trade concerns were raised in the TBT Committee. Figure 137 shows the distribution of measures maintained by Members in different regions that were raised as specific trade concerns in the TBT Committee.

Positively, African WTO Members had the lowest number of specific TBT measures raised as being of concern to other Members, at eight (or 2.9 per cent) of specific trade concerns raised in the TBT Committee. Three (or 7.1 per cent) of African WTO membership, that is, Egypt (4), South Africa (3) and Tunisia (1) accounted for the measures by African Members. The measures maintained by African Members mostly related to labelling requirements. This suggests that Africa in fact remained the "least trade protectionist region" with specific regard to the use of NTBs.[123] The objectives that African Members put across to justify their measures included: harmonization and health and safety. Annex XI: 1 shows the specific trade concerns by African Members.

(i) Specific Trade Measure Concerns Raised by African WTO Members

A number of African WTO Members have expressed concerns in the TBT Committee with specific measures maintained by other Members that could impact their exports. Annex XI: 2 shows the measures with which African Members raised concerns in the

[123] Least trade protectionist does not necessarily mean the most open. A market may be open in trade terms, but less accommodating and business friendly because of a range of other trade negative factors such as corruption, insecurity, rule of law and governance issues, low level and inefficient trade infrastructure etc.

period analysed. Twelve African Members (or 28 per cent) expressed concerns about 6 measures (or 2.1 per cent of all specific concerns raised in the Committee) in the 15 year period studied. These were Botswana, Burundi, Egypt, Kenya, Malawi, Mauritius, Mozambique, South Africa, Tanzania, Uganda, Zambia and Zimbabwe. The concerns expressed broadly related to transparency; time to adapt measures; measures presumed to create unnecessary barriers to trade; complexity of measures; uncertainty and further information and clarification of measures.

17. The Committee on Subsidies and Countervailing Measures

Article 24 of the Agreement on Subsidies and Countervailing Measures (SCM Agreement) established a Committee on Subsidies and Countervailing Measures (SCM Committee). The SCM Agreement establishes rules and disciplines governing different categories of subsidies. It identifies prohibited subsidies, actionable subsidies and non-actionable subsidies. The SCM Agreement also specifies procedures for dispute settlement panels and remedies in demonstrated instances where subsidies cause serious prejudice. The Committee carries out responsibilities as assigned to it under the Agreement or by Members and affords Members the opportunity of consulting on any matter relating to the operation of the Agreement or to the furtherance of its objectives.

The level of participation/engagement of African WTO Members was analysed and compared to Members from other regions with regard to the following indices:

- Oral statements in the Committee;
- Written submissions/proposals; and,
- Notification count.

(a) *Oral Statements in the Committee*[124]

Figure 138 shows the distribution of statements by Members in different regions in the SCM Committee in the period 1995–2010.

African WTO Members have underlined as priority the area of WTO regular work covered by the Agreement on Subsidies and Countervailing Measures. Their stated position to justify this area as one of trade policy priority relates to their immediate post-Uruguay Round reaction to achieve "fairness, equity and a level playing field in the WTO".[125] The overall approach has been to seek to "normalize" the conditions of competition as affected by unrestrained use of subsidies. This same position has been repeated by African WTO Members, in coordination with low-income developing countries, in the context of the monitoring mechanism established by the Director-General on trade-related measures taken to contain and mitigate the effects of the 2008–2009 Global Financial and Economic Crisis. Tightly constrained national budgets (fiscal resources) prevent African Members from maximal use of subsidies. However, their trade policy position has been to ensure the disciplined and constrained use of subsidies by devel-

[124] Minutes of the Committee on Subsidies and Countervailing Measures, G/SCM/M/1 to 75.

[125] See footnote 2 in chapter four.

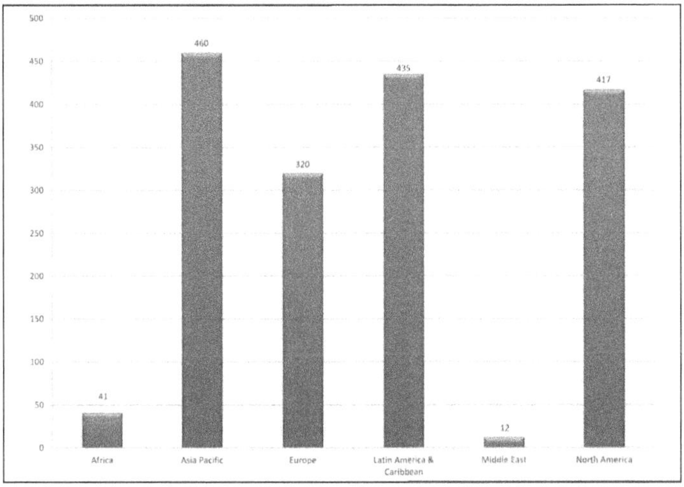

Figure 138. Statements in the SCM Committee (1995–2010).

oped Members. The objective therefore has been for a high level of engagement, at least with regard to advocacy in interventions in the SCM Committee. This is an area that African WTO Members have identified as being of systemic priority.

However, African Members' statements were low at a total of 41 (or 2.4 per cent) of the total number of oral statements in the SCM Committee. African Members' statements were also low *per se* in relation to statements from Members in all other regions, with the exception of the Middle East. Eleven African WTO Members (or 26 per cent of African WTO membership) accounted for the 41 statements. These Members were: Egypt (15); Mauritius (7); South Africa (7); Kenya (3); Tunisia (2); Côte d'Ivoire (2); Cameroon (1); Ghana (1); Morocco (1); Namibia (1), and, Zimbabwe (1). These African Members form part of the universe of active African delegations in the Organization's activities. Egypt and South Africa were the African WTO Members that had initiated CVD actions and South Africa ranked fifth amongst WTO Members in the initiation of CVD actions.

African WTO Members' individual oral statements were low in relation to individual statements by Members in other regions. In rank order, the highest number of statements in the SCM Committee were made by: the US (321), EU (248), Japan (99), Canada (96), Australia (74), China (68), Mexico (59), Brazil (48), Argentina (45), and, Colombia (44).

The substance of African WTO Members interventions in the SCM Committee related to the review of their CVD legislation; the status of subsidy notification; expression of concern with burdens faced in meeting notification obligations; responses to questions posed to them about their semi-annual reports on countervailing actions; and implementation issues and concerns under the SCM Agreement. Furthermore, in their statements, they sought extension of the transition period in Article 27.4 of the SCM for the phasing out of export subsidy programmes; the review of Article 27.6 (export competitiveness of a product); the review of Annex VII of the SCM, and, to respond to concerns raised by other Members about country programmes instituted (for example, the case of the South African Motor Industry Development Programme).

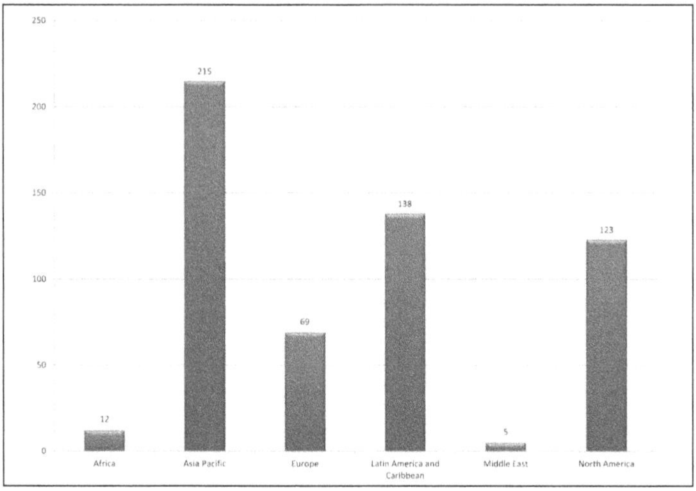

Figure 139. SCM submissions/proposals.

(b) *Written Submissions/Proposals to the SCM Committee*[126]

Figure 139 shows the distribution of written submissions/proposals by Members in different regions in the period 1995–2010. In the period reviewed, African WTO Members submitted a total of twelve (12) proposals or 2.1 per cent of the total number of proposals to the SCM Committee. This was low *per se*. The number of written submissions/proposals was also low relative to proposals by Members in other regions with the exception of the Middle East. Written submissions/proposals by African Members were made by seven (or 16 per cent) of African membership. The seven Members were: Egypt (3), Mauritius (2), South Africa (2), Tunisia (1), and a joint proposals/submissions by Uganda, Tanzania, and, Zimbabwe et al. (4).

The substance of submissions by African Members were replies to questions posed to them regarding their SCM legislation. African Members also highlighted implementation issues and concerns under the SCM Agreement in submissions made. They also highlighted difficulties faced in meeting notification obligations; and, requested for the extension of the transition period in Article 27.4 of the SCM Agreement on the phasing out of export subsidies for developing countries.

Disaggregated data showed that in rank order, most written submissions/proposals in the Committee were made by the US (83), Hong Kong, China (61), EU (50), Australia (48), Canada (40), Korea (30), and, India (29). Most of these Members have high systemic interest with regard to SCM legislation or regulations adopted by other WTO Members that could impact their trade. Most submissions by Members in other regions were in the form of questions posed to other Members on laws and regulations on SCM and written responses to questions received. Submissions were also made in the context

[126] Committee on Subsidies and Countervailing Measures, G/SCM/W/1 to 553.

of the review of the SCM; subsidy notifications, implementation issues and concerns under the SCM Agreement, extension of the transition period for the phase out of export subsidies for developing countries and China's Transitional Review Mechanism.

(c) *Submission of Required Notifications*[127]

(i) Notification of Countervailing Duty Legislation

Article 32.6 of the SCM Agreement requires Members to notify to the Committee changes in their laws and regulations relevant to the Agreement and in the administration of such laws and regulations. As of April 2010, thirty-two countries had not yet made a notification of their laws and regulations to the SCM Committee. The level of compliance with notification of countervailing duty legislation by Members, in different regions, in the period from 1995 to April 2010 was as follows:

- North America, Europe – 100 per cent of its membership
- Latin America and Caribbean, Middle East – 88 per cent of its membership
- Asia Pacific – 86 per cent of its membership
- Africa – 48 per cent of its membership

With 48 per cent of its membership having complied with this notification obligation, Africa's level of compliance was the lowest and the poorest across all regions. Twenty-two African WTO Members (or 52 per cent) had not complied with the obligation to notify the existence or non-existence of countervailing duty legislation. These were: Angola, Botswana, Burkina Faso, Cape Verde, Central African Republic, Congo, Democratic Republic of Congo, Côte d'Ivoire, Djibouti, Gabon, Gambia, Guinea Bissau, Mali, Mauritania, Mozambique, Niger, Rwanda, Sierra Leone, Swaziland, Tanzania, and, Togo. This number was poor in relation to the other regions that had Members that had not notified their national legislation: 14 per cent of Members from Asia Pacific; and 12.5 per cent of Members from the Latin America and Caribbean and Middle East regions respectively.

The effort and input level required for notification are not difficult and non-burdensome. Members notify existent legislation and provide the text, or notify to indicate the absence of any legislative and/or regulatory software. Where there is no legislation, the notification is in the form of a letter stating the fact of non-existence of legislation. This does not entail specialized technical knowledge and skills.

(ii) Notification of Competent Authority

Article 25.12 of the SCM Agreement stipulates that Members shall notify to the Committee the competent authorities to conduct countervailing duty investigations in their territories and the domestic procedures that govern the initiation and conduct of such investigations.

[127] Committee on Subsidies and Countervailing Measures, *Notification Requirements under the Agreement on Subsidies and Countervailing Measures*, G/SCM/W/546/Rev.1, 16 April 2010.

As of April 2010, sixty-seven (67) WTO Members had made this notification to the Committee. The level of compliance with notification of Competent Authority by Members in different regions in the period from 1995 to April 2010 was as follows:

- North America – 100 per cent of its membership
- Europe – 90 per cent of membership
- Latin America and Caribbean – 65 per cent of membership
- Asia Pacific – 57 per cent of membership
- Middle East – 38 per cent of membership
- Africa – 28 per cent of membership

With 28 per cent of its membership (or 12 out of 42) having submitted this notification, African WTO Members had the poorest level of compliance. The 12 Members that had submitted notifications were: Angola, Egypt, Ghana, Kenya, Morocco, Namibia, Nigeria, South Africa, Tunisia, Uganda, Zambia, and, Zimbabwe. Thirty African WTO Members were yet to notify. It is observed that the same African Members that had not notified their competent authorities had also not complied with the requirement to notify CVD legislation, presumbly that would establish a competent authority.

(iii) Notification of Subsidies

Article 25.1 of the SCM Agreement provides that, without prejudice to the provision of Article XVI: 1 of GATT 1994, Members shall notify their subsidies no later than 30 June of each year. However, based on a May 2001 Committee Decision, Members are now required to submit this information to the Committee every second year.

The distribution of compliance with the notification of subsidies in the period 1995–2009 by Members in different regions was as follows:

- North America – 100 per cent of membership
- Latin America and Caribbean – 94 per cent of membership
- Europe – 90 per cent of membership
- Asia Pacific – 79 per cent of membership
- Middle East – 75 per cent of membership
- Africa – 57 per cent of membership

In the period studied, a total of thirty-two (32) Members had not notified their subsidies to the SCM Committee as required. Eighteen (18) African countries had not notified their subsidies. This was the highest. By contrast, 14 Members from other regions had not notified: 6 from Asia-Pacific; 4 in Europe and 2 each in the Middle East and Latin America and Caribbean regions.[128]

[128] Annex B of document G/SCM/W/546/Rev.1. **African countries** were: Angola, Cape Verde, Central African Republic, Chad, Congo, Democratic Republic Congo, Djibouti, Gabon, Guinea Bissau, Kenya, Lesotho, Mauritania, Mozambique, Niger, Rwanda, Sierra Leone, Tanzania, and, Togo. **Asia-Pacific** (Bangladesh, Cambodia, Maldives, Nepal, Solomon Islands, Tonga, and, Vietnam); **Europe** (FYR Macedonia, Kyrgyz Rep., Moldova) **Middle East** (Kuwait, Kingdom of Saudi Arabia) **Caribbean** (Guyana, Haiti).

The overall state of compliance with subsidy notification provisions of Article 25 was repeatedly the subject of discussion in the Committee.[129] For a number of African Members that had provided information on subsidies, the notifications were out-dated. For these African Members, the "most recent" period dated back to ten years for the period between 1995 and 2002. The problem therefore of a low level of compliance with notification obligations was worsened by the obsolescence of previous notification. In the period analysed, only Burkina Faso and Mauritius had recent notifications.

(iv) Semi-Annual Reports on Countervailing Duty Actions[130]

Article 25.11 of the SCM Agreement requires Members to notify, without delay, all preliminary and final actions taken with respect to countervailing duties. It also provides that Members shall submit, on a semi-annual basis, reports on any countervailing duty actions taken in the preceding six months.

To ascertain the level of commitment to semi-annual reporting on countervailing duty actions, two specific recent periods were selected for comparative analysis in this study. These two periods were: (i) from 1 July to 31 December 2009; and, (ii) from 1 January to 30 June 2010. Table 1 in Annex XII shows the level of compliance by Members in different regions in providing semi-annual reports. Members either reported actions taken or reported that no actions had been undertaken or made a one-time notification.

African WTO Members' level of compliance was the lowest and poorest with only 28 per cent of them either submitting a report of action taken, or a report of no action, or making a one-time notification. Compliance was also low in comparison with the 100 per cent notification for North America; 92 per cent for Europe; 59 per cent for Latin America and Caribbean; 53 per cent for Asia Pacific; and, 50 per cent for the Middle East.

Africa had the most number of Members that had not complied with this notification obligation. Thirty-two African WTO Members (or 76 per cent of its membership) had not complied with the obligation for the required periods in 2009/2010. This was the poorest in comparison to other regions with Members that had not complied. These were: Middle East, four Members (or 50 per cent); Asia Pacific, thirteen Members (or 46 per cent); Latin America and Caribbean, thirteen Members (or 40 per cent); and Europe, three Members (or 7.4 per cent).

The recurring question, similar to other specifically identified core areas of regular work, is why is there an inverse relationship between the level of engagement/participation in identified areas of systemic and commercial interests for African WTO Members, on the one hand, and the time and sustained effort invested, on the other? Explanatory factors have varied across different areas of regular work. Specific to the SCM Committee, why has the level of participation (number of oral statements, written submissions/

---

129 Minutes of the Subsidies Committee in G/SCM/M/24, 25, 27 as cited in document G/SCM/W/546/Rev.1.

130 Data is based on Annex E of the Annual Report of the Committee on Subsidies and Countervailing Measures, of 29 October 2010, G/L/937.

proposals, and notifications) been low in contrast to the priority attached to this area of regular work by African WTO Members?

Analysis of the data gathered and results of interviews again reinforce the combined propositions that the level of participation/engagement of African WTO Members was low as the level of specialized complexity increased. But this explanatory factor does not stand alone. Associated explanations, based on data analysis, also reinforced discontinuous professional engagement, scope for increased professional diligence and continued laxity in Geneva-capital coordination. The analysed trends in the section that follows further describes the reality of low levels of participation and the continued plausibility of the suggested propositions.

(d) *Trends in the Use of Countervailing Measures*[131]

(i) Initiations of Countervailing Actions

Reporting Members (Figure 140 (b))

A relatively small number of WTO Members – 20 Members (counting the European Union as one) – had been involved in initiation of countervailing investigations in the period analysed.

With 17 (or 6.8 per cent) of the total number of initiations of countervailing actions, African WTO Members initiated the lowest numbers of countervailing actions. Two (or 4.7 per cent) of 42 African Members initiated countervailing actions in a 15 year period studied. These actions were accounted for by Egypt (4) and South Africa (13). Expectedly, Africa's use of this trade remedy instrument as a trade policy tool was the lowest, with the exception of South Africa which ranked as one of the top five initiators of countervailing actions. Why has there been low usage of this trade policy instrument? As explained in the other two areas of trade remedy engagement by African WTO Members, this low level of countervailing action was partly explained by absence of domestic infrastructure (legislation, competent authorities), the low level of specialized capacity, and, the overall longstanding problem of the inability in African trade policy to match policy priorities with corresponding technical action.

Members with the highest initiations in the period studied were US (104), EU (56), Canada (24), South Africa (13) and Australia (11).

(ii) Countries Subject to Initiation

Figure 141 shows the distribution of Members in different regions that had been subject to countervailing investigations in the period 1995 to December 2009.

Expectedly, African WTO Members were low level targets for countervailing duty investigations. Exports from only one (1) African Member, South Africa, were the subject of countervailing initiations in the period reviewed. Why this?

A possible core explanatory factor for Africa as a low-level target of countervailing duty investigations is that the SCM Agreement provides more favourable treatment for least developed countries (LDCs) in terms of exemption from the prohibition on export

[131] http://www.wto.org/english/tratop_e/scm_e/scm_e.htm

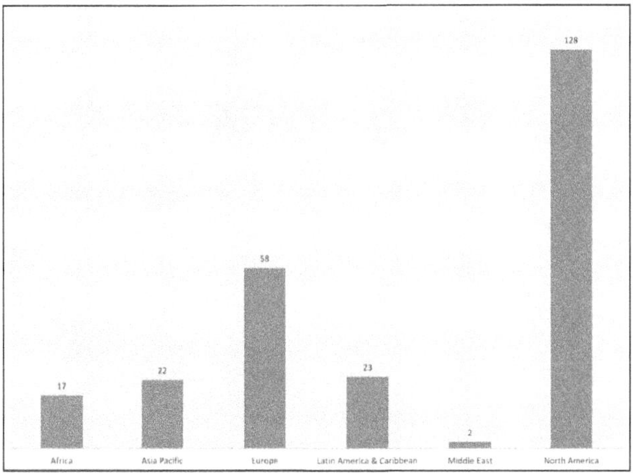

Figure 140. Countervailing initiations (1/1/1995–30/6/2010).

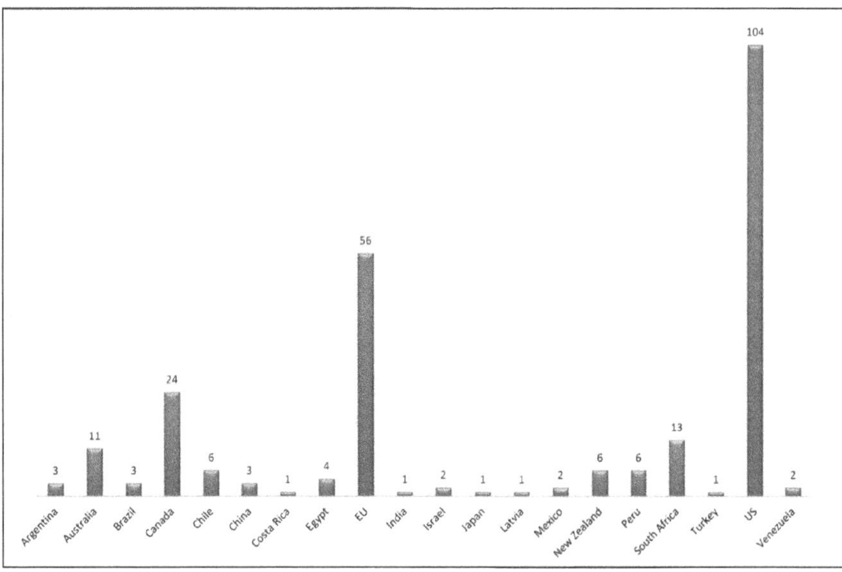

Figure 140 (b). Countervailing initiations by reporting member (1/1/95–30/06/2010).

subsidies, and a longer time period to phase out import-substitution subsidies. These S&D provisions probably accounted for the minimal level of investigations against African exports. In addition, there was also more favourable treatment with respect to actionable subsidies. For example, certain subsidies related to developing country Members' privatization programmes were not actionable multilaterally. With respect to countervailing measures, developing country Members' exporters were entitled to more favourable treatment with respect to the termination of investigations where the level of subsidization or volume of imports was small. Most African countries would therefore benefit from these special and differential treatment provisions, including the exemptions mentioned.

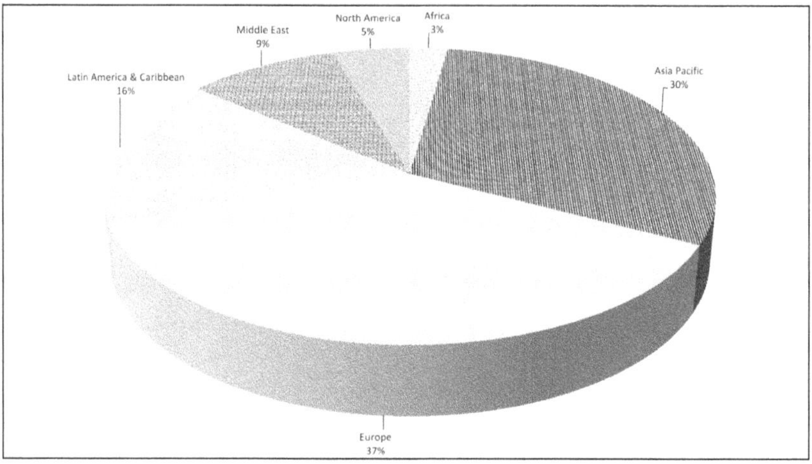

Figure 141. Members subject to countervailing initiations by region (1/1/1995–31/12/2009).

Finally, the level of Africa's trade share and trade flows remain low. They do not pose a threat, nor have they caused material injury to the manufacturing interests in its trading partners. Only South Africa had taken SCM trade remedy action against other African countries.

(iii) Imposition of Countervailing Measures

Data points to the fact that countervailing measures were not automatically imposed for all investigations initiated. Only fifteen (15) WTO Members were involved in the imposition of countervailing measures. Figure 142, shows the distribution of Members in different regions that imposed countervailing measures in the period 1995–June 2010.

African WTO Members imposed the lowest number of countervailing measures, after the Middle East whose Members did not imposed countervailing measures. South Africa was the only African Member which imposed measures against other trading partners, accounting for the 5 measures imposed by African WTO Members. These actions by South Africa continued to reflect its industrial capacity in comparison to other African countries, "emergent" market status and indicated an area of trade defence for South Africa (in contrast to its areas of trade offence, such as agriculture). South Africa was also the only African country whose exports were subject to countervailing measures – four times, by New Zealand and the United States, twice each.

18. The Committee on Sanitary and Phytosanitary Measures

The objective of the Agreement on Sanitary and Phytosanitary Measures (SPS Agreement) is to safeguard and improve human health, animal health, and, phytosanitary situations in WTO Member States and establish a multilateral framework of rules and disciplines to guide the development, adoption, and enforcement of SPS measures so as to minimize negative trade effects. The Agreement also has as its objective to promote

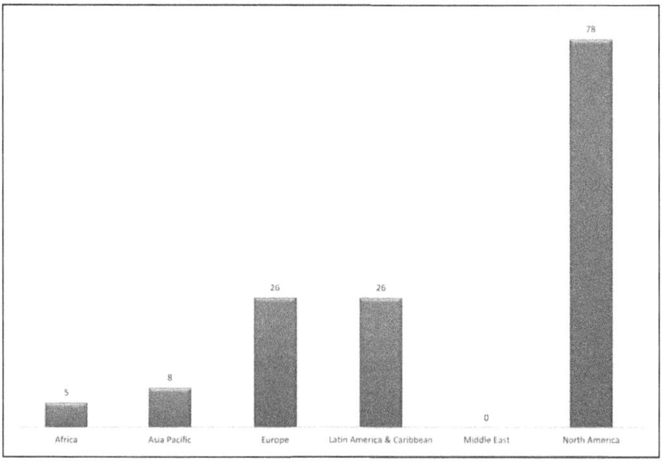

Figure 142. Countervailing measures (1/1/95–30/6/2010).

the use of harmonised SPS standards between Members on the basis of international standards, guidelines and recommendations developed by the relevant international standard setting bodies. Article 12 of the SPS Agreement established a Committee to administer the Agreement and provide a regular forum for consultations.

The level of participation/engagement of African WTO Members compared to Members from other regions in the SPS Committee was analysed with regard to the following indices:

- Oral statements in the Committee;
- Written submissions/proposals; and,
- Notification count
- Specific trade concerns in the Committee.

The SPS area of WTO regular work is one of the clutch issues to which African WTO Members have attached priority. They have done so for several reasons. First, the area of SPS is closely related to agriculture and as a consequence the export of African agricultural (tropical) products to global markets. Second, SPS measures have been reviewed and dealt with in the framework of international standards and, in reality, developed-country market standards,[132] which have challenged the vast majority of African countries. Third, African exports have been directly affected by international standards with specific impacts on the livelihood and well-being of their agricultural exporters. As a result, this is an area of WTO regular work where their specific trade interests have been affected and market realities have constrained their engagement. Finally, the facts also indicate that African priority trade interests in this area have been energized, at particular moments, by civil society. Within this framework, wider analysis has drawn the strong

[132] This includes private standards by enterprises in developed country markets that source supplies from developing country exporters.

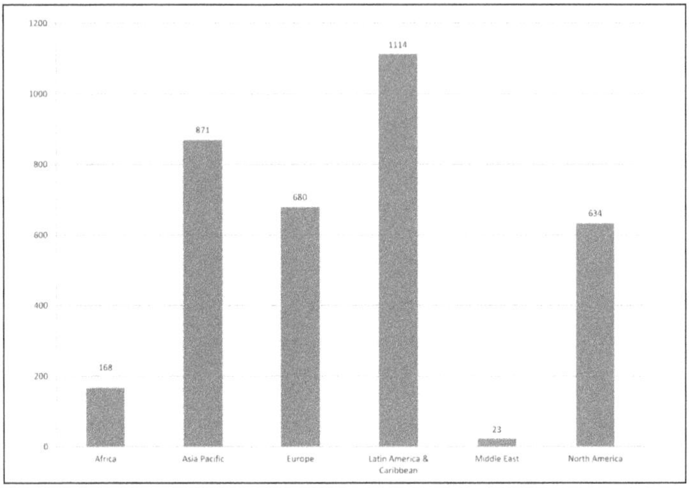

Figure 143. Statements in the SPS Committee (1995–2010).

relationship between SPS measures, on the one hand, and the new forms of murky and resurgent protectionism, on the other. These factors have influenced their individual levels of engagement.

(a) *Oral Statements in the SPS Committee*[133]

Figure 143 shows the distribution of oral statements in the SPS Committee by Members in different regions in the period 1995–2010. In spite of the priority attached to this area of regular work, and its impact on their exports, African Members' oral interventions in the SPS Committee was low at 168 (or 4.8 per cent) of the total number of statements in the Committee. Their statements were also low *per se* as a proportion of statements by Members from other regions, with the exception of the Middle East. However, it is notable that twenty-seven (or 64 per cent), a relatively higher proportion of African WTO Members, accounted for the 168 statements.[134]

African WTO Members' individual statements were low in relation to individual statements by Members in other regions and also low in relation to their identified priority. Their statements ranged from 1 to 7, with the exceptions of Egypt (49), South Africa (21), and, Senegal (13). In rank order, the highest numbers of statements in the SPS Committee were made by: EU (614), US (416), Canada (218), Argentina (211), Chile (174), Brazil (164), China (153), Australia (149), Japan (104), and, New Zealand (99).

---

133 Summary Records of SPS meetings: R1 to R 61.

134 Benin(4); Cameroon (3), Côte d'Ivoire (3); Djibouti (1); Egypt (49); Gabon (1); Gambia (1); Ghana (1); Guinea (2); Kenya (19); Madagascar (4); Malawi (7); Mali (6); Mauritania (2); Mauritius (7); Morocco (3); Mozambique (2); Namibia (2); Niger (1); Rwanda (1); Senegal (13); Sierra Leone (2); South Africa (21); Tanzania (1); Uganda (1); Zambia (7); and, Zimbabwe (4).

Content analysis of statements showed that African WTO Members intervened in the SPS Committee to express concerns about specific trade measures maintained by other Members that negatively impacted on their exports. They made statements on the difficulties they faced in implementing SPS regulations adopted by Members. They pointed to difficulties and constraints revolving around finance, scientific and legal capacity constraints and infrastructure. They expressed the difficulties they faced in regulating SPS trade-related risks due to lack of risk assessment expertise. In their statements, they proposed that they be allowed to restrict access on the basis of the precautionary principle[135] and not strictly risk assessment analysis.

African Members also intervened in the Committee to explain and/or respond to questions posed by Members on SPS regulations/measures they maintained. They also sought the "full implementation of S&D provisions in the SPS Agreement". In this context, some African Members actively engaged in the discussions on the SPS Agreement and developing countries. This item exists as a specific agenda item in the regular work of the SPS Committee. African Members also intervened in the discussions on specific SPS Agreement topics such as equivalence, regionalization and pest and disease free areas. African Members intervened to provide information on national SPS initiatives, including the establishment of national SPS committees and to share national experiences on the implementation of the SPS Agreement. They also intervened to raise concerns about their low participation levels in international standard-setting organisations in the SPS area: the Codex Alimentarius Commission; the International Office of Epizootics, and International and regional organizations operating within the framework of the International Plant Protection Convention (IPPC). In this context, some African Members made the case for Africa-specific "international standards" in areas such as animal health e.g. for African Horse Sickness.

In the period 2009–2010, African Members intervened in the discussions on private standards. They expressed concerns about the difficulties they faced in adapting to numerous private standards and the resultant impact on market access for their exports. They intervened in the Committee to seek SPS technical assistance for the implementation of the Agreement, including the establishment of the necessary domestic infrastructure. African Members also intervened on the subject of observership of bodies to the SPS Committee, where they supported applications for observership for African regional bodies including ECOWAS, SADC and the ACP.

(b) *Written Submissions/Proposals in the SPS Committee*[136]

Figure 144 shows the distribution of written submissions/proposals in the SPS Committee by Members in different regions in the period 1995–2010.

The number of written submissions/proposals by African Members was lower than the number of statements they had made in the Committee. With 70 (or 9.4 per cent) of

[135] The reference has been to Article 5.7 of the SPS Agreement.

[136] Committee on Sanitary and Phytosantitary Measures, G/SPS/W/1 to 255.

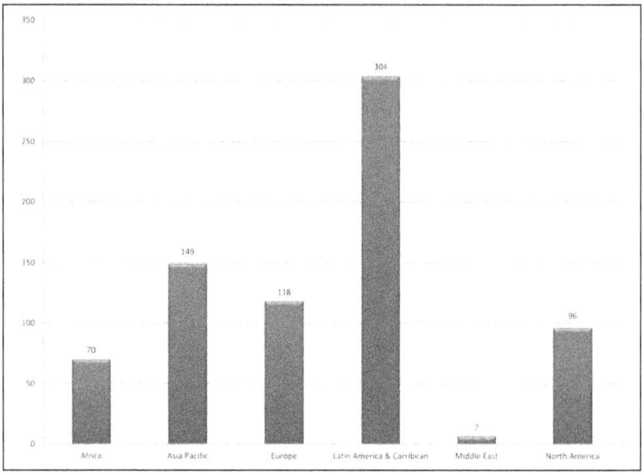

Figure 144. SPS submissions/proposals 1995–2010.

the total number of submissions/proposals, African WTO Members' proposals/submissions to the SPS Committee were low. Their proposals were also low in relation to the number of proposals/submissions by Members in all other regions, with the exception of the Middle East. Twenty-eight (or 67 per cent) of African WTO membership accounted for these submissions/proposals.[137] Although several African WTO Members tabled at least one proposal, the number of individual written submissions/ proposals were low, compared to those from Members in other regions, and ranged between 1 and 6. Again, the paradox is that of incommensurability between priority attachment on the one hand and matching statements, submissions/proposals on the other.

The substance of written submissions/proposals related to concerns with measures maintained by other Members that African Members considered as potentially impacting on their exports. Proposals and submissions were also centred on the agenda items of "the SPS Agreement and developing countries"; "implementation of the SPS Agreement"; and, "regionalization under Article 6 of the SPS Agreement", including the concept of pest and disease free areas. African Members contributed case studies about their national enquiry points and national notification authorities in the context of the discussions on enhancing transparency. They informed the SPS Committee about national SPS initiatives and of measures instituted in the wake of outbreaks of epidemics. They also informed the Committee of their "health status" in relation in diseases. Submissions also included requests for the development of Africa-specific standards by standards-setting

[137] Benin (1); Burkina Faso (1); Burundi (1); Cameroon (3); Central African Republic (1); Chad (1); Congo (1); Côte d'Ivoire (1); Egypt (9); Gabon(1); Gambia (3); Kenya (3); Madagascar (4); Malawi (3); Mauritania (3); Mauritius (4); Morocco (5); Niger (1); Nigeria (2); Rwanda (1); Senegal (3); South Africa (6); Tanzania (1); Togo (1); Tunisia (1); Uganda (3); Zambia (6); Zimbabwe (1).

bodies and responses to a questionnaire on SPS technical assistance including technical assistance needs.

(c) *Submission of Required Notifications*[138]

(i) Designation of National Notification Authorities

Annex B, paragraph 9, of the SPS Agreement obliges Members to designate a single central governmental authority as responsible for the implementation of notification procedures. As of 2010, one hundred and forty (140) WTO Members out of 153 had designated an "SPS Notification Authority. The level of compliance with the notification of national authorities by Members in different regions in the period 1995–September 2010 was as follows:

- North America – 100 per cent of membership
- Europe – 100 per cent of membership
- Middle East – 100 per cent of membership
- Latin America and Caribbean – 100 per cent of membership
- Asia Pacific – 89 per cent of membership
- Africa – 76 per cent of membership

As of December 2010, ten (or 24 per cent) WTO African Members had not notified their National Notification Authorities. These were: Cape Verde, Central African Republic, Chad, Congo, Côte d'Ivoire, Ghana, Guinea, Guinea Bissau, Niger and Togo. This was a poor record for an area of expressed trade policy priority. Members in all other regions had complied with this obligation, with the exception of Asia Pacific where three Members had not complied.

(iii) Designation of Enquiry Points

Annex B, paragraph 3, of the SPS Agreement requires that each Member establish an Enquiry Point responsible for the provision of answers to all reasonable questions and of relevant documents. As of 2010, one hundred and forty eight (148) WTO Members out of 153 had provided the WTO with the contact information of their Enquiry Point. The level of compliance with the notification of enquiry points by Members in different regions in the period 1995–September 2010 was as follows:

- North America – 100 per cent of membership
- Europe– 100 per cent of membership
- Middle East– 100 per cent of membership
- Latin America and Caribbean– 100 per cent of membership
- Asia Pacific– 96 per cent of membership
- Africa – 90.5 per cent of membership

138 Overview Regarding the Level of Implementation of the Transparency Provisions of the SPS Agreement, Note by the Secretariat, G/SPS/GEN/804/Rev.3, 7 October 2010.

As of December 2010, 9.5 per cent of African WTO membership had not notified an enquiry point.[139]

(iii) Submission of Regular Notifications

Under the SPS Agreement, the notification system is designed to inform other Members about new or changed regulations that may significantly affect trade. The procedures to be followed by Members are elaborated in Annex B, paragraphs 5 to 8, and the 2002 transparency procedures. The two main types of notifications are regular notifications and emergency notifications. In addition, addenda, corrigenda or revisions can be issued subsequent to an original regular or emergency notification.

In the period 1 January 1995 to 30 June 2010, a total of 11,622 notifications were submitted. As of 15 September 2010, one hundred and three (103) Members out of 153 (67 per cent) had submitted at least one notification to the WTO.

Figure 145 shows the distribution of regular SPS notifications by Members in different regions in the period 1995–2010.

With 120 (or 1.4) of the total number of SPS regular notifications, African Members had the least number of notifications. This was the lowest in comparison to all regions. Fourteen (or 33 per cent) of African WTO membership accounted for the 120 notifications. Most notifications of SPS measures were made by Egypt (31); Morocco (26) and, South Africa (23).

Adherence to and respect of international standards and, in market reality also, private SPS standards are critical for the exports of African and other developing countries. As a consequence, African countries have been sensitive and tended to be commercially compliant with the standards in their trading partners in the developed country markets to which their principal exports are destined. They have therefore been constrained to comply with all the market standards of these countries to ensure the access of their exports. For these three African Members (Egypt, Morocco and South Africa) their relatively higher levels of development are more sensitive to the needs and requirements of their domestic populations, tourist industries and rising standards of living. The other African WTO Members which notified SPS measures were: Benin (5); Botswana (3); Gambia (2); Kenya (3); Madagascar (8); Mauritius (5); Malawi (1); Senegal (7); Tanzania (1); Uganda (1), and, Zambia (4).

The individual number of notified SPS measures by African Members was low *per se*, and low in relation to the individual number of measures notified by Members in other regions. In rank order the most measures in the period studied were notified by the US (2082), Brazil (712), Canada (527), China (472), Korea (363), EU (357), and EU members, (197); New Zealand (351), Chile (321), Peru (308), and, Japan (256). In general, these Members have higher GDP levels than most WTO Members. This outcome reinforces a proposition in this study, "tested in the data analysis in the TBT regular work," that the higher the level of development the stricter the regulatory framework for measures to safeguard the health and welfare of domestic populations.

---

[139] These were: Central African Republic, Chad, Congo, and, Guinea Bissau.

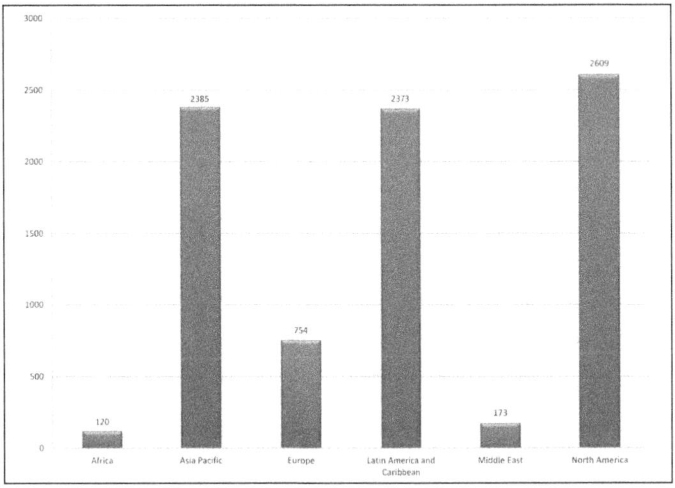

Figure 145. Regular SPS notifications (1995–2010).

(d) *Specific Trade Concerns Raised in the SPS Committee*[140]

Since 1995, WTO Members have notified to the SPS Committee SPS measures that they have maintained. In reaction to these measures, members have raised "specific trade concerns". Figure 146 is a combined chart that shows the regional distribution of SPS measures that have caused concern to other Members[141] and the regional distribution of Members that expressed "specific trade concerns", in the period 1995–2009.[142]

With a total of six (or 1.8 per cent) specific trade concerns raised in the SPS Committee, African WTO Members had the lowest number of specific SPS measures of concern to other Members. Statistically, African Members had the lowest number of trade measures and expectedly, the lowest number of specific concerns registered against these measures. Three (or 7.1 per cent) of African WTO membership accounted for these measures against which concerns were registered by other Members. These were: Egypt (2), Gabon (1), and, South Africa (3). The measures of concern maintained by African Members related to animal health, human health and food safety. Annex XIII: 1 shows the specific trade concerns maintained by African Members and the Members expressing concerns against these measures. A number of African Members expressed concern in the SPS Committee about measures maintained by other Members that could potentially

---

140 Committee on Sanitary and Phytosanitary Measures, *Specific Trade Concerns, Note by Secretariat*, G/SPS/GEN/204/Rev. 10, 10 February 2010.

141 Europe (103); Asia Pacific (102); Latin America and Caribbean (67); North America (39); Middle East (11); and, Africa (6).

142 Although the total number of specific trade concerns is listed as 290 in the period 1995–2009 for the purpose of this study, every measure/concern is attributed to the number of Members maintaining the measure/raising the concern.

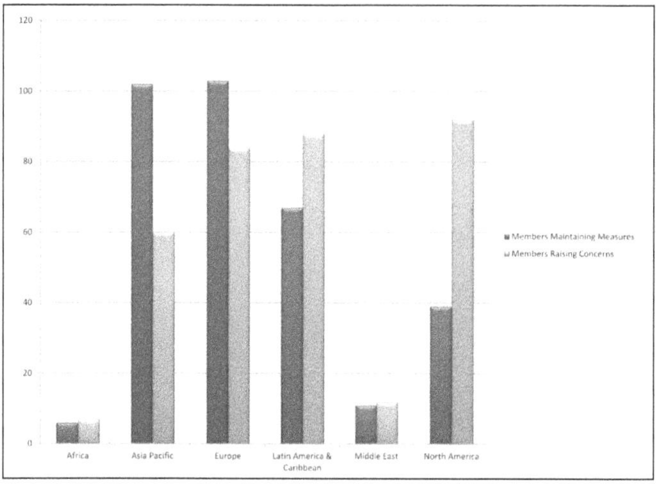

Figure 146. Specific trade concerns (1995–2009).

impact, or were impacting on their exports. Annex XIII: 2 shows the measures against which African Members raised concerns. Seven (or 16.6 per cent) African WTO members expressed concern with six measures mostly maintained by the European Union, Africa's largest trading partner. These Members were: Egypt (1); Tanzania (1); South Africa (1); Senegal (2); Gambia (1), and, Côte d'Ivoire (1). African Members raised fewer concerns with measures maintained by other Members in proportion to concerns raised by Members in other regions.

(i) Specific Trade Concerns Supported by African Members

Four (or 9.5 per cent) African WTO membership supported specific trade concerns raised by other Members with a potential impact on their exports. These were Benin, Kenya, South Africa and Egypt. Annex XIII: 3 shows the specific trade concerns that African Members supported.

(e) *Overall Observations*

As with other key areas of WTO regular work to which African WTO Members attach priority, the question re-occurs: why is the level of engagement low (across the indices of statements, submissions/proposals, notifications) in inverse relationship to the high level of priority attached to this area of regular WTO work?

Across the related areas of regular work, similar explanatory factors re-apply. In the case of the SPS Committee, the level of engagement has been low across the various indices, with the exception of the notification of enquiry points, directly related to the ability to export. The relationship between enquiry points and export ability, relates to market information and "traceability" of the SPS history of exports. It is evident that there is horizontal feature of low levels of engagement, even in an area with direct effects on the ability for exports and import revenue. First, because the data indicated a high level of enquiry point notification, Geneva-capital coordination, as a stand-alone factor, offered a necessary but insufficient explanation. If there had been a low level of enquiry points, Geneva-capital coordination, as an explanatory factor, may have been more robust. Evidently, other factors were at play. Second, the low level of African engagement appeared to reinforce the typical pattern in areas of specialized complexity, real or apparent. The more specialized and complex the subject, the lower the level of engagement. Third, the review of data and interview results, continued to highlight the vital importance of the variable of professional diligence and commitment. It is recommended that this may be one of these areas where targeted technical assistance from multiple sources (particularly, from import markets) may play a key role in improving the level of engagement. The WTO Secretariat in partnership with other international organizations and standard-setting bodies has increased technical assistance. These need to be further scaled-up. The uniqueness of the SPS area is that the major markets have been insistent that international (and in many instances) higher levels of national SPS standards are met because of electoral pressure from domestic consumer constituencies for "quality imports". It is argued in this study that although protectionist influences may be in play, there has been a positive effect with regard to the relative increases in African SPS standards and the increased level of consciousness that SPS standards matter. It is argued that one of the positive aspects of this pressure and constraint has been the high levels in the notifications of enquiry points and the high level of awareness amongst African WTO Members in this area of regular work.

It is partly this awareness that has also led to the recent increased participation of African WTO Members in the SPS Committee, with capital-based officials attending meetings. But, the level of their participation is still low relative to all regions in this study. It is recommended, as with other areas of regular WTO work, that African Members must urgently increase Geneva-capital coordination. They need to either establish or make more effective their standing national committees to coordinate the position of government with that of industry. There is a continuing failure to operate credibly at domestic levels of coordination with relevant, real time stream of instructions to African negotiators at the WTO.

19. Participation of African Countries in Plurilateral Committees

There are two WTO plurilateral committees – on government procurement and trade in civil aircraft.

(a) *The Committee on Government Procurement*

The Agreement on Government Procurement (GPA) which was negotiated during the Uruguay Round is the only legally binding Agreement in the WTO, focusing on the subject of government procurement. It is a plurilateral treaty administered by a Committee on Government Procurement, which includes the WTO Members that are Parties to the GPA, and thus have rights and obligations under the Agreement.

The purpose of the GPA is to open up as much government procurement business as possible to international competition. It is designed to make laws, regulations, procedures and practices regarding government procurement more transparent and to ensure they do not protect domestic products or suppliers, or discriminate against foreign products or suppliers. There are general rules and obligations and schedules of national entities, in each member country whose procurement is subject to the Agreement. A large part of the general rules and obligations concern tendering procedures.

(i) Signatories to the Agreement

In the period analysed, the Agreement had 28 members.[143] No African country was a member of the GPA.

(ii) Observers

In the period analysed there were 23 observer governments to the GPA.[144] Cameroon was the only African observer. Nine observers were negotiating accession to the GPA. No African country was in the process of negotiating GPA accession.

(iii) Participation in the Work of the Committee

Given that in the period analysed, no African country was a member of the GPA and only one African country – Cameroon – was an observer and, was not negotiating accession to the Agreement. Given this situation, no analysis was undertaken of the participation of African countries in this committee relative to other regions.

(b) *Committee on Trade in Civil Aircraft*

The Agreement on Trade in Civil Aircraft is a plurilateral agreement signed by a smaller number of WTO Members. The Agreement aims to eliminate import duties on all aircraft, other than military aircraft, as well as on all other products covered by the agreement (civil aircraft engines and their parts and components, all components and sub-assemblies of civil aircraft, and flight simulators and their parts and components).

(i) Signatories to the Agreement[145]

In the period 1995 to 2010, there were 31 signatories to the Agreement: Albania, Canada, the European Union (the following 20 EU Member States are also Signatories to the Agreement on Trade in Civil Aircraft in their own right: Austria, Belgium, Bulgaria, Denmark, Estonia, France, Germany, Greece, Ireland, Italy, Latvia, Lithuania, Luxembourg,

---

143 Canada, EC, Hong Kong China, Iceland, Israel, Japan, Korea, Liechtenstein, Netherlands with respect to Aruba, Norway, Singapore, Switzerland, Chinese Taipei and the United State. Source: http://www.wto.org/english/tratop_e/gproc_e/memobs_e.htm#partie.

144 Albania, Argentina, Armenia, Australia, Bahrain, Cameroon, Chile, China, Colombia, Croatia, Georgia, India, Jordan, Kyrgyz Republic, Moldova, Mongolia, New Zealand, Oman, Panama, Saudi Arabia, Turkey and Ukraine.

145 WT/L/805; 773 – Annual Reports of the Committee for 2010 and 2009 respectively.

Malta, the Netherlands, Portugal, Romania, Spain, Sweden and the United Kingdom), *Egypt*, Georgia, Japan, Macao China, Norway, Switzerland, Chinese Taipei and the United States.

(ii) Observers

In the period 1995 to 2010, WTO Members with observer status in the Committee were: Argentina, Australia, Bangladesh, Brazil, Cameroon, China, Colombia, Gabon, Ghana, India, Indonesia, Israel, the Republic of Korea, Mauritius, Nigeria, Oman, Saudi Arabia, Singapore, Sri Lanka, Trinidad and Tobago, Tunisia, Turkey and the Ukraine. In addition the Russian Federation was also an observer. The IMF and UNCTAD are also observers.

(iii) Participation in the Work of the Committee

Given that only one African country – Egypt was a Member of the Committee, no analysis of the participation of African countries in this committee relative to other regions was undertaken. It is only observed that six African countries had observer status in this Committee.

CHAPTER SIX

PARTICIPATION – WTO DISPUTE SETTLEMENT

1. African Participation in the WTO Dispute Settlement System[1]

In previous chapters, this study gathered and analysed data on the "level of African participation" in the areas of negotiations and WTO regular-committee work. In this chapter, primary data gathered and analysed evaluates the level of participation of African WTO Members in the dispute settlement system, as the most important pillar of the rules-based multilateral trading system. The level of African participation was analysed across the following indices:

- complainant participation;
- respondent participation;
- third party participation;
- panellist participation;
- Appellate Body member participation.

The WTO dispute settlement system was the most important result from the Uruguay Round of multilateral trade negotiations. It is the foundation of the system. Article 3.2 of the DSU sets out the cardinal objective namely that:

> The dispute settlement system of the WTO is a central element in providing security and predictability to the multilateral trading system. The Members recognise that it serves to preserve the rights and obligations of Members under the covered agreements, and to clarify the existing provisions of those agreements in accordance with customary rules of interpretation of public international law...

It is argued in this study that low to limited levels of participation in the WTO dispute settlement system results in significant gaps in understanding the entirety of the functioning of the rules-based trading system and, in many instances, failures in effective participation. It is from this argument that the level of participation of African WTO Members was evaluated.

[1] The list of disputes that African WTO Members have been involved in is provided in Annex XIV.

As designed and by its track record over the past 15 years, the WTO dispute settlement system has established itself as the most powerful pillar in the World Trade Organization, and as one of the most, if not, the most powerful institutions in international law. The dispute settlement system has been described as "the perpetual motion of the WTO mechanism" and "the most prolific of all international dispute settlement systems".[2] This study shares the position by Professor Jackson that the dispute settlement system (the judicial arm) has had its authority and power magnified by the continuing inability of the legislative arm (WTO membership in the Ministerial Conference and the General Council) to "legislate"; that is conclude the Doha Round to either establish new rules, or close the lacuna in existing rules or clarify existing rules.

Legal scholars have argued that the WTO, and more specifically the dispute settlement system is one of the most intricate and profound legal component of international economic law, linked to general international law. (Jackson, John, 2006). The key elements that have established the dispute settlement system as the most powerful judicial organ in contemporary international economic law are compulsory jurisdiction over the "Covered Agreements", the automaticity of the WTO dispute settlement system with automatic establishment of panels; adoption of panel and appellate body reports with absolute exclusion of blockage, the appeal process culminating in the Appellate Body, and, an international law obligation for compliance through domestic adjustment of WTO-inconsistent measures (or, compensation and/or retaliation).

The concept that the WTO is about "the rule of law", with all Members governed by the trade laws, is anchored on the functioning of the dispute settlement system. In this framework, scholars observed and hoped that a more legalistic system would encourage developing country Members, including African Members, to more effectively participate in WTO dispute settlement compared to the GATT "power-based" system where their participation had been minimal. It was also observed that the WTO dispute settlement system worked to the advantage of all Members, particularly the weak ones, who in the past lacked political and economic clout to enforce their rights and protect their interests. The WTO dispute settlement system has been described as one where "right perseveres over *might*.[3] Some have argued that the expectations of enhanced participation were attributed to the legal reforms ushered in by the WTO dispute settlement system, particularly "automaticity" of the system. Several scholars observed that automaticity of DSU procedures made it more difficult for economically powerful Members to "bully" economically weaker Members into giving up their legal

[2] H.E. Yonov Frederick Agah, 2010 Chairman of the WTO Dispute Settlement Body, *WTO Dispute Settlement Body Developments in 2010*, Fourth Annual Update on WTO Dispute Settlement, at the Graduate Institute of International and Development Studies, 8 March 2010.

[3] Lacarte- Muro. J and Gappah. P. *Developing Countries and the WTO legal and Dispute Settlement System*, Journal of International Economic Law (2000) 395–401. Croome, (1995) highlights that the main players wanted a binding and stronger system to deal with the increased range and complexity of issues, while developing countries supported the system because it was rules-based and not power-based.

complaints, because if they wished to have a legal ruling, it required less diplomatic confrontation.[4]

It has also been argued that the evidence suggests that developing countries view the dispute settlement system as not merely a forum for the righting of specific wrongs but also as a means to enhance their ability to participate fully in the WTO, even if they never participate in dispute settlement proceedings.[5]

In conception and design, in track record and jurisprudence, the dispute settlement system stands on *terra firma*, with its authority reinforced and enhanced, insulated from politics and controversy and, key to understanding and functioning in the rules-based system. Against this background, what has been the level of African WTO Members' participation?

2. Complainant Participation[6]

The WTO dispute settlement process is trigged by a request for consultations (Article 4, DSU). As of December 2010, a total of 419 complaints had been filed in the WTO by 444 complainants. Figure 147 shows the distribution of complainants in different regions in the period 1995–2010.

African WTO Members had not initiated a dispute in the WTO since the inception of the Organization. What accounts for this situation and does it impair Africa's ability for effective participation in the WTO?

First, it has been argued that developing countries, especially those in Africa, have less interest in pursuing dispute settlement proceedings in order to uphold or clarify systemic principles of WTO law, because they trade extensively under preferential arrangements that constitute waivers or exceptions to the general WTO principles.[7]

Second, there is the factor of the high cost of WTO dispute settlement. Exorbitant costs involved in bringing and defending a case have been cited by a number of observers as a

---

[4] Hudec R. *The adequacy of WTO Dispute Settlement Remedies – a developing country perspective*, in Hoekman et al., Development, Trade and the WTO – a hand book, pg. 81–91; Delich V, Developing Countries and the WTO Dispute Settlement System, in Hoekman et al., Development, Trade and the WTO – a hand book, pgs 71–80.

[5] Meagher Nial, notes that the ACWL's records indicate that approximately three-quarters of opinions provided concern systemic issues of WTO law or measures taken or planned by the WTO Members seeking the advice itself. *Representing Developing Countries in WTO Dispute Settlement Proceedings*, in Bermann and Mavroids, *WTO Law and Developing Countries*, Colombia Studies in WTO Law and Policy, Cambridge University Press, 2007.

[6] Plaintiffs in municipal law.

[7] Meagher Nial, *Representing Developing Countries in WTO Dispute Settlement Proceedings*, in Bermann and Mavroids, *WTO Law and Developing Countries*, Colombia Studies in WTO Law and Policy, Cambridge University Press, 2007. This view was restated by H.E. Yonov Agah, Chairman of the WTO Dispute Settlement Body in 2010, in response to a question about Africa's very low participation levels. Fourth Annual Update on WTO Dispute Settlement (see footnote 2).

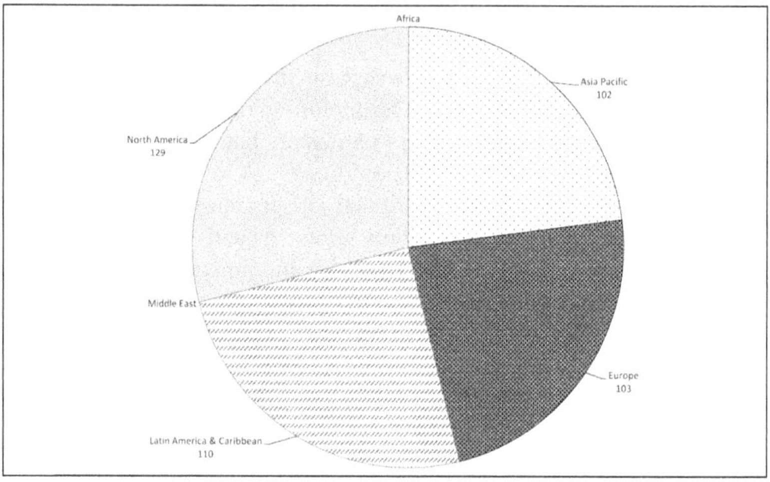

Figure 147. WTO dispute settlement: Complainants (1995–2010).

hindering factor.[8] Costs ranging between US$500,000 to US$ 1 Million have been quoted as minimum. In addition, it has been observed that a WTO Member faces three primary types of costs in determining whether to institute a dispute: direct out-of-pocket costs for hiring outside counsel; costs for hiring and dedicating government personnel with expertise to oversee and provide necessary support in bringing a complaint; and, the opportunity cost of expending scare government resources and personnel time against use in other social priorities. It has been noted that because poorer countries have more limited resources and perhaps immediate economic and social priorities, they are particularly likely to perceive WTO legal costs to be significant, especially where future benefits are uncertain.[9] This study suggests that although these explanations are plausible, they require adjustment in several respects. For instance, in the period reviewed, the dispute settlement system had functioned for over a 15 year period. This is more than an adequate time for African WTO Members to have trained and developed competent WTO trade-law counsels that can bring complaints in those areas where their benefits and/or their rights have either been nullified or impaired. Furthermore, the Advisory Centre on WTO Law exists, to provide legal advice and support.[10] In addition, several law firms have continued to offer pro-bono legal services to African WTO Members, including in bring cases if they so wish. It has also been argued that high cost should not

[8] Gabilondo, 2001; Busch and Reinhardt 2003; Zunckel, 2005; Gappah, 2005; Ewelukwa 2005; Shaffer 2003; Mosoti 2006; Low 2007; Meagher, Niall, 2007; Nordstrom and Shaffer, 2008.

[9] Nordstrom and Shaffer (2008).

[10] It has been observed that the ACWL charges fees for support in dispute settlement proceedings based on a fixed time budget for each stage of a dispute and an hourly rate that varies according to the income level and trade share of the developing country involved. It is estimated that ACWL fees are roughly 20 per cent of those charged by private law firms. However, all other legal advice is provided free of charge. Meagher (2007) at footnote 5.

be a hindering factor. The US- Upland cotton case involving Benin and Chad is cited as an example. In this regard it has been observed that networks available from organisations such as the Advisory Centre on WTO Law and UNCTAD show that there are trade law firms and research organisations willing to provide pro bono or lower cost rates to poor countries. In addition, it has been argued that the financial returns liberated from reforming the perversions of the trading system make it an infinitely possible cost/benefit decision to initiate a dispute as a fully paying client.[11] It is argued in this study that the evidence reviewed suggests that although there are cost constraints, other factors are also in play. There is more to legal capacity for dispute settlement initiation than the variable of financial/cost constraints.

Third, the combined lack of technical expertise and the associated costs have been argued as a limitation to dispute settlement initiation. Some scholars have stressed that it is during the "upstream" stage that these elements play an important role. This is because information about the case has to be gathered and analysed in order to make an informed decision whether or not it is worth pursuing a case.[12] Again the question that logically arises is, as plausible as these explanations are, for how long over time do they retain cogency and relevance. While plausible in the early years of dispute settlement, the strength of these arguments become weaker over time.

Fourth, it has been argued that effectively functioning trade policy infrastructures is critical for engagement in dispute settlement. Government/industry coordinating frameworks and institutional linkages between private companies and government officials, such as in the US and the EU, has provided originating impetus for dispute settlement system. This is a relevant argument. In general, such structures, even when extant, are weak in most African countries.

Fifth, the habit of dispute initiation and dispute settlement has also been argued. Due to less frequent use of the WTO dispute settlement system, developing countries have less incentive to deploy resources to develop internal legal expertise.[13] This is also an argument of relevance, related to a key hypothesis in this study that delegations from municipal systems *unaccustomed to the rule of law*, with fragile democracies and weak governance structures have been inactive and/or ineffective.[14]

Sixth, this study argues that a strong explanatory factor is the cost in time and staying power, the latter related to the factor of political reluctance. As illustrated in the US-Upland case there is an interrelated dynamic of WTO dispute settlement, political staying power and trade negotiations process. In this case, two (Benin and Chad) of the Cotton-Four countries (Benin, Burkina Faso, Chad, and, Mali) took third party rights. At a February 2011 Workshop on WTO Dispute Settlement, the Doha Negotiations and the WTO Cotton Case, the Cotton-Four actively examined the option of

---

11 Zunckel (2005); US, Brazil Agree on Framework Regarding WTO Cotton Dispute, June 2010, http://www.ustr.gov/about-us/press-office/press-releases/2010/june/us-brazil-agree-framework-regarding-wto-cotton-disput.

12 Hoekman and Mavroidis (2000).

13 Shaffer (2003).

14 See Chapter 1.

either initiating a dispute against trade-distorting cotton US subsides, building on the Brazilian case against US subsidies on upland cotton, or continuing to invest in the Doha agriculture negotiations.[15] The Brazilian delegation actively participated at this workshop, as panellist and presented detailed factors to assist C4 decision making for either option. It is notable, that one of the factors that potential dispute initiating delegations should take into account, as suggested by the Brazilian delegation at the workshop, is the "time of process" and sustained position over time. The Brazilian delegation suggested that the Cotton-Four fully consider all options, highlighting in particular the fact that it took Brazil 10 years from the initiation of the dispute, through the panel and Appellate Body process, the Article 21.5 compliance procedures, the arbitrators ruling and the final 21 June 2010 Framework Agreement with the US, to obtain final satisfaction.[16] The Brazilian delegation posed the question as to how many Members could have the staying power to wait 10 years with associated costs in time and resource before final satisfaction. It is argued in this study that beyond the more theoretical reasons argued by scholars and reviewed in this chapter, the results of this workshop, describes in greater reality the factors of greater operative relevance that influence a potential dispute settlement initiator from whether to initiate a WTO dispute settlement process or not.

Relatedly, it has also been argued that political reluctance exists on the part of small developing countries, such as African countries, to initiate cases against large trading partners. This has been cited as a hindering factor in instituting cases. It has been argued that African countries are subjects to the vagaries and pressures of global asymmetries. Many African countries receive aid or some form of development assistance from richer countries. This situation erodes their strength to litigate.[17] However, other scholars cautiously dissent, arguing that threat of retaliation is more ambiguous.

Seventh, there is a question of effective enforcement of a ruling in favour of a small country against a larger trading partner. It is argued that such a situation is a hindering factor.[18] The remedy of withdrawal of equivalent concessions in particular has been highlighted as one where only the economically powerful would have leverage to use. To the contrary, use of this remedy would hurt the economically weak. In this regard it has been noted that the majority of African countries are dependent on continuing trade relations with the rest of the world to whom they supply mostly commodities or unprocessed goods and therefore have no "alternatives" for retaliation. However, the enforcement issues arising in the case of Antigua and Barbuda on Gambling to an extent mitigates this argument. On 21 June 2007, Antigua and Barbuda requested authorization from the DSB, pursuant to Article 22.2 of the DSU, to suspend the application to the United States

---

15 *Atelier de réflexion sur le règlement des différends: Un atout ou une contrainte pour la négociation? Le cas du Coton à l'OMC, samedi 12 février 2011.*

16 US-Brazil Framework Agreement on WTO Cotton dispute, June 21, 2010. http://www.ustr.gov/about-us/press-office/press-releases/2010/june/us-brazil-agree-framework-regarding-wto-cotton-disput.

17 Mosoti (2006).

18 Shaffer (2003); Mosoti (2006); Low (2007).

of concessions and related obligations of Antigua and Barbuda under the GATS and the TRIPS Agreement. In the Article 22.6 arbitration, the arbitrator determined the annual level of nullification or impairments of benefits accruing to Antigua as US$21 million and that Antigua may request authorization from the DSB to suspend obligations under the TRIPS Agreement at a level not exceeding US$21 million annually.[19] The facts therefore suggest that the operative factor goes beyond the "size" or "economic weight" of the country, but to the larger factor of trade policy willingness, determination to invoke the system and sustain the process until satisfaction. This goes beyond whether a country is big or small. This also relates the importance of professional diligence and commitment to invoke and operate in a system of laws.

Eighth, it has also been observed that although the WTO is multilateral, it is based on a collection of bilateral bargains in which countries trade "concessions". The purpose of the dispute settlement procedure and of renegotiation provisions more generally is to preserve reciprocity. It has therefore been argued that since many developing countries (including those in Africa) have never participated in this horse trading on a substantive scale, the WTO dispute settlement system is in a basic sense not relevant to them, although they can to some degree still avail themselves of it.[20]

Finally, a number of scholars argue that the probability of having disputable trade measures is proportional to the diversity of a country's exports over products and partners. Shares in world trade, number of traded products and trading partners are determinants of participation in WTO dispute settlement. The hypothesis therefore is that the more diversified a country's exports are the greater the chances of initiating complaints and vice versa.[21] It has been noted that because individual developing countries are less active traders, they are less likely to be repeat players in WTO litigation. African countries have a small share of world trade and most of their exports receive preferential treatment in major markets, accounting for their inactive participation in WTO dispute settlement.[22] Regression analysis for this study provided support to suggest that the higher a Members' trade share or GDP, the higher the likelihood of instituting a dispute to preserve the negotiated balance of concessions, including on market access, agreed in the WTO Agreements. (See charts 11 and 12 in Annex III).

19 United States – Measures Affecting the Cross-Border Supply of Gambling and Betting Services, WT/DS285.

20 Ethier. W.J. *Comment on Patrick Low's "Is the WTO Doing Enough for Developing Countries*, in Bermann George and Mavroidis Petros, WTO Law and Developing Countries, Colombia Studies in WTO Law and Policy, Cambridge University Press 2007 at pg. 360.

21 See Gabilondo, 2001; Bown and Hoekman, 2005; Nordstrom, 2005; Horn et al., 1999; Low, 2007.

22 Shaffer (2003); Kessie and Apea (2006).

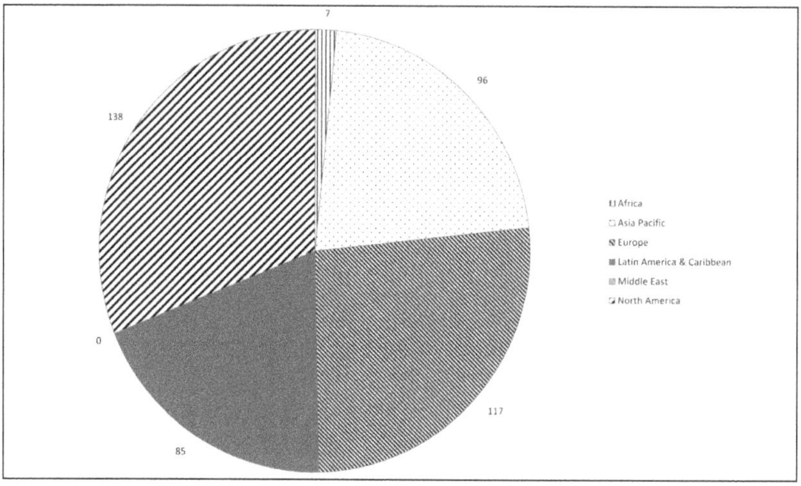

Figure 148. WTO dispute settlement: Respondents (1995–2010).

3. Respondent Participation[23]

Figure 148 shows the distribution of participation as respondents in WTO dispute settlement by Members in different regions, in the period 1995–2010.

Most analysis of poor countries' lack of engagement in WTO dispute settlement has focused on the hurdles of initiating complaints or taking third-party roles. This has ignored the dimension of developing countries as *respondents* in the system. The argument has been made that the failure of WTO Members to enforce the provisions of trade agreements against low income countries reduces the value of participation for these Members. Data analysed in this study showed that African WTO Members had had the lowest number of respondents in WTO dispute settlement. Two African Members (or 4.7 per cent of its membership), accounted for the seven times that African Members had been respondents. These Members were Egypt (4 times); and South Africa (3 times). By contrast Members in the North America; Europe; Latin America and Caribbean and Asia Pacific had been respondents in most of the disputes initiated. No Member from the Middle East, had been respondent.

The question is why has there been a low level of complaints initiated against low-income developing countries; in order words, why the low level of respondents in this group of the membership? The factors applied in explaining the low level of initiating disputes by African WTO Members also largely apply in explaining the low level of respondents amongst African WTO Members. In addition, three possible explanations have been posited. Low-income countries have made limited market access commitments. In addition, they can invoke various provisions on special and differential treatment with regard to the application of specific rules. It has also been argued that litigation against

[23] Defendants in municipal law.

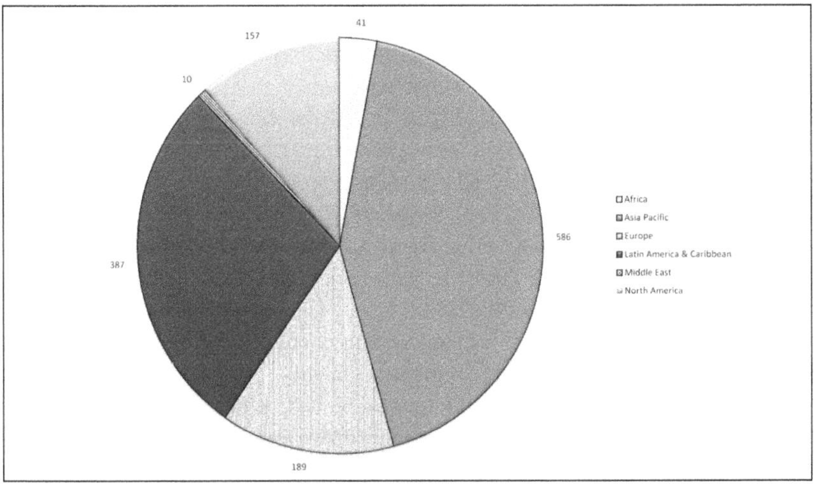

Figure 149. WTO dispute settlement: Third-party participation (1995–2010).

these countries is "expensive" in economic terms in contrast to the potential gains to a foreign exporter which may be too small to compensate for the cost of litigation.

Furthermore, litigation is politically expensive, as many governments, especially high-income countries, may not prefer to be seen as "picking on" a poor country for WTO violations.[24]

4. Third-Party Participation

Article 10.2 of the DSU provides that any WTO Member, having substantial interest in a matter before a panel and having notified its interest in a timely manner to the DSB, shall have the opportunity to be heard and to make written submissions to the panel. Third parties are invited to present their views at a special session of the first substantive meeting of the panel and only receive the first written submission of parties to the dispute. The submissions of third parties are provided to the parties to a dispute.

Figure 149 shows the distribution of participation as third-parties in WTO dispute settlement by Members in different regions, in the period 1995–2010.

There were a total of 1370 third-party positions taken by participants in the dispute settlement process between 1995 and 2010, of which African WTO Members accounted for 41 (or 2.9 per cent). This was a very low percentage of participation for an area that carries huge dividends in understanding the functioning of the rules-based trading system. It is strongly argued that this low level of participation has magnified negative

[24] See Bown and Hoekman (2007); Ethier's (2007); Bown Chad P. and Hoekman Bernard M., Developing Countries and Enforcement of Trade Agreements, Why Dispute Settlement is not Enough, Policy Research Working Paper 4450, The World Bank, Development Research Group, Trade Team, 2007 (also citing Davis and Bermeo (2006)).

effects in other areas of WTO work. It is also argued in this study that the lower the level of engagement in the dispute settlement system, such as in invoking third-party rights, the lower the overall level of systemic effectiveness.

The sixteen (or 38 per cent) of African WTO membership that undertook third-party rights in the 15 year period studied were: Benin (1); Cameroon (1); Chad (1); Côte d'Ivoire (4); Egypt (6); Ghana (1); Kenya (3); Madagascar (3); Malawi (3); Mauritius (6); Nigeria (1); Senegal (2); South Africa (2); Swaziland (3); Tanzania (3), and, Zimbabwe (1). These Members are part of the limited universe of African WTO Members that are active in the WTO. The areas where they took third party rights were consistent with their identified areas of systemic and commercial interests. These areas included cotton, sugar, shrimp-turtle (trade and environment and systemic issues regarding extra-territoriality of domestic laws), bananas, and trade remedies.

Some scholars have observed that the involvement of African countries as third parties has in most cases merely been observer. Only in few instances have African countries made substantive submissions.[25] But, this position has evolved as illustrated in the cases of Benin and Chad in the US-Upland Cotton dispute.

The regression results of this study did not suggest a strong positive correlation between trade shares or GDP level and third party participation. This was an interesting finding; which confirmed the value of the practice of systemic interventions. It has been argued that developing countries' understanding of and participation in the dispute settlement system can make an important contribution to their overall ability to benefit from their rights and obligations under the WTO Agreements.[26] As a consequence, it is recommended that African WTO Members should intervene more as third parties regardless of (low) level of trade share. A Members' trade share or GDP level did not seem relevant for third party participation. Whether a Members' trade share was high, medium, low or very low did not seem to matter. (See Annex III, charts 15, 16, 31, and, 32).

5. Panellist-Participation

The adjudication of disputes in the WTO is by *ad hoc* panels, which are quasi-judicial bodies. Panels are not standing bodies, but are composed for each dispute. Article 6 of the DSU provides that if a complaining party so requests, a panel shall be established at the latest at the DSB meeting following that at which the request first appeared as an item on the DSB's agenda, unless at that meeting the DSB decides by consensus not to establish a panel.

Article 8 of the DSU provides that panels are usually composed of three panellists, unless the parties to the dispute agree to a panel composed of five panellists, within 10 days from the establishment of the panel. Articles 8.1 and 8.2 provide that panels shall be composed

---

[25] Mosoti V. *Africa in the First Decade of WTO Dispute Settlement*, Journal of International Economic Law, 1 of 27. Nigeria in the US-Shrimp-Turtle case; Egypt in EC-Bed Linen case; Benin and Chad in the US-Upland Cotton case. In addition Morocco submitted an amicus curiae brief in the EC-Sardines case.

[26] Meagher (2007) at footnote 7.

of well-qualified governmental and/or non-governmental individuals, including persons who have served on or presented a case to a panel, served as a representative of a Member or representative to the Council/Committee of any covered agreement or its predecessor agreement, or in the Secretariat, taught or published on international trade law or policy, or served as a senior trade policy official of a Member. Panel Members have to be selected with a view to ensuring the independence of the members, a sufficiently diverse background and a wide spectrum of experience.

The WTO Secretariat maintains an indicative list of governmental and non-governmental individuals possessing the prescribed qualifications, from which panellist may be drawn as appropriate. Members suggest names of governmental and non-governmental individuals for inclusion on the indicative list, providing relevant information on their knowledge of international trade and of the sectors/subject matter of the covered agreements. However, it is not necessary to be on the indicative list to be proposed to serve on a panel.

Panellists serve in their individual capacities and not as government representatives, nor as representatives of any organisation. Members are forbidden from giving instructions or seeking to influence panellist with regard to matters before them. The Rules of Conduct for the Understanding on Rules and Procedures Governing the Settlement of Disputes, lays down *inter alia* rules for self-disclosure and confidentiality that govern panellists, arbitrators, Appellate Body Members and Secretariat staff working on WTO disputes.[27]

(a) *Panellist Participation by Region*[28]

Figure 150 shows the distribution of panellists by region in the period 1995–2010.

There were a total of 706 panellist positions in the dispute settlement process between 1995 and 2010, of which African WTO Members accounted for 43 positions (or 6.0 per cent). This was also a very low percentage of engagement in light of the overall increasing role of developing countries as panellists.[29] It was also low in relation to the number of panellist-positions held by Members from other regions.

Data showed that 263 positions had been held by the Asia-Pacific region; 177 positions by Europe; 148 positions by the Latin American and Caribbean region; 49 by North America and 12 by the Middle East region. The Asia-Pacific; Europe and Latin American regions had each had panellists from at least five different countries.[30] In the Middle-East,

---

27 WT/AB/WP/6, Working Procedures for Appellate Review, Annex II, Rules of Conduct for the Understanding on Rules and Procedures Governing the Settlement of Disputes.

28 Author's calculations from http://ada-mssql-db2/dsweb2/Home.aspx.

29 Citing worldtradelaw.net, H.E. Yonov Agah noted that, "An interesting statistic for 2010 relates to panellists. Historically, in the 15 years of WTO dispute settlement, a little less than half of the panellists have come from developing countries. He noted that at the end of 2010, 21 of the 33 panellists serving on active panels were from developing countries.

30 Country of origin of panellists by regions has been: **Africa** (Egypt, Mauritius, Morocco, South Africa); **Asia Pacific** (Australia, Bangladesh, Hong Kong, China, India, Indonesia, Japan, Korea, Malaysia, New Zealand, Pakistan, Philippines, Singapore, Thailand, China, and, Chinese Taipei); **Europe** (Austria, Belgium, Bulgaria, Czech Rep, Finland, France, Germany, Hungary, Iceland,

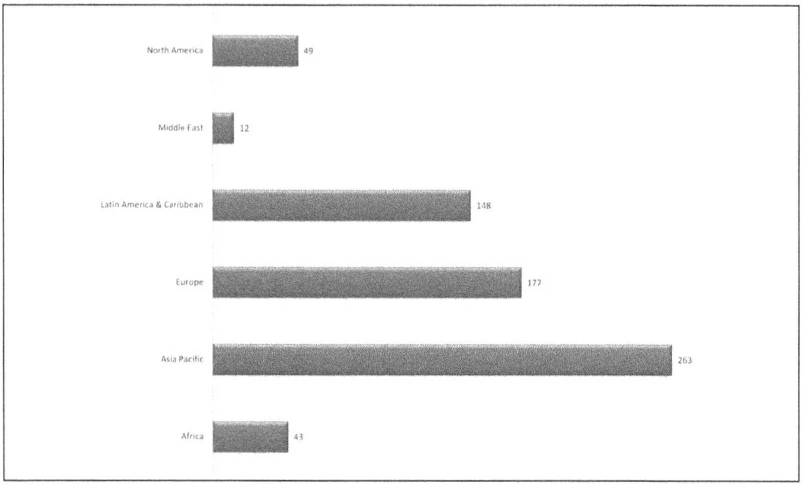

Figure 150. WTO dispute settlement panellists (1995–2010).

panellists originated from Israel. Panellists from Africa had originated from only four countries – Egypt, Mauritius, Morocco and South Africa. Egypt (14) and South Africa (22) had had more panelist positions. Mauritius and Morocco had a total of seven positions.

The requirements for panellists already identified, does not entail originating from a major trading Member. The core requirement is well-qualified individuals with experience in trade law and policy. None of the typical factors explaining Africa's low level of participation in the WTO appear to be operative in explaining the low level of panellists, except for what appears to be a long-standing systemic habit of drawing on panellists from the traditional regional pools. Remedying this situation is a combined duty for the WTO Secretariat, including the Director-General ex-officio on the one hand, and, African governments that nominate panellists on the other. Urgent action on both sides will be mutually reinforcing. On the part of African delegations, there is a duty to nominate to the roster of panellists competent and experienced individuals. On the side of the Secretariat and the Director-General, there is wide scope for increasing the number of Africans both nominated and appointed (in those cases where the disputants cannot reach an agreement) to panels. An increased number of panellists from Africa should have many positive knock-on effects, including enhancing Africa's ownership and membership of the rules-based trading system.

Ireland, Italy, Netherlands, Norway, Poland, Portugal, Slovenia, Sweden, Switzerland, and, United Kingdom); **Latin America & Caribbean** (Argentina, Brazil, Chile, Colombia, Costa Rica, Ecuador, Jamaica, Mexico, Panama, Peru, Uruguay, Venezuela); **Middle East** (Israel); **North America** (Canada; United States).

6. Appellate Body Members

The Appellate Body is composed of seven persons, three of whom serve on a case. Appellate Body Members are appointed by the Dispute Settlement Body for a four-year term and each person can be reappointed once. Terms are staggered, ensuring that not all Members begin and complete their terms at the same time. Members of the Appellate Body are persons of recognised authority, with demonstrated expertise in law, international trade and the subject matter of the covered agreements generally. They are unaffiliated with any government.

Regional Overview of Members of the Appellate Body (1995–2010)

Article 17.3 provides that appellate body membership shall be broadly representative of membership in the WTO. The table below shows the country of origin of Appellate Body members as they have evolved over the time period 1995 to 2010.

1995	2000	2001	2003	2006	2007	2009	2010
United States	United States	United States	United States	United States	United States	United States	United States
New Zealand	India	India	India	India	China	China	China
Germany	Germany	EC	EC	EC	EC	EC	EU
Egypt	Egypt	Egypt	Egypt	Egypt	South Africa	South Africa	South Africa
Philippines	Philippines	Australia	Australia	South Africa	Philippines	Philippines	Philippines
Uruguay	Uruguay	Brazil	Brazil	Brazil	Brazil	Mexico	Mexico
Japan	Japan	Japan	Japan	Japan	Japan	Japan	Japan

The table above shows that the rule with regard to appellate body members being broadly representative of the membership had been observed. In the period analysed the following additional observations were drawn: (i) The Asia-pacific region always maintained one-third of the composition of AB members; (ii) there had so far been no Appellate Body Member from the Middle-East region; (iii) the North American region had only had representation from the United States; (iv) members of the Appellate Body from Africa had originated from only two countries – Egypt (having served the most), and South Africa; (v) members of the Appellate Body from the Latin American and Caribbean Region had originated from three countries – Uruguay, Brazil and Mexico, and (vi) Appellate Body Members from the Asia-Pacific region had originated from more countries in comparison to other regions – New Zealand, Australia, Philippines, Japan, India and China. Members from the Philippines and India had served the most.

In conclusion, the dispute settlement system is the *pierre angulaire* of the rules-based Multilateral Trading System. Over a 15 year period the credibility of the WTO has come to rest on this pillar. In many respects, it is the key that opens the door to a complete understanding of the how the System functions and was designed to function. It is argued that participation in the dispute settlement system has a leverage effect in the overall systemic level of participation in the three areas of negotiations, regular work and dispute settlement *per se*. Systemic engagement in the dispute settlement system, through the allocation of resources/delegations, yields dividends in capacity, specialization and knowledge of the system, far greater than the equivalent amount of resources allocated to the other two areas of WTO work. The dispute settlement system pursuant to Article 3.2 of the DSU has been the central element in the security and predictability of the system, through its rulings that stand implicitly or explicitly on jurisprudence. This is the core of the system. As a consequence, this study strongly recommends that based on the analysis, African WTO Members would be better served to concentrate and increase their resources by systemically increasing third party participation and being more active in the Dispute Settlement Body, in their allocation of resources in the choices that must be made between regular work, negotiations and dispute settlement.

CHAPTER SEVEN

CONCLUSION

1. Research Focus and Findings

The purpose of this research was to explore, beyond prevailing perceptions and impressions, the level and substantive content of individual and collective participation of the 42 African Members at the WTO, from 1995 when the WTO was established to 2010, in the three core areas of WTO activities: the Doha negotiations, WTO regular committee work, and dispute settlement. Although this research undertook an empirical approach, it was legally grounded as its main focus was on participation in the World Trade Organization – a rules-based system grounded on legal Agreements binding on every Member. The value and systemic importance of participation rests on the fact that multilateral trade rules serve an important domestic political-economic function. Increasingly they form part of national strategies of external liberalization. Binding reciprocal commitments engender the necessary locking in of policy, forestalling domestic policy reversals and uncertainty and unpredictability of national trade policy. It is therefore important to participate in the shaping of trade rules that will ultimately require domestic implementation. For instance, in regular committee work, Members' engagement is focused on administering the rules that bind all Members in a system of balanced rights and obligations. In trade negotiations, such as the on-going Doha negotiations, legal texts emerge from technical drafting processes underscoring the value of actively participating and contributing to shaping final outcomes that would be legally binding on each Member. Members would have to implement the results. In dispute settlement, although the ability for effective engagement and participation in panel and Appellate Body work inter-alia depend on expert and competent legal capacity in delegations, it is equally important to participate from a systemic view point and contribute to the shaping of "precedents" of the Dispute Settlement Body.

Over time, variations have existed in the levels of participation by African WTO Members in these three areas. However, data analysed, supplemented by extensive interviews, showed that in the 15-year period studied, African participation was nominal, minimal and largely ineffectual in relation to African WTO Trade Policy objectives,[1] substantive

[1] Reference was made to Declarations/Communiqués by African Trade Ministers on WTO issues from which cross-cutting African WTO trade objectives were inferred, listed in Annex V. One of

qualitative content of proposals/submissions that reinforce the rules-based system, and, compared to the level of engagement by Members from other regions. The assessed level of engagement was also related to the significant "size" of African WTO Members *per se*.

Although regression suggested statistical correlation between the variables of trade shares and GDP, on the one hand, with the levels of engagement/participation on the other, the logical relationships between variables were much more complex. It did not always logically follow that a Member with a low trade share and GDP would have a low level of engagement/participation. The relationships were not always entirely clear, nor was there clarity in the direction of causality. Was a Member's level of engagement/participation low (such as for African Members/LDCs) because trade shares and GDP levels were low? Or, should the level of engagement/participation of a Member with low trade shares and GDP be high (very active) for the reason of wanting to increase trade shares and GDP? The position argued in this study is that historically, the engagement/participation of Members had been *more about* the rules *qua* rules and defined by participation to level the conditions of competition, to ensure stable, predictable and non-discriminatory rules, and *less about* market access.[2] Also argued in this study is that Members, such as African Members and LDCs, with low trade shares and GDP levels have a greater incentive for more active participation than Members with higher trade shares and GDP levels. The analysis of the data in this research clearly indicated that there was an African engagement/participation problem. The research argued that at the core of the problem was the persisting orientation to special and differential treatment.

The cardinal research question investigated was why individual and collective African participation in the World Trade Organisation was nominal, minimal and largely ineffectual in relation to the group's size, Members' participation from other regions and even on those questions African Members had identified as priorities. Related questions addressed were: whether the existence of the WTO African Group had made any difference in the level and substantive content of African participation? Why, after 15-years of supposedly accumulated experience and capacity-building, the level of African engagement/participation had not been significantly scaled-up. Data analysed[3] indicated that WTO-specific technical assistance and capacity building increased from a total of 324 activities in 2000 (the selected baseline) by 281 per cent to a total of 1235 activities in 2005 and by 366 per cent to 1513 activities in 2010. These were massive increases in technical assistance and capacity building by the WTO Secretariat alone, excluding very many other TA/CB suppliers. Finally, there are policy-relevant considerations: will the

---

the dimensions associated with assessing the participation of any country or group of countries in the WTO is to determine their objectives. Methodologically, it was difficult for this research to ascertain what individual governments were seeking to achieve. Although Declarations and Communiqués of African Trade Ministers were the fall back option to determine objectives and priorities, it was virtually insurmountable and difficult to coherently tabulate uniform or unitary African trade policy objectives which hardly exist. A greater discussion of the objectives would be useful in any further research on this topic.

[2] The situation in the Doha Round has been different, with in some cases, a higher than previous level focus on market access in relation to rules.

[3] See Annex VI for the grand total and individual African country disaggregation.

future of African Members' participation at the WTO resemble the past 15 years and what will be the implications for the balance of rights and obligations acting as a spur to trade growth in Africa?

(a) *Building on Previous and Current Research*

Valuable foundation research, in the first ten years of the WTO, cleared the underbrush in investigating and assessing the level of developing country participation in the Organization. The host of explanations of developing country participation, in the immediate aftermath of the establishment of the GATT/WTO, identified such factors as a starting baseline of passivity, defensiveness and the orientation towards exceptions (Hudec, 1987, edited in 2009 and 2011; Whalley, 1982; Srinivasan, 1998); technical capacity and financial constraints (Blackhurst, Lyakurwa, and Oyejide 2000), disinterest with the original GATT agenda (Page, 2001); and, the assertion that the rules-based system was "a rich man's club" and, consequently, the implication that developing countries were either excluded or had no incentive for active engagement/participation. Many of these explanations that were formulated with regard to developing countries in general, tended to be "applied" to the participation of African countries without precise adaptation. These broad applications, although theoretically useful, raised further questions that required deeper research. Furthermore, these studies were also characterized by the fact that they either focused very broadly on developing countries' participation in the functioning of the WTO, or specifically in either, the separate areas of the Doha negotiations, or WTO dispute settlement, with little or no comparative analysis across time. Since the establishment of the WTO, a considerable proportion of the WTO research agenda has been dominated by the Doha negotiations and dispute settlement. These have provided valuable insights. However, research gaps were evident such as in the area of comparative analysis of "levels of participation" across more disaggregated groupings of WTO Members and different areas of WTO work.

This research contributed to filling some of the gaps in research. It undertook a combined, simultaneous comparative analysis of "levels of participation" across the three core areas of the Doha negotiations; WTO regular committee work; and, dispute settlement. This level of African participation was researched across these three areas comparatively. It built on aspects of existing work, broadly analysing developing country participation and went further. It developed specific explanations for the "level and quality content" of African participation across the three areas of WTO core work. It gathered evidence over a longer and more recent 15-year period from 1995 to 2010. It undertook comparative analysis with Members' engagement from other regions. It questioned prevailing explanations for Africa's low level of participation, such as limited experience, low levels of expertise and capacity constraint, which may have been relevant in the initial years of the WTO, but diminish in explanatory strength over time. Paradoxes were examined such as why very low levels of participation also existed in areas of identified WTO trade policy priorities by African Members individually and collectively. It is expected that the results of this research should assist African WTO Members in critically reviewing their participation in the past 15 years, addressing their participatory weaknesses, and, identifying specific areas to which they could allocate more resources and, invest greater efforts in order to significantly scale-up their systemic participation.

Although there have been variations and exceptions, the level of African WTO Members' engagement in the period analysed, in the three areas of the Doha Negotiations, WTO regular committee work and dispute settlement remained low with regard to the totality of analysed engagement, in relation to the group's significant size, on identified priorities and compared to Members participation from other regions. Participation was nominal with regard to the meagreness of concrete results on rules-specific areas with wide scope for greater effectiveness.[4] There is no correct or ideal level of participation *ex ante*, either for African WTO Members, or for Members from other regions. However, emerging from the comparative analysis of levels of participation were differences ranging across the scale of those on lower and higher rungs, as a consequence of the activity levels for the group *per se* and as proportions of the totality of the "level of engagement/participation indices" developed for the analysis in each of the three core areas examined. The "level of engagement/participation" concept was evaluated on a range of selected indices in the three areas[5]. In the Doha negotiations, assessments were made on the basis of *statements made*, *submissions/proposals* and *chairmanships*. In regular work, data were analysed inter-alia on *statements made*, *submissions/proposals*, *responses to mandated notifications*, *chairmanships*, *discussants roles* in trade policy reviews and, *formulation of questions* (beyond "solidarity statement"). Beyond these, additional specific variables were analyzed, depending on the subject matter and mandate of a committee. Assessments in dispute settlement revolved around activities of "*initiation of disputes*", *respondents to dispute initiation*, *panellist function*, *Appellate Body positions*, and systemic *third party positions*.

Why was the level of African WTO Members' participation low and rare specific instances of relatively high levels of engagement not sustained? This study addressed this question. It argued that, since the establishment of the WTO, across the three core areas of work, the minimal participation of African WTO Members (in contrast to its large membership share and at variance with its identified areas of priority) was explained by the continuing inertia of a "special and differential exemption orientation[6]"; misalignment in coordinating capital-driven domestic trade policy and economic reforms with the African WTO "Geneva frontline"; misallocation of negotiators within core areas of work; and, to a lesser extent, specialized capacity handicaps. It was also observed that the degree of engagement and impact of participation of African WTO Members was explained by the extent of personal commitment and professional engagement of individual negotiators despite existing constraints and weaknesses. However, this research identified a few instances of relatively high levels of participation by African WTO Members of which the most evident were in the areas of cotton, TRIPS and Public Health, and to a lesser extent, SPS and TBT, all in the two core area of negotiations and regular WTO committee work. In these areas, particular African negotiators, with demonstrable,

[4] Beyond the statistical conclusion that the level of engagement/participation of African WTO Members has been low, nominal and largely ineffective, the responses in the questionnaires administered to selected African WTO delegates reinforce this conclusion. See Annex II (methodology) for how engagement was quantified in this research.

[5] See AnnexII-Methodology

[6] For clarity, Special and differential treatment encompasses and is largely than the narrower concept of preferences, the latter specifically applying to market access.

relatively higher levels of individual engagement, were evident from a limited universe of African WTO Members including Benin, Burkina Faso, Chad, Mali (the C4), South Africa, Egypt, Mauritius, Kenya, Uganda, Zambia, Zimbabwe, Rwanda and Nigeria.

Furthermore, the study argued that negotiators from municipal systems with fragile democracies and weak governance structures were inactive and ineffectual in WTO engagement. (Charts 33–42 in Annex III). Within this overarching explanatory framework, specific variables intervened in different combinations in the three areas of work to influence the levels of engagement. For instance, low levels of trade shares (*ipso facto* low level of commercial interest) tended to suggest explanations for low levels of engagement in MFN market access negotiations. (Charts 1–8 in Annex III) However, for African Members the low trade share level was largely accounted for by a higher proportion of preferential trade. Low trade shares also appeared to suggest low dispute settlement participation with the exception of third party participation (charts 15 and 16 in Annex III). "Competitiveness rankings"[7] of individual African countries, when high, suggested why their level of engagement across the three areas studied compared to the most active in any region, regardless of trade share and GDP. Tunisia and Mauritius were examples. These examples strongly suggested that the variable of economic/trade competitiveness had intervened to modify/influence the variable of low trade shares in explaining performance in regular work and negotiations. Analysis of the data indicated that modest to high rankings in economic competitiveness were associated with active engagement and performance in WTO regular work and negotiations over and above low trade shares.

Comparing the three areas, the overall analysis of the data indicated that the "level of engagement" had been relatively higher in the area of Doha negotiations, where there had been a degree of compensation for individual Member weaknesses through "coalitional" behaviour. Engagement levels had also been relatively higher in specific areas where support had been provided by non-WTO multilateral institutions, civil society and, in some cases, the pro-bono support of law firms. The results of African WTO Members' engagement in the specific areas of TRIPS, cotton and to a lesser extent SPS and TBT provided justifying evidence. However, beyond these exceptional cases, the net level of engagement remained low. In other words, the analysis suggested that in the few cases of relatively high levels of engagement, the *activity engine* had come from "elsewhere". While *per se* this had been useful as a process of "jump starting" engagement/ participation, this had neither been sustained by African WTO Members nor been fully owned. One of the reasons for this inability to sustain a high level of participation was that there were still huge gaps in a fundamental understanding of the technical balance of rights and obligations and the direction of accumulating jurisprudence of the rules-based system.

From the total number of 42 African WTO Members, a limited universe, ranging between 15 and 20, had been individually active in the two core areas of the Doha negotiations and WTO regular committee work. These included: Benin, Burkina Faso, Chad, Côte d'Ivoire, Egypt, Gabon, Ghana, Kenya, Lesotho, Mali, Mauritius, Morocco, Namibia, Nigeria, Senegal, South Africa, Tanzania, Tunisia, Uganda, Zambia and, Zimbabwe. This limited number further diminished in the area of dispute settlement to about sixteen

[7] The World Economic Forum: Global Competitiveness Index 2010–2011 was used for this study.

African Members effectively participating in WTO dispute settlement (Benin, Cameroon, Chad, Côte d'Ivoire, Egypt, Ghana, Kenya, Madagascar, Malawi, Mauritius, Nigeria, Senegal, South Africa, Swaziland, Tanzania and Zimbabwe).

(b) *Core Area of Work: Doha Negotiations*

The Doha Round is the ninth Round of trade negotiations in the multilateral rules-based trading system since the launch of the first round in Geneva in 1947. African countries were marginally involved in the Uruguay Round (1986–1994), of which they considered the results unbalanced and not taking account of their trade and development interests. From 1995 to the Third WTO Ministerial Conference in Seattle (1999), African WTO Members actively opposed the launch of a new trade round until, in their view, "implementation corrections" to the Uruguay Round results had taken place. The reversal of their position to commit to a new Round of negotiations came much later in 2001. Thereafter African WTO Members have retained a high level of rhetorical and declaratory commitment to the Doha Round. The question therefore is why the actual level of technical engagement was minimal, nominal and largely ineffective. This research identified several findings.

First, a key finding based on the data analysed in chapter 4 showed that the level of African participation/engagement in the Doha Round negotiations, although low, was relatively higher than in the other two core areas of regular committee work and dispute settlement. The Doha Round was launched six years after the establishment of the WTO. The negotiations generated excitement as the most seductive area of work. It was seen as an opportunity to correct perceived imbalances from the Uruguay Round results. The negotiating atmosphere *per se* was heady. Furthermore, many of the African Members "confused" the negotiations with the regular work of the Organization and, as a consequence, accorded the negotiations priority over other areas of core work. To a large extent for many of the African "newcomers" to the rules-based system, the negotiations became synonymous with the regular work of the Organization. It also has to be borne in mind that with the exception of a few African countries, notably Egypt, Morocco, Nigeria, South Africa, Tunisia and Zimbabwe, there was no pre-existing core precedent group of African trade negotiators in the GATT/WTO system. In reality, the "Doha-Group" of African trade negotiators was the "first real generation" of multilateral trade negotiators. This explains in part the relatively higher level of participation of African WTO Members in the negotiations over and above regular work and dispute settlement.

Second, the research showed imbalances in the allocation of resources by African WTO Members amongst the core areas. It is obvious that individual Members have to make a choice in the allocation of resources (negotiators, funding, time, intellectual effort etc.) amongst the three core areas. There are no right or wrong choices. The question however revolves around efficiency, returns to resources invested and the approach that provides greater leverage effects in understanding and operating the system. The debate is likely to continue as to whether multilateral negotiations over a ten year period, with uncertain outcomes, and punctuated by periods of no activity and deadlock should command absolute priority in the allocation of resources. Although "negotiating a good bargain" is the ideal, the record shows that the practice and the outcome of "bargains" are more tempered, complex and the gains therefore largely dependent more on domestic reforms and less on the quality of negotiated bargains.

Third, African participation in the Doha negotiations manifested in specific forms. Although there was a limited degree of robust individual activity by some in the small universe of active African WTO Members, the principal form of negotiating engagement was through "coalitional" behaviour. African WTO Members operated in a wide range of intra-regional, inter-regional and issue-specific coalitions to compensate for their individual weakness. This form of engagement seemed more effective than their individual activity in relation to their negotiating objectives. The analysis, as in chapter 4 indicates this behaviour as the preferred form of engagement in the negotiations on agriculture including cotton, non-agricultural market access (NAMA), trade facilitation, TRIPS, and, development issues, in particular. Despite its weaknesses, the African Group had utility. It had pooled scarce resources, created synergies, provided a necessary forum for African countries to exchange views and coordinate with other groupings and provided weight for common African representation in consultations and meetings. The latter is part of the "constituency" system, which has become the *modus operandi* in WTO work to facilitate consensus decision-making amongst WTO membership. The African Group continues to have an important role on cross-cutting and issues of general interest to its Members. The combined results of interviews and responses to questionnaires strongly indicated that the effectiveness of the African Group had been moderate in trade negotiations. Although the Group gave support to decisions in favour of LDCs, most of which are African countries, LDCs themselves preferred to pursue their interests within their dedicated forum – the Least Developed Countries' Consultative Group.

Fourth, one of the findings in this study was African trade policy priority areas in the negotiations. African WTO Members accorded priority to specific negotiating areas. These revolved around agriculture; cotton; trade facilitation; special & differential treatment (LDC waivers, DFQF, preferences); policy-space and development issues. With the exception of cotton, proposals tabled by African Members, individually and collectively sought differentiated treatment and were in a number of instances rhetorical, declaratory and counteractive against proposals from other groups.

Finally, although the African Group has produced some results and achieved some gains from its collective engagement, on balance, the results from the 15 year period analysed have been disappointing largely because of the persistence with an exemption-seeking orientation.[8] There were gains in expression of common group positions, invitation for representation at limited consultations, contributions to systemic transparency improvements, and, counteractive proposals. However, progress in the Round so far suggested that more effective engagement and results were produced when individual group members acted in inter-regional coalitions to build consensus, such as on trade facilitation, through individual African Member initiatives for example South Africa and Kenya on the TRIPS amendment and, when the African Group gave support to sharper, formulated initiatives, for example by the Cotton-Four and LDCs on duty free, quota free market access.

[8] Osakwe, Chiedu (2011), *Developing Countries and GATT/WTO Rules: Dynamic Transformations in Trade Policy Behaviour and Performance*, (forthcoming).

(c) *Core Area of Work: Regular Committee Work*

In the architecture of the rules-based system, if dispute settlement is the foundation, regular committees, are the structures within which the rules are administered, implemented and custom/practice emerge. Regular committee work to administer existing rules and disciplines under the Covered Agreements namely, Annex 1A (Multilateral Agreements on Trade in Goods); Annex 1B (GATS); Annex IC (TRIPS); Annex 2 (DSU); Annex 3 (TPRM); and, Annex IV (Plurilateral Trade Agreements) of the Marrakesh Agreement Establishing the WTO, takes place in a number of WTO bodies. Broadly, the Agreements define the objectives and establish the principles that govern the specific area covered by that Agreement. They provide the balance of rights and obligations, exceptions to the rules including any special and differential treatment, structures to administer the agreement, notification requirements, dispute settlement provisions and technical assistance.

First, at its core, the level of engagement by African WTO Members in regular committee work was low. However, there were exceptions and variations, reflecting relatively higher levels of participation, in particular WTO bodies. The Committee on Trade and Development best reflected the latter. In the CTD, African WTO Members intervened with a high number of 776 oral statements only lower than statements by Members in the Asia Pacific (906) and Latin America and Caribbean region (808), but higher than statements by Members in Europe (583); North America (541), and the Middle East (36). Yet, these were rarely followed up with concrete written proposals to achieve consensus and concrete outcomes. In the TRIPS Council, the level of engagement was similarly high with regard to oral statements made. Again, the problem emerged with regard to failure with follow up, as exemplified with TRIPS and Public Health where for instance as of December 2010, only five African Members (Mauritius, Egypt, Morocco, Zambia and Uganda) had notified their acceptance of the amendment to the TRIPS Agreement.[9] This is why; analysis in this study of "the level of engagement" reviewed data across the three indices of: i) statements made; (ii) submissions/proposals; and, (iii) fulfilment of notification obligations.

Second, a major findings in this study was that effective and robust membership is undermined by obligations and commitments not implemented. Unimplemented obligations render a Member vulnerable and weaken its engagement/participation with the reduction of that membership to *nominalism*. The level of engagement/participation not only includes acts of commission, but also acts of omission. The detailed review, in this research, of the level of engagement and specific participation on the minutiae of obligations and commitments revealed huge gaps, even after 15 years of membership. Several examples emerged in this research. A few of them included the three areas of trade remedies, rules of origin, import licensing, services, and agriculture notifications. This should be a major cause of concern for individual WTO African WTO Members and the WTO African Group. The question that emerges is how much has actually changed since

[9] Since December 2010, Senegal (18 January 2011); Rwanda (12 December 2011); and, Togo (13 March 2012) had also notified their acceptance of the Protocol amending the TRIPS Agreement. Thirty-four African WTO Members are yet to do the same.

the starting point in 1995, with specific regard to this core area of participation in WTO regular committee work?

Third, one of the findings of this research was that the nature of regular committee work (different from the Doha negotiating environment) constrained Members to participate individually, different from the coalitional behaviour in the Doha negotiations. African WTO Member participation in regular work was, therefore, individual and non-coalitional with the exception of a few bodies such as the General Council and TRIPS Council. Part of the explanation is that the nature and substance of work although linked are "different". Regular work involves the implementation of obligations and commitments already accepted and the promotion of very specific interests affecting Members individually, within the context of already established rules in the area of the Agreement being administered by a committee. Differently, in "negotiations", the dynamics for bargaining are different, linked to the "balance of trade and economic power" and where coalitions are more necessary than usual for negotiating gains.

Fourth, analysis of the data (in chapter five) indicated that over the past 15 years, the priorities of African WTO Members in regular committee work fell into three broad categories, namely: i) process and appointments; ii) substance; and, iii) technical assistance. In particular, priorities revolved around textiles and clothing matters particularly with regard to the expired Agreement on Textiles and Clothing; outstanding implementation issues under Uruguay Round Agreements; TRIPS and Public Health; LDCs' matters; agriculture, customs valuation; SPS; TRIMS and local content issues; subsidy use; services (mandatory certification work on individual schedules of commitments or acceptance of protocols on basic telecommunications and/or financial services, GATS Article II MFN exemptions); balance of payments consultations on import prohibition restrictions; trade and development matters; and, accession matters.

Fifth, another finding in this study was the pattern of African WTO participation, reflecting the puzzling paradox of very low levels of participation in areas of high WTO trade policy priorities. The committees on Agriculture, Rules of Origin, SPS, TBT, and Import Licensing best reflected this paradox. For example, in the Import Licensing Committee, most chaired by African delegates, participation did not improve but actually remained at its low base starting point. This is also a committee not requiring specialized expertise. Paradoxically, many African countries have employed import licensing as a trade policy instrument yet participation in the Committee has remained very low. The Committee on Rules of Origin was also chaired by Nigeria in the first few years of the WTO. This remains an area with direct commercial and systemic interest for African Members. However, only Egypt, Morocco and Mauritius had actively engaged. Overall, individual and group African participation remained low.

Sixth, the explanations for the level and peculiar character of African engagement in regular WTO work are neither mono-causal nor simple. Data gathered and analysed point to particular factors, operating in different combinations in various areas of regular work. For instance, in the areas of specialized complexity such as safeguards, anti-dumping, subsidies and countervailing measures, the level of engagement tended to be low with high levels of complexity. In the areas of SPS, TBT and TRIMS, where African Members have drawn tight linkages to their ability for market access (SPS, TBT) and development (TRIMS, local content requirements), participation was also low. Analysis of the data, supplemented by interviews, suggested a combination of failures in Geneva-capital coordination, misalignment of legislation-based domestic reforms, and, the trade policy engagement in the Geneva "front-line".

Seventh, in market access-related areas of regular work, results of regression analysis suggested that the variable of economic competitiveness had intervened to modify/influence the variable of low trade shares in explaining the relative levels (and behaviour) of individual African WTO Members in regular work. Although the results of the regression suggested a positive correlation between trade shares and participation in regular committee work (through oral statements/interventions/proposals) indicating that the higher a Member's trade share, the higher the number of interventions/statements, exceptions existed. In these instances, Members with higher trade shares made fewer interventions. For example, South Africa, with the highest trade share amongst WTO African Members of 0.68%, intervened only thrice in the CTD in the period studied. Others with lower trade shares made relatively more interventions. For example Kenya, with a trade share of 0.08%, was an example of an African Member with the several interventions in the TNC and CTD. Most African Members barely participated; all of them have low trade shares (less than one per cent). However, modest to high rankings in economic competitiveness[10] was associated with active engagement and performance in WTO regular work and negotiations, even within low to minimal levels of trade shares. The participation of Mauritius best exemplified this engagement behaviour.

Eighth, a key finding that reoccurred over the 15 year period of analysis was the "critical" importance of the personal commitment and professionalism which go beyond the normally analysed "technical" explanatory variables. The review of data and interview results strongly suggested a wide scope for improvements in sustained professional diligence and commitment, distinct from intelligence and ability. No volume and quality increase in technical assistance and capacity building will mitigate this challenge. The solution lies in individual commitments and conviction to sustained professional improvements and engagement regardless of "other factors".

Ninth, on process and appointments, there was a high level of focus and engagement by African WTO Members on the issues relating to appointment of WTO Directors-General; waivers under Article IX of the WTO Agreement; WTO observerships; representation at limited group consultations; "bottom-up" effective participation of Members and corollary issues; and, share of chairmanships. The effort invested on the appointment of WTO Directors-General is linked to job creation and appointments that normally follow with the election of a new Director-General. In addition, there is the attention attendant on elections; elections normally create periodic opportunities to review and "refresh" the System; lobby for positions; and, the constant quest to "rebalance" the WTO Secretariat.

Tenth, there were two aspects of the findings on chairmanships that were relevant namely: (a) distribution; and, (b) who chairs? There were specific findings on the regional distribution of chairmanships, and which Member or regional group held and retained particular chairmanships. These have raised vital systemic questions in both areas of regular work and the Doha negotiations. It is useful to look at this cross-cutting issue

[10] World Economic Forum: Global Competitiveness Index 2010–2011.

together. The questions that have arisen have frequently conflated process but also substantive issues.

Chairmanships in regular work and the Doha negotiations are of vital systemic importance, although ceremonial in limited instances. Some comparison is useful. Chairmanships provide vantage positions to understand the issues, manage and steer regular work or negotiations in specific directions within the constraints of a Member-driven System. Regular body chairmanships are annual with scope for renewal. In contrast, DDA chairmanships are only renewed with the exit of a chairperson from Geneva. The struggle over chairmanships has revolved to some extent around setting the agenda and "deciding" when to bring an issue to decision-making. Although the chairmanships struggles in both regular work and negotiations have been more latent than overt, it continues to reflect on the cardinal question of the level of engagement of individual Members in the context of their regions. The comparison of the data on chairmanships, across 15 years of WTO regular committees and 10 years of DDA negotiations revealed results as follows:

Region	Regular Committee Chairmanships (1995–2010)	DDA Negotiating Group Chairmanships (2002–2010)
Africa	78	6
Asia Pacific	156	45
Europe	167	11
Latin America & Caribbean	94	34
Middle East	4	0
North America	30	3

Europe, with a very high level of activity and engagement, including commercial and systemic interests to safeguard, had the most chairmanships in regular committee work, followed by Asia Pacific and Latin America and the Caribbean. Africa's number of chairmanships of regular committee work since the establishment of the WTO only ranked above North America and the Middle East. Typically, as indicated in the data analysed the North American region hardly vies for chairmanships.

In the chairmanships of DDA negotiating groups, since effective negotiations begun in 2002, the Asia Pacific region had had the most chairmanships, followed by Latin America and the Caribbean and Europe. Several reasons could account for the Asia Pacific region having the most chairmanships in DDA negotiating bodies. This region is currently the most economically dynamic. Its trade negotiators in the DDA negotiations, in contrast to traditional cultural attitudes, have been aggressive, ambitious and engaged. The region combines robust, fast-growing economies with trade negotiators with strong offensive and defensive orientations in the Doha negotiations. Africa had six chairmanships only higher than North America with three and the Middle East with no chairmanships over the eight year period analyzed. Although DDA negotiating chairmanships were initially of "higher profile", in the aftermath of the launch of the negotiations, over time, their shine has diminished and Members acknowledge the fact that chairmanships of regular bodies and DDA negotiating groups are of approximate and equal importance.

The finding on who chairs revealed an interesting pattern. The analysis of the data showed that the more technical, specialised, experienced professionally motivated the delegates (in a delegation), the higher the share of chairmanships. This was also obvious in the pattern that had emerged from the limited universe of African WTO Members that repeatedly accounted for the largest share of chairmanships within the African Group. Specifically, the more technical and specialized individuals in this limited universe of African countries had been systemically accepted to chair even the perceived most "complex" of the regular bodies such as trade remedies bodies, trade in financial services, regional trade agreements, trade in civil aircraft etc. In the final analysis, appointments to chairmanships did come down to the professional quality of the individual delegate. The lesson is that individual negotiators assigned to African WTO Member missions in Geneva must be top-class quality.

Eleventh, African WTO Members accorded horizontal priority to technical assistance, capacity building and the Aid for Trade agenda that emerged in the context of the Doha Round. In some areas, greater knowledge improved the understanding of African WTO Members of the opportunities and potential benefits in several areas of regular work, such as the TRIPS Agreement. In other areas, limited knowledge of the rules and failure to understand the connections to benefits deepened low levels of participation. It has been argued in this study that the technical assistance and capacity building factor to explain levels of participation could only be plausibly argued in the first five years of the establishment of the WTO. The position is maintained in this research that this factor should be invoked to a much lesser extent to explain participatory levels in the fifteenth year of the Organization.

(d) *Core Area of Work: WTO Dispute Settlement*

The dispute settlement system has been variously described as a pillar, the foundation, "the crown jewel", and being one of the central elements of the rules-based trading system. Analyses have been undertaken, at various stages, over the past 15 years to evaluate several aspects of its functioning, effectiveness, use by (developed and developing) Members and scope for improvement. Performance rating on the functioning of the DSU has ranged from successful, reasonable to impressive.[11] Several of those involved in "guardianship functions" have taken the position that the dispute settlement system has played a central role in clarifying and enforcing legal obligations in various Agreements (Wilson, Bruce, 2005: 15). The unique strength of the WTO dispute settlement system, universally acknowledged, is that it establishes a compulsory and binding process of adjudication. As noted also, the System was designed to ensure credibility and fairness, through its insulation from the pressure of Members and Secretariat. Specifically, it has been argued that although there is scope for improvement, no one has yet been able to prescribe better

---

[11] Professor Jackson has argued that the Appellate Body is unique in international law and that the jurisprudence it has developed is impressive in comparison to either national or international tribunals. Conference on the WTO at Ten: Governance, Dispute Settlement, and Developing Countries, Colombia University, April 2006: http://www.sipa.columbia.edu/wto/html/papers.html.

with regard to basic fundamentals (Yerxa, Rufus, 2005: 5). The dispute settlement system has contributed to the credibility of the WTO as an institution (Hughes, Valerie, 2006).[12]

This study examined the level of participation by African WTO Members in the dispute settlement system, as part of the broader evaluation by scholars and commentators of the use of the DSU. There were several key findings.

First, existing data analysed showed that over the 15-year period, from 1995–2010, developed countries had been *complainants* in 57.4 per cent of disputes, while developing countries had been complainants in 62 per cent of disputes. On the *respondents* side, the data showed that developed countries had been respondent in 61 per cent of cases, while developing countries had been respondent in 56.1 per cent of all disputes.[13]

In this regard, one key finding was that even as developed and developing country use of the DSU had increased over time and therefore lent greater credibility to the functioning of the System, African WTO Members had not been part of this trend. In the use of the dispute settlement system, the level of African participation had been abysmally low. Data gathered and analysed to assess the level of participation by African WTO Members, over the 15-year period, indicated the following:

- complainant participation – 0;
- respondent participation – 7 (Egypt, South Africa);
- third party participation – 41 (16 African Members);[14]
- panellist participation – 42 (Egypt, Mauritius, Morocco and South Africa); and,
- Appellate Body member participation – (Egypt and South Africa).

Second, a key finding from the regression analysis was that there was no strong positive correlation between trade shares and third party participation. This was an interesting finding; which confirmed the value of the practice of systemic engagement/participation. As a consequence, it is recommended that African WTO Members should systemically intervene more regardless of (low) level of trade share. A Members' trade share did not seem relevant for third party participation in the dispute settlement system. Whether a Members' trade share was high, medium, low or very low did not seem to matter.

Third, analysis of the data showed that this low level of participation had "ripple" effects in other areas of WTO work. Based on this observation, one of the strong arguments in this study is that this low level of DSU participation has magnified negative effects; and the corollary argument that the lower the level of engagement in the dispute settlement system, such as in invoking third-party rights, the lower the overall level of systemic effectiveness. Why has participation of African WTO Members been low?

Fourth, several factors were considered to be at play in explaining the very low level of African participation in the dispute settlement system. Some of the factors, it appeared, had been more argued and conceptualized with minimal bearing on empirical reality. Analysis of the situation and interviews with non-lawyer delegates, who have

---

12 Hughes Valerie (2006), Conference on the WTO at Ten: Governance, Dispute Settlement, and Developing Countries, Colombia University, April 2006: http://www.sipa.columbia.edu/wto/html/papers.html.

13 Author's own calculations.

14 Benin, Cameroon, Chad, Côte d'Ivoire, Egypt, Ghana, Kenya, Madagascar, Malawi, Mauritius, Nigeria, Senegal, South Africa, Swaziland, Tanzania and, Zimbabwe.

participated in the WTO dispute settlement system over time, suggested that the high cost factor had been overstated. It is correct that the service charges of law firms are high. However, as pointed out by many observers, WTO law is "diplomatic law", of the kind that allows competent technical participation by professionally diligent diplomats (non-lawyers). This has been the case with delegations such as India, Brazil and several others. As a related point, it is worth noting that many top law firms are also recruiting non-lawyers in recognition of the diplomatic character and interdependence between lawyers and trade diplomats in WTO dispute settlement. In addition, assuming high cost, the establishment of institutions like the Advisory Centre on WTO Law (ACWL) had further reduced the plausibility of the high cost arguments. Furthermore, there are law firms that provide, pursuant to their charters, pro bono legal services. Finally, it is also argued in this study that for identified areas of priority with systemic value such as dispute settlement, governments should allocate appropriate resources, regardless of costs if they deem it in their best judgement, necessary, to "litigate". This study argues that the cost of WTO dispute settlement is not prohibitive.

Fifth, other factors, while plausible, at the initial stage of research and theorizing of African participation, have diminished in relevance with the passage of time. This is the case with the development of specialized capacity through technical assistance, training and capacity building. While specialized dispute settlement expertise was expectedly low in the first five years of the WTO, this factor cannot be retained to explain continuing low levels of African Member participation in the dispute settlement system in the fifteenth year of the Organization.

Ascertaining the combination of critical variables presented one of the key challenges in this research. Based on data gathered and analysed, it has been argued in this study that the low level of participation of African Members in the dispute settlement system is strongly influenced by "the cost in time and staying power", a "mind-set reluctance to litigate" against major trading partners, "disputable trade measures" and, sustained, cumulative diligent professional engagement. Professional diligence and commitment are vital in invoking and operating a system of laws.

An implication that has arisen from this low level of participation of African WTO Members in the dispute settlement system are the significant gaps in understanding the entirety of the functioning of the rules-based trading system and, in many instances, failures in effective participation.

This is why it has been argued in this study that the understanding and effective use of the dispute settlement system are key and indispensable for the understanding and effective use of the rules-based multilateral trading system. The WTO's dispute settlement system provides deeper technical, jurisprudence-based insights into the workings of this system. It is argued that African WTO Members would be best served by focusing on the rules *qua* rules, rather than exceptions with the risk of unravelling the balance of rights and obligations. Strategically, while it would be necessary to allocate resources and invest energy in regular work (to administer existing rules), and negotiations (to formulate new rules), the greater and more rational investments on balance, should be systemically in dispute settlement through increased third-party participation and more active engagement in the Dispute Settlement Body (to better work the system and contribute to evolving jurisprudence).

2. Recommendations

A range of recommendations result from this study. They revolve around the principal African actors at the WTO, the process and substance of African WTO participation, emergent best practices and, technical assistance and capacity building. The conclusion underlines the importance of trade policy and reform for African growth, development, the rule of law and governance issues.

First, of the 42 African Members of the WTO, only a limited universe of them were relatively active. This comprised a range of approximately 15 to 20 African WTO Members. These have emerged to set the foundation of Africa's participation at the WTO. It is recommended that this foundation be strengthened. Other African Members African Members should continue to build on this foundation, as work in progress, to improve the level of Africa's effective participation at the WTO. What has worked? To scale-up their level of engagement/participation, all WTO African Members need to more closely study the rare instances of effective engagement analysed in this study and more closely examine the reasons for the better, higher levels of their fellow African delegations in the limited universe of active WTO Members. The WTO presents Africa with the perfect forum to combine law, policy, domestic reform and governance issues to achieve the dual goals of delivering on national priorities and, at the same time, strengthen their engagement in institutions for global law and governance.

Second, possibly because most African Members are least-developed countries, there was a preponderant focus on special and differential treatment. This has served developing countries badly (Hudec, Robert, 2011), and African countries equally badly (Osakwe, Chiedu, 2011). It is recommended, based on the results and findings in this study that African WTO Members would be best served by focusing on the rules *qua* rules, rather than exceptions with the risk of unravelling of the balance of rights and obligations, in the rules-based multilateral trading system. Strategically, it is recommended that they understand and accept the necessity for the equal investment of energy in regular work (to administer existing rules), negotiations (to formulate new rules) and dispute settlement (to contribute to evolving jurisprudence, particularly in areas of hiatus in rule-making). Resources constraints to engage in all core WTO activities or the paradox of "rational ignorance"[15] by not devoting significant resources to the WTO should not be viewed in isolation but in the broader context of benefits that would ultimately accrue. While it is true that the policy objectives or priorities are never entirely clear or straight forward in the face of multiply challenges that confront policy makers, it is argued and recommended that greater engagement in the rules-based multilateral trading system and global economy would carry greater welfare and competitiveness gains. It is argued in this study that, however one analyses the resource factor, it is a mistake and is irrational for African policy makers not to focus on multilateral institutions such as the WTO to assist them with their domestic reform efforts. WTO Agreements which are legally

[15] Pauwelyn Joost, Report on the PhD thesis of Joan Apecu Laker, 4 September 2011; Hoekman Bernard, Report on Joan Laker Apecu, African Participation at the WTO: Legal and Institutional Aspects – 1995 to 2010, 2 September 2011.

binding would engender the necessary locking in of policy and forestall policy reversals and uncertainty and unpredictability in national trade policy and domestic markets.

Third, a key finding from the regression analysis confirmed the value of systemic engagement and participation. There was no strong positive correlation between trade shares and third party participation. This was an interesting finding. As a consequence, it is recommended that African WTO Members should intervene more regardless of (low) level of trade share. Therefore, the view that because of a low trade share (around 3 per cent) Africa's participation in the WTO as illustrated by the data in this study is "higher than expected/predicted" is not shared by this research.[16] It is argued to the contrary based on the data that under conditions of lesser trade and greater poverty, African WTO Members should achieve higher levels of participation. For example, a Members' trade share did not seem relevant for third party participation in the dispute settlement system. Whether a Members' trade share was high, medium, low or very low did not seem to matter. The fact of low trade shares and GDP levels should not be used as grounds to seek derogations or operate at lower levels of the functioning of the system.

Fourth, although the three core areas of work are uniquely interrelated: negotiations ("legislature"), regular committee work ("executive"), and, dispute settlement ("adjudicature"), it is recommended that more intensive participation in a specific core area can be leveraged for greater systemic payback. This is why one of the key conclusions and recommendation of this research was that a more involved and deeper engagement in the area of dispute settlement particularly through increased third-party participation and more active engagement in the Dispute Settlement Body (through greater deployment of African Trade negotiators) should yield greater systemic benefits with knock on effects for the other two areas of regular work and negotiations.

Fifth, trade policy is singularly effective when linked to domestic reform processes and tightly anchored on coordination between capital authorities and African Permanent Missions to the WTO. This is why the recommendation is made for stronger linkages between domestic reforms for competitiveness with effective WTO participation/engagement. It is argued in this study that it would be a mistake and irrational for African policy makers not to focus on multilateral institutions such as the WTO to assist them with their domestic reforms. The example of Mauritius in this study strongly suggested that the variable of domestic economic/trade competitiveness through domestic reforms has intervened to modify/influence the variable of low trade shares in explaining performance in regular work and negotiations. Analysis of the data indicated that modest to high rankings in economic competitiveness are associated with active engagement and performance in WTO regular work and negotiations over and above low trade shares.

Sixth, many struggles have been played out in the rules-based system over chairmanships, ranging from trivial, to ceremonial and substantive. It is recommended that Africa's "struggles" in the competition for chairmanships should be substantively and strategically focused. It is also recommended that, African WTO Members should accord approximate equal regard in seeking chairmanships of both regular bodies (to administer

[16] Hoekman Bernard, Report on Joan Laker Apecu, African Participation at the WTO: Legal and Institutional Aspects – 1995 to 2010, 2 September 2011.

existing rules) and negotiating bodies (for the formulation of new rules). None is more important. The tenure of negotiating chairmanship is longer, as agreed by Members, for greater predictability and less disruption in the negotiations, whereas, there is an annual turnover for regular committee chairmanships almost in keeping with a "Buggins' turn system".

Seventh, there will always be demand for training, technical assistance and capacity building that will exceed supply. But even so, data analysed in this research indicated the existence of core sources of supply. The key challenge for African WTO Members is to ensure that their use of technical assistance, capacity building and training is strategically directed to areas of low participation, weaknesses, focus on country priorities (e.g. through Aid for Trade or the EIF) to address factors that impede trade, investment and employment creation, "bigger bang for the buck", builds on best practices, and is cumulative with real time feedback into actual work in progress. This recommendation has been the case in several areas reviewed below, in the areas of trade policy review and TRIPS.

In the TRIPS area, technical assistance and capacity building were targetted and specialized. The nature of the challenge that African WTO Members had to address involved the mobilization of available resources on offer in multilateral, regional institittions and, civil society. African engagement was more focused and driven. Two key factors explain why Africa's engagement in the area of TRIPS regular work became reinforced. At the start, was the analytic support that better connected for Africa the provisions of the TRIPS Agreement on the one hand, with their domestic interest, on the other. This was exemplified by biodiversity, geographical indications, patenting of life forms, and identification of priority needs by LDCs to implement the TRIPS Agreement etc. This was followed by the clear identification of the opportunities in the Agreement and the flexibility it provided for addressing the catastrophic public health crisis in Africa. In this latter, discussions and negotiations provided impetus to regular work. At the beginning, the content of this support from civil society was for African delegations to challenge and resist IP consideration in WTO regular work. This situation however changed as understanding was improved for the African delegations and an African Ambassador was appointed to chair the TRIPS Council. As knowledge improved, and specialized capacity developed, and African delegations begun to associate themselves with the stability of the system, and utilization of its benefits, participation improved. Training and capacity building in the TRIPS area were real and involved all relevant assistance providers. It was on-going with instant integration into actual negotiations. This is a best practice of technical assistance and capacity building linked to "negotiations".

The Trade Policy Review process provides a best practice for technical assistance and capacity building, in a partnership between the WTO Secretariat and a Member under review in the area of regular work. The result of this specific relationship has enormously contributed to deepening desperately urgent specialized trade policy capacity in African countries. Specifically, to prepare for a country's trade policy review, the Secretariat prepares its own report and the Member to be reviewed also prepares its report. Largely the report preparatory process is mutually reinforcing, even if not necessarily convergent in all cases. In the African preparatory processes, the data gathered and analysed, supplemented by interviews indicated that African Members had used it as a learning process including specially for specialised capacity building. It is therefore recommended that regardless of the prescribed frequency for trade policy reviews for African countries, most of which are LDCs, more frequent reviews would serve them best in substance, training and learning. The relationship between the WTO Secretariat and African Members over the selection of trade policy discussants is a related good example for learning and engagement. It is recommended in this study that continued wide scope remains to reduce Africa's capacity constraints in the WTO through significantly scaled-up mutual reinforcement of trade policy reviews and Secretariat trade capacity building. The Secretariat should designate more African negotiators to participate as discussants in trade policy reviews. With the passage of time, knowledge and experience and increased participation in the institutional functioning of the rules-based multilateral trading system, African WTO Members should get better at "working" the system.

There is also a "training" best practice. Drawing from the WTO Universities and Chairs Programme, one of the specific recommendations in this study is to develop sustained and specialized trade policy capacity. Universities in Africa urgently need to establish particular modules and curricula on trade and economic policy, negotiations and trade dispute settlement. The WTO Chairs Programme which aims to support and promote trade-related academic activities by universities and research institutions in developing and least-developed countries is a good starting point. Academic institutions awarded WTO Chairs receive support in the following areas: course preparation, teaching, research and outreach activities. In the period examined, five universities in Africa had been chosen to hold WTO Chairs.[17]

Eighth, in the period analysed, 92.8 per cent of African WTO Members were physically established in Geneva at the WTO. This was a vast improvement from the 50 per cent of those physically established in 1995 at the establishment of the WTO. Only three remained non-resident, although there are others in the process of accession. What is important however is that physical establishment of trade policy negotiators, on site, at the WTO in Geneva carry effects for the effectiveness and quality of legal and institutional participation/engagement in the rules-based multilateral trading system. As a consequence it is recommended that for continued improvements in legal and institutional participation, physical establishment in Geneva should attain 100 per cent. In a legal system with a clear balance of rights and obligations, effective engagement and participation cannot be from a distance. In addition, African WTO Members would be best served if their delegates/representatives in their strategic missions such as Addis Ababa (African Union), Brussels, New York, Beijing, Tokyo, Washington and other such stations frequently participated in the three core areas of WTO regular work, negotiations and dispute settlement in Geneva. Their WTO counterparts could equally monitor trade work in these strategic stations and other "economic" organizations. It is equally important that more African regional economic communities and regional bodies with mandates that relate to the work of the WTO actively participate and contribute to the work of the WTO African Members beyond observership in WTO bodies. All this could

[17] These were: Kenya (University of Nairobi); Mauritius (University of Mauritius); Morocco (Mohammed V University – Souissi); Namibia (University of Namibia); Senegal (Cheikh Anta Diop University).

help to reinforce coherence, coordination and effective follow-up in the major centres of trade co-operation for African countries and reduce scope for contradiction or gaps in positions.

Ninth, while the focus of this study has primarily been on African States or public officials, it is recommended that African governments should enhance their engagement with non-state actors where there is greater scope for improvement to systematically institutionalize and strengthen co-operation in WTO participation. Non-state actors would play important roles in improving African WTO participation and engagement for instance by acting as conduits back to society to understand WTO rights and obligations and their impacts on society livelihoods; promoting messages to local communities on the benefits of trade; and, helping governments in monitoring if their trade partners are living up to their WTO commitments. More importantly, there is value in bringing different views to the table for legitimacy of actions and social coherence and to reduce social collision. It is argued in this study that the responsibility to engage with and fully with national civil society and private sector rests with each national government. Adequate channels of communication with business constituencies with a stake in open predictable markets should be strengthened. WTO African Members should embrace this cooperation, with real time feedback to their Geneva frontlines.

Finally, concluding thoughts, on the future of African Members' participation at the WTO and the implications for the balance of rights and obligations acting as a spur to trade growth in Africa. It is difficult to forecast with certainty the future of African Trade Policy and negotiating engagement at the WTO. Although there have been some improvements in the past 15 years, overall the performance has remained disappointing without much evidence that the future will be better than the past. The ability to manage effective national trade policies has always been linked to sustained and coordinated domestic reform. This domestic trade policy reform can be trigged by WTO binding rules. This could have the impact of locking-in policy and forestalling policy reversals and uncertainty and unpredictability in national trade policy and domestic markets. The view that the WTO mechanism reinforces the credibility of domestic policy reform in the eyes of the exporter, importer or investor and that International Agreements strengthen the hand of governments and shift the balance of interest group politics within the domestic sphere is shared by this study.[18]

This is why it has been argued that effective Geneva-capital coordination, up to date information on relevant trade policy issues and much higher levels of diligent and expert professional engagement will underpin any improvements in Africa's trade policy future – that is – a change in orientation. Although this research acknowledges there are other important foundation stones and pillars supporting the edifice of outward-oriented trade policy[19] and it that shares the view that a significant increase in exports and a big rise in export diversification of African countries is important, for without export industries to push them governments do not have the constituency that in practice drives the WTO

18 Razeen Sally (2000), Developing Country Trade Policy Reform and the WTO, Cato Journal, Vol 19, No. 3.

19 Ibid.

engagement of the countries that engage more proactively,[20] it is argued in this study that factors such as improved governance, improved professionalism, improved Geneva-capital coordination are equally important because it is such defects that could translate into a muddling-through effect on the international trade policy scene. It is argued that it is this domestic change in orientation that will drive export dynamism. Trade policy and specifically WTO participation require more attention. Trade is the engine for growth. The near consensus and positive links between trade and growth are well established in the literature. Openness to trade is associated with faster growth and countries that trade grow much faster than those that are closed. (Dollar, 1992; Sachs and Warner, 1995; Panagariya, 2003). The rules-based Multilateral Trading System has functioned since 1947 to regulate and drive and open the multilateral trading system and has contributed to global welfare, development and poverty reduction, including through linkages to domestic reform. It is argued that the participation of African Members in the WTO would increase if they better made these linkages. It is the understanding and application of these linkages that would make the difference between the past and the future level of African participation at the WTO. Sustained and more intensive policy-relevant research is required for the improvement of Africa's level of engagement and participation in the WTO.

The last word has not been said and this will always remain work in progress.

[20] Hoekman Bernard, Report on Joan Laker Apecu, African Participation at the WTO: Legal and Institutional Aspects – 1995 to 2010, 2 September 2011.

ANNEXES

Annex I: Regional Groupings of WTO Members for Purposes of This Research

Region	Countries
Africa (42)	Angola, Benin, Botswana, Burkina Faso, Burundi, Cameroon, Cape Verde, Central African Republic, Chad, Congo, Cote d'Ivoire, Democratic Republic of Congo, Djibouti, Egypt, Gabon, Gambia, Ghana, Guinea, Guinea Bissau, Kenya, Lesotho, Madagascar, Malawi, Mali, Mauritania, Mauritius, Morocco, Mozambique, Namibia, Niger, Nigeria, Rwanda, Senegal, Sierra Leone, South Africa, Swaziland, Tanzania, Togo, Tunisia, Uganda, Zambia, Zimbabwe
Asia-Pacific (28)	Australia, Bangladesh, Brunei Darussalam, Cambodia, China, Fiji, Hong Kong China, India, Indonesia, Japan, Korea, Macao China, Malaysia, Maldives, Mongolia, Myanmar, Nepal, New Zealand, Pakistan, Papua New Guinea, Philippines, Singapore, Solomon Islands, Sri Lanka, Chinese Taipei, Thailand, Tonga, Vietnam
Europe (41)	Albania, Armenia, Austria, Belgium, Bulgaria, Croatia, Cyprus, Czech Rep, Denmark, Estonia, European Communities, Finland, FYR, Macedonia, France, Georgia, Germany, Greece, Hungary, Iceland, Ireland, Italy, Kyrgyz Rep, Latvia, Liechtenstein, Lithuania, Luxembourg, Malta, Moldova, Netherlands, Norway, Poland, Portugal, Romania, Slovak Rep, Slovenia, Spain, Sweden, Switzerland, Turkey, Ukraine, United Kingdom
Latin America and the Caribbean (32)	Antigua and Barbuda, Argentina, Barbados, Belize, Bolivarian Rep of Venezuela, Bolivia, Brazil, Chile, Colombia, Costa Rica, Cuba, Dominica, Dominican Rep, Ecuador, El Salvador, Grenada, Guatemala, Guyana, Haiti, Honduras, Jamaica, Mexico, Nicaragua, Panama, Paraguay, Peru, St Kitts and Nevis, St Lucia, St Vincent and the Grenadines, Suriname, Trinidad and Tobago, Uruguay
Middle East (8)	Bahrain, Israel, Jordan, Kuwait, Oman, Qatar, Saudi Arabia, United Arab Emirates
North America (2)	Canada, United States

Annex II: Methodology Used

This is a study of the "levels of participation and engagement" of African WTO Members across the three core areas of activity in the WTO: the Doha negotiations; regular WTO committee work; and, dispute settlement, over a 15 year period (1995–2010). Although data was gathered and analysed across all WTO Members, African WTO Members constitute the case study of this research.

Previous research had largely adopted a "silo approach" in the investigation of African WTO participation; with a distinct focus on each area with virtually no comparison. This was understandable particularly in the first few years of the existence of the WTO. However, the passage of time provides insights gained from comparative analysis. In this study, the level of African participation is researched across the three areas comparatively. It is suggested that the uniqueness of this study revolves around the inter-related treatment of the three core areas, testing the same explanatory factors across the three areas and over the 15 year existence of the WTO. Areas of work in the WTO are not stand alone. A proper understanding of the engagement and participation of any one Member in any area is enabled by a fuller understanding of the inter-relationships between the particular characteristics of the three core areas: negotiations (trade economics, bargaining and diplomacy); regular work (trade law and implementation); and, dispute settlement (international law, trade law, and, adjudication).

Although this research takes an empirical approach, it is legally grounded as its main focus is on participation in the World Trade Organization – a rules-based system grounded on legal Agreements binding on every Member. The value and systemic importance of participation rests on the fact that multilateral trade rules serve an important domestic political-economic function. Increasingly they form part of national strategies of external liberalization. Binding reciprocal commitments engender the necessary locking in of policy, forestalling domestic policy reversals and uncertainty and unpredictability of national trade policy. It is therefore important to participate in the shaping of trade rules that will ultimately require domestic implementation. For instance, in regular committee work, Members' engagement is focused on administering the rules that bind all Members in a system of balanced rights and obligations. In trade negotiations, such as the on-going Doha negotiations, legal texts emerge from technical drafting processes underscoring the value in actively participating and contributing to shaping final outcomes that would be legally binding on each Member party to the negotiations. Each member would have to implement the results. In dispute settlement, although the ability for effective engagement and participation in panel and Appellate Body work inter-alia depend on expert and competent legal capacity in delegations, it is equally important to participate from a systemic view point and contributing the shaping of the "precedents" of panels and the Appellate Body.

Methodologically, a range of specific analytic tools were applied. These included statistical and substantive content analysis, comparative analysis with Members in other regions, questionnaires, interviews and "the participant/observer" role of the author.

The dependent variable specified is: "level of engagement/participation" of African WTO Members. This variable is specifically defined for measure in the area of **negotiations** as the:

- number of DDA chairmanships,
- number and quality of individual and co-sponsored proposals/submissions,
- number and quality of individual, co-sponsored and group proposals/submissions
- interventions/statements[1]

This variable is specifically defined for measure in **regular committee work** inter-alia as:

- number of chairmanships,
- number of proposals/submissions,
- number of interventions/statements,
- notifications (regular). Beyond these, additional specific variables were analyzed, depending on the subject matter and mandate of a committee.

This variable is specifically defined for measure in **dispute settlement** as:

- number of chairmanships,
- initiation of disputes(complainant roles)
- respondent (defendant) roles,
- third party roles
- panellist roles.
- Appellate Body Member roles

Methodologically, there are several dimensions associated with assessing the participation of any country or group of countries in the WTO. The first is to determine the objectives, that is, what participation is aimed at; second is to document and quantify participation and engagement and third to assess effectiveness.

Although an exhaustive discussion of objectives would be useful, this was not the focus of this study. But, this research did recognise that there is a relationship between objectives on the one hand, and effectiveness of African engagement on the other. However, in this research and based on the empirical data, the evidence indicated that the more critical factors for assessing effectiveness levels of African engagement were inter-alia Geneva-Capital coordination, information on relevant trade policy issues and professional expertise and diligence. These defects can translate into muddling-though stance on the international trade policy scene.[2] In addition, there was the methodological challenge and almost virtually insurmountable difficulty in coherently tabulating uniform or unitary African trade policy objectives. In light of this challenge, this research fell back to the objectives and priorities of Declarations of African Union Trade Ministers listed in Annex V.

In order to reach conclusions on the "level of engagement/participation", percentage calculations were made for African WTO Members across the foregoing defined variables in relation to: (i) the size of African WTO membership totalling 42; (ii) in comparison to the engagement of individual Members from other regions; (iii) as a percentage of the engagement by all participating Members on a particular variable analysed; and, (iv) qualitative assessments about the level of participation in specific relationship to

1 This was only done for the TNC and not its subsidiary bodies. From about 2007 work in most negotiating bodies took place mainly in informal mode with no official records.

2 Razeen Sally, *Developing Country Trade Policy Reform and the WTO*, Cato Journal, Vol. 19, No. 3, 2000.

areas identified as top priority by African WTO Members in their declarations; statements; and, submissions.

Determining whether observed level of engagement was high or low requires a clear benchmark, ideally based on some theory on the determinants of participation that would generate a prediction of what one would expect to observe. However, it is argued in this research that benchmarks should be seen more as "variables" and "not constants". A more theoretical approach would lead down the path of drawing on theories dealing with benchmarks for judgements on higher or lower levels of engagement. But, the approach in the specific circumstances of the primary data gathered and the explanatory variables used in this study which have combined "personality" variables with trade (import and export), income and market shares, and direct observations lent itself to greater pragmatism in assessing the levels of engagement and less theory. In other words, greater pragmatism and less metrics, but clearly acknowledging that both are important in judging levels of engagement.

A methodological question wrestled with in this research was whether there was "a right amount of participation expected". The conclusion reached was that although there was no "right amount of participation" expected *ex ante* for African WTO Members, African participation was self-evidently low *per se*. The question of "level of participation" is neither *purely statistical* nor can the answer be *purely judgemental*. Both numbers and judgements equally apply in reaching the conclusion about the low, nominal and largely ineffectual level of African WTO Member participation. The "expectation" on participation is linked to "effectiveness", the "optimization" of the number of African WTO Members and "maximization" of available resources in regular work, negotiations and dispute settlement. Although it might be argued that with a share of world trade of around 3 per cent, African WTO participation is higher than expected (predicted) it is firmly argued in this study that under conditions of lesser trade and greater poverty, African Members should achieve higher levels of participation. In addition in practice what might matter in terms of incentives to participate could be product or issue specific or centres on specific markets or trading partners. And, it is true and one must accept that data can be interpreted differently. The glass can either be half full or half empty. The incentive question is certainly critical and deserves greater attention in further research.

Linked to the methodological question of the "right" amount of participation and the substantive research focus of the level of engagement, were the related issues of "quantity" and "quality" of engagement, as investigated in statements made and proposals submitted. Quantity and quality stand in contrast. In the data analysed, there was a "quality" question in contrast to the "quantity" of tabled proposals and statements made. This research made judgements about quality, revolving around the factors of substantive content, attraction of consensus and, tangible outcomes from proposals and submissions. As defined for this study, in a consensus based decision making system, the higher the quality, the higher the number and likelihood of tangible outcomes. Quality was construed as a function of ability of a proposal/submission to bridge the gaps, narrow the differences and approach consensus. This is in the nature of the System.

Data was gathered from relevant WTO bodies. Minutes and summary records of WTO bodies falling under the category of regular work from 1995 to 2010 were examined. For the Doha negotiations, minutes, summary records and lists of proposals were reviewed from 2002–2010. For both regular committee work and the Doha negotiations, reports and records of committees and Secretariat reports were referred to as primary sources. Data on notifications and specific trade concerns were assessed from relevant reports of respective committees. In addition data was collected from specific WTO databases, including the SPS and TBT Information Management Systems; Dispute Settlement database and the ITTC activities database.

Questionnaires were administered to African WTO delegates, but with very low rate of returns. Thirty-seven (37) questionnaires were administered to African delegates through the coordinator of the African Group to cover the universe of the 37 African WTO Members, resident in Geneva, and that participate at the weekly meetings of the WTO African Group. After nearly one year of reminders, there was a poor return of nine (or 23% of Geneva-resident African WTO Members). The poor returns corroborate the thesis of minimal, nominal and largely ineffective levels of participation. The questionnaire and results are annexed. (See Annex IV for the model questionnaire specifically structured for this study and the results).

A number of interviews were conducted, although only approximately 15 were critical.[3] These were conducted with African Ambassadors, African trade negotiators, coordinators of the African Group, and, WTO Secretariat officials.

Research strives for the highest levels of rigour and objectivity to reduce bias, but this always remains a challenge. Analyses of the data were undertaken through statistics (counting, totalling, averages, percentages, and, regression; the latter used to cross-check conclusions reached through the logic of the evidence and arguments).

A number of the results from the regression analysis provide interesting insights. Several independent/explanatory variables were applied in various combinations in this study. Regression analysis was employed with regard to three independent/explanatory variables: trade share; GDP Per Capita; and, democracy level. These explanatory variables were applied to the dependent variable of "level of engagement and participation".

The results of the regression are set out in Annex III.

Trade Shares

Trade shares were based on internal calculations.[4] The ranking excluded intra-EU trade. Regression results for the explanatory variable of "trade shares" suggested the following with regard to the dependent variable of "level of engagement and participation":

(i) Interventions, Statements and Proposals: Regular work and negotiations (Charts 1–8)

- A positive correlation between trade shares and statements/interventions/proposals in regular work and in negotiating engagement. The results showed that the higher a Members' trade share, the higher the number of interventions/statements, although this was mediated with competitiveness rankings as was illustrated in the case of Mauritius.

---

3 Arsene Balihuta, Chiedu Osakwe, Edwini Kessie, Nelson Ndirangu, Dan Owoko, Peter Pedersen, Katjipuka Benjamin, Nadir Alikhan, Rishikesh Mavroidis Suja, Madja Petschen, Stefania Bernabe, El Hachimi Said, Kim Eki, Zainab Mchumo, Moira Redecker.

4 Calculations of trade shares were done specifically for this study with the assistance of colleagues in the WTO Statistics unit.

- Exceptions seemed to exist where Members with high trade shares made fewer interventions. This was the case for South Africa with the highest trade share in Africa of 0.68 %, but making fewer interventions than other African Members with lower trade shares, on development questions in the Committee on Trade and Development.
- Exceptions also existed where those with low trade shares made relatively more interventions. This was the case for Kenya with a relatively lower trade share of 0.08%, but with the most interventions by an African Member in the TNC and General Council.
- Most African Members barely intervened. All of them have low trade shares (less than one per cent).
- One African Member with a trade share of 0.4%, Egypt, (relatively high by African standards) had the highest level of African Members' interventions in regular work (the General Council).
- Other factors, beyond trade share level, or in combination, were also at play such as the experience and diligence of individual diplomats, professional exposure, tenure, commercial stake in subject area.

(ii) Dispute settlement:

- Complainants: the results suggested that, in general, the higher a Members' trade share, the higher the number of times a Member was likely to institute a dispute against another Member/s. Trade shares of all African WTO Members are very low. They have not instituted any complaints against any Member/s. (Charts 11 and 12)
- Respondents: the results suggested that the higher a Members' trade share, the higher the number of times disputes were instituted against that Member. However few exceptions existed where Members with relatively low trade shares had been "sued" a couple of times, for example Dominican Republic with a trade share of 0.10% had been sued 7 times. (Chart 13). With very low trade shares, only two African Members have been respondents in WTO dispute settlement. These were Egypt and South Africa (Chart 14)
- Third Parties: the result did not suggest a strong positive correlation between trade shares and third party participation. (Charts 15 and 16). This is an interesting finding; which confirms the value of the practice of systemic interventions. As a consequence, it is recommended that African WTO Members should intervene more regardless of (low) level of trade share. A Members' trade share did not seem relevant for third party participation. Whether a Members' trade share was high, medium, low or very low did not seem to matter. However, for African Members whose trade shares are in general very low, the number of third party participation has been lower than that of other Members in the low trade share category (less than one per cent).
- Other factors, beyond the level of a Members' trade share, or in combination, were at play with regard to decisions to undertake third party participation.

GDP per Capita

GDP Per Capita (GDP per Capital (current $ US) was based on figures in the World Bank Database – World Development Indicators. Regression results for the explanatory variable of GDP suggested the following with regard to the dependent variable of "level of engagement and participation":

(i) Interventions, Statements and Proposals: Regular work and negotiations (Charts 17–24)

- Overall, a positive correlation between GDP per capita and statements/interventions/proposals in regular work and in negotiating engagement seemed to exist. The results suggested that a higher a Members' GDP per capita, the higher the number of interventions/

statements, although this was mediated with competitiveness rankings as was illustrated by the case of Mauritius.
- African Members with low GDP intervened less. Very few exceptions existed where no more than two (2) African Members with low GDP shares registered relatively higher levels of intervention/proposals. This was case for Benin and Burkina Faso; again confirming the argument, based on the facts, that low trade and GDP shares should not necessarily inhibit systemic engagement/participation.

(ii) Dispute settlement.

With regard to dispute settlement the regression showed a mixed result as follows:

- Complainants: the result did not seem to suggest a strong positive correlation between GDP and participation as complainant. A Members' GDP did not seem to matter much. Whether a Members' GDP was high, medium, low or very low seemed irrelevant for participation as complainant. Some Members with very high GDP levels had not been complainants in WTO dispute settlement; some with very low GDP had also not been complainants (the case for all African WTO Members). However, some Members with relatively low GDP levels had been complainant on a number of occasions, while those with "medium" level GDP had also been complainant more times than those with higher levels. (Charts 27 and 28)
- Respondents: the results suggested a positive correlation between GDP levels and number of times a Member was respondent, only for African Members (the two Members that have been respondents). (Chart 30). For all other Members, the correlation was not positive. (Chart 29). The results suggested that GDP levels did not appear to influence behaviour as respondents. Irrespective of GDP levels, Members had been or not been respondents. In other words the nature of the functioning is very "systemic", regardless of levels of trade and economic development.
- Third Parties: the result did not seem to suggest a strong positive correlation between GDP and third-party participation. A Members' GDP did not seem to influence behaviour as third-party. Whether a Members' GDP was high, medium, low or very low appeared to be of little relevance for third-party participation. (Charts 31 and 32).

(iii) Mission Size:

- Although the results showed that in the minority of cases, the higher the GDP, the larger the mission size, in the majority of cases, the result suggested that GDP did not affect mission size. (Chart 25). Some Members with low GDP had mission sizes larger than or comparable to with those Members with higher GDP levels. This is the case for Nigeria and Kenya. (Chart 26)

Democracy Level

A Members' democracy level was based on the Economist Intelligence Unit's Democracy Index 2010. The scores measured the level of democracy as follows: full democracies (score 10–8); flawed democracies (scores 7.9–6); hybrid regimes (scores 5.9–4); authoritarian regimes (scores below 4). Regression results for the explanatory variable of "democracy level" suggested the following with regard to the dependent variable of "level of engagement and participation":

(i) Interventions, Statements and Proposals (Regular work and negotiations) and Mission Size

- Most African Members ranked low (i.e. less democratic) as per the EIU democracy index and intervened less in regular work and negotiating engagement. (Charts 34, 36, 38,40)
- The results suggested that the less democratic a Member was, the less the level of interventions/participation.
- There were some exceptions where a few that were ranked low had intervened more (for instance Djibouti with a score of 2.2 had intervened 34 times in the General Council and Egypt with a score of 3.07 had intervened 218 times). There were also opposite exceptions where those that ranked high (more democratic) had made very few statements. (For example, Iceland with a score of 9.65 had made only 5 interventions in the CTD in the 15 years studied. Cape Verde, with a score of 7.94 had not intervened in the CTD)
- The results seemed to suggest that a Members' level of democracy did not affect mission size. (Charts 41 and 42)
- Other factors in combination with the level of democracy seem to be at play.

ANNEX III: REGRESSION RESULTS

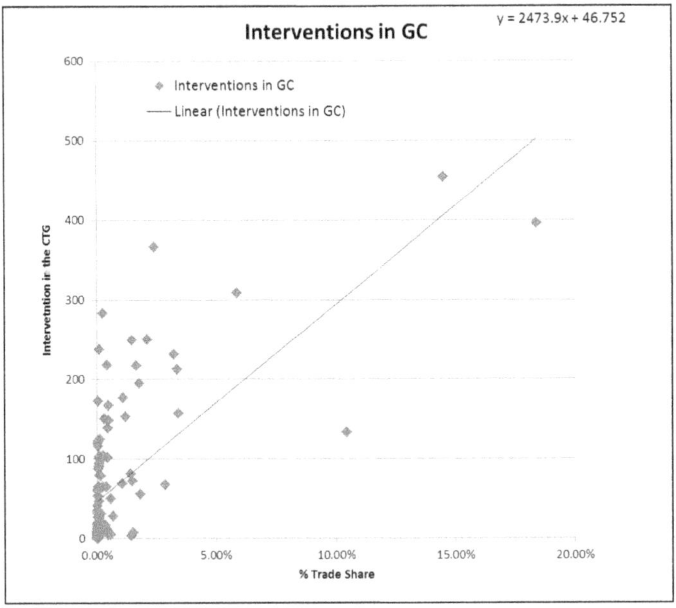

Chart 1. Trade shares and regular WTO work (interventions in the General Council) by all members.

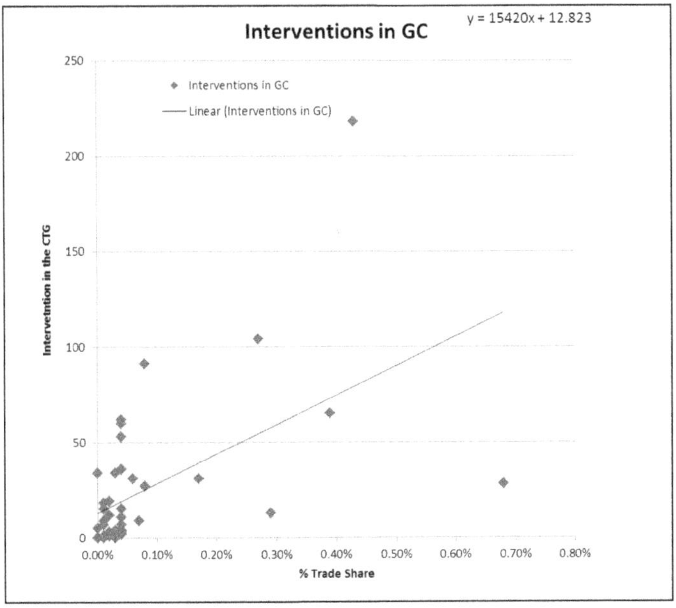

Chart 2. Trade shares and regular WTO work (interventions in the General Council) by African WTO members.

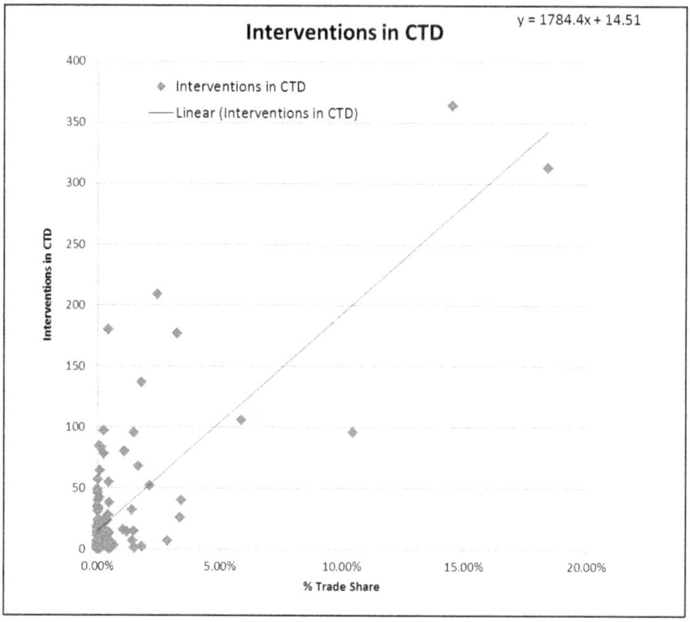

Chart 3. Trade shares and regular WTO work (interventions in the CTD) by all members.

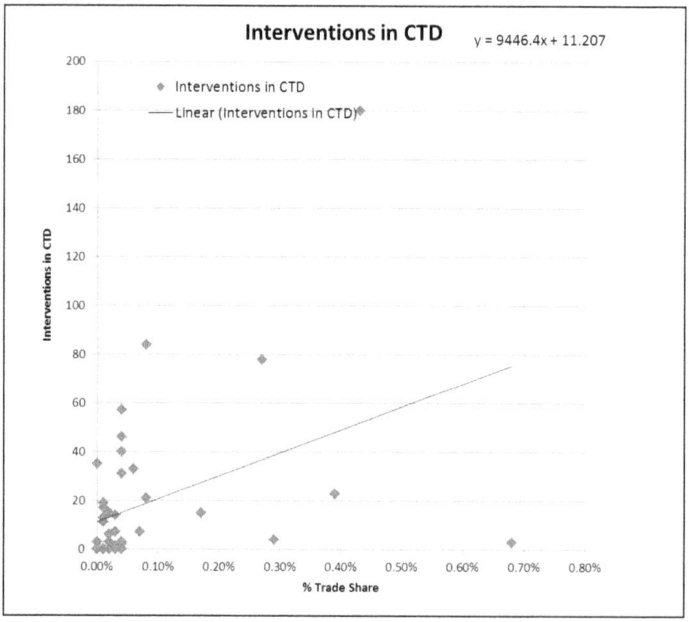

Chart 4. Trade shares and regular WTO work (interventions in the CTD) by all African WTO members.

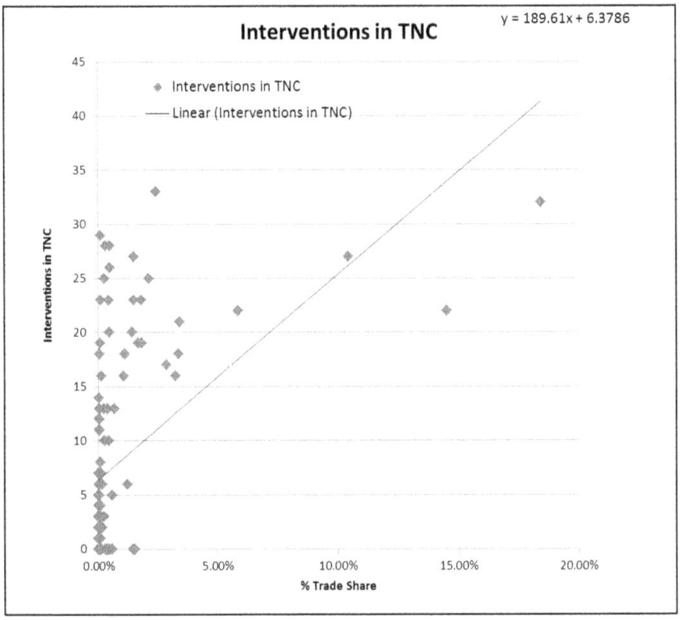

Chart 5. Trade shares and negotiating engagement (interventions in the TNC) by all members.

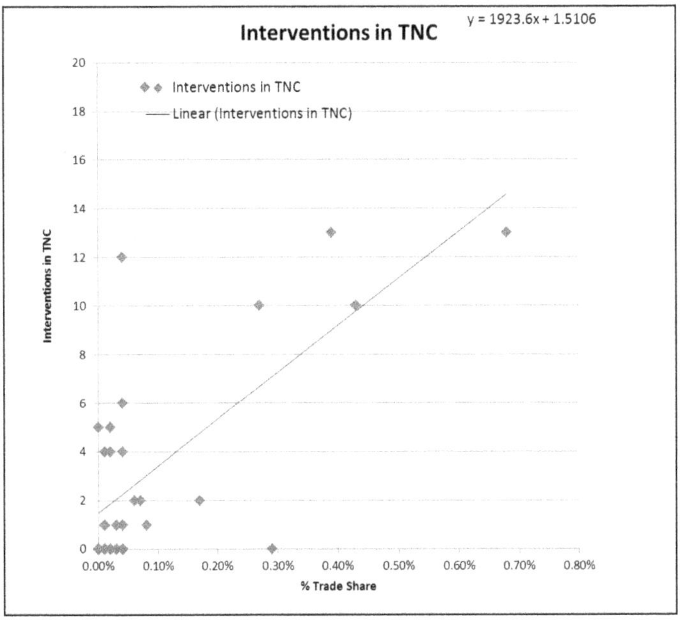

Chart 6. Trade shares and negotiating engagement (interventions in the TNC) by African WTO members.

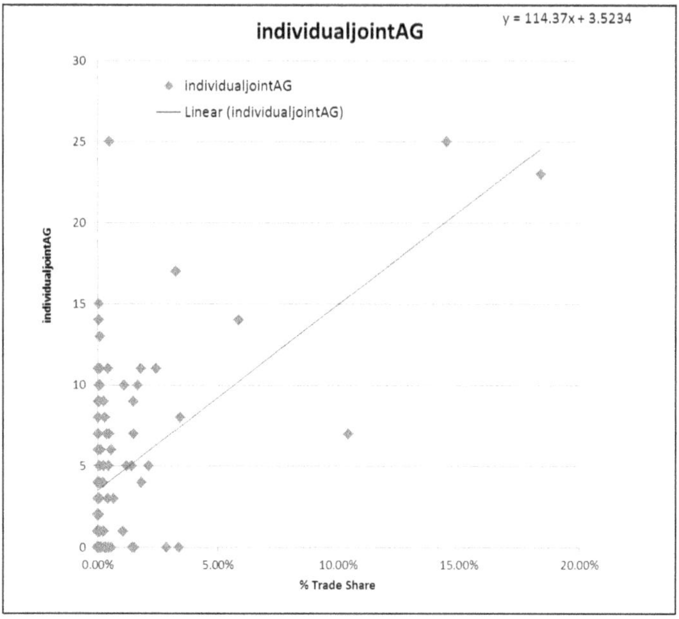

Chart 7. Trade shares and negotiating engagement (agriculture proposals) by all members.

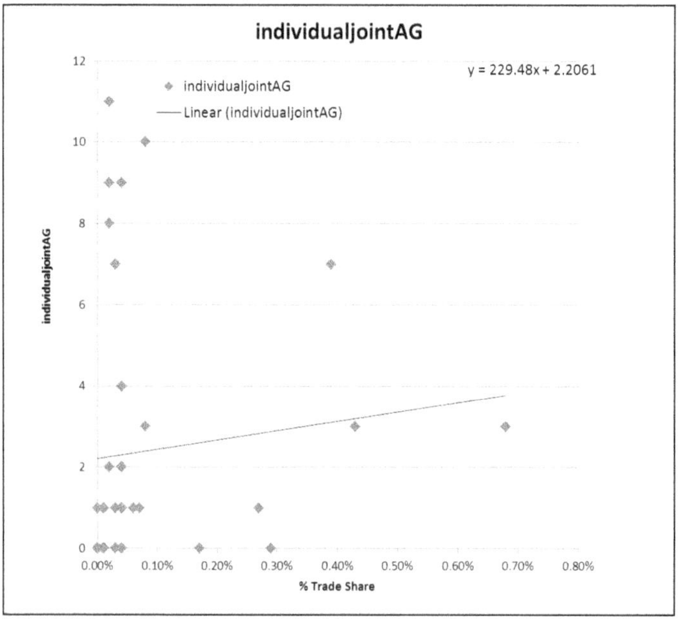

Chart 8. Trade shares and negotiating engagement (agriculture proposals) by African WTO members.

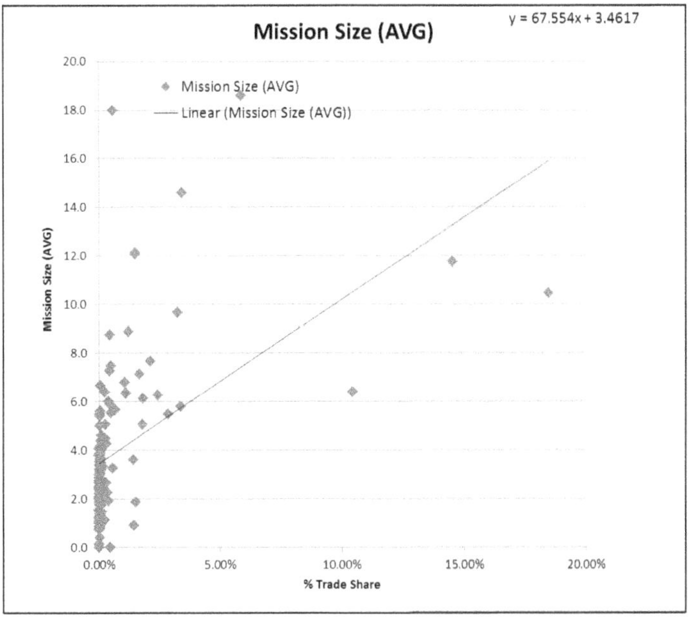

Chart 9. Trade shares and mission size, all members.

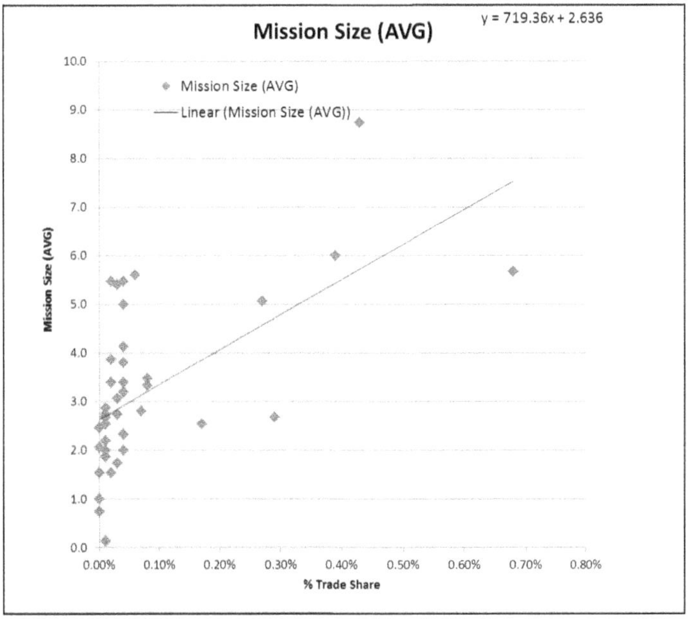

Chart 10. Trade shares and mission size African WTO members.

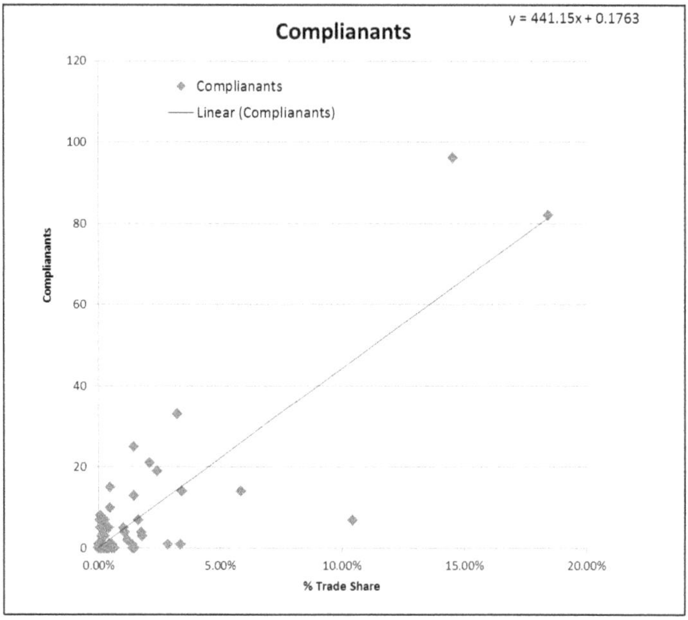

Chart 11. Trade shares and complainants, all members.

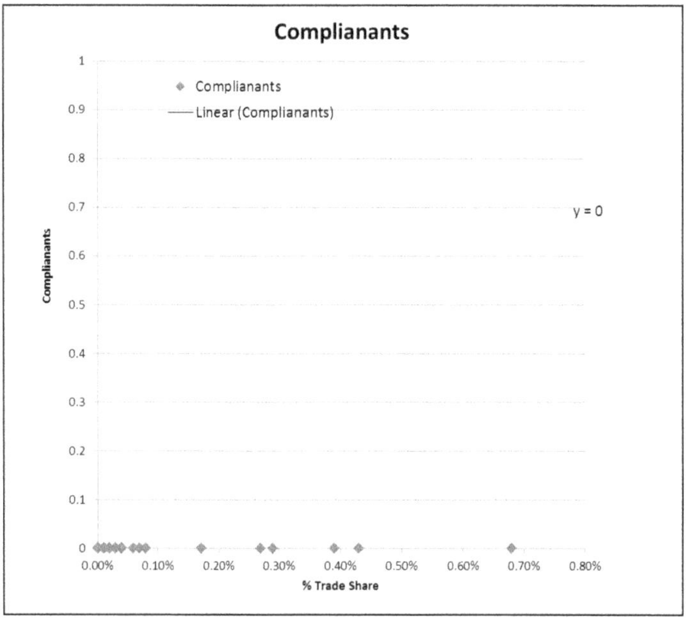

Chart 12. Trade shares and complainants, African WTO members.

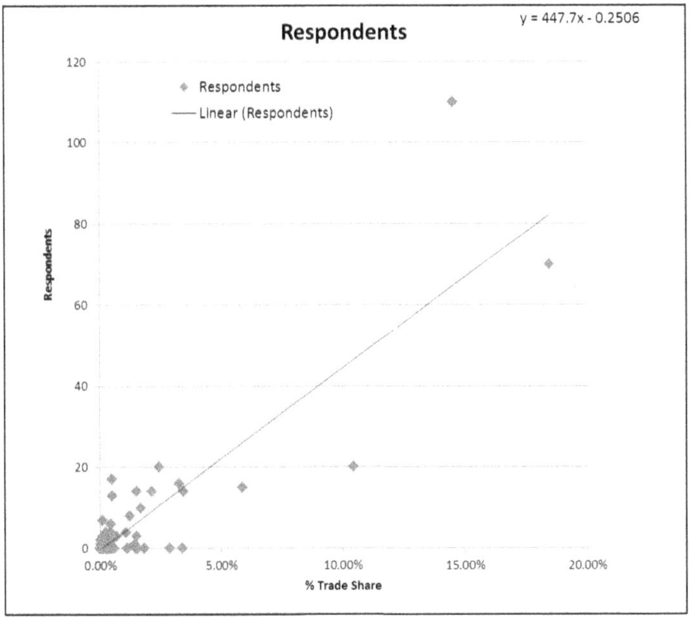

Chart 13. Trade shares and respondents all members.

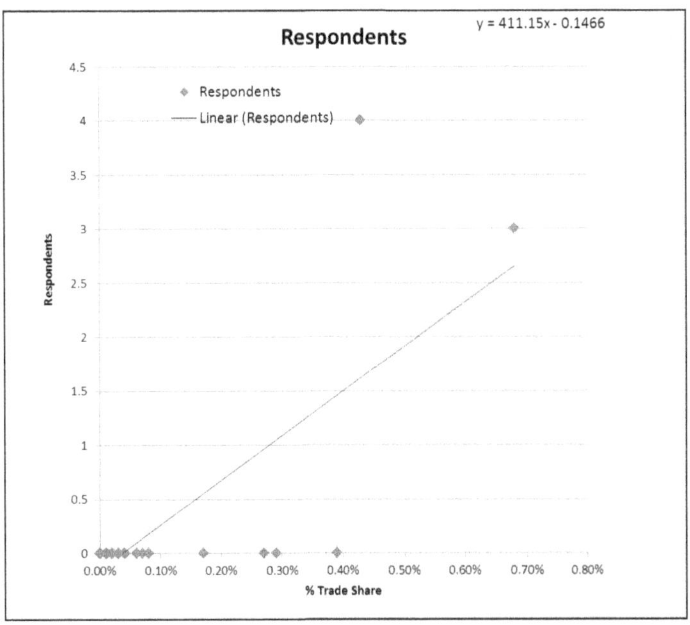

Chart 14. Trade shares and respondents, African WTO members.

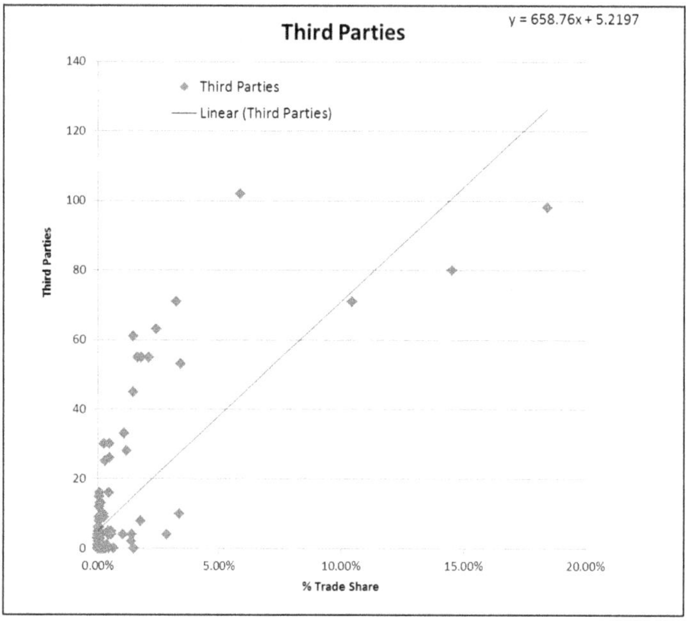

Chart 15. Trade shares and third parties, all members.

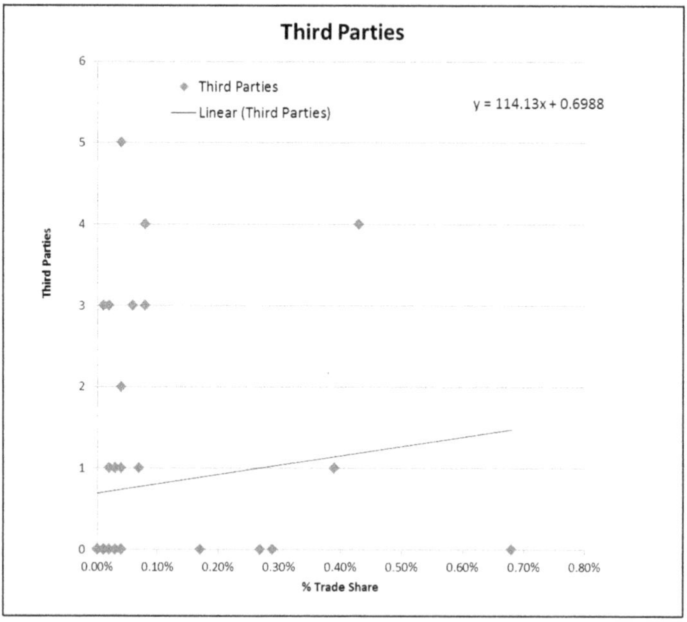

Chart 16. Trade shares and third parties, African WTO members.

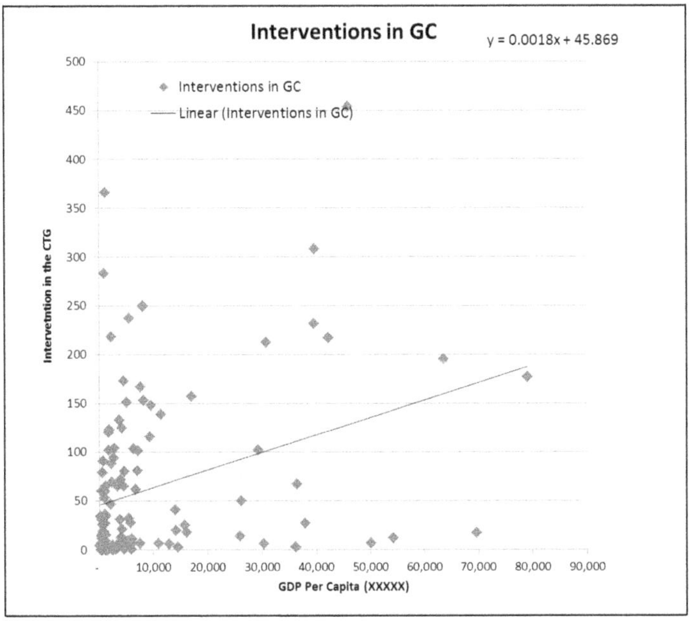

Chart 17. GDP and regular WTO work (interventions in the General Council) by all members.

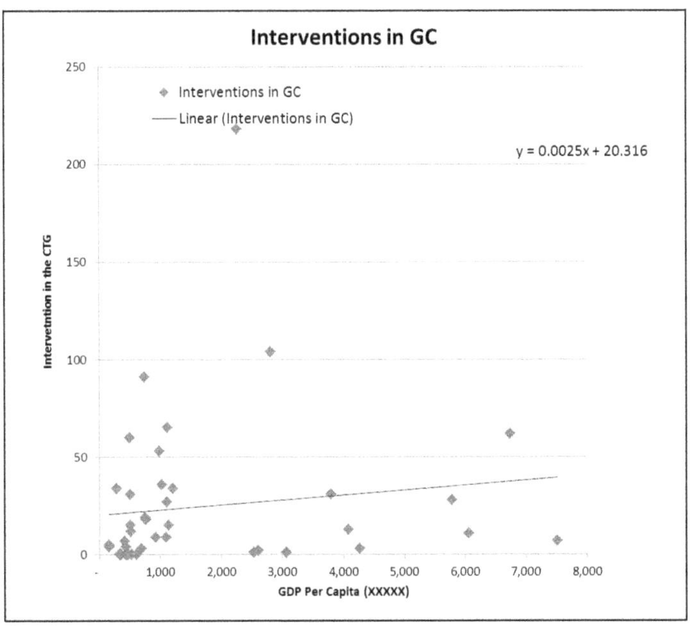

Chart 18. GDP and regular WTO work (interventions in the General Council) by African WTO members.

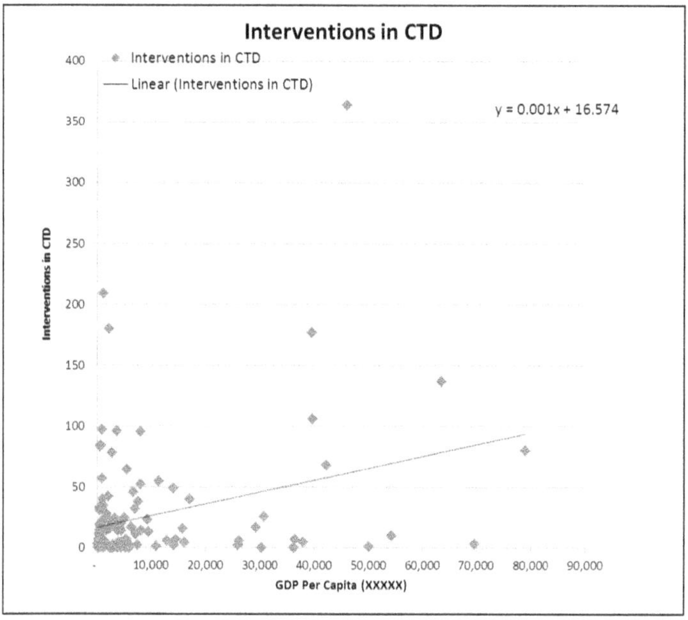

Chart 19. GDP and regular WTO work (interventions in the CTD) by all members.

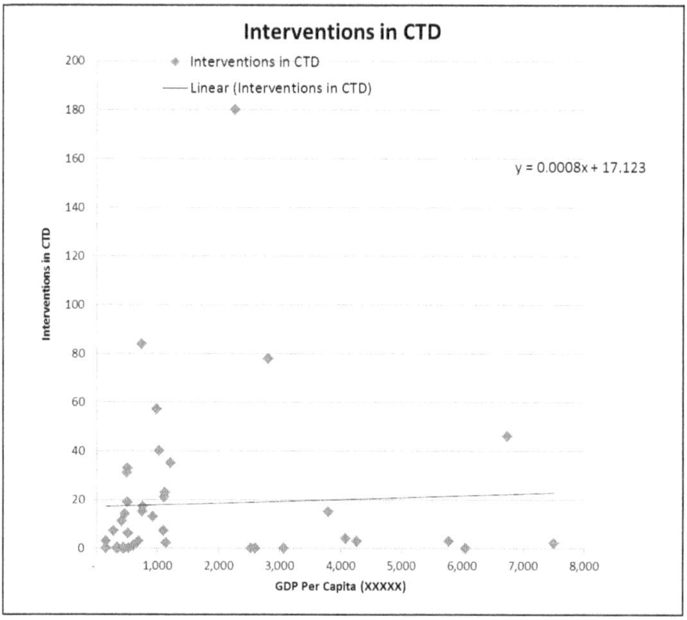

Chart 20. GDP and regular WTO work (interventions in the CTD) by African WTO members.

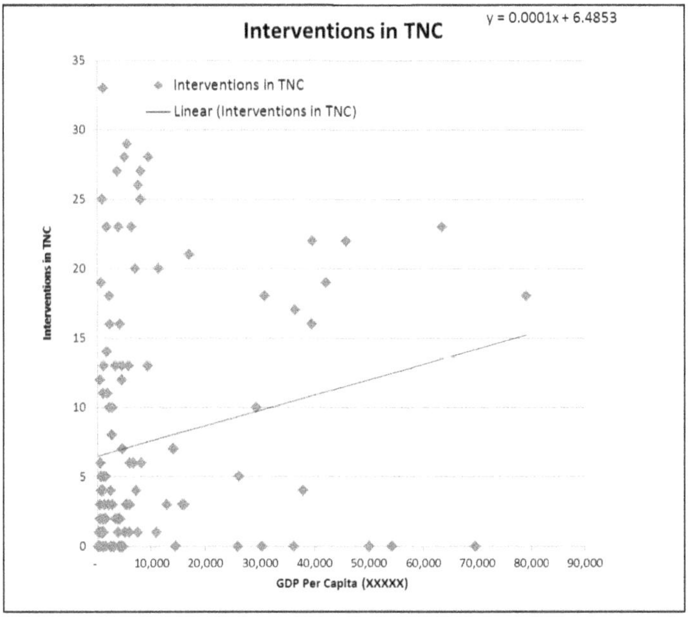

Chart 21. GDP and negotiating engagement (interventions in the TNC) by all members.

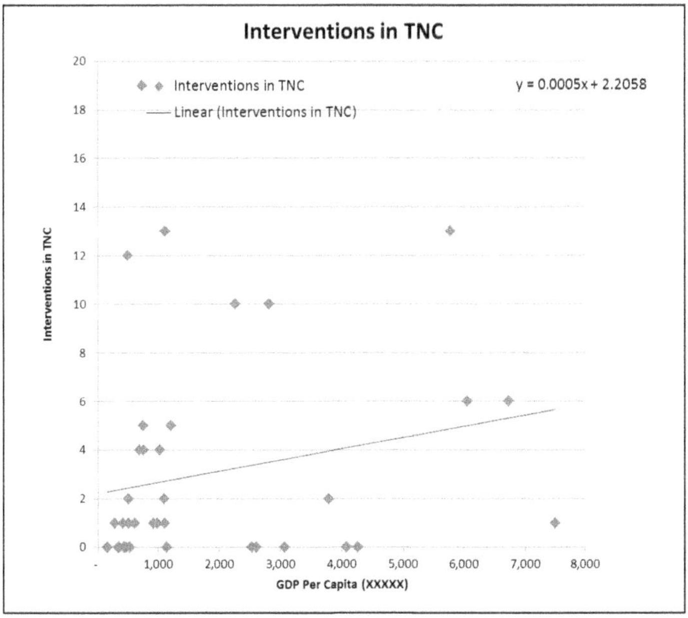

Chart 22. GDP and negotiating engagement (interventions in the TNC) by African WTO members.

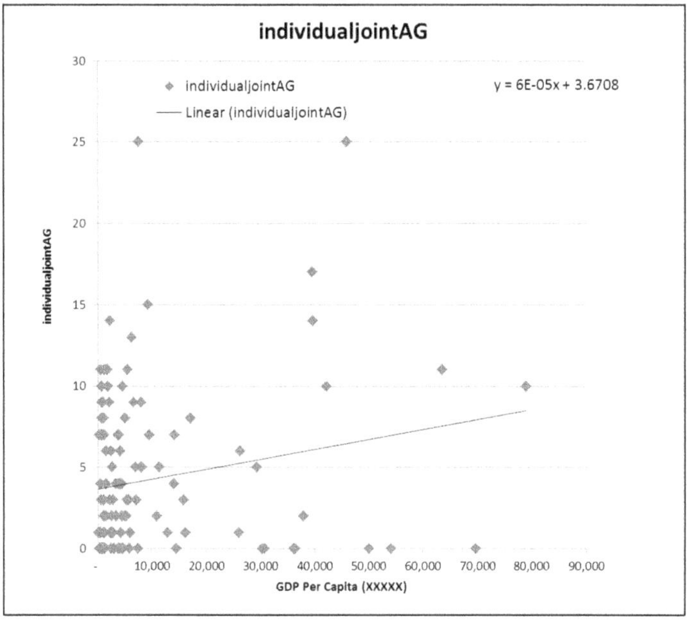

Chart 23. GDP and negotiating engagement (agriculture proposals) by all members.

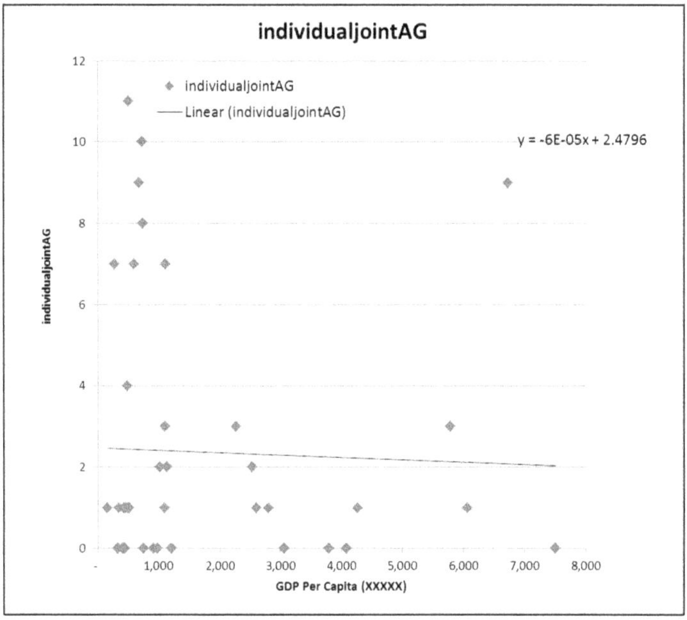

Chart 24. GDP and negotiating engagement (agriculture proposals) by African WTO members.

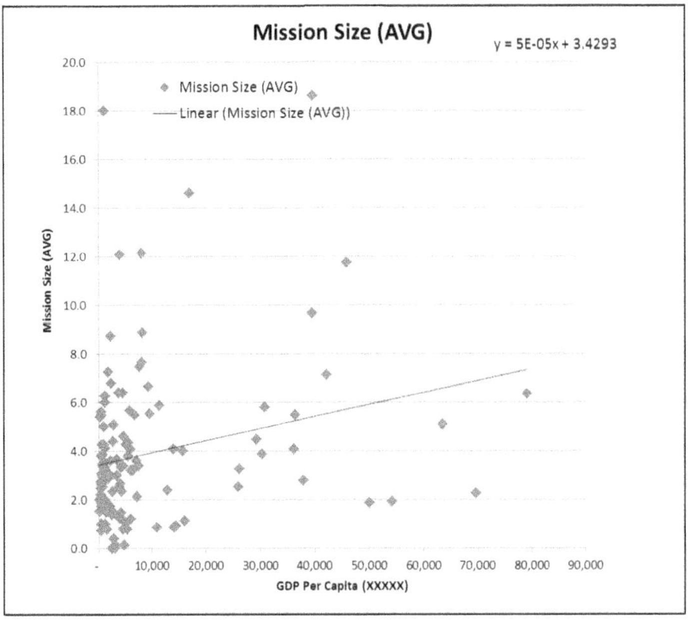

Chart 25. GDP and mission size, all members.

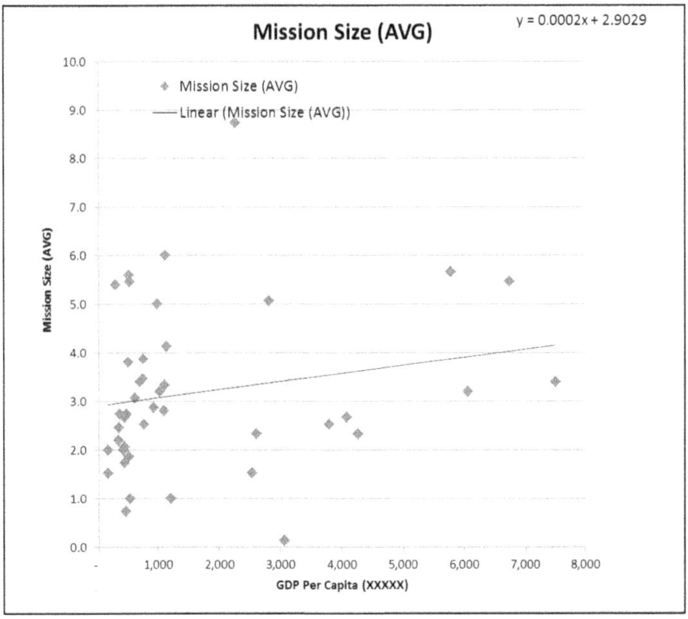

Chart 26. GDP and mission size, African WTO members.

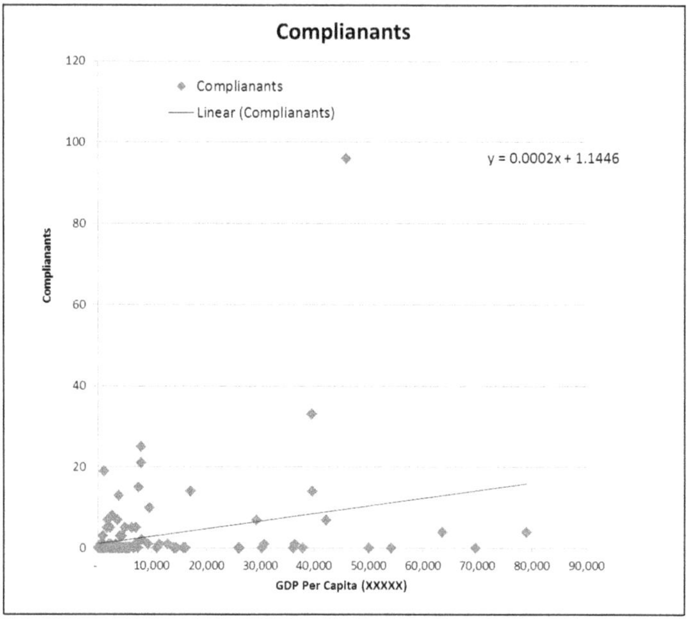

Chart 27. GDP and complainants, all members.

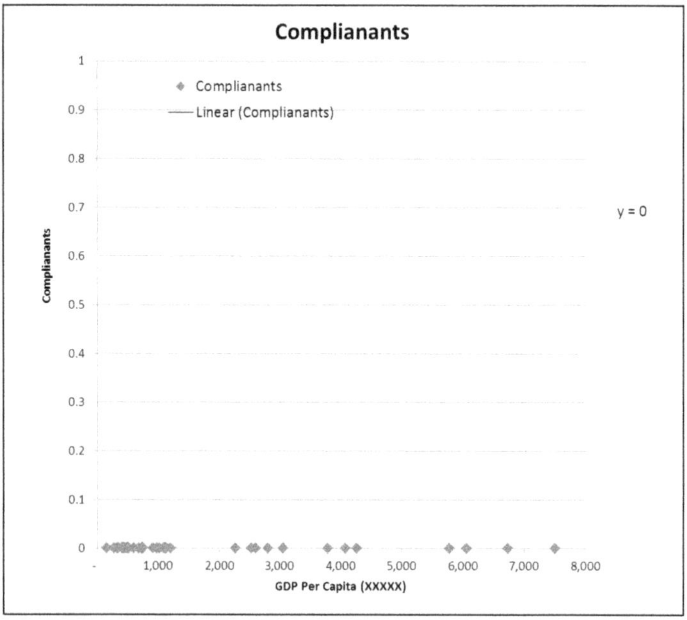

Chart 28. GDP and complainants, African WTO members.

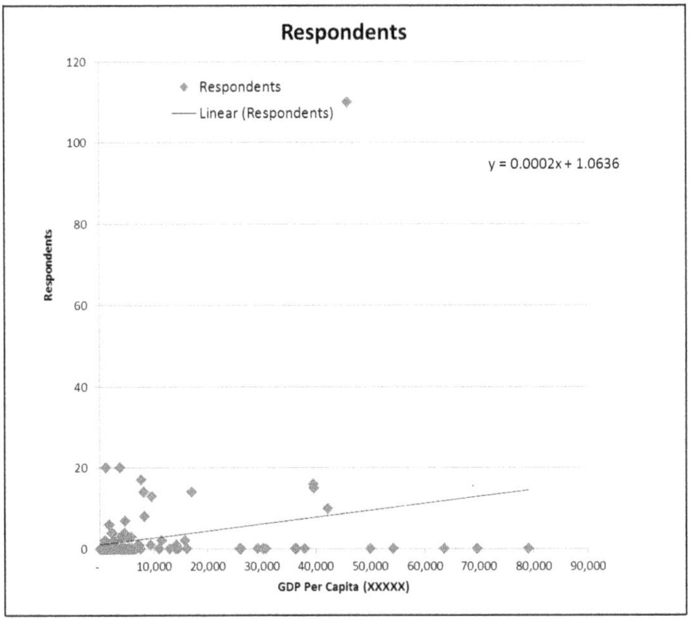

Chart 29. GDP and respondents all members.

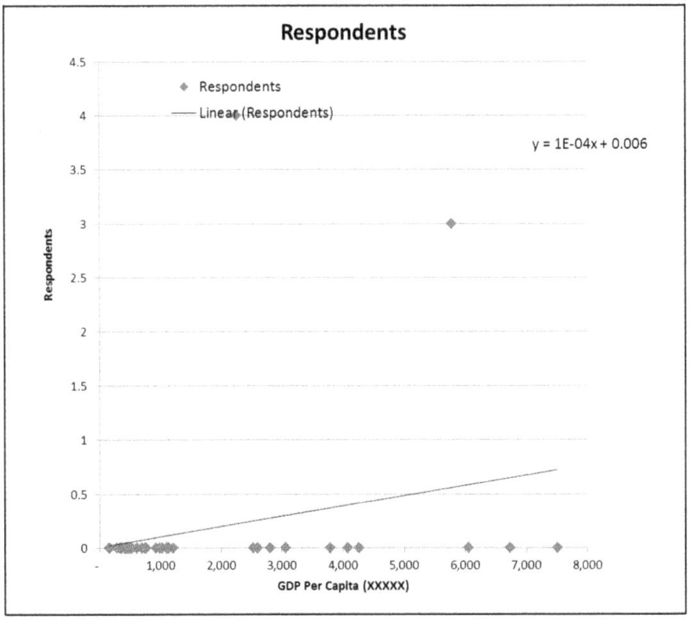

Chart 30. GDP and respondents, African WTO members.

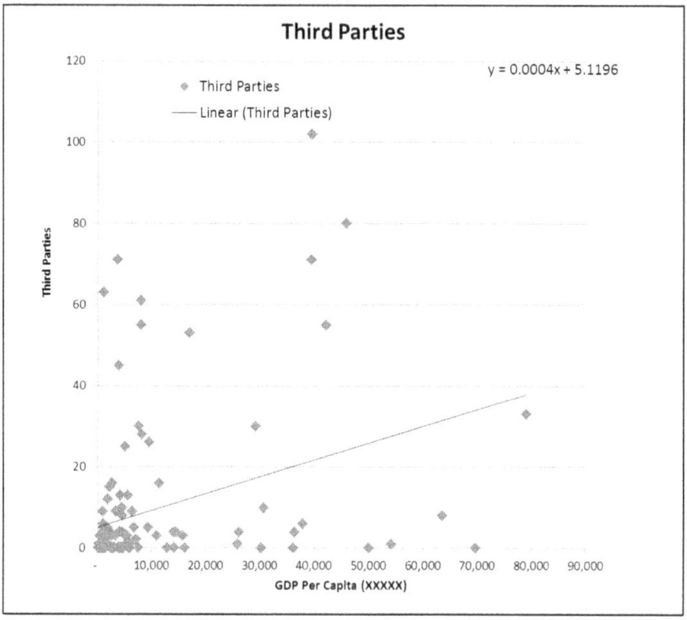

Chart 31. GDP and third parties, all members.

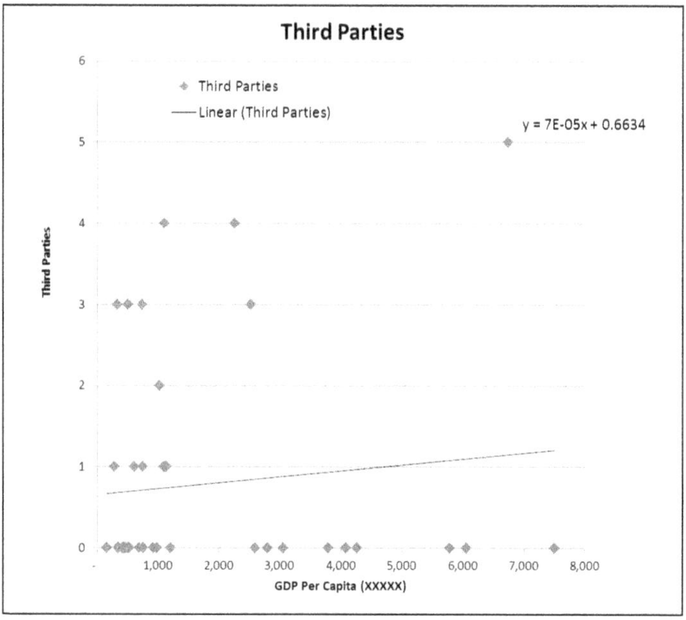

Chart 32. GDP and third parties, African WTO members.

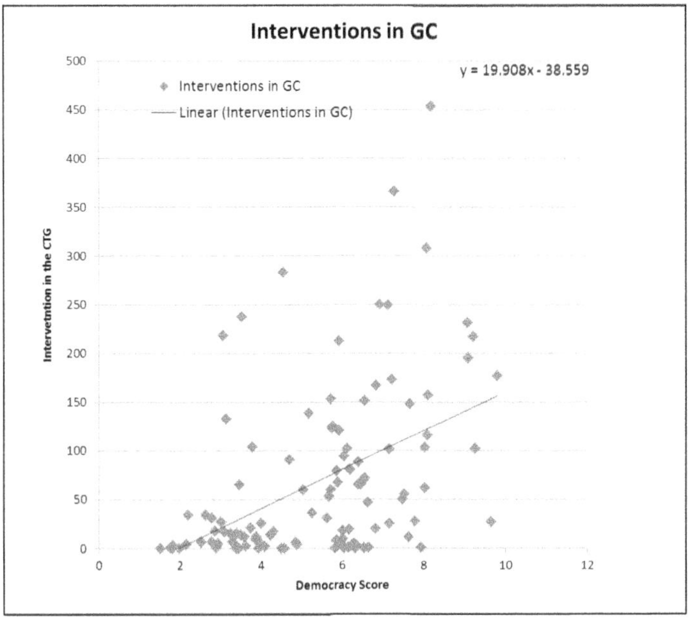

Chart 33. Democracy level and regular WTO work (interventions in the General Council) by all members.

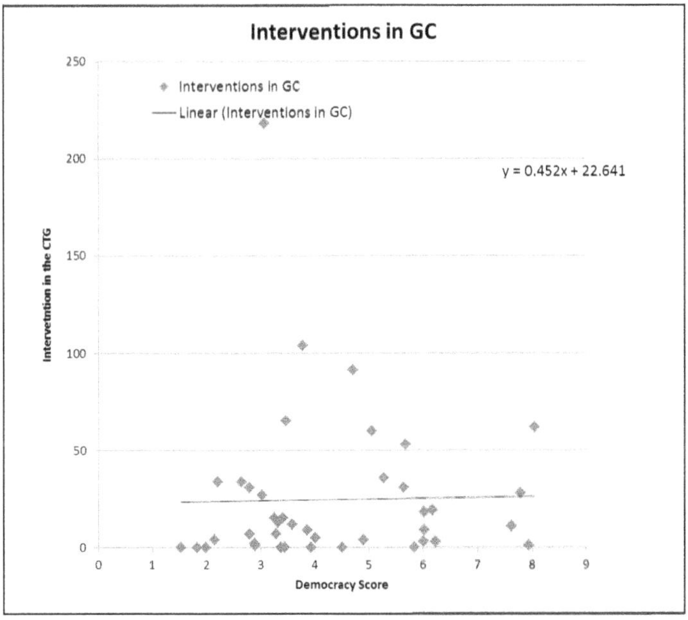

Chart 34. Democracy level and regular WTO work (interventions in the General Council) by African WTO members.

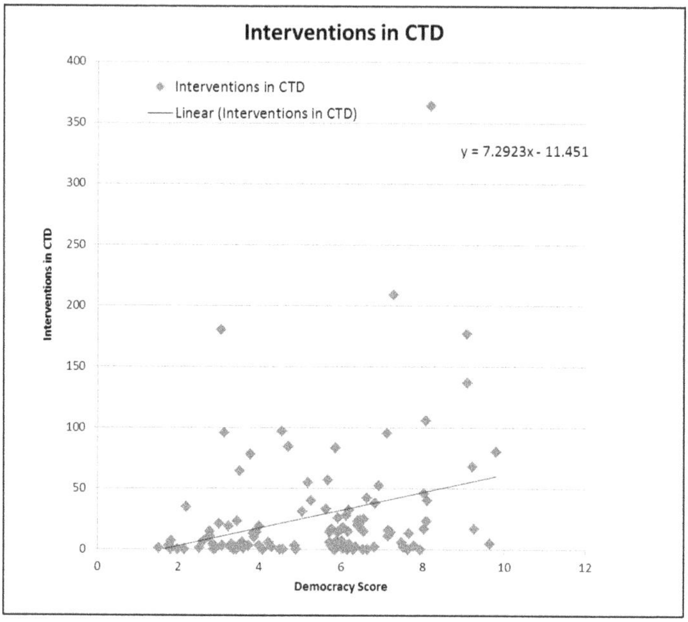

Chart 35. Democracy level and regular WTO work (interventions in the CTD) by all members.

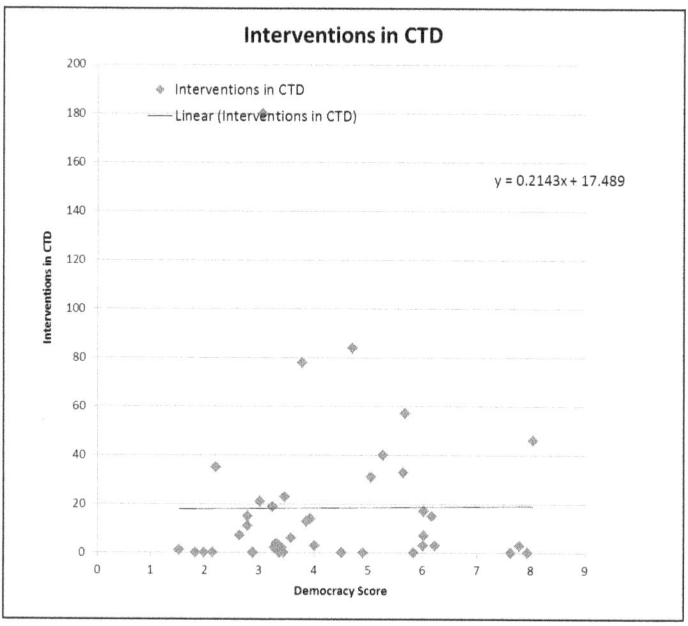

Chart 36. Democracy level and regular WTO work (interventions in the CTD) by African WTO members.

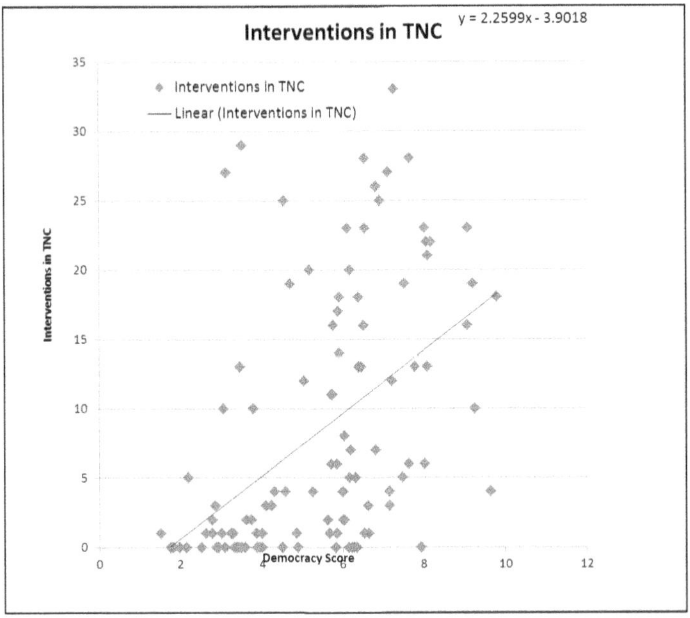

Chart 37. Democracy level and negotiating engagement (interventions in the TNC) by all members.

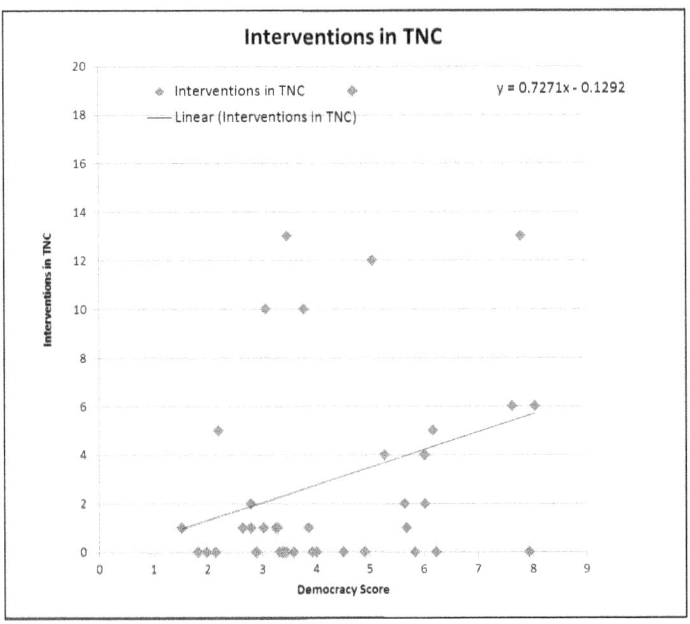

Chart 38. Democracy level and negotiating engagement (interventions in the TNC) by African WTO members.

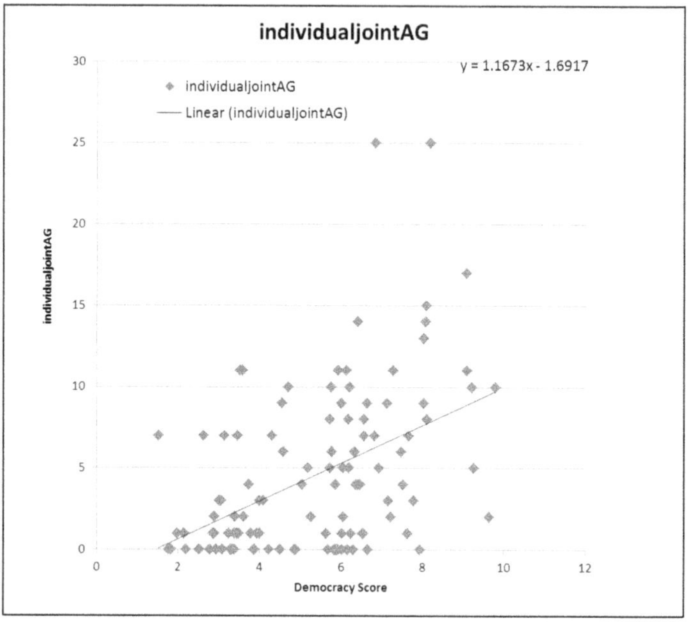

Chart 39. Democracy level and negotiating engagement (agriculture proposals) by all members.

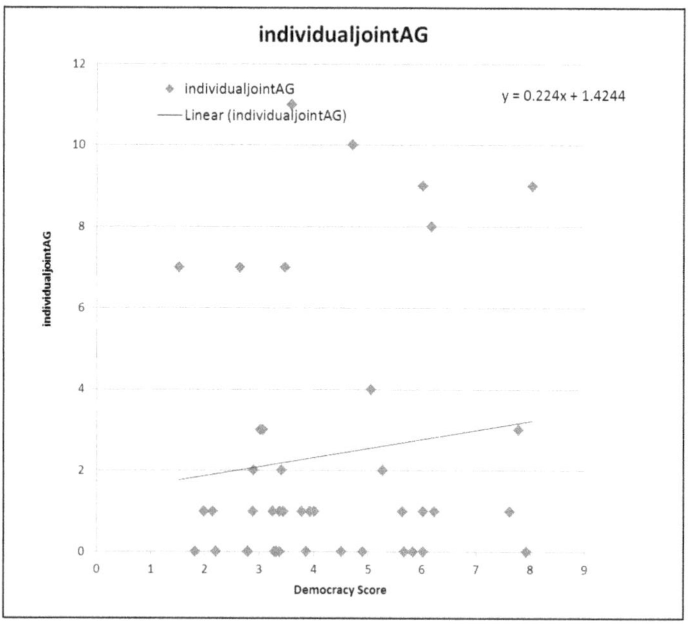

Chart 40. Democracy level and negotiating engagement (agriculture proposals) by African WTO members.

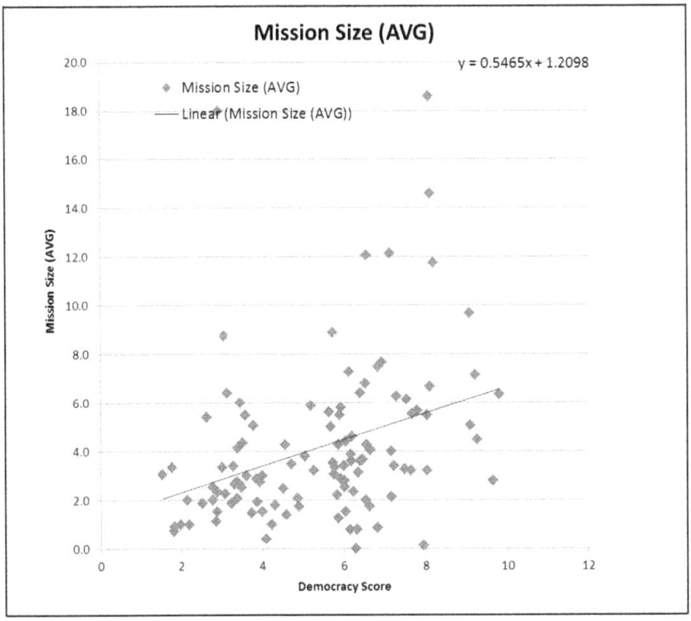

Chart 41. Democracy level and mission size, all members.

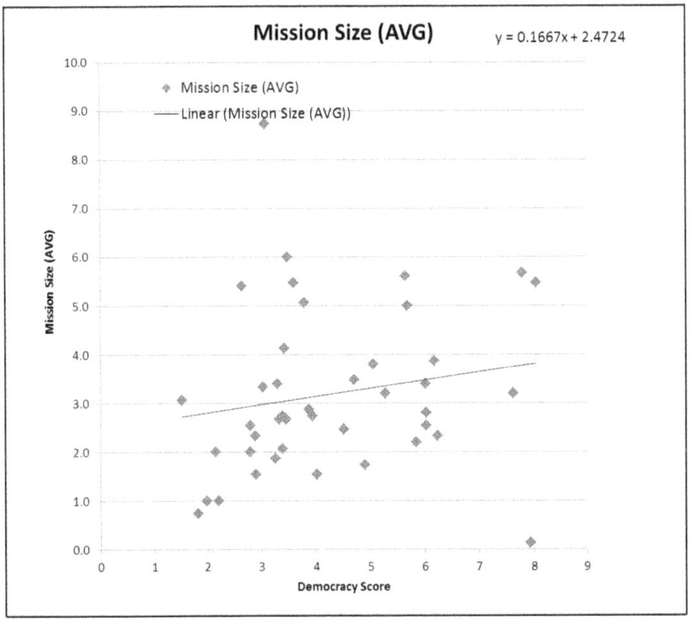

Chart 42. Democracy level and mission size, African WTO members.

Annex IV: Questionnaire and Results

"African Participation at the WTO – Legal and Institutional Aspects"

PART I: CAPACITY-RELATED MATTERS

A. Mission to the WTO

1. Do you have a Diplomatic Mission specifically assigned to WTO work and if so where is it located? Geneva ☐ Brussels ☐ Capital ☐ Other location

B. Resources and Workload

2. What is the size of your Mission to the WTO?
   Professional staff
   Administrative/Support staff

3. If your Mission's professionals divide their time of work between the WTO and other Organizations in Geneva, how much time, on the average, do they spend on WTO work in a month?
   20–30% ☐ 40–60% ☐ 70–100% ☐

4. Which Government Ministries/Departments are your Professionals assigned to WTO duties from?

a. Ministry/Department of/ Trade/ Commerce ☐	b. Ministry of/Department of/Foreign Affairs ☐
c. Ministry/Department of Finance/ Economy ☐	d. Ministry of Justice/Legal Affairs ☐
e. Office of the President/Prime Minister ☐	f. Other Government Ministry/ Department (Please Specify) ☐

5. Is there a Trade Lawyer/Legal adviser assigned to your diplomatic mission?
   Yes ☐ No ☐

C. Co-Operation with Other Delegations in Geneva

6. As an African delegation, list any 5 delegations (which may be African or non-African) with which you cooperate closely

....

....

....

7. What is the nature of your co-operation with other delegations in Geneva in the course of performing your WTO-related duties?
   a. Co-sponsoring draft proposals/decisions ☐
   b. Membership of informal negotiating groups (example African Group, G-20, G-33, G-10, ACP) ☐
   c. Dispute settlement (example third party rights) ☐
   d. Representation under the "Constituency System" (speaking for and reporting back to the "Constituency"). ☐
   e. Exchange of Information ☐
   f. Others (please specify).

8. What have been your main motivations for co-operation?
   a. "Education": better understanding and grasp of WTO rules. ☐
   b. "Fairness": correction of imbalances and anomalies in the rules – "a fairer trading multilateral trading system". ☐
   c. "Trade Capacity Building": obtaining trade capacity in key areas of negotiations or regular WTO work (such as agriculture, SPS, TBT, trade policy formulation, trade remedies, customs valuation, implementation – notification obligations, cotton development assistance etc). ☐
   d. "Flexibility": maximizing flexibility possibilities in rules (seeking derogation from rules, special and differential treatment, etc). ☐
   e. "Capacity Deficit": compensating for capacity deficit (human capital constraint in individual missions). ☐
   f. "Protection" of commercial interests by "blocking" unfavourable proposals. ☐
   g. Any other, please specify

9. In relation to the objectives of the African Group to coordinate its positions and implement the decisions by African Union (AU) Trade Ministers, how would you assess the "effectiveness" and "level of co-operation" in the African Group?
   Very satisfactory ☐ Satisfactory ☐ Unsatisfactory ☐ Work in progress. ☐

10. Do you face any challenges or difficulties in co-operation with other African delegations?
    a. Divergent commercial and trade policy interests. ☐
    b. Country/ "membership category" (example: LDCs, SVE, RAM, developing country, etc). ☐
    c. Language differences. ☐
    d. Logistic constraints. ☐
    e. Opposition to extraneous issues in a delegation's position originating from "elsewhere". ☐
    f. Opposition to "free-riders". ☐
    g. Any other, please specify

    Briefly elaborate on your responses

11. Identify specific suggestions for improving or strengthening co-operation on WTO matters amongst African delegations?
    a. Substance
    b. Logistics
    c. Language
    d. Coordination
    e. Focal Points
    f. Role of AU Permanent Observer Mission
    g. Contributions from other multilateral institutions
    h. Contributions from civil society and others
    i. Please specify any other.

D. Support from Capitals

12. Rate the support for your delegation on WTO matters in relation to funding, policy analysis, instructions, freedom to negotiate, strengthened delegation for negotiating cycles, etc.
    Very Satisfactory ☐ Satisfactory ☐ Moderate ☐ Minimal ☐ Non-existent ☐
    Elaborate on your answer above

PART II: PARTICIPATION IN WORK OF WTO REGULAR BODIES

E. Participation in the Work of WTO Regular Bodies

13. Rate the level of your delegation's participation in the WTO's regular bodies?
    Very Satisfactory ☐ Satisfactory ☐ Moderate ☐ Minimal ☐ Non-Existent ☐
    Elaborate on your answer above

14. What areas of WTO place the greatest demands on the resources of your mission and what areas of WTO work most preoccupies your delegation? Please tick as appropriate.
    a. **General Council** ☐
    b. **Trade in Goods**
       Agriculture Issues ☐ Balance of Payments ☐ Sanitary and Phytosanitary (SPS) ☐ Technical Barriers to Trade (TBT) ☐
       Trade Related Investment Measures (TRIMs) ☐ Anti-dumping ☐
       Customs Valuation ☐ Pre-shipment inspection ☐ Rules of Origin ☐
       Import licensing ☐ Subsidies and Countervailing ☐ Safeguards ☐
       State Trading Enterprises ☐
    c. **Trade in Services**
       Market access ☐ Domestic Regulation ☐ GATS Rules (subsidies, government procurement, safeguards) ☐ Specific Commitments0 Financial Services ☐
    d. **TRIPS Issues (Please specify area/s)**
    e. **Dispute Settlement** ☐
    f. **Trade Policy Reviews** ☐
    g. **Accession Matters** ☐

h. **Trade and Development** ☐
i. **Regional Trade Agreements** ☐
j. **Expansion of Trade in Information Technology Products** ☐
k. **Trade and Transfer of Technology** ☐
l. **Trade, Debt and Finance** ☐
m. **Plurilateral Agreements (Please specify)**

15. Has your country raised any trade concern in any WTO Committees/bodies. Illustrate such as with regard to Avian Flu, East African fish exports to the EU, notification obligations, SARs, TRIPS amendment, etc.
    Yes ☐ No ☐
    If yes, specify what the nature of the problem was

16. Has your delegation chaired/ or is chairing any WTO regular body or committee, if so which one?

F. Participation in Plurilateral Committees/ Sectoral-Type Agreements

17. Is your country signatory to any Plurilateral/Sectoral-type Agreement? If so, which agreement?
    a. Transparency in Government Procurement ☐
    b. Agreement on Civil Aircraft ☐
    c. Information Technology Agreement ☐

18. Is your country an observer to any of the above plurilateral/ sectoral-type committee? If yes, please specify the committee/s

19. What is your delegation's view on the co-existence of "critical mass" agreements (plurilaterals/sectoral agreements) with multilateral agreements?
    Very useful and practical ☐ Useful and impractical ☐
    Not useful and impractical ☐
    Elaborate on your response with any additional comments.

G. Notification Obligations

20. Assess your delegation's performance in meeting its notifications obligations under various WTO Agreements?
    Very satisfactory ☐ Satisfactory ☐ Not satisfactory ☐
    Elaborate on your response with any additional comments

21. Under which Agreement/s does your delegation notify most frequently?

22. What specific challenges does your delegation face in complying with its notification obligations?
    a. Financial ☐ b. No instructions ☐ c. Domestic coordination difficulties ☐ d. Logistic ☐ e. Human resource deficit ☐ f. Lack of knowledge on how to Notify ☐ g. Complicated notification requirements ☐ h. All of the above ☐

23. Has your country sought technical assistance from the WTO Secretariat to meet its notification obligations? If so, which areas was assistance provided?

24. Do you have any suggestions on what could be done to strengthen and improve Members' compliance with notification obligations?

H. Accession of African Countries to the WTO

25. Is your delegation an original WTO Member in 1995?
Yes ☐ No ☐

26. Did your delegation accede to WTO membership after 1995? (If you answer YES to this question, please also answer the next question).
Yes ☐ No ☐

27. How would you assess the process of your country's accession to the WTO?
Very satisfactory ☐ Satisfactory ☐ Not satisfactory ☐
Elaborate on your response with any additional comments below:

28. In your view, have the LDCs' Accession Guidelines assisted the accession process for Least Developed African countries?
Yes ☐ No ☐

29. Has your delegation actively participated in accession working parties, such as through market access demands or related proposals? If so, which ones?

PART III: DISPUTE SETTLEMENT AND SURVEILLANCE MECHANISMS

I. Participation in WTO Dispute Settlement

30. Has your delegation participated in WTO dispute settlement? If so identify the form and nature of participation (examples: complainant, defendant, third party rights, panellist, expert, arbitrator, AB Member, participation in the DSB through statements, tabling of proposals, decision-making, etc.)

31. Has your country used Good Offices, Conciliation, Mediation under DSU Article 5 or resorted to Article 25 Arbitration or external arbitration or any other dispute settlement mechanism in the context of regional trade agreements to resolve any WTO dispute/s?
Yes ☐ No ☐

32. If yes, please specify the specific WTO trade concern and which mechanism was resorted to?

33. In what ways, is your delegation involved in the ongoing DSU reform process?
    a. Individual Member proposal(s) ☐
    b. Group proposal(s) ☐

c. Statement in support of proposal(s) ☐
d. Comments on proposal(s) ☐
e. Other

34. Identify the specific areas in which your delegation has participated in the ongoing process of DSU reform
a. Third Party Rights Enhancement ☐
b. Panel Composition ☐
c. Remand ☐
d. Mutually Agreed Solutions ☐
e. Strictly Confidential Information ☐
f. Sequencing ☐
g. Post-retaliation ☐
h. Transparency/Amicus Curiae Briefs ☐
i. Timeframes ☐
j. Developing Country Interests including Special and Differential Treatment ☐
k. Flexibility and Member Control ☐
l. Effective Compliance ☐
m. Cost of WTO Dispute Settlement ☐

35. Has your delegation benefitted from Article 27.2 of the DSU on the obligation by the WTO Secretariat to provide legal advice to developing countries in dispute settlement? Yes ☐ No ☐

36. Has your delegation had recourse to the services of the Advisory Centre on WTO Law (ACWL)? Yes ☐ No ☐

37. If not, do you think that it would be advisable for a legal fund to be established to fund the participation of least developed and other low-income developing countries?

J. Surveillance – Trade Policy Review Mechanism (TPRM)

38. Since your delegation's membership of the WTO, how many times has your country's trade policy been reviewed? Please indicate a specific number.

39. Has your delegation actively participated in the trade policy review of other Members? If yes, indicate how
a. Discussant ☐ b. Statement(s) ☐ c. Question/Enquiries ☐
d. Participation in consultation by TPRB Chairman/Secretariat ☐ e. Any other

40. Do you agree with the view that the TPRM could be quicker and more cost effective for your delegation in enhancing its institutional engagement and resolving its trade concerns in the WTO than use of the WTO dispute settlement?
Yes ☐ No ☐ Both are equally effective ☐ Not applicable ☐

PART IV: DOHA NEGOTIATIONS

K. Participation in the WTO Doha Round of Negotiations

41. Is your delegation an active participant in the DDA negotiations? Yes ☐ No ☐

42. Please indicate the forms of participation by ticking against any of the choices below.
    a. Individual Member Proposals Tabled ☐
    b. Co-sponsorship of Group proposals ☐
    c. Chairmanship of Negotiating Groups ☐
    d. Coordinator of Informal Negotiating Coalitions/Regional Groups ☐
    e. Green Room participation. ☐
    f. Invitation to specific Chair consultations (examples Services" Enchilada" consultations, walk-in-the woods or fireside chats in agriculture, etc). ☐
    g. Negotiating "focal points" ☐
    h. Friend of the Chair(s) ☐

43. Indicate in rank order the negotiating priorities of your delegation (1–9)
    Agriculture
    Non-Agricultural Market Access
    Services
    Trade Facilitation
    TRIPS
    Special and Differential Treatment
    Trade and Environment
    Rules/Fisheries
    DSU

44. What challenges has your delegation been confronted with in its participation in the Doha negotiations?
    a. Domestic coordination ☐
    b. Analytic capability ☐
    c. Complexity of issues ☐
    d. Size of delegation ☐
    e. Pressure from major trading partners ☐
    f. Absence of Principal Supplier Status/Market Size limitation ☐
    g. Expertise deficit ☐
    h. Logistic support for delegations/Funding ☐
    i. Frequent turnover of Professionals ☐
    j. Turnover of Trade Ministers ☐

L. General

Please provide any additional relevant comments in relation to the participation of African Countries in the WTO system in this section

Table (*cont.*)

Country	2000	2001	2002	2003	2005	2005	2006	2007	2008	2009	2010	Total
Mali	8	7	27	28	30	32	27	36	32	35	33	**295**
Mauritania	2	10	29	35	39	37	35	31	25	32	32	**307**
Mauritius	9	11	25	29	31	33	29	37	38	47	46	**335**
Morocco	7	9	24	26	39	31	43	39	28	45	39	**330**
Mozambique	9	8	29	33	35	39	35	39	28	43	39	**337**
Namibia	9	8	23	25	22	25	22	23	11	26	33	**227**
Niger	8	9	28	31	30	27	28	27	27	26	20	**261**
Nigeria	9	8	21	28	28	27	29	32	28	46	31	**287**
Rwanda	6	5	23	25	27	27	28	33	19	33	30	**256**
Senegal	8	7	25	35	28	28	27	29	34	37	41	**299**
Sierra Leone	6	5	26	25	25	27	23	23	8	36	26	**230**
South Africa	12	8	21	25	27	30	25	29	25	46	43	**291**
Swaziland	7	9	20	25	25	31	22	27	26	33	37	**262**
Tanzania	12	11	31	32	33	42	28	42	27	41	38	**337**
Togo	7	6	27	27	28	28	24	23	21	25	31	**247**
Tunisia	9	8	25	29	38	36	36	32	32	48	42	**335**
Uganda	11	9	31	34	33	39	39	38	27	52	44	**357**
Zambia	9	8	23	31	29	28	33	42	36	38	43	**320**
Zimbabwe	11	9	31	25	26	33	28	24	22	32	36	**277**
Total	**324**	**307**	**1023**	**1144**	**1235**	**1267**	**1190**	**1269**	**1130**	**1542**	**1513**	**11944**

Annex VII: Description of Groups That African Members Associate with in the Doha Negotiations (Figure 48)[6]

Groups	Description / issues	Countries
ACP	**African, Caribbean and Pacific** countries with preferences in the EU **Nature:** geographical **Issues:** preferences, etc.	**WTO members (58):** Angola, Antigua & Barbuda, Barbados, Belize, Benin, Botswana, Burkina Faso, Burundi, Cameroon, Cape Verde, Central African Rep., Chad, Congo, Côte d'Ivoire, Cuba, Congo (Democratic Rep.), Djibouti, Dominica, Dominican Rep., Fiji, Gabon, Gambia, Ghana, Grenada, Guinea, Guinea Bissau, Guyana, Haiti, Jamaica, Kenya, Lesotho, Madagascar, Malawi, Mali, Mauritania, Mauritius, Mozambique, Namibia, Niger, Nigeria, Papua New Guinea, Rwanda, St Kitts & Nevis, St Lucia, St Vincent & the Grenadines, Senegal, Sierra Leone, Solomon Islands, South Africa, Suriname, Swaziland, Tanzania, Togo, Tonga, Trinidad & Tobago, Uganda, Zambia, Zimbabwe **WTO observers (10):** Bahamas, Comoros, Equatorial Guinea, Ethiopia, Liberia, Samoa, São Tomé and Principe, Seychelles, Sudan, Vanuatu **Not WTO members or observers (11):** Cook Islands, Eritrea, Kiribati, Marshall Islands, Micronesia, Nauru, Niue, Palau, Somalia, Timor-Lesté, Tuvalu
African group	All **African** WTO members **Nature:** regional **Issues:** general	**WTO members (42):** Angola, Benin, Botswana, Burkina Faso, Burundi, Cameroon, Cape Verde, Central African Rep., Chad, Congo, Congo (Democratic Rep.), Côte d'Ivoire, Djibouti, Egypt, Gabon, Gambia, Ghana, Guinea, Guinea Bissau, Kenya, Lesotho, Madagascar, Malawi, Mali, Mauritania, Mauritius, Morocco, Mozambique, Namibia, Niger, Nigeria, Rwanda, Senegal, Sierra Leone, South Africa, Swaziland, Tanzania, Togo, Tunisia, Uganda, Zambia, Zimbabwe

[6] Adapted by author for this study from the list of country groups on the WTO website- www.wto.org.

Table (*cont.*)

Groups	Description / issues	Countries
G-90	**African Group + ACP + least-developed countries** **Issues:** general	**WTO members (65):** Angola, Antigua & Barbuda, Bangladesh, Barbados, Belize, Benin, Botswana, Burkina Faso, Burundi, Cambodia, Cameroon, Cape Verde, Central African Rep., Chad, Congo, Côte d'Ivoire, Cuba, Congo (Democratic Rep.), Djibouti, Dominica, Dominican Rep., Egypt, Fiji, Gabon, Gambia, Ghana, Grenada, Guinea, Guinea Bissau, Guyana, Haiti, Jamaica, Kenya, Lesotho, Madagascar, Malawi, Maldives, Mali, Mauritania, Mauritius, Morocco, Mozambique, Myanmar, Namibia, Nepal, Niger, Nigeria, Papua New Guinea, Rwanda, St Kitts & Nevis, St Lucia, St Vincent & the Grenadines, Senegal, Sierra Leone, Solomon Islands, South Africa, Suriname, Swaziland, Tanzania, Togo, Trinidad & Tobago, Tunisia, Uganda, Zambia, Zimbabwe **WTO observers (14):** Afghanistan, Bahamas, Bhutan, Comoros, Equatorial Guinea, Ethiopia, Laos, Liberia, Samoa, São Tomé & Principe, Seychelles, Sudan, Vanuatu, Yemen **Not WTO members or observers (11):** Cook Islands, Eritrea, Kiribati, Marshall Islands, Micronesia, Nauru, Niue, Palau, Somalia, Timor-Lesté, Tuvalu
Least developed countries (LDCs)	Least developed countries: the world's poorest countries. The WTO uses the UN list. **Issues:** general	**WTO members (32):** Angola, Bangladesh, Benin, Burkina Faso, Burundi, Cambodia, Central African Rep., Chad, Congo (Democratic Rep.), Djibouti, Gambia, Guinea, Guinea Bissau, Haiti, Lesotho, Madagascar, Malawi, Maldives, Mali, Mauritania, Mozambique, Myanmar, Nepal, Niger, Rwanda, Senegal, Sierra Leone, Solomon Islands, Tanzania, Togo, Uganda, Zambia **WTO observers (12):** Afghanistan, Bhutan, Comoros, Equatorial Guinea, Ethiopia, Laos, Liberia, Samoa, São Tomé & Principe, Sudan, Vanuatu, Yemen
Small, vulnerable economies (SVEs) – rules	Sponsors of TN/RL/W/226/Rev.5 **Issues:** Rules (fisheries subsidies)	**WTO members (15):** Barbados, Cuba, Dominica, Dominican Rep., El Salvador, Fiji, Honduras, Jamaica, Maldives, Mauritius, Nicaragua, Papua New Guinea, St Lucia, St Vincent & the Grenadines, Tonga

Table (*cont.*)

Groups	Description / issues	Countries
Recently acceded members (RAMs)	Recently acceded members (RAMs), ie, countries that negotiated and joined the WTO after 1995, seeking lesser commitments in the negotiations because of the liberalization they have undertaken as part of their membership agreements. Excludes least-developed countries because they will make no new commitments, and EU members **Issues:** general	**WTO members (19):** Albania, Armenia, Cape Verde, China, Croatia, Ecuador, FYR Macedonia, Georgia, Jordan, Kyrgyz Rep., Moldova, Mongolia, Oman, Panama, Saudi Arabia, Chinese Taipei, Tonga, Ukraine, Viet Nam
Cairns group	Coalition of agricultural exporting nations lobbying for agricultural trade liberalization. **Issues:** agriculture	**WTO members (19):** Argentina, Australia, Bolivia, Brazil, Canada, Chile, Colombia, Costa Rica, Guatemala, Indonesia, Malaysia, New Zealand, Pakistan, Paraguay, Peru, Philippines, South Africa, Thailand, Uruguay
G-10	Coalition of countries lobbying for agriculture to be treated as diverse and special because of non-trade concerns (not to be confused with the Group of Ten Central Bankers) Issues: agriculture	**WTO members (9):** Chinese Taipei, Rep. Korea, Iceland, Israel, Japan, Liechtenstein, Mauritius, Norway, Switzerland
G-20	Coalition of developing countries pressing for ambitious reforms of agriculture in developed countries with some flexibility for developing countries (not to be confused with the G-20 group of finance ministers and central bank governors, and its recent summit meetings) **Issues:** agriculture	**WTO members (23):** Argentina, Bolivia, Brazil, Chile, China, Cuba, Ecuador, Egypt, Guatemala, India, Indonesia, Mexico, Nigeria, Pakistan, Paraguay, Peru, Philippines, South Africa, Tanzania, Thailand, Uruguay, Venezuela, Zimbabwe
G-33	Also called **"Friends of Special Products"** in agriculture. Coalition of developing countries pressing for flexibility for developing countries to undertake limited market opening in agriculture **Issues:** agriculture	**WTO members (46):** Antigua & Barbuda, Barbados, Belize, Benin, Bolivia, Botswana, China, Congo, Côte d'Ivoire, Cuba, Dominica, Dominican Rep., El Salvador, Grenada, Guatemala, Guyana, Haiti, Honduras, India, Indonesia, Jamaica, Kenya, Rep. Korea, Madagascar, Mauritius, Mongolia, Mozambique, Nicaragua, Nigeria, Pakistan, Panama, Peru, Philippines, St Kitts & Nevis, St Lucia, St Vincent & the Grenadines, Senegal, Sri Lanka, Suriname, Tanzania, Trinidad & Tobago, Turkey, Uganda, Venezuela, Zambia, Zimbabwe

Table (*cont.*)

Groups	Description / issues	Countries
Cotton-4	West African coalition seeking cuts in cotton subsidies and tariffs **Issues:** agriculture (cotton)	**WTO members (4):** Benin, Burkina Faso, Chad, Mali
NAMA 11	Coalition of developing countries seeking flexibilities to limit market opening in industrial goods trade **Issues:** NAMA	**WTO members (10):** Argentina, Brazil, Egypt, India, Indonesia, Namibia, Philippines, South Africa, Tunisia, Venezuela
'Paragraph 6' countries	Group of countries with less than 35% of non-agricultural products covered by legally bound tariff ceilings. They have agreed to increase their binding coverage substantially, but want to exempt some products. (In paragraph 6 of the first version of the NAMA text, later paragraph 8.) **Issues:** NAMA	**WTO members (12):** Cameroon, Congo, Côte d'Ivoire, Cuba, Ghana, Kenya, Macao China, Mauritius, Nigeria, Sri Lanka, Suriname, Zimbabwe
Trade Facilitation Core Group of Developing Countries	Group of developing countries and LDCs that have been particularly wary of taking on new, difficult-to-implement commitments. Interested *inter alia* in effective S&D and capacity building commitments in the trade facilitation negotiations	Bangladesh, Botswana, Cuba, Egypt, India, Indonesia, Jamaica, Kenya, Malaysia, Mauritius, Namibia, Nepal, Nigeria, Philippines, Rwanda, Tanzania, Trinidad & Tobago, Uganda, Venezuela, Zambia and Zimbabwe
'W52' sponsors	Sponsors of TN/C/W/52, a proposal for "modalities" in negotiations on geographical indications (the multilateral register for wines and spirits, and extending the higher level of protection beyond wines and spirits) and "disclosure" (patent applicants to disclose the origin of genetic resources and traditional knowledge used in the inventions). The list includes as groups: the EU, ACP and African Group. * Dominican Rep. is in the ACP and South Africa is in the African Group, but they are sponsors of TN/IP/W/10/Rev.2 on geographical indications **Issues:** Intellectual property (TRIPS)	**WTO members (109):** Albania, Angola, Antigua & Barbuda, Austria, Barbados, Belgium, Belize, Benin, Botswana, Brazil, Bulgaria, Burkina Faso, Burundi, Cameroon, Cape Verde, Central African Rep., Chad, China, Colombia, Congo, Côte d'Ivoire, Croatia, Cuba, Cyprus, Czech Rep, Congo (Democratic Rep.), Denmark, Djibouti, Dominica, Dominican Rep.*, Ecuador, Egypt, Estonia, EU, Fiji, Finland, FYR Macedonia, France, Gabon, Gambia, Georgia, Germany, Ghana, Greece, Grenada, Guinea, Guinea Bissau, Guyana, Haiti, Hungary, Iceland, India, Indonesia, Ireland, Italy, Jamaica, Kenya, Kyrgyz Rep., Latvia, Lesotho, Liechtenstein, Lithuania, Luxembourg, Madagascar, Malawi, Mali, Malta, Mauritania, Mauritius, Moldova, Morocco, Mozambique, Namibia, Netherlands, Niger, Nigeria, Pakistan, Papua New Guinea, Peru, Poland, Portugal, Romania, Rwanda, St Kitts &

Table (*cont.*)

Groups	Description / issues	Countries
		Nevis, St Lucia, St Vincent & the Grenadines, Senegal, Sierra Leone, Slovak Rep., Slovenia, Solomon Islands, Spain, Sri Lanka, Suriname, Swaziland, Sweden, Switzerland, South Africa*, Tanzania, Thailand, Togo, Tonga, Trinidad & Tobago, Tunisia, Turkey, Uganda, United Kingdom, Zambia, Zimbabwe
TRIPS Joint proposal	Sponsors of TN/IP/W/10/Rev.2 proposing a database that is entirely voluntary ../../Pickett/AppData/Local/Microsoft/Windows/Temporary Internet Files/Content.Outlook/PMMCV1CJ/www.wto.org/trips **Issues:** TRIPS GI register	**WTO members (19):** Argentina, Australia, Canada, Chile, Costa Rica, Dominican Rep., Ecuador, El Salvador, Guatemala, Honduras, Japan, Korea, Mexico, New Zealand, Nicaragua, Paraguay, Chinese Taipei, South Africa, US

Annex VIII: WTO Member Trade Policy Reviews (1995–2010)[7]

Africa	Asia Pacific	Europe	Latin America & Caribbean	Middle East	North America
Angola (1)	Australia (3)	Albania (1)	Antigua &	Bahrain (2)	Canada (5)
Benin (3)	Bangladesh (2)	Armenia (1)	Barbuda (2)	Israel (2)	United
Botswana (3)	Brunei Darussalam (2)	Bulgaria (1)	Argentina (2)	Jordan (1)	States (7)
Burkina Faso(2)	China (3)	Croatia (1)	Belize (1)	Oman (1)	
Burundi (1)	Chinese Taipei (2)	Cyprus (1)	Barbados (2)	United Arab	
Cameroon (3)	Fiji (2)	Czech	Brazil (4)	Emirates (1)	
Central African	Hong Kong China (4)	Republic (2)	Bolivia (2)	Qatar (1)	
Republic (1)	India (3)	European	Chile (3)		
Chad (1)	Indonesia (3)	Union (7)	Colombia (2)		
Congo (1)	Japan (7)	Georgia (1)	Costa Rica (3)		
Cote d'Ivoire (1)	Korea (4)	Hungary (1)	Dominica (2)		
Djibouti (1)	Macao, China (2)	Iceland (2)	Dominican		
D.R. Congo (1)	Malaysia (4)	Kyrgyz	Republic (3)		
Egypt (3)	Maldives (2)	Republic (1)	Ecuador (1)		
Gabon(2)	Mongolia (1)	Liechtenstein (3)	El Salvador (3)		
Gambia (2)	New Zealand (3)	Norway (4)	Guatemala (2)		
Ghana (2)	Pakistan (2)	Poland (1)	Guyana (2)		
Guinea (2)	Papua New	Romania (2)	Grenada (2)		
Kenya (2)	Guinea (1)	Slovak	Haiti (1)		
Lesotho (2)	Philippines (2)	Republic (2)	Honduras (2)		
Madagascar (2)	Singapore (4)	Slovenia (1)	Jamaica (2)		
Malawi(2)	Sri Lanka (2)	Switzerland (4)	Mexico (3)		
Mali (3)	Solomon Islands (2)	Turkey (3)	Nicaragua (2)		
Mauritania (1)	Thailand (4)		Panama (1)		
Mauritius (3)			Paraguay 82)		
Morocco (3)			Peru (2)		
Mozambique (2)			St. Kitts &		
Namibia (3)			Nevis (2)		
Niger (2)			St. Lucia (2)		
Nigeria (2)			St Vincent and the		
Rwanda (1)			Grenadines (2)		
Senegal (2)			Suriname (1)		
Sierra Leone (1)			Trinidad &		
South Africa (3)			Tobago (2)		
Swaziland (3)			Uruguay (2)		
Tanzania (2)			Venezuela (2)		
Togo (2)					
Tunisia (1)					
Uganda (3)					
Zambia (3)					

[7] Adapted by the Author for this study from the Annual Report of the Trade Policy Review Body, 2010.

Annex IX: Overview of Notification Requirements in the Agreement on Agriculture

The requirements and formats for notifications under Article 18:2 and other relevant provisions of the Agreement on Agriculture are set out in WTO document G/AG/2.

In the area of *market access*, Table MA: 1 notifications relate to the implementation of tariff and other quota commitments. This notification was required to be submitted by all Members with tariff and other quota commitments. Table MA: 2 notifications relate to imports under tariff and other quotas and are required to be submitted annually by Members with tariff and other quota commitments specified in their schedules of commitments. Table MA: 5 notifications relate to the special safeguard under Articles 5.7 and 18.2 of the Agreement on Agriculture. These are required to be submitted annually by Members which have reserved the right to have recourse to the special safeguard provisions.

With regard to *domestic support*, Table DS: 1 notifications are required to be submitted annually by Members with base and annual commitments levels specified in their schedules of commitments. All other Members are required to submit an annual Table DS:1 notification provided that in the case of a developing country only supporting tables DS:1-3 may be required (measures exempt from reduction – green Box measures; special and differential treatment/development programmes; direct payments under production limiting programmes – blue box). Least developed countries are requested to submit supporting tables DS: 1-3 only every other year. Where no support exists, a statement to this effect should be submitted.

With regard to *export subsidies*, Table ES: 1 notifications relate to subsidized exports, food aid and annual commitment levels which Members with base and annual commitments levels specified in their schedules of commitment should submit annually. Members with no such scheduled commitments are required to submit a notification annually in the form of a statement confirming that no export subsidies exist or, in the case of developing countries using certain export subsidies pursuant to Article 9.4 in the form of supporting table ES: 2.

Notifications on total exports in the context of export subsidy commitments under Articles 10 and 18.2 of the Agreement are required to be submitted annually by Members with export subsidy commitments specified in their schedules and by "significant exporters". The format is laid out in Table ES: 2.

Food aid volumes in the context of export subsidy commitments are required to be submitted annually by all donors for donated products except for those products where information must be notified under Table ES: 1. No nil return is required. Finally, food and other aid in the context of the Marrakesh Decision are required from all donor Members in respect of actions taken within the framework of the Decision on Measures concerning the Possible Negative Effects of the Reform Programme on Least-Developed and Net Food-Importing Developing Countries. No "nil" return is required. The format for this notification is laid out in Table NF: 1.

Annex X: Member Notification of Anti-Dumping Semi-Annual Reports (2009–2010)

Figure 100

Regions	Africa (42 Countries)	Asia-Pacific (28 countries)	Europe (41 countries)	Latin America & Caribbean (32 countries)	Middle East (8 countries)	North America (2 countries)
Semi-Annual Report	Egypt, South Africa	Australia, China, India, Indonesia, Korea, New Zealand, Pakistan, Philippines, Chinese Taipei, Thailand	European Union, Turkey, Ukraine	Argentina, Brazil, Chile, Colombia, Costa Rica, Jamaica, Mexico, Panama, Peru	Israel	Canada, United States
Report of no action taken	Morocco, Nigeria	Fiji, Japan, Malaysia	Albania, Armenia, Croatia, F.Y.R. Macedonia, Moldova, Norway	Cuba, Dominican Rep., Ecuador, El Salvador, Guatemala, Honduras, Trinidad & Tobago, Venezuela	Jordan, Oman, Qatar	
One time Notification	Burkina Faso, Burundi, Cape Verde, Central African Rep, Djibouti, Gabon, Madagascar, Mali, Mauritius, Mozambique, Rwanda, Tanzania	Brunei Darussalam, Hong Kong China, Macao, China, Maldives, Mongolia, Nepal, Sri Lanka	Liechtenstein, Switzerland	Barbados, Belize Dominica, Grenada, Guyana, Haiti, St. Kitts & Nevis, Suriname		
No report submitted	Angola, Benin, Cameroon, Chad, Congo, Cote d'Ivoire, D.R. Congo, Gambia, Ghana, Guinea, Guinea Bissau, Kenya, Lesotho, Malawi, Mauritania, Namibia, Niger, Senegal, Sierra Leone, Swaziland, Togo, Tunisia, Uganda, Zambia, Zimbabwe	Bangladesh, Cambodia, Myanmar, Papua New Guinea, Singapore, Solomon Islands, Tonga, Vietnam	Georgia, Iceland, Kyrgyz Rep.	Antigua & Barbuda, Bolivia, Nicaragua, Paraguay, St. Lucia, St. Vincent & Grenadines, Uruguay	Bahrain, Saudi Arabia, Kuwait, United Arab Emirates	

Annex XI.1: TBT Specific Trade Concerns Maintained by African WTO Members

Specific Trade Concern	When concern first raised
Tunisia – Labelling and Presentation of Pre-packaged food	25 June 2009
South Africa – Labelling and Advertising of Foodstuff	20 March 2008
South Africa – Labelling requirements for textiles, clothing and leather goods	22 December 2005
South Africa – Regulation on Iced Desserts and Ice creams	17 October 2002
Egypt – National Standards on the Certification of the Hide of Leather Footwear	19 May 2000
Egypt – Decree on the Labelling of Meat	31 March 1999
Egypt – Technical Regulation on Labelling of Textile Products	31 March 1999
Egypt – Regulations on Tyres	20 June 1997

Annex XI.2: Specific Trade Measures That African WTO Members Have Raised Concerns About

Measure	Stated Objective of Measure	African Members expressing concern	Nature of concerns expressed
Canada – Bill C-32 amendment to Tobacco Act	Protection of human health or safety	Burundi, Kenya, Malawi, Mozambique, Zimbabwe, Uganda, Egypt, Tanzania, Zambia	Discrimination, further information, clarification, transparency, unnecessary barrier to trade
European Communities-Regulation on the Registration, Evaluation and Authorization of Chemicals (REACH),	health and/or safety; environment	Botswana, Egypt and South Africa	transparency; time to adapt; unnecessary barrier to trade; complexity; uncertainty and further information and clarification

Table (*cont.*)

Measure	Stated Objective of Measure	African Members expressing concern	Nature of concerns expressed
European Communities-Regulation on Certain Wine Sector Products	quality, prevention of deceptive practices; harmonisation, protection of legitimate interests of the producers; ensuring the smooth operation of the international market	South Africa	transparency, time to adapt, unnecessary barrier to trade, discrimination, further information and clarification, and intellectual property
European Communities-Directive 2002/95/EC on the restriction of the use of certain hazardous substances in Electrical and Electronic Equipment (RoHS) and Directive 2002/96/EC on Waste Electrical and Electronic Equipment (WEEE).	health and/or safety, environment and harmonization	Egypt	transparency, time to adapt, lack of certainty, further information, clarification
The European Communities – Dangerous Chemical Substances: Draft Commission Directive amending, for the 30th time, Council Directive 67/548/EEC	classification and labelling requirements, testing methods for dangerous chemical substances are health and/or safety; environment; harmonisation	South Africa and Zimbabwe	transparency, time to adapt, unnecessary barrier to trade, rationale, lack of scientific evidence and precaution
European Communities – Dangerous Chemical Substances: Draft Commission Directive amending for the 31st time, Council Directive 67/548/EEC	classification and labelling requirements, testing methods for dangerous chemical substances are health and/or safety; environment; harmonisation	Botswana, Mauritius, Zimbabwe and South Africa	transparency, time to adapt, unnecessary barrier to trade, rationale, lack of scientific evidence and precaution

Annex XII: Member Notification of Countervailing Semi-Annual Reports (2009–2010)

Regions	Africa (42 Countries)	Asia-Pacific (28 Countries)	Europe (41 countries)	Latin America & Caribbean (32 countries)	Middle East (8 countries)	North America (2 countries)
Semi-Annual Report	South Africa	Australia, China, India, New Zealand	EU	Peru		Canada, United States
Report of no action taken	Egypt, Morocco, Namibia	Brunei Darussalam, Japan, Korea, Malaysia, Philippines, Chinese Taipei, Thailand	Albania, Armenia, Croatia, FYR Macedonia, Moldova, Norway, Turkey, Ukraine	Brazil, Chile, Colombia, Costa Rica, Cuba, Dominican Rep., Ecuador, El Salvador, Guatemala, Honduras, Jamaica, Mexico, Trinidad & Tobago, Venezuela	Israel, Jordan, Oman, Qatar	
One time Notification	Botswana, Burkina Faso, Burundi, Mozambique, Senegal, Sierra Leone,	Hong Kong China, Macao China, Mongolia, Sri Lanka	Liechtenstein, Switzerland	Barbados, Guyana, St Kitts & Nevis, Suriname		
No report	Angola, Benin, Cameroon, Cape Verde, Central African Rep., Chad, Congo, D. R. Congo, Cote d'Ivoire, Djibouti, Gabon, Gambia, Ghana, Guinea, Guinea Bissau, Kenya, Lesotho, Madagascar, Malawi, Mali, Mauritania, Mauritius, Niger, Nigeria, Rwanda, Swaziland, Tanzania, Togo, Tunisia, Uganda, Zambia, Zimbabwe	Bangladesh, Cambodia, Fiji, Indonesia, Maldives, Myanmar, Nepal, Pakistan, Papua New Guinea, Singapore, Solomon Islands, Tonga, Vietnam	Georgia, Iceland, Kyrgyz Rep.	Antigua & Barbuda, Argentina, Belize, Bolivia, Dominica, Grenada, Haiti, Nicaragua, Panama, Paraguay, St Lucia, St Vincent & Grenadines, Uruguay	Bahrain, Kuwait, Saudi Arabia, United Arab Emirates	

Annex XIII

Annex XIII.1: SPS Specific Trade Concerns Maintained by African WTO Members

Measure of Concern	Stated Objective	Members expressing concern
Egypt's restrictions on canned tuna imports containing genetically modified organisms (GMOs)	food safety	Thailand
South Africa's prohibition on bone-in beef imports from EC member states	protection of human and animal health	European Union
South Africa- Restrictions on beef and pork	protection of human and animal health	Brazil
Egypt – Restrictions on heat-treated products in relation to avian flu	protection of human and animal health	European Union
Gabon – Import restrictions on pork products due to Influenza A/H1N1	Protection of human and animal health; provisional measure	Mexico
South Africa – Import restrictions on fresh pork meat and beef	protection of human and animal health	Brazil

Annex XIII.2: SPS Specific Trade Concerns Raised by African WTO Members

Measure	Member maintaining Measure	African Members expressing Concern	Nature of Concern/s
Maximum levels for certain contaminants (aflatoxins) in foodstuffs	European Union	Gambia, Senegal	Use International Standards/Harmonization Technical Assistance
Directive 2000/42 on pesticide residues	European Union	Côte d'Ivoire	Time to adapt, S&D and TA needs
Restrictions on Egyptian potatoes	European Union	Egypt	protection against the disease *pseudomomas solanacearum*, severely restricted imports
EC Directive 2001/661/EC on foot and mouth disease	European Union	South Africa	South Africa and Namibia are identified as zones free from FMD without vaccination by the OIE. The EC restrictions on imports from areas within FMD control zone of South Africa.

Table (*cont.*)

Measure	Member maintaining Measure	African Members expressing Concern	Nature of Concern/s
Rapid Alert System regarding mango imports	European Union	Senegal	Small fruit and vegetable farmers affected. Sought waiver from EC directive
Trade restrictions in response to cholera	European Union	Tanzania	Restrictions having severe economic effects on economy

Annex XIII.3: SPS Specific Trade Concerns Raised by Other WTO Members and Supported by African WTO Members

Specific Trade Concern	Member Raising concern	Nature of Concern/s	African Member Support
Application and Modification of EC regulation on Novel Food	Colombia	– amount of information on the safety of these traditional food products required by the EC regulation and the costs to undertake scientific studies were not proportional to health risks and were excessive especially for small scale farmers and exporters	Benin
Regulation on Genetically Modified Food and Feed	US	– lengthy food safety review for all biotech food and biotech feeds which would also need to be labelled; – no distinction between health and environment and perceived consumer desires; – more trade restrictive than necessary and create difficulties for exporting countries; – consideration of the safety of GM products should be on the basis of risk assessment as provided in the SPS Agreement.	Egypt
EC measures on Cut Flowers	Ecuador Israel	– scientific grounds for the measures; – risk analysis; – methods to be used at entry ports; – special treatment for developing countries and possible alternative methods	Kenya

Table (*cont.*)

Specific Trade Concern	Member Raising concern	Nature of Concern/s	African Member Support
EC regulation on Ocratoxin A (OTA) in coffee	Colombia	– impact of the measure on marketing of coffee in Europe. – Scientific justification for the levels set of OTA	Kenya
EureGAP certification requirements for bananas	Saint Vincent and the Grenadines	– cost implications of these private standards huge especially for small, vulnerable economies	Kenya, South Africa and Egypt
EU criteria for protected zones	Uruguay	EC decision to eliminate the criteria for protected zones within the European Communities might result in a strengthening of phytosanitary requirements for the whole Community. This could also have negative consequences for citrus fruit exports from Chile. Request for clarification of the scientific basis for this proposal	South Africa
Measures for cirtrus canker	Argentina	recognition of equivalent certification systems South Africa was free from citrus canker	South Africa
Maximum levels of certain contaminants (aflatoxins) in foodstuffs	Gambia, Senegal et al.	EC proposal to set new maximum levels for aflatoxins would impose severe restrictions on trade while not resulting in a significant reduction in health risk to consumers. The proposal did not seem to be based on a proper risk assessment. Furthermore, the proposed sampling procedure was unduly costly, burdensome and unjust	South Africa
Import restrictions on bovine semen and embryos, milk and milk products	Argentina		South Africa

Annex XIV: Disputes Involving African WTO Members

Country	Dispute(s)	Role
Benin	US-Subsidies on Upland Cotton (compliant by Brazil)	Third Party
Cameroon	EC-Regime for the Importation, Sale and Distribution of Banana (compliant by Ecuador, Guatemala, Honduras, Mexico and US)	Third Party
Chad	US-Subsidies on Upland Cotton (compliant by Brazil)	Third Party
Côte d'Ivoire	EC-Regime for the Importation, Sale and Distribution of Banana (compliant by Ecuador, Guatemala, Honduras, Mexico and US)	Third Party
	EC-Export Subsidies on Sugar (compliant by Australia)	Third Party
	EC-Export Subsidies on Sugar (compliant by Brazil)	Third Party
	EC-Export Subsidies on Sugar (compliant by Thailand)	Third Party
Egypt	Egypt-Import Prohibition on Canned Tuna with Soybean Oil (complaint by Thailand)	Respondent
	Egypt-Definitive Anti-dumping Measures on Steel Rebar from Turkey (compliant by Turkey)	Respondent
	Egypt-Measures Affecting Imports of Textiles and Apparel Products (complaint by US)	Respondent
	Egypt-Anti-dumping duties on Matches from Pakistan (compliant by Pakistan)	Respondent
	EC-Anti-dumping duties on Imports of Cotton-type Bed Linen from India (compliant by India)	Third Party
	EC-Provisional Safeguard Measures on Imports of Certain Steel Products (compliant by US)	Third Party
	Turkey-Measures Affecting the Importing of Rice (compliant by US)	Third Party
	US-Continued Existence and Application of Zeroing Methodology (compliant by EC)	Third Party
Ghana	EC-Regime for the Importation, Sale and Distribution of Banana (compliant by Ecuador, Guatemala, Honduras, Mexico and US)	Third Party
Kenya	EC-Export Subsidies on Sugar (compliant by Australia)	Third Party
	EC-Export Subsidies on Sugar (compliant by Brazil)	Third Party
	EC-Export Subsidies on Sugar (compliant by Thailand)	Third Party
Madagascar	EC-Regime for the Importation, Sale and Distribution of Banana (compliant by Ecuador, Guatemala, Honduras, Mexico and US)	Third Party
	EC-Export Subsidies on Sugar (compliant by Australia)	Third Party
	EC-Export Subsidies on Sugar (compliant by Brazil)	Third Party
	EC-Export Subsidies on Sugar (compliant by Thailand)	Third Party

Table (*cont.*)

Country	Dispute(s)	Role
Malawi	EC-Export Subsidies on Sugar (compliant by Australia)	Third Party
	EC-Export Subsidies on Sugar (compliant by Brazil)	Third Party
	EC-Export Subsidies on Sugar (compliant by Thailand)	Third Party
Mauritius	Mexico-Anti-dumping Investigation of High Fructose Corn Syrup (HFCS) from the US (compliant by the US)	Third Party
	EC-Conditions for the Granting of Tariff Preferences to Developing Countries (complaint by India)	Third Party
	EC-Export Subsidies on Sugar (compliant by Australia)	Third Party
	EC-Export Subsidies on Sugar (compliant by Brazil)	Third Party
	EC-Export Subsidies on Sugar (compliant by Thailand)	Third Party
Nigeria	US-Import Prohibition of Certain Shrimp and Shrimp Products (complaint by India, Malaysia, Pakistan and Thailand)	Third Party
Senegal	EC-Regime for the Importation, Sale and Distribution of Banana (compliant by Ecuador, Guatemala, Honduras, Mexico and US)	Third Party
	US-Import Prohibition of Certain Shrimp and Shrimp Products (complaint by India, Malaysia, Pakistan and Thailand)	Third Party
South Africa	South Africa-Anti-dumping Duties on Certain Pharmaceutical Products from India (complaint by India)	Respondent
	South Africa –Definitive Anti-dumping Measures on Blanketing from Turkey (complaint by Turkey)	Respondent
	South Africa – Anti-dumping Measures on uncoated Wood Free Paper (complaint by Indonesia)	Respondent
Swaziland	EC-Export Subsidies on Sugar (compliant by Australia)	Third Party
	EC-Export Subsidies on Sugar (compliant by Brazil)	Third Party
	EC-Export Subsidies on Sugar (compliant by Thailand)	Third Party
Tanzania	EC-Export Subsidies on Sugar (compliant by Australia)	Third Party
	EC-Export Subsidies on Sugar (compliant by Brazil)	Third Party
	EC-Export Subsidies on Sugar (compliant by Thailand)	Third Party
Zimbabwe	EC-Measures Affecting Asbestos and Products containing Asbestos (compliant by Canada)	Third Party

Annex XV: Share of GDP of African Countries accounted for by Trade in Commercial Services

Africa: Trade in commercial services as percentage of GDP (percentage)

	1995	2000	2001	2002	2003	2004	2005	2006	2007	2008	2009
Exports	5.0	5.4	5.7	6	6.2	6.2	**5.7**	5.5	5.6	5.5	5.3
Imports	6.8	6.6	7.3	7.4	7	7.2	**7.3**	7.5	8.3	9.2	5.6
Total (Exports + imports)	11.8	11.9	12.9	13.4	13.2	13.4	**13**	13	13.9	14.7	13.9

Note: Figures in bold indicate a methodological break in series.
Source: WTO estimates and IMF, WEO database for GDP.

REFERENCES

Agah, Yonov Frederick (2010). *WTO Dispute Settlement Body Developments in 2010*, Presentation at the Fourth Annual Update on WTO Dispute Settlement, at the Graduate Institute of International and Development Studies, 8th March 2010.

Alavi Amin (2007). *African Countries and the WTO's Dispute Settlement Mechanism*, Development Policy Review, 2007, 25 (1): 25–42.

Arcand Jean-Louis (2011). Report on Joan Apecu's PhD Dissertation, 5 September 2011.

Aryeetey, Devarajan, Kanbur and Kasekende, *The Oxford Companion to the Economics of Africa*, Oxford University Press, 2012.

Bermann George and Mavroidis Petros (2007). *WTO Law and Developing Countries*, Colombia Studies in WTO Law and Policy, Cambridge University Press 2007.

Bhagwati Jagdish, *Reshaping the WTO*, Far Eastern Economic Review, Jan/Feb 2005.

Blackhurst, R., Lyakurwa, B. and Oyejide, A. (2000). *Options for Improving Africa's Participation in the WTO*, The World Economy 23,4. pgs. 491–510.

Blackhurst and Lyakurwa, *Markets and Market Access for African Exports: Past, Present and Future Directions*, in Oyejide and Lyakurwa, Africa and the World Trading System, selected issues of the Doha Agenda, Vol. 1, at pg. 55.

Bown Chad P. and Hoekman Bernard M. (2007). *Developing Countries and Enforcement of Trade Agreements, Why Dispute Settlement is not Enough*, Policy Research Working Paper 4450, The World Bank, Development Research Group, Trade Team, 2007.

Bown, Chad P. (2005). *Participation in WTO Dispute Settlement: Complainants, Interested Parties and Free riders*, World Bank Economic Review, Vol. 19, pgs 287–310.

Busch, Marc L., and Eric Reinhardt. (2003). *Developing Countries and General Agreement on Tariffs and Trade/World Trade Organisation Dispute Settlement*, Journal of World Trade 37(4):719–735.

Canutu Otaviano (2010). *Recoupling or Switchover? Developing Countries in the Global Economy*, in: The Day After Tomorrow. A Handbook on the Future of Economic Policy in the Developing World. The World Bank, 2010.

Chadha et al. (2000). *Developing Countries and the Next Round of WTO Negotiations*, World Economy, Vol. 23, Issue 4, pgs 431–611.

Chantal Thomas, Joel P. Trachtman (2009). *Developing Countries in the WTO Legal System*, Oxford University Press (9, 10, 11, 16, 74, 104, 146).

Collier, P. (2006). *Why the WTO is deadlocked: And What Can be Done About It*, The World Economy, 29(10):1423–1449.

Croome. J. *Reshaping the World Trading System, A history of the Uruguay Round*, Kluwer Law International.

Dollar, David (1992). *Outward-Oriented Developing Economies Really Grow More Rapidly: Evidence from 95 LDCs, 1976–198*, in Economic Development and Cultural Change 40(4); 1992.

Dollar, David and Kraay, Art (2000). *Growth is Good for the Poor*, 2000.

Delich V (2002). *Developing Countries and the WTO Dispute Settlement System*, in Hoekman et al., Development, Trade and the WTO- a hand book, pgs 71–80.

Draper Peter and Nkululeko Khumalo (2005). *Towards a Fairer WTO*, South African Institute for International Affairs, 2005.

Dunoff Jeffrey (2007). *What is Wrong with Inactivity?* Comment on Nordstrom's Developing Countries in the WTO, in Bermann George and Mavroidis Petros, WTO Law and Developing Countries, Colombia Studies in WTO Law and Policy, Cambridge University Press 2007. pg. 186–194.

Ethier. W.J. (2007). *Comment on Patrick Low's "Is the WTO Doing Enough for Developing Countries,* in Bermann George and Mavroidis Petros, WTO Law and Developing Countries, Colombia Studies in WTO Law and Policy, Cambridge University Press 2007 at pg. 360.

Ewelukwu, Uche U., *African States, Aggressive Multilateralism and the WTO Dispute Settlement System- Politics, Process, Outcomes and Prospects*, University of Arkansas School of Law.

Finger Michael and Schuler Philip (2002). *Implementation of WTO Commitments: The Development Challenge*, in Hoekman et al., Development, Trade and the WTO, A Hand book, The World Bank, at pg. 493.

Fisher Bob (2006). *Preference Erosion, Government Revenues and Non-tariff Trade Barriers*, the World Economy (2006).

Gabilondo, Jose Luiz Perez (2001). *Developing Countries in the WTO Dispute Settlement Procedures*, Journal of World Trade 35 (4): 483–488.

Hakan Nordstrom (2007). *Participation of Developing Countries in the WTO- New Evidence Based on 2003 Official Records,* in Bermann George and Mavroidis Petros, *WTO Law and Developing Countries*, Colombia Studies in WTO Law and Policy, Cambridge University Press 2007.

Hakan Nordstrom and Gregory Shaffer (2008). *Access to Justice in the World Trade Organisation: a case for a small claims procedure?* World Trade Review, October 2008.

Hoekman B. (2010). *Changing Developing Country Trade Policies, Performance and WTO engagement*, World Bank and CEPR, paper based on presentation at the American Society of International Law Conference, "International Economic Law in a Time of Change", University of Minnesota Law School, Minneapolis, November 18–20, 2010 at the occasion of the launch of the re-issue of Robert Hudec's book – *Developing Countries in the GATT Legal System.*

Hoekman, Bernard (2011). Report on Joan Laker Apecu, African Participation at the WTO: Legal and Institutional Aspects – 1995–2010, 2 September 2011.

Hoekman B. and Kostecki M., *The Political Economy of the World Trading System*, 2nd edition, Oxford, Oxford University Press.

Hoekman B., Matoo A. and English P. (2002). *Development, Trade and the WTO- a Hand Book*, The World Bank.

Hoekman, Bernard M., and Mavriodis Petros C. (2001). *WTO Dispute Settlement, Transparency and Surveillance*, In Developing Countries and the WTO, edited by Bernard Hoekman and Will Martin. Oxford: Blackwell.

Horn, Henrik, Hakan Nordstrom and Mavroidis Petros C. (1999). *Is the Use of the WTO Dispute Settlement System Biased?* CEPR Discussion paper 2340. London: Centre for Economic Policy Research.

Hudec Robert (1987). *Developing Countries in the GATT Legal System.* London: Trade Policy Research Centre. Re-issued in 2010 by Cambridge University Press.

——. (1987). *Developing Countries in the GATT Legal System*, edited with an afterword by Joel P. Trachtman (2009), Rowman and Littlefield for the Cordell Hull Institute, Washington, D.C.

Hudec R. *The adequacy of WTO Dispute Settlement Remedies- a developing country perspective*, in Hoekman et al., Development, Trade and the WTO- a hand book, pg. 81–91.

Hughes Valerie (2006). Conference on the WTO at Ten: Governance, Dispute Settlement, and Developing Countries, Colombia University, April 2006: http://www.sipa.columbia.edu/wto/html/papers.html.

Ismail, Faizel (2009). *Reforming the World Trade Organization, Developing Countries in the Doha Round*, CUTS and Friedrich Ebert Stiftung.

Jackson H. John (2006). *Sovereignty, the WTO and Changing Fundamentals of International Law*, Cambridge University Press.

Jensen Micheal Friis (2007). *African demands for special and differential treatment in the Doha Round: An assessment and analysis*, Development Policy Review, 2007, 25 (1): 91–112.

Jensen Micheal Friis and Gibbon Peter (2007). *Africa and the WTO Doha Round: An Overview*, Development Policy Review, 2007, 25(1): 5–24.

Kessie Edwini (2007). *The Legal Status of Special and Differential Treatment Provisions under the WTO Agreements*, in Bermann George and Mavroidis Petros, *WTO Law and Developing Countries*, Colombia Studies in WTO Law and Policy, Cambridge University Press 2007.

Kessie Edwini and Apea Yvonne, (2006). *The Participation of African Countries in the Multilateral Trading System*, African Yearbook of International Law, 9–66.

Kanitz Roberto (2010). *Managing Multilateral Trade Negotiations: The Role of the WTO Chairman*, Cameron May International Law and Policy.

Krueger, Anne O. (1990). *Trends in Trade Policies of Developing Countries, the Direction of Trade Policy*: Papers in Honour of Isaiah Frank (ed), Charles S. Pearson and James Riedel, Cambridge, Mass, Blackwelll, 1990: 87–107.

Lacarte-Muro and Gappah Pettina (2000). *Developing Countries and the WTO Legal and Dispute Settlement System, A View from the Bench*, Journal of International Economic Law.

Low Patrick (2007). *Is the WTO Doing Enough for Developing Countries?* in Bermann George and Mavroidis Petros, *WTO Law and Developing Countries*, Colombia Studies in WTO Law and Policy, Cambridge University Press 2007.

Low Patrick, Mchumo Zainab and Muyambo Vonai (2006). *Africa in the World Trading System: Prospects and Challenges*, Paper prepared for conference on Accelerating Africa's Development – Five Years into the 21st Century, African Development Bank, Tunis, 22–24 November, 2006.

Lyakurwa, Africa and the World Trading System, Selected Issues of the Doha Agenda, Volume 1, pg. 11.

Lyakurwa W. (2005). *Africa and the World Trading System*, Selected Issues of the Doha Agenda, Volume 1.

Manduna, Calvin (2005). *Daring to Dispute: Are There Shifting Trends in African Participation in WTO Dispute Settlement?* TRALAC Trade Brief No.3/2005.

Manzoor, Ahmed (2009). *Negotiating Mechanisms, the various interest groups and their functioning*, presentation to senior Vietnamese trade negotiators, IDEAS Centre, 23 September 2009.

Markham, Jesse W. (1955). *The per se Doctrine and the New Rule of Reason*, Southern Economic Journal, Vol. 22, No. 1 (Jul., 1955), pp. 22–31.

Meagher, Niall (2007). *Representing Developing Countries in WTO Dispute Settlement Proceedings*, in Bermann and Mavroidis, WTO Law and Developing Countries, Colombia Studies in WTO Law and Policy, Cambridge University Press.

Michalopoulos, C. (1999). *The participation of Developing Countries in the WTO*, World Bank Policy Research Discussion Papers.

——. (1999). *The Developing Countries in the WTO*" The World Economy, 22, 1. pgs 117–143.

Moore M. (1999). *Africa and the multilateral trading system: challenges and opportunities*, Address by Mike Moore, at the Conference of African Trade Ministers, Algiers, 23 September 1999, available at http://www.wto.org/english/news_e/spmm_e/spmm07_e.htm.

Mosoti Victor (2006). *Africa in the First Decade of WTO Dispute Settlement*, Journal of International Economic Law.

——. (2003). *Does Africa need the WTO Dispute Settlement System?* ICTSD, March 2003.

Narlikar, Armita (2004). *Developing Countries and the WTO*, in Brain Hocking and Steven McGuire (eds), Trade Politics, 2nd edn, London: Routledge.

——. (2006). *Fairness in International Trade Negotiations: Developing Countries in the GATT and WTO*, the World Economy (2006).

Ng'ong'ola Clement (2005). *African Member States and the Negotiations on Dispute Settlement Reform in the World Trade Organisation, TRALAC Working Paper 11/2005.*

Njinkeu Dominique (2004). *Uniform Treatment for Africa in the DDA*, World Trade Review, 2004.

Nordstrom Hakan (2003). *Participation of Developing Countries in the WTO- new evidence based on 2003 official records*, National Board of Trade, Stockholm, Sweden.

Octaviano Canuto and Marcelo Giugale (2010), *The Day After Tomorrow*, A Handbook on the Future of Economic Policy in the Developing World, The World Bank.

Ohiohenuan, J.F. (2005). *Capacity Building Implications of Enhanced African Participation in Global Trade Rules-Making and Arrangements*, in Oyejide and Lyakurwa, Africa and the World Trading System, selected issues of the Doha Agenda, pg. 355.

Osakwe, Chiedu (2001). *Poverty Reduction and Development: The Contribution of Trade, Macroeconomic and Regulatory Policies*, 10th Joseph Mubiru Memorial Lecture organized by the Bank of Uganda, 14 December 2001.

Osakwe, Chiedu (2010). *Developing Countries and GATT Rules: Dynamic Transformations in Trade Policy Behaviour and Performance*, American Journal of International Law (November 2010, forthcoming) paper based on presentation at the American Society of International Law Conference, "International Economic Law in a Time of Change", University of Minnesota Law School, Minneapolis, November 18–20, 2010 at the occasion of the launch of the re-issue of Robert Hudec's book – *Developing Countries in the GATT Legal System*.

Oyejide, A.T. (1990). *Africa and the Uruguay Round*, the World Economy 13, 3.

Page Sheila (2001). *Developing Countries in GATT/WTO Negotiations*, Overseas Development Institute.

Panagariya, Arvind. (2003). *Think Again. International Trade*, Foreign Policy, Columbia University, www.columbia.edu.

Park, Young Duk and Georg Umbricht. (2001). WTO *Dispute Settlement 1995–2000: A Statistical Analysis*. Journal of International Economic Law: 4: 213–230.

——. (2001). WTO *Dispute Settlement 1995–2001: A Statistical Analysis*. Journal of International Economic Law: 4: 221–244.

Pauwelyn Joost (2011). Report on the PhD thesis of Ms Joan Apecu Laker, 4 September 2011.

Petersmann Ernst-Ulrich, *Addressing institutional challenges to the WTO in the new millennium: a longer-term perspective*: Journal of International Economic Law 8 (3), 647–665.

Polaski Sandra (2006). *Winners and Losers, Impact of the Doha Round on Developing Countries*, Carnegie Endowment for International Peace.

Rajapatirana, Sarath (2000). *The Trade Policies of Developing Countries* Recent Reforms and New Challenges, The AEI Press, Publishers for the American Enterprise Institute, Washington, D.C.

Razeen, Sally (2000). *Developing Country Trade Policy Reform and the WTO*, Cato Journal, Vol. 19, No.3.

Roderick Abbott (2007). *Are developing countries deterred from using the WTO Dispute Settlement System? Participation of Developing Countries in the DSM in the years 1995–2005*, ECIPE Working Paper No. 01/2007.

Rorden Wilkinson and James Scott (2008). *Developing country participation in the GATT: a reassessment*: World Trade Review (2008) 7: 3, 473–510.

Sachs, Jeffrey, and Andrew M. Warner. (1995). *Natural Resources and Economic Growth*. Development Discussion Paper No: 517a. Harvard Institute for International Development, Cambridge Massachusetts, 1995.

Shaffer, Gregory (2003). *How to make the WTO Dispute Settlement System work for developing countries*. Geneva: ICTSD Resource Paper No.5.

Sharer R. (2000). *Special and Differentiated Treatment and Economic Reforms in Developing Countries*, Paper presented to the WTO Conference on Special and Differential Treatment for Developing Countries, Geneva, 7 March 2000.

Srinivasan T.N. (2000), *Developing Countries and the Multilateral Trading System: From the GATT to the Uruguay Round and the Future*, Boulder Co. West view Press.

Tractchman P. Joel (2009). *Developing Countries in the GATT/WTO legal system by Robert E Hudec edited with an afterword by Joel P Tracthman, Rowman and Littlefield for Cordell Hull Institute, Washington D.C.*

Vyborny Katherine (2007). *What Could the Doha Round Mean for Africa?* Carnegie Endowment for International Peace.

Wang Z. and Winters L., *Africa's Role in the Multilateral Trade Negotiations*, World Bank Policy Research Working Paper, November 1997, p. 25.

Yeo, Stephen, *Trade Policy in Sub-Saharan Africa: Lessons from the Uruguay Round Experience.* In Oyejide.

Yerxa, R. and Wilson, B., (2005). *Key Issues in WTO Dispute Settlement, The First Ten Years*, Cambridge University Press.

Zunckel, H., (2005). *The African Awakening in United States-Upland Cotton,* Journal of World Trade 39(6):1071–1093.

List of WTO Documents

World Trade Organization, *the Legal Texts, the Results of the Uruguay Round of Multilateral Trade Negotiations*, Cambridge University Press, 1999.

World Trade Organization, the Doha Round Texts and Related Documents, 2009.

World Trade Organisation, Understanding on Rules and Procedures Governing the Settlement of Disputes.

World Trade Organisation (2004), *The Future of the WTO: Addressing Institutional Challenges in the new Millennium*, Report of the Consultative Board to the Director-General Supachai Panitchpakdi.

World Trade Organization, Annual Report 2010.

World Trade Organization, Annual Report 1998.

World Trade Organization, *World Trade Report 2008.*

World Trade Organization, *International Trade Statistics 2008.*

World Trade Organization, *International Trade Statistics 2009.*

World Trade Organisation, *International Trade Statistics 2010.*

World Trade Organization, *The Blue Book*, 1995–2009 (2003, 2004 not produced).

World Trade Organization, *Guidelines for Appointment of Officers to WTO Bodies*, WT/L/31.

World Trade Organization, General Council, *Minutes of Meetings*, WT/GC/M/1–129.

World Trade Organization, General Council, *Working Documents, Submissions, Proposals*, WT/GC/W/1–628.

World Trade Organization, Trade Policy Review Body, *Annual Report 2008*, WT/TPR/232.

World Trade Organization, Trade Policy Review Body, *Rules of Procedure for Meetings of the Trade Policy Review Body*, WT/TPR/6/Rev.2.

World Trade Organization, Trade Policy Review Body, *Minutes of Meetings*, WT/TPR/M/1–235.

World Trade Organization, Trade Policy Review Body, *Arrangements for Review Meetings*, WT/TPR/1–270.

World Trade Organization, Trade Policy Review Body, *Communication from Discussants*, WT/TPR/D/1–83.

World Trade Organization, Council for Trade in Goods, *Minutes of Meetings*, G/C/M/1–104.

World Trade Organization, Council for Trade in Services, *Minutes of Meetings*, S/C/M/1–101.

World Trade Organization, Council for Trade in Services, *Working Documents, Submissions, Proposals*, S/C/W/1–329.

World Trade Organisation, Council for Trade in Services, *Overview of Notifications made under relevant GATS provisions*, Informal Note by the WTO Secretariat, 21 June 2010.

World Trade Organization, Council for Trade Related Aspects of Intellectual Property Rights, *Minutes of Meetings*, IP/C/M/1–64.

World Trade Organization, Council for Trade Related Aspects of Intellectual Property Rights, *Working Documents, Submissions, Proposals*, IP/C/W/1–553.

World Trade Organization, Council for Trade Related Aspects of Intellectual Property Rights, *Timeliness and Completeness of Notifications and Other Information Flows*, Note by Secretariat, IP/C/W/543, 22 October 2009.

World Trade Organization, Protocol of Accession of Cape Verde to the World Trade Organization, WT/L/715 and Report of the Working Party, WT/ACC/CPV/30.

World Trade Organization, Committee on Trade and Development, Decision of the General Council, 31 January 1995, WT/L/46.
World Trade Organization, Committee on Trade and Development, *Minutes of Meetings*, WT/COMTD/M/1–80.
World Trade Organization, Committee on Trade and Development, *Working Documents, Submissions, Proposals*, WT/COMTD/W/1–176; WT/COMTD/1–72.
World Trade Organization, Committee on Agriculture, Decision of the General Council, 31 January 1995, WT/L/43.
World Trade Organization, Committee on Agriculture, *Summary Records of Meetings*, G/AG/R/1–60.
World Trade Organization, Committee on Agriculture, *Working Documents, Submissions, Proposals*, G/AG/W/1–80.
World Trade Organization, Committee on Agriculture, *Compliance with Notification Obligations*, Note by the Secretariat, G/AG/GEN/86/Rev.4, 17 November 2010.
World Trade Organization, Committee on Anti-dumping Practices, *Minutes of Committee*, G/ADP/M/1–39.
World Trade Organization, Committee on Anti-dumping Practices, *Working Documents, Submissions, Proposals*, G/ADP/W/1–483.
World Trade Organization, Report (2010) of the Committee on Anti-Dumping Practices to the Council for Trade in Goods, G/L/935, 28 October 2010.
World Trade Organization, Committee on Customs Valuation, *Minutes of Meetings*, G/VAL/M/1–50.
World Trade Organization, Committee on Customs Valuation, *Working Documents, Submissions, Proposals*, G/VAL/W/1–199.
World Trade Organization, Report (2010) of the Committee on Customs Valuation to the Council for Trade in Goods, G/L/942, 10 November 2010.
World Trade Organization, Committee on Import Licensing, *Minutes of Meetings*, G/LIC/M/1–32.
World Trade Organization, Committee on Import Licensing, *Working Documents, Submissions, Proposals*, G/LIC/W/1–37.
World Trade Organization, Report (2010) of the Committee on Import Licensing to the Council for Trade in Goods, G/L/941, 9 November 2010.
World Trade Organization, Committee on Market Access, Decision of the General Council of 31 January 1995, WT/L/47.
World Trade Organization, Committee on Market Access, *Minutes of Committee*, G/MA/M/1–52.
World Trade Organization, Committee on Market Access, *Working Documents, Submissions, Proposals*, G/MA/W/1–104.
World Trade Organization, Committee on Market Access, *Notifications under the Decision on Reverse Notification of Non-Tariff Measures, G/MA/NTM/W/3/Rev.1.*
World Trade Organization, *Decision on Notification Procedures for Quantitative Restrictions adopted by the Council for Trade in Goods on 1/December/1995* G/L/60.
World Trade Organization, *Supply of Information to the Integrated Database for Personal Computers*, Decision of the General Council, WT/L/225.
World Trade Organization, Committee on Market Access, *Timeliness and Completeness of Notifications, Notifications of Quantitative Restrictions, Note by Secretariat*, 2 April 2009, JOB (09/33).
World Trade Organization, Committee on Market Access, *Status of Submission to the Integrated Database, Note by Secretariat*, G/MA/IDB/2/REV.32, 6 October 2010.
World Trade Organization, Committee on Market Access, *Framework to enhance IDB notification compliance, Note by Secretariat*, 2 June 2009, JOB (09)/43/Rev.1.
World Trade Organization, Committee on Rules of Origin, *Minutes of Meetings of the Committee*, G/RO/M/1–55.
World Trade Organization, Committee on Rules of Origin, *Working Documents, Submissions, Proposals*, G/RO/1–138.

World Trade Organization, Committee on Rules of Origin, *Sixteenth Annual Review of the Implementation and Operation of the Agreement on Rules of Origin, Note by Secretariat*, G/RO/70, 17 December 2010.

World Trade Organization, Committee on Rules of Origin, *Integrated Negotiating Text for the Harmonization Work Programme, Technical Issues to be Resolved in the Committee, Note by Secretariat*, 11 April 2007.

World Trade Organization, Committee on Safeguard Measures, *Minutes of Meetings of Committee*, G/SG/M/1–38.

World Trade Organization, Committee on Safeguard Measures, *Working Documents, Submissions*, Proposals, G/SG/W/1–215.

World Trade Organization, Report (2010) of the Committee on Safeguard Measures to the Council for Trade in Goods, G/L/936, 22 October 2010.

World Trade Organization, Committee on Trade Related Investment Measures, *Minutes of Meetings of Committee*, G/TRIMS/M/1–30.

World Trade Organization, Committee on Trade Related Investment Measures, *Working Documents, Submissions, Proposals*, G/TRIMS/W/1–80.

World Trade Organization, *Notifications under Article 5.1 of the Agreement on Trade Related Investment Measures by States and Separate Customs Territories Eligible to become Original WTO Members that accept the WTO Agreement after its entry into force*, WT/L/64.

World Trade Organization, Committee on Technical Barriers to Trade, *Minutes of Meetings of Committee*, G/TBT/M/1–51.

World Trade Organization, Committee on Technical Barriers to Trade, *Working Documents, Submissions, Proposals*, G/TBT/W/1–333.

World Trade Organization, Committee on Technical Barriers to Trade, *Fifteenth Annual Review of the Implementation and Operation of the TBT Agreement, Note by Secretariat*, 5 February 2010.

World Trade Organization, Committee on Technical Barriers to Trade, *Specific Trade Concerns Raised in the TBT Committee, Note by the Secretariat*, G/TBT/GEN/74/Rev.6, 19 October 2010.

World Trade Organization, Committee on Subsidies and Countervailing Measures, *Minutes of Meeting of Committee*, G/SCM/M/1–75.

World Trade Organization, Committee on Subsidies and Countervailing Measures, *Working Documents, Submissions, Proposals*, G/SCM/W/1–553.

World Trade Organization, Committee on Subsidies and Countervailing Measures, *Notification Requirements under the Agreement on Subsidies and Countervailing Measures*, G/SCM/W/546/Rev.1, 16 April 2010.

World Trade Organization, Report (2010) of the Committee on Subsidies and Countervailing Measures to the Council for Trade in Goods, G/L/937, 29 October 2010.

World Trade Organization, Committee on Sanitary and Phytosanitary Measures, *Summary Records of Meetings of the Committee*, G/SPS/R/1–61.

World Trade Organization, Committee on Sanitary and Phytosanitary Measures, *Working Documents, Submissions, Proposals*, G/SPS/W/1–255.

World Trade Organization, Committee on Sanitary and Phytosanitary Measures, *Overview Regarding the Level of Implementation of the Transparency Provisions of the SPS Agreement, Note by Secretariat*, G/SPS/GEN/804/Rev.3 7 October 2010.

World Trade Organization, Committee on Sanitary and Phytosanitary Measures, *Specific Trade Concerns, Note by Secretariat*, G/SPS/GEN/204/REV.10, 10 February 2010.

World Trade Organization, *Working Procedures for Appellate Review, Annex II, Rules of Conduct for the Understanding on Rules of Procedure Governing the Settlement of Disputes.*

World Trade Organization, Negotiating Group on Market Access, *List of Documents, Note by Secretariat*, TN/MA/S/16/Rev.10.

World Trade Organization, Negotiating Group on Trade Facilitation, *List of Documents, Note by Secretariat*, TN/TF/W/106/Rev.13.

World Trade Organization, Committee on Trade and Environment – Special Session, *List of Documents, Note by Secretariat*, TN/TE/INF/4/Rev.14.

World Trade Organization, Committee on Trade and Environment – Special Session, *Africa Group Proposal for the Establishment of a Group of Experts on Trade and Environment*, JOB (08/38).
World Trade Organization, Dispute Settlement Body – Special Session *Negotiations on the Dispute Settlement Understanding, Proposal by the African Group*, TN/DS/W/15.

List of Databases

Economist Intelligence Unit (2010), Democracy Index 2010: Democracy in Retreat, http://graphics.eiu.com/PDF/Democracy_Index_2010_web.pdf.
World Trade Organization, Documents online, http://docsonline/gen_search.asp.
World Trade Organization, Legal Affairs Division Internal Database, http://ada-mssql-db2/dsweb2/Home.aspx.
World Trade Organization, SPS Information Management System, http://spsims.wto.org/.
World Trade Organization, TBT Information Management System, http://tbtims.wto.org/.
World Trade Organization, Institute for Training and Technical Cooperation Activities Database, http://wtotrta/Public/BasicSearch.aspx.
World Trade Organization, Anti-dumping Gateway, http://www.wto.org/english/tratop_e/adp_e/adp_e.htm.
World Trade Organization, Subsidies and Countervailing Measures Gate way http://www.wto.org/english/tratop_e/scm_e/scm_e.htm.
World Trade Organization, Safeguards Gateway http://www.wto.org/english/tratop_e/safeg_e/safeg_e.htm.
World Bank, World Development Indicators, http://data.worldbank.org/data-catalog/world-development-indicators.
World Economic Forum, *Global Competitiveness Index 2010–2011*, http://gcr.weforum.org/gcr2010/.

INDEX

www.ingramcontent.com/pod-product-compliance
Lightning Source LLC
LaVergne TN
LVHW020651300926
849161LV00004B/889